Blockchain + Antitrust

Blockchain + Antitrust
The Decentralization Formula

Thibault Schrepel

Associate Professor, Department of Transnational Legal Studies, VU Amsterdam University, the Netherlands, and Faculty Affiliate, The CodeX Center, Stanford University, USA

Cheltenham, UK • Northampton, MA, USA

Published by
Edward Elgar Publishing Limited
The Lypiatts
15 Lansdown Road
Cheltenham
Glos GL50 2JA
UK

Edward Elgar Publishing, Inc.
William Pratt House
9 Dewey Court
Northampton
Massachusetts 01060
USA

Paperback edition 2022

A catalogue record for this book
is available from the British Library

Library of Congress Control Number: 2021943534

This book is available electronically in the **Elgar**online
Law subject collection
http://dx.doi.org/10.4337/9781800885530

ISBN 978 1 80088 552 3 (cased)
ISBN 978 1 80088 553 0 (eBook)
ISBN 978 1 0353 0681 7 (paperback)

Printed and bound by CPI Group (UK) Ltd, Croydon, CR0 4YY

Contents

Preface

We have all heard about the butterfly effect. The idea that the flapping of such tiny wings can change a trajectory is fascinating; but it is terrifying too.

In April 2018, while I was still living in Paris, I received an email from a soon-to-become friend working at the Organisation for Economic Co-operation and Development (OECD). I had just published an article on predatory innovation, a subject I explored during my Ph.D. He wanted to discuss the concept and asked if we could meet. To spice up the discussion a bit, we rendezvoused in a bar I liked in the *9eme arrondissement*. We ordered a few old fashioneds and discussed predatory innovation. The discussion ended up on the subject of blockchain. I had written a few paragraphs about it in my Ph.D., and although I do not recall who introduced the subject, I remember having fun debating it.

A few weeks after this meeting, I had an interview for my first academic position. I did not mention blockchain. Little did I know it would become one of my fascinations just a few weeks after that.

The OECD had invited me to its first panel on the subject. I so decided to write an article discussing blockchain from the perspective of monopolization practices. I understand how curious this might seem. If you are interested in something, why only discuss its downsides? I certainly owe this approach to my training as a lawyer, always eager to identify legal issues where others may see opportunities. I continued my efforts the following year, publishing an article on collusion and smart contracts.

It took me some time (two years, in fact) before realizing that I was still exploring "blockchain antitrust" not because of a particular passion for anti-competitive practices, but because of the technology's complementary relationship with antitrust. Once this intuition had become clear to me, I decided to write a book to investigate it further.

My articles on anticompetitive practices serve as the centerpiece of this manuscript. One cannot foster a long-lasting cooperation merely by sweeping the sticking points under the carpet. On top of that, one must clarify why and how blockchain and antitrust could benefit from one another. Knowing that there are icebergs on the way is necessary, but not sufficient; the rudder must also (and above all) be oriented in the right direction.

The challenge that lies ahead of us is a moving target, as the relationship between blockchain and antitrust is certainly not static. The law evolves with technological advancements. Blockchain, in particular, is undergoing multiple evolutions – Darwin would have been fascinated. But luckily, the general dynamic between blockchain and antitrust remains the same.

With this book, I am taking you with me on the journey toward the "+" symbol that shines out from the middle of its title. I know how provocative this may appear. Increasing the common good is not (only) a matter of mathematics. Moreover, "+" is not a very useful command in most computer languages. Finally, it does not fit well with the concept of legal primacy that has long led lawyers to ignore possible cooperation with other fields and social drivers.

I am also aware of how curious it is for a jurist to add up the law with a technology born to escape it. But if I try nonetheless, it is because I am convinced that a cooperation between blockchain and antitrust represents a real opportunity to increase the common good. I must also confess my attraction to blockchain's inherent ideology. Blockchain allows for individual empowerment. Over the years, I found myself imagining a freer, more decentralized world. I do not know if we will get there one day; but I am pleased to be now dreaming about it in more concrete terms.

These aspirations and research have led me to explore various environments and to forge many friendships. In particular, I want to thank Dirk Auer for his suggestions; Vitalik Buterin and Nicolas Petit for our numerous discussions; Italo Leone, Shimal Kapoor, Kirill Ryabtsev, Ian Fraser and Chiara Pescetto for their assistance; the people at Stanford University CodeX Center for their support; the people at the International Center for Law & Economics for their friendship; the people at Utrecht University for their financial support; and all the participants with whom I exchanged during conferences at Stanford University, Harvard University, the University of California, Berkeley, New York University, the University of Amsterdam, the European University Institute, Bocconi University, the University of Siena, Maastricht University, the Seoul National University, the College of Europe, Northeastern University, Saint Mary University, the Technical University of Munich, Roma Tre University, the University of Zagreb, the University of Provence Aix-Marseille, IE, the Vrije Universiteit Brussel, Stockholm University and the University of Lucerne. People working in institutions based in Brazil, India, Spain, France, Hong Kong, Belgium, the United Kingdom and the United States, at the OECD, at the French Parliament, and at the Italian, French, Dutch and German competition agencies have also greatly contributed to my thinking. Finally, and most importantly, this book was possible only thanks to the unshakeable support of my parents and my other half, Mégane.

Introduction: the decentralization formula

It's nothing new. The relationship between law and technology has already existed for several millennia. Human behaviors in society have been defined by written rules since antiquity; while technology – a means to fulfill a purpose – is even older. And both the law and technology are dynamic because they are designed by humankind, for humankind. Describing their relationship as ancestral and evolutionary is an understatement. In fact, technology has been regulated since the very existence of the Rule of Law. For example, the Code of Hammurabi (1754 BC) regulated the negligent opening of a canal for irrigation by a man. It imposed compensation for the misuse of this technology.[1]

What is new is the importance of law and technology interaction, especially for digital technologies. The prevalence of computer code in organizing society is growing every day. Whether we educate or entertain ourselves, shop, communicate with friends, arrange trips or look for specific information, digital technologies are increasingly shaping the realm of possibilities. They are the bedrock upon which our modern societies are built.

Moreover, many digital technologies (are developed to) escape the rule of law; or at least, (to) prevent its full application.[2] Every day, these technologies – such as blockchain – advance a little bit faster, become autonomous from humans and increasingly determine the organization of our societies. Although the law remains (one of) the primary constraint(s) on human behavior, it can no longer prevail unconditionally on digital architectures. West Coast code (computer programming) is acquiring the means to oppose East Coast code (legislation and regulations). For these reasons, a confrontational approach to law and technology no longer maximizes the common good, as it has in centuries past.

Whatever one thinks about the new importance of code in society, it justifies a novel approach to "law and technology." This book is an argument about the need for cooperation between the two. To paraphrase Sun Tzu,[3] faced with the

---

[1]   Code of Hammurabi, Article 55 (1754 BC).
[2]   Thibault Schrepel, "Anarchy, State, and Blockchain Utopia: Rule of Law versus Lex Cryptographia," in *General Principles and Digitalisation* (Hart Publishing, 2020).
[3]   Sun Tzu, *L'art de la Guerre*, trans. Francis Wang (Flammarion, 1972).

danger of a destructive confrontation, only collaboration "like the right hand with the left hand" will maximize the common good.[4]

That cooperation can take different forms, depending on the nature of the relationship between laws and technologies. I distinguish three situations: two at each end of the spectrum depicted in Figure 0.1, and one in the middle.

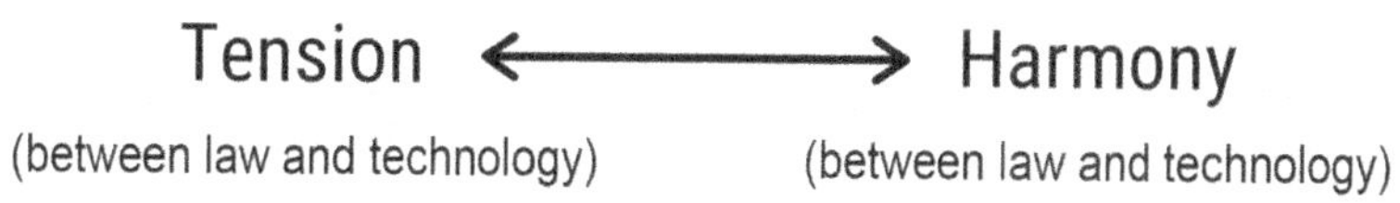

Tension ⟵⟶ Harmony
(between law and technology)   (between law and technology)

Figure 0.1   A scale of the relationship between law and technology

First, there are situations in which technology systematically opposes the law. The left side of the spectrum represents these. Here, one must first analyze whether the aim pursued by the technology benefits the common good and under what circumstances. If that is the case, one must change the law to enable the technology. If not, collaboration between law and technology should lead to the domination of the rule of law. Two outcomes are possible: either redirecting the technology or outlawing it altogether. All discussions regarding blockchain applications designed to evade the rule of law are located on this spectrum's left side.

Second, law and technology may have an ambiguous relationship, where they oppose and complement each other in different aspects. In that case, collaboration seeks to enable the – necessarily partial – achievement of two different objectives without putting either at risk. The example of blockchain and privacy protection is telling in this respect. While blockchain's immutable nature is difficult to reconcile with the right to rectification or erasure, block-chain's encryption makes it possible to protect transactions' identity (as I will explain).

Finally, there are situations in which law and technology pursue the same aim. The right side of the spectrum represents these. Here, one must ensure that each can rely on the other. This is notably the case for blockchain and antitrust

---

[4]   In this book, common good maximization will be analyzed from the angle of competitiveness. It should also be addressed from a more human rights perspective. The idea that technology can also liberate citizens from oppressive states is a signifi-cant point that George Orwell dodged in his famous *1984*, yet an important one embod-ied by blockchain.

law. While from time to time they will be antagonistic, they will mostly benefit from cooperation. One must identify which confrontations may endanger blockchain or antitrust law, and determine how they can be eliminated while maintaining their complementary aspects.

This paradigm is new for antitrust law. Private companies have long been (and still are) pursuing a different goal than antitrust agencies. That explains why tech giants are at the heart of many recent cases. Regardless of the merits of these decisions, and although one may regret the confrontational approach taken by the legal and tech communities, there is a logical explanation.

While the vast majority of these companies' activities benefit consumers, some end up reducing consumer welfare because tech giants are not pursuing that objective. Like all other companies, they are guided by profit maximization; whereas antitrust law aims to protect consumers by ensuring the proper functioning of markets. These two agendas are generally aligned, but are sometimes at odds with each other. As we shall see together, the creation of the Sherman Act resulted from the desire to respond to the practices of large companies (e.g., Standard Oil). At the heart of their relationship is a fundamental mistrust, resulting in the spending of immense financial and human resources.

Things are different for antitrust law and blockchain. They are complementary. On the one hand, antitrust law protects the competitive process by eliminating forms of coercive control. On the other hand, blockchain seeks to eliminate centralized and vertical forms of control (and disrupt such existing structures). In a sense, antitrust law aims to constrain the exercise of power through the rule of law; while blockchain seeks to do so through technical means. And while some entities running on blockchain ecosystems are profit driven, the technology architecture (tends to) align their goals with antitrust law. Both end up taking part in the decentralization of transactional power. They do not speak the same language, but they share the same ambition.

It goes even further than this. Besides seeking the same aim, the combination of antitrust law and blockchain can maximize their common goal to a degree that would be unthinkable if they were acting on their own. The same is true for all interactions in the first quadrant (top-right corner) of Figure 0.2 – that is, where a body of laws and technology naturally pursue the same aim[5] and seek cooperation.

This book addresses that first quadrant. Collaboration between law and technology is instinctively appealing; after all, who would not want them to benefit from each other? But I fear that dissenting voices will become more pressing

---

[5] That statement is deterministic, _see_ Thibault Schrepel, "Law and Technology Realism," MIT Computational Law Report, August 14, 2020, https://perma.cc/C5VU -DKD4.

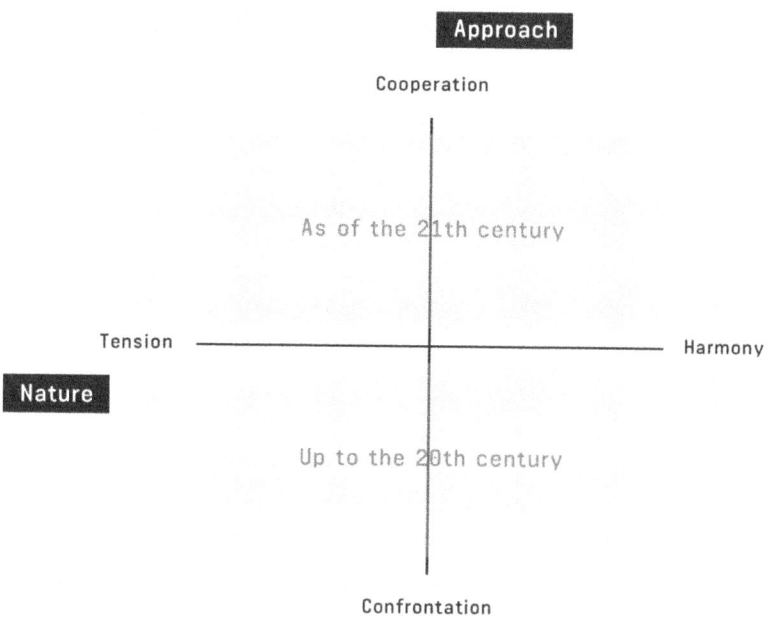

Figure 0.2   Law and technology interactions through the years

when talking about the terms of this collaboration. The return to reality will be difficult; as in any marriage, the alliance of antitrust law and blockchain will require mutual concessions.

My goal is thus to convince readers that efficiencies arise from collaboration between antitrust law and blockchain (the big picture); and that this should guide the treatment of all interactions (the small picture), including negative ones. The book's title reflects that intention. Whereas the classical conception of the rule of law tends towards a "Blockchain vs. Antitrust" approach, I want to set the terms for a "Blockchain + Antitrust" approach, where technology is aligned with regulators' intentions.

The task before me is not an easy one; I approach it with the utmost humility. First, it is necessary to change the mentalities of both legal scholars and technologists. This can be done by highlighting the mutual benefits that stem from cooperation between each of the two communities. A single book won't be enough to achieve that goal; the process will take many years. In the meantime, the use of blockchains to violate antitrust law will create numerous tensions. The same will go for the other antitrust infringements committed within blockchain ecosystems.

The confrontational approach must nonetheless be resisted, mainly because a non-cooperative application of antitrust law would have the effect of reducing blockchain's usefulness. Thus, it would give the impression that blockchain is not a valuable ally in achieving the common aim. Policymakers should not fall into this negative spiral.

With that in mind, and since the best defense is to attack, this book discusses the frictions between blockchain and antitrust law. It explains how blockchains can (be used to) infringe antitrust law. In other words, while blockchain technology has many benefits, it also has flaws and limitations. This book lays bare all of these features and interactions. It examines what I refer to as "blockchain antitrust" – that is, potential antitrust infringements by and within blockchains.[6] It also discusses how cooperation between these two spheres could take place in that context.

Here is our roadmap. The first part shows that blockchain and antitrust law share a common aim: decentralization. The second part shows that blockchain could still (be used to) infringe antitrust law and create artificial forms of centralization. In the third part of the book, I analyze how to tackle these infringements while making sure not to diminish blockchain's role as an ally.

---

6   Thibault Schrepel, "Is Blockchain the Death of Antitrust Law? The Blockchain Antitrust Paradox," Georgetown Law Technology Review 3, no. 2 (2019): 281, 292.

PART 1 – A COMMON AMBITION

The concept of decentralization is at the core of this first part of the book. I explore its contours and the different means to achieve it. The analysis first focuses on technology (blockchain) before moving on to the rule of law (antitrust). The two are eventually combined after analyzing the objectives they pursue and the means they deploy to do so.

This method reveals that blockchain and the law could become strong allies. Not only do they complement each other, but they also share a common objective: that of decentralizing economic opportunities. This alliance is an emergent, bottom-up phenomenon. It is not the result of market design or social planning; quite the contrary.

Against this backdrop, I first explore the roots of blockchain technology. From Stewart Brand to the cypherpunks, the "founding fathers" of blockchain technology sought to create a "new" world in which the individual is empowered by the right tools (Chapter 1). I then analyze how this vision has been technically translated within the blockchain ecosystem. I expose blockchain technology's core characteristics – what I call the "blockchain toolbox"– in this context (Chapter 2). I then study the dynamism of the blockchain environment and seek to understand the competitive forces that shape it (Chapter 3). I show that blockchain ecosystems are built around the objective of decentralization which is a key parameter of competition between them.

This leads me to question the actual meaning(s) of decentralization. After identifying the type of decentralization that blockchain communities pursue, I then question whether their vision can realistically be achieved (Chapter 4). This leads me to analyze each level of a blockchain ecosystem. I further explain that antitrust law can provide decisive support in pursuing this objective (Chapter 5). Despite the fact, I outline several reasons why blockchain and antitrust could oppose each other and why we should follow a different path.

1. Blockchain: from ideology to implementation

1   BLOCKCHAIN THROUGH THE AGES

Blockchain is a relatively new technology,[1] whose origins are to be found in the so-called "cypherpunk" movement that grew out of an old van in California in the 1960s. Understanding the ideology behind blockchain is a requirement for anyone wanting to apply the law without hindering the technology. I invite you to embark on this journey with me.

1.1   Blockchain's Premises… in a Van

"Don't mourn, organize."[2]

The setting: California, 1968. Stewart Brand and his wife, Lois Jennings, go on a road trip across America.[3] They plan on going to educational fairs with a truck full of tools and equipment – such as for "drilling a well, or grinding flour."[4] They also carry a small library of books written by Robert Heinlein, the dean of twentieth century science fiction. They have a lot of unique items for sale, so Brand quickly initiates the creation of a catalog to help potential buyers find their way around the inventory. A few weeks after returning from their road trip, he opens a shop in Menlo Park, not far from San Francisco. The hippie youth are riding on the 1967 "Summer of Love" euphoria. Brand quickly becomes one of their gurus. He is about to initiate the "do it yourself" (DIY) culture.

---

[1]   Emmanuel G. Mesthene, "Some General Implications of the Research of the Harvard University Program on Technology and Society," Technology and Culture 10, no. 4 (1969) (defining "technology" as "the organization of knowledge for the achievement of practical purposes").

[2]   Carole Cadwalladr, "Stewart Brand and the Whole Earth Catalog, The Book That Changed the World," The Guardian, May 4, 2013, https://perma.cc/4KHE-XKFF.

[3]   Andrew Kirk, *Counterculture Green* (University of Kansas Press, 2007): 48.

[4]   Kevin Kelly, *Cool Tools: A Catalog of Possibilities* (Cool Tools, 2013): 4.

Brand's store is a significant success. More products are added and the catalog expands. In Fall 1968, the Portola Institute (an education nonprofit in Menlo Park) gives Brand the platform to spread his message. Together, they publish the first official issue of the Whole Earth Catalog. The magazine's name comes from a campaign Brand ran in 1966, when he publicly asked NASA to publish the first image ever taken of the "Whole Earth." The magazine's aim is that "anyone on Earth can pick up a telephone and find out the complete information on anything."[5] In 1969, the fall issue of the catalog specifies:

> We are as gods and might as well get good at it. So far, remotely done power and glory—as via government, big business, formal education, church—has succeeded to the point where gross defects obscure actual gains. In response to this dilemma and to these gains a realm of intimate, personal power is developing—power of the individual to conduct his own education, find his own inspiration, shape his own environment, and share his adventure with whoever is interested. Tools that aid this process are sought and promoted by the WHOLE EARTH CATALOG.[6]

The Whole Earth Catalog rapidly gains popularity, with more than 1 million copies printed in just a few months.[7] It promotes a new social order empowering the individual[8] – letting him "conduct his own education, find his own inspiration, shape his own environment, and share his adventure with whoever is interested,"[9] after acquiring the right tools. Publication ceases in 1972, but Brand's influence continues to grow. Steve Jobs will call it "one of the bibles of [a] generation,"[10] but Brand is already aiming toward cyberspace. He is about to create the "internet before the internet."[11]

In 1984, Brand publishes the first issue of the *Whole Earth Software Catalog and Review*. That is when he first writes about "[c]omputers and their

---

[5]   Quote taken from the movie *Ecological Design: Inventing the Future*, directed by Brian Danitz and Chris Zelov (1994), https://perma.cc/C3HS-3N6W.

[6]   Stewart Brand, *Whole Earth Catalog: Access to Tools*, Fall 1969 (Portola Institute Inc., 1969).

[7]   Jan-Felix Schrape, "The Promise of Technological Decentralization: A Brief Reconstruction," Society 56 (2019): 31, 32.

[8]   Anna Wiener, "The Complicated Legacy of Stewart Brand's 'Whole Earth Catalog'," The New Yorker, November 16, 2018, https://perma.cc/YN4E-4K5R.

[9]   *Id.*

[10]   Stanford University, "Text of Steve Jobs' Commencement Address," Stanford News, June 14, 2005, https://perma.cc/H5J8-PFT4.

[11]   John Markoff, "A Free and Simple Computer Link", The New York Times, December 8, 1993, https://perma.cc/HJ4D-GZRJ.

Figure 1.1   *Whole Earth Catalog, Spring 1969*

programs," with the ambition of opposing centralized forms of production.[12] He also creates The Whole Earth 'Lectronic Link (The WELL) in 1985,[13] a mailing list still in operation to this day. In 1989, he further starts *The Electronic Whole Earth Catalog*, which is distributed on CD-ROM. Brand

---

[12]   Stewart Brand, *Whole Earth Software Catalog* (Quantum Press/Doubleday, 1984); for more on that, *see* Fred Turner, *From Counterculture to Cyberculture: Stewart Brand, the Whole Earth Network, and the Rise of Digital Utopianism* (University of Chicago Press, 2006).

[13]   Jan-Felix Schrape, "The Promise of Technological Decentralization. A Brief Reconstruction," Society 56 (2019): 31, 32.

hails computers as one of the tools of personal liberation. Years later, a technology writer for the *New York Times* describes him as "the first person to understand cyberspace." Brand not only coins the term "personal computer"[14] and the phrase "information wants to be free,"[15] but also contributes to the emergence of the Web 2.0.[16]

Brand's influence is still visible to this day. TED's curator confides that Brand has been his "intellectual hero"[17] for numerous years. Kevin Kelly – the creator of *Wired* magazine, known for his support of early cyber-libertarian communities – has said the Whole Earth Catalog inspired the genesis of his magazine.[18] And Jeff Bezos has donated $42 million to a project by the Long Now Foundation, of which Brand is the president.[19]

Not surprisingly, Brand is regularly on the side of blockchain communities or quoted by them. In November 2018, he took part in a conference organized in Prague by the Ethereum Foundation.[20] The DIY culture he has helped to flourish is that of the blockchain communities which are developing infrastructures outside of government circuits. Brand wants every individual to access emancipating tools. Blockchain communities want to emancipate themselves from current transactional methods; this explains why they draw inspiration from Brand. In that sense, his influence is very much visible, even if it is only indirect (i.e., does not directly concern blockchain architectural choices). He contributed to the decentralized philosophy of Web 2.0; while blockchain communities want to implement this into Web 3.0.

[14] John Markoff, *What the Dormouse Said: How the Sixties Counterculture Shaped the Personal Computer Industry* (Penguin, 2006).
[15] Brand, *Whole Earth Software Catalog*; Stewart Brand, *The Media Lab: Inventing the Future at M.I.T.* (Penguin Books, 1989).
[16] Jan-Felix Schrape, "The Promise of Technological Decentralization. A Brief Reconstruction," Society 56 (2019).
[17] Carole Cadwalladr, "Stewart Brand and the Whole Earth Catalog, The Book That Changed the World," The Guardian, May 4, 2013, https://perma.cc/A9ZJ-LTGH.
[18] *Id.*
[19] Anna Wiener, "The Complicated Legacy of Stewart Brand's 'Whole Earth Catalog'," The New Yorker, November 16, 2018, https://perma.cc/YN4E-4K5R; Stewart Brand, personal website, https://perma.cc/4WNS-HG6S.
[20] Ethereum Foundation, "A Conversation with Stewart Brand (Devcon4)," YouTube, December 11, 2018, https://perma.cc/45XA-QRCB.

1.2   The Cypherpunks are *Not* Coming to Get You

Satoshi Nakamoto first introduced blockchain in his article "Bitcoin: A Peer-to-Peer Electronic Cash System" published on October 31, 2008.[21] It resulted from decades of research[22] strongly dominated by a cyber-libertarian ideology, finding its roots in the Whole Earth Catalog.[23] More specifically, blockchain can be traced back to the work of the cypherpunks: cyber-libertarians writing code.[24]

In the 1970s, for the first time, cryptographic methods became accessible to civilians.[25] For example, Rivest, Shamir and Adleman showed how two persons could use public–private key encryption and digital signatures to ensure communication integrity.[26] In 1982, David Chaum, an American com-

---

[21]   Satoshi Nakamoto does not use the word "blockchain" once in the famous Bitcoin white paper.

[22]   The Satoshi Nakamoto Institute indicates: "Bitcoin was not forged in a vacuum. These works serve to contextualize Bitcoin into the broader story of cryptography and freedom," *see* "Literature," Satoshi Nakamoto Institute, https://perma.cc/YE9W -9YBY.

[23]   For a thorough analysis of all the technical and technological advances that are combined in the blockchain, *see* Arvind Narayanan and Jeremy Clark, "Bitcoin's Academic Pedigree: The Concept of Cryptocurrencies is Built from Forgotten Ideas in Research Literature," Communications of the ACM 15, no. 2 (2017) ("nearly all of the technical components of bitcoin originated in the academic literature of the 1980s and '90s"), concluding on page 17 that "Nakamoto's genius, then, wasn't any of the individual components of bitcoin, but rather the intricate way in which they fit together to breathe life into the system."

[24]   Nathaniel Whittemore, "'Economics Will No Longer Be the Handmaiden of Politics': A History of the Cypherpunks, Feat. Jim Epstein," Coindesk, November 4, 2020, https://perma.cc/53A2-U3PU (discussing a 2020 documentary on the cypherpunk movement explaining how it ties with blockchain). Also, see ReasonTV, "Bitcoin and the End of History," YouTube, October 28, 2020, 15:55, https://perma.cc/B9DX -K3AK.

[25]   Gábor Soós, "Smart Decentralization? The Radical Anti-Establishment Worldview of Blockchain Initiatives," Smart Cities and Regional Development (SCRD) Journal 2, no. 2 (2018): 17. *See*, for example, Vinton G. Cerf and Rachel E. Kahn, "A Protocol for Packet Network Intercommunication," IEEE Transactions on Communications 22, no. 5 (1974) (introducing a protocol that "supports the sharing of resources that exist in different packet switching networks"). *See also* Whitfield Diffie and Martin E. Hellman, "New directions in cryptography," IEEE Transactions on Information Theory 22, no. 6 (1976) (discussing applications of teleprocessing). Lastly, *see* William P. Wardlaw, "The RSA Public Key Cryptosystem," in *Coding Theory and Cryptography*, ed. David A. Joyner (Springer, 2000) (explaining the RSA—Rivest, Shamir, Adleman—cipher algorithm).

[26]   Ronald Linn Rivest, Adi Shamir and Leonard Max Adleman, "A Method for Obtaining Digital Signatures" (1978).

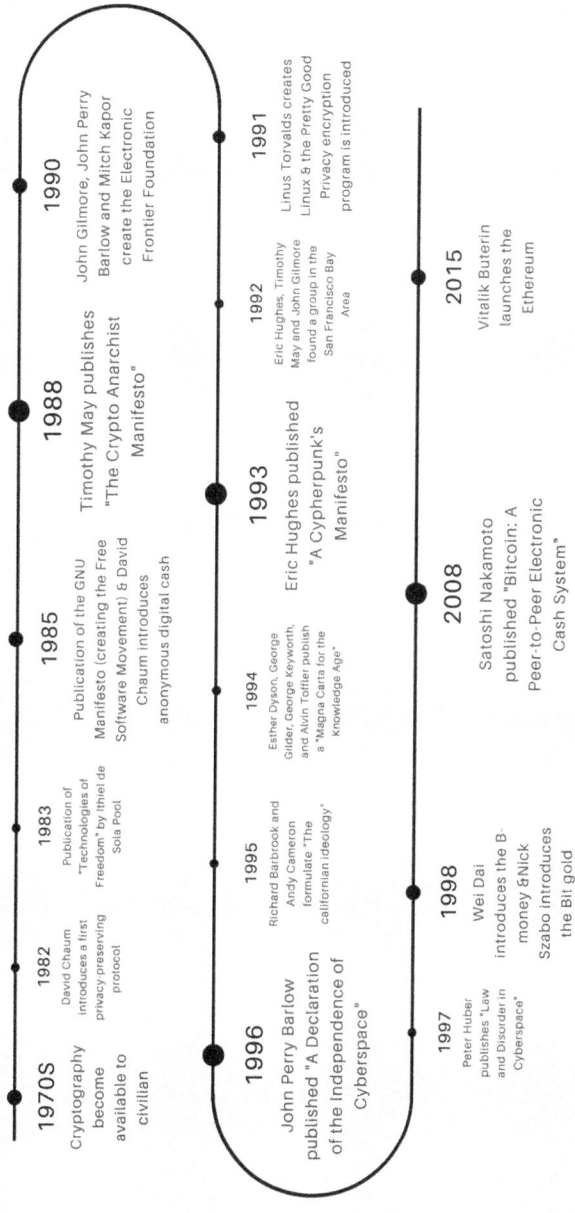

Figure 1.2   A timeline of cyberlibertarianism

puter scientist, published his thesis which he had written at the University of
Berkeley. Entitled "Computer Systems Established, Maintained, and Trusted
by Mutually Suspicious Groups,"[27] it introduced a new protocol that harnessed
cryptographic tools to protect private information.[28]

A year after, in 1983, Ithiel de Sola Pool – then a professor at Massachusetts
Institute of Technology (MIT) – published a book entitled *Technologies of
Freedom*,[29] in which he analyzed the impact of several technologies on free
speech and freedom of the press. The objective was clearly stated: technology and freedom go hand in hand. Two years later, David Chaum published
"Security without Identification: Transaction Systems to Make Big Brother
Obsolete," an article in which he introduced anonymous digital cash.[30] Here
again, freedom was mainly intended as freedom from the government. In
the same vein, the GNU Manifesto was introduced the same year, starting
the Free Software Movement. It argued that: "[T]here is no intrinsic right to
intellectual property. The kinds of supposed intellectual property rights that the
government recognizes were created by specific acts of legislation for specific
purposes."[31] It was deeply libertarian.

A few years later, in 1988, Timothy May published "The Crypto Anarchist
Manifesto" in which he called for further action.[32] It read:

> Computer technology is on the verge of providing the ability for individuals and
> groups to communicate and interact with each other in a totally anonymous manner.
> … The methods are based upon public-key encryption, zero-knowledge interactive
> proof systems, and various software protocols for interaction, authentication, and
> verification. … But only recently have computer networks and personal computers
> attained sufficient speed to make the ideas practically realizable.

---

[27]   David Lee Chaum, "Computer Systems Established, Maintained, and Trusted by
Mutually Suspicious Groups" (Ph.D diss., University of California, Berkley, 1982).
[28]   It followed Ralph C. Merkle, "Protocols for Public Key Cryptosystems," IEEE
Symposium on Security and Privacy (1980).
[29]   Ithiel de Sola Pool, *Technologies of Freedom* (Harvard University Press, 1984).
For context, *see* Gábor Soós, "Smart Decentralization? The Radical Anti-Establishment
Worldview of Blockchain Initiatives" (2018): 17.
[30]   David Chaum, "Security Without Identification: Transaction Systems to make
Big Brother Obsolete," Communications of the ACM 28, no. 10 (1985), an article
in which he introduced anonymous digital cash. It followed David Chaum, "Blind
Signatures for Untraceable Payments," in *Advances in Cryptology: Proceedings of
Crypto 82*, ed. David Chaum et al. (Springer, 1983).
[31]   Richard Stallman, "The GNU Manifesto," LINFO, March 1985, https://perma
.cc/86AR-JE5X.
[32]   Timothy C. May, "The Crypto Anarchist Manifesto," Activism, May 1988,
https://perma.cc/5NE5-VRJA. For more, *see* Daniel Eszteri, "Bitcoin: Anarchist
Money or the Currency of the Future," Studia Iuridica Auctoritate Universitatis Pecs
Publicata 151, no. 23 (2013).

... The State will of course try to slow or halt the spread of this technology, citing national security concerns, use of the technology by drug dealers and tax evaders, and fears of societal disintegration. Many of these concerns will be valid; crypto anarchy will allow national secrets to be trade freely and will allow illicit and stolen materials to be traded. An anonymous computerized market will even make possible abhorrent markets for assassinations and extortion. Various criminal and foreign elements will be active users of CryptoNet. But this will not halt the spread of crypto anarchy. ... Arise, you have nothing to lose but your barbed wire fences!

In his signature, Timothy May linked "Crypto Anarchy" to the "collapse of governments." His manifesto would be quoted several thousand times. Two years later, in April 1990, the Federal Bureau of Investigation questioned John Perry Barlow (lyricist of the Grateful Dead) about stealing and distributing the code of Macintosh ROMs. He recounted his experience on The WELL (the newsletter created by Brand) and obtained financial support from John Gilmore and Steve Wozniak (Apple's co-creator). The idea of the Electronic Frontier Foundation was born. And in July of the same year, Gilmore, Barlow and Mitch Kapor created the Electronic Frontier Foundation. They aimed to provide legal and financial support to people that were subjected to unfounded legal threats regarding internet civil liberties.

Then came Linux in 1991 as one of the first major concrete outputs accessible to the public. Linus Torvalds released the operating system's kernel under a GNU General Public License. Linux was perfectly in line with the 1985 GNU Manifesto. And Phil Zimmerman's encryption program, Pretty Good Privacy, was also made freely available in 1991. Things started to become more concrete. The following year, Eric Hughes, May and Gilmore formed a group and agreed to meet every month at Gilmore's company premises in the San Francisco Bay Area. Jude Milhon, an American hacker also known as St. Jude, attended one of the first meetings.[33] She described the group as being "cypherpunks," derived from "cipher" and "cyberpunk." Hughes reused the term in 1993 in his "Cypherpunk's Manifesto."[34] It read:

Privacy is necessary for an open society in the electronic age. Privacy is not secrecy. A private matter is something one doesn't want the whole world to know, but a secret matter is something one doesn't want anybody to know. Privacy is the power to selectively reveal oneself to the world. ...

---

[33] Steven Levy, "Crypto Rebels," Wired, February 1, 1993, https://perma.cc/C8FX -9479.

[34] Eric Hughes, "A Cypherpunk's Manifesto," March 9, 1993, https://perma.cc/ F3AK-C52W.

We cannot expect governments, corporations, or other large, faceless organizations to grant us privacy out of their beneficence. It is to their advantage to speak of us, and we should expect that they will speak. To try to prevent their speech is to fight against the realities of information. Information does not just want to be free, it longs to be free. Information expands to fill the available storage space. ...

We the Cypherpunks are dedicated to building anonymous systems. We are defending our privacy with cryptography, with anonymous mail forwarding systems, with digital signatures, and with electronic money. Cypherpunks write code. We know that someone has to write software to defend privacy, and since we can't get privacy unless we all do, we're going to write it. We publish our code so that our fellow Cypherpunks may practice and play with it. Our code is free for all to use, worldwide. We don't much care if you don't approve of the software we write. We know that software can't be destroyed and that a widely dispersed system can't be shut down.

Cypherpunks deplore regulations on cryptography, for encryption is fundamentally a private act. The act of encryption, in fact, removes information from the public realm. Even laws against cryptography reach only so far as a nation's border and the arm of its violence. Cryptography will ineluctably spread over the whole globe, and with it the anonymous transactions systems that it makes possible.

Importantly, and perhaps more aggressively, Esther Dyson, George Gilder, George Keyworth and Alvin Toffler published "A Magna Carta for the Knowledge Age" in 1994.[35] The authors quoted the "libertarian icon" Ayn Rand[36] and pointed out that cyberspace:

spells the death of the central institutional paradigm of modern life, the bureaucratic organization. (Governments, including the American government, are the last great redoubt of bureaucratic power on the face of the planet, and for them the coming change will be profound and probably traumatic.)

From these writings came "The Californian Ideology," introduced a year later by Richard Barbrook and Andy Cameron.[37] It was arguably better embedded

---

[35]   Esther Dyson, George Gilder, George Keyworth and Alvin Toffler, "Cyberspace and the American Dream: A Magna Carta for the Knowledge Age," Future Insight, August 1994. www.pff.org/issues-pubs/futureinsights/fi1.2magnacarta.html. For background information, *see* Gabor Soos, "Smart Decentralization? The Radical Anti-Establishment Worldview of Blockchain Initiatives" (2018): 36.
[36]   Esther Dyson, George Gilder, George Keyworth and Alvin Toffler, "Cyberspace and the American Dream: A Magna Carta for the Knowledge Age," Future Insight, August 1994, https://perma.cc/AG2X-FKTW.
[37]   Richard Barbrook and Andy Cameron, "The Californian Ideology," Science as Culture 6, no. 1 (1996): 44. For background information, *see* Gabor Soos, "Smart Decentralization? The Radical Anti-Establishment Worldview of Blockchain Initiatives," Smart Cities and Regional Development (SCRD) Journal 2, no. 2 (2018): 37.

in Silicon Valley's free-market technology mindset. And in 1996, John Perry Barlow published "A Declaration of the Independence of Cyberspace."[38] He argued as follows:

> Governments of the Industrial World, you weary giants of flesh and steel, I come from Cyberspace, the new home of Mind. On behalf of the future, I ask you of the past to leave us alone. You are not welcome among us. You have no sovereignty where we gather.

> We have no elected government, nor are we likely to have one, so I address you with no greater authority than that with which liberty itself always speaks. I declare the global social space we are building to be naturally independent of the tyrannies you seek to impose on us. You have no moral right to rule us nor do you possess any methods of enforcement we have true reason to fear.

> Governments derive their just powers from the consent of the governed. You have neither solicited nor received ours. We did not invite you. You do not know us, nor do you know our world. Cyberspace does not lie within your borders. Do not think that you can build it, as though it were a public construction project. You cannot. It is an act of nature and it grows itself through our collective actions.

> You have not engaged in our great and gathering conversation, nor did you create the wealth of our marketplaces. You do not know our culture, our ethics, or the unwritten codes that already provide our society more order than could be obtained by any of your impositions.

> You claim there are problems among us that you need to solve. You use this claim as an excuse to invade our precincts. Many of these problems don't exist. Where there are real conflicts, where there are wrongs, we will identify them and address them by our means. We are forming our own Social Contract. This governance will arise according to the conditions of our world, not yours. Our world is different.

> Cyberspace consists of transactions, relationships, and thought itself, arrayed like a standing wave in the web of our communications. Ours is a world that is both everywhere and nowhere, but it is not where bodies live.

> We are creating a world that all may enter without privilege or prejudice accorded by race, economic power, military force, or station of birth. We are creating a world where anyone, anywhere may express his or her beliefs, no matter how singular, without fear of being coerced into silence or conformity.

> Your legal concepts of property, expression, identity, movement, and context do not apply to us. They are all based on matter, and there is no matter here. Our identities

---

Also, *see* Richard Barbrook and Andy Cameron, "The Californian Ideology", in *Crypto Anarchy, Cyberstates, and Pirate Utopias*, ed. Peter Ludlow (The MIT Press, 2001): 363 (describing the "Californian ideology" as a "bizarre fusion of the culture bohemianism of San Francisco with the high-tech industries of Silicon Valley").

[38] John Perry Barlow, "A Declaration of the Independence of Cyberspace," Electronic Frontier Foundation, February 8, 1996, https://perma.cc/CYB7-DYMB.

have no bodies, so, unlike you, we cannot obtain order by physical coercion. We believe that from ethics, enlightened self-interest, and the commonweal, our governance will emerge. Our identities may be distributed across many of your jurisdictions. The only law that all our constituent cultures would generally recognize is the Golden Rule. We hope we will be able to build our particular solutions on that basis. But we cannot accept the solutions you are attempting to impose. ...

We will create a civilization of the Mind in Cyberspace. May it be more humane and fair than the world your governments have made before.

In the wake of the Declaration, Peter Huber, a Harvard and MIT graduate, published *Law and Disorder in Cyberspace* in 1997. The book – whose subtitle read: "Abolish the FCC and Let Common Law Rule the Telecosm" – was making a more technical point,[39] namely defending the abolition of the Federal Communications Commission in favor of common law.

Finally, a year later, in 1998, Wei Dai and Nick Szabo both introduced models of cryptographic coins – B-money and Bit gold, respectively – which were very similar to what Bitcoin would become.[40] These two digital currencies thus brought two decades of ideological and cryptographic research to fruition, building on top of the research mentioned in this section. The blockchain ecosystem has continued to flourish since then, but the core ideology remains the same – at least for now.[41] This ideological tradition has technical implications that I will explain in Chapter 2. In turn, these technological underpinnings have important ramifications for economic policy and regulation.

---

[39]   Peter Huber, *Law and Disorder in Cyberspace: Abolish the FCC and Let Common Law Rule the Telecosm* (Oxford University Press, 1997).

[40]   Satoshi Nakamoto quotes Wei Dai in her/his/their/its white paper, *see* Satoshi Nakamoto, "Bitcoin: A Peer-To-Peer Electronic Cash System," (2008), https://perma .cc/TGE8-H4DQ. For more, *see* Daniel Eszteri, "Bitcoin: Anarchist Money or the Currency of the Future," Studia Iuridica Auctoritate Universitatis Pecs Publicata 151, no. 23 (2013). According to the Ethereum White Paper, Wei's "proposal was scant on details as to how decentralized consensus could actually be implemented," *see* Ethereum, "A Next-Generation Smart Contract and Decentralized Application Platform," GitHub: 4, https://perma.cc/ZTR8-8PUF. Also, Nick Szabo, "Secure Property Titles with Owner Authority," Phonetic Sciences, https://perma.cc/3U4A -5NPT.

[41]   Catalina Goanta and Marieke Hopman, "Crypto Communities as Legal Orders," Internet Policy Review 9, no. 2 (2020): 4.

2   TODAY'S COMMUNITY: ANOTHER VAN STORY

The blockchain community is growing exponentially. Despite this, the majority of its members remain true to the main ideology of Brand's era. A specific episode of crisis management reminds us of this vividly.

2.1   One Big Community?

Another setting: 17 September 2018, seaside (the location remains a secret).

"Awemany" wakes up in his van (yes, a van, again!). He is part of the Bitcoin Unlimited team, a full-node implementation for the Bitcoin and Bitcoin Cash networks. That morning, he wants to work on implementing the "Checkdatasig/-Verify opcodes" that his team intends to activate on the Bitcoin Cash network in November. Around noon, he stumbles upon a problem in the way code counts signature operations in Bitcoin ABC, a full-node implementation of the Bitcoin Cash protocol. Awemany performs additional tests and writes a note to himself: "BitcoinABC does not check for duplicate inputs when processing a block, only when inserting a transaction into the mempool." He adds: "This is dangerous as blocks can be generated with duplicate transactions and then sent through, e.g., compact block missing transactions and avoid hitting the mempool, creating money out of thin air." The stakes are high. Awemany may have put his finger on "the most catastrophic bug in recent years, and certainly one of the most catastrophic bugs in Bitcoin ever."[42] The Bitcoin blockchain could validate a block with double spending, which would put its entire integrity at risk.[43]

A few minutes have passed. Awemany's tests are now complete. The problem seems to come from Bitcoin Core, the developers in charge of proposing changes to the Bitcoin "constitutional" code. Instead of taking advantage of the bug, or revealing it publicly in a forum to jeopardize Bitcoin, Awemany alerts five Bitcoin Core developers. He does so despite the fact that he works mainly on Bitcoin Cash, a fork of the original Bitcoin (more on this later). Both communities are constantly taunting each other on social networks (Reddit, Twitter...). They are in competition, yes; but Awemany wants fair competition. "Let's continue competing. Let's civilly inform each other of bugs. May

---

[42] Awemany, "600 Microseconds," Medium, September 22, 2018, https://perma.cc/T478-2LCB.

[43] Double spending occurs when a Bitcoin user spends the same token twice. It puts the blockchain integrity, and usefulness, at risk.

the best chain win," he will say later on. Oh… and he also owns a few Bitcoins, which may help.[44]

By 2:57 p.m., Pieter Wuille, Greg Maxwell and Wladimir Van Der Laan of Bitcoin Core, deadalnix of Bitcoin ABC and sickpig of Bitcoin Unlimited are made aware of the problem. Awemany has included his Bitcoin address in his email to them, hoping for "a little performance bonus." Eighteen minutes later, Greg Maxwell shares the report sent by Awemany to Cory Fields, Suhas Daftuar, Alex Morcos and Matt Corallo, four Bitcoin Core developers. At 5:47 p.m., Matt Corallo "officially" identifies two issues: a denial of service (DoS), as identified by Awemany; and a "critical inflation vulnerability." He has identified a way to duplicate one Bitcoin infinitely on top of the double-spending issue, going beyond an initial cap of 21 million mined Bitcoins.[45]

Luckily, both problems have "the same root cause and fix."[46] A little more than an hour later, a patch is created. It now needs to be deployed on the Bitcoin blockchain; but, as we will see later, the Bitcoin Core team doesn't have the power to unilaterally impose such a change (unlike how Apple can impose a minor update on its iPhone). For that reason, Matt tries to get in touch with Slushpool's chief executive officer to ask him to apply the patch without further delay. Slushpool is "the world's first Bitcoin mining pool," and has over 180 000 active workers on the Bitcoin blockchain, giving it significant sway over the network's development.[47] Matt finally reaches him at 8:30 p.m. The update is implemented at 8:48 p.m.

2.2   Crisis Management … and Collusion?

Let's explore how this crisis was handled. Just after 9:00 p.m., an alert was sent to Bitcoin ABC that a patch would be posted publicly around 10:00 p.m. For the first time, all the blockchain participants were informed of the issue; but rather than revealing the two vulnerabilities, the choice was made to mention only the most minor part: the DoS bug. When the message was finally sent

---

[44]   Awemany, "600 Microseconds," Medium, September 22, 2018, https://perma .cc/T478-2LCB ("[U]nfortunately [I] still own a (for my poor soul significant) amount of BTC and for that reason and others do not like having bugs in Core either.")

[45]   Alyssa Hertig, "The Latest Bitcoin Bug Was So Bad, Developers Kept Its Full Details a Secret," CoinDesk, September 21, 2018, https://perma.cc/E4K6-K7FW.

[46]   "CVE-2018-17144 Full Disclosure," Bitcoin Core, September 20, 2018, https:// perma.cc/VM3Q-D2NJ.

[47]   Slushpool.com, https://perma.cc/KM9X-MKC3.

at 9:47 p.m., the critical inflation vulnerability was omitted. Bitcoin Core explained:

> In order to encourage rapid upgrades, the decision was made to immediately patch and disclose the less serious Denial of Service vulnerability, concurrently with reaching out to miners, businesses, and other affected systems while delaying publication of the full issue to give times for systems to upgrade.[48]

The next day, on September 18, 2018, one participant posted banners on Bitcointalk and Reddit, "urging people to upgrade." The day after, the Bitcoin Core mailing list distributed "an additional message urging people to upgrade." Bitcoin Optech did the same, prompting users to "[u]pgrade to Bitcoin Core 0.16.3 to fix denial-of-service vulnerability."[49] It was not until September 20, 2018 that David Jaenson, a Qtum developer, discovered that the patch addressed not one but two problems – the DoS vulnerability *and* the critical inflation vulnerability. At that point,[50] the Bitcoin Core team could no longer deny the truth: it was primordial that a majority of Bitcoin miners update their software to prevent the exploitation of the vulnerability. At the same time, they were also trying to determine whether some had already exploited this glitch. After all, it had been there for 18 months.[51]

Fortunately, the answer seemed to be negative. Nevertheless, the community was very keen to ensure that all miners had implemented the patch. Someone posted a new message on Reddit: "New info escalates importance: upgrading to 0.16.3 is REQUIRED."[52] It said: "You should not run any version of Bitcoin Core other than 0.16.3. Older versions should not exist on the network. If you know anyone who is running an older version, tell them to upgrade it ASAP." The danger was indeed that, should two versions of the software run concomitantly, the blockchain would split. Putting them back together would have caused all the transactions validated under the old software to be lost.[53] Once

---

[48]   "CVE-2018-17144 Full Disclosure," Bitcoin Core, September 20, 2018, https://perma.cc/VM3Q-D2NJ.
[49]   Bitcoin Optech, "Bitcoin Optech Newsletter #13," September 18, 2018, https://perma.cc/B53H-F66P.
[50]   Hacker News, September 20, 2018, https://perma.cc/JH8Z-YFPA.
[51]   Aaron van Wirdum, "The Good, the Bad and the Ugly Details of One of Bitcoin's…," Bitcoin Magazine, September 21, 2018, https://perma.cc/Q2YY-HM76.
[52]   Theymos, "New info escalates importance: upgrading to 0.16.3 is REQUIRED," Reddit, www.reddit.com/r/Bitcoin/comments/9hkoo6/new_info_escalates_importance _upgrading_to_0163/.
[53]   Alyssa Hertig, "The Latest Bitcoin Bug Was So Bad, Developers Kept Its Full Details a Secret," CoinDesk, September 21, 2018, www.coindesk.com/the-latest -bitcoin-bug-was-so-bad-developers-kept-its-full-details-a-secret.

again, network integrity was at risk; and once again, things luckily turned out fine.

A few days later, Bitcoin subreddit moderator Theymos minimized the event: "Even if the bug had been exploited to its full extent, the theoretical damage to stored funds would have been rolled back." Bitcoin Core's Pieter Wuille made the same point.[54] Still, the worst had been avoided thanks to Awemany. The community hoped that he "and other Bitcoin developers, despite disagreements and some squabbles, will continue this practice." Nothing could be less certain. Oversights that resulted from an overflow of confidence – probably a "young, cocky Core developer, a new 'master of the universe' wreaking havoc by sheer arrogance and hubris"[55] – may have compromised the entire Bitcoin blockchain.

Ultimately, this story reveals a key weakness of decentralized systems where tasks are not always clearly defined. However, some would say that the same weakness is also a strength, pushing each member of the community to verify others' work. It results from the original Stewart Brand ideology: empowering individuals, without asking institutions or governments for help. The blockchain community, for now, has handled this responsibility well. It responded quickly to challenges and activated the right defense mechanisms. This is no small feat; after all, "moments of crisis uncover where actual power lies in a system."[56] I will return to this when discussing collusion in Part 2.

3   CHAPTER SUMMARY AND BEYOND

In this first chapter, I have shown that blockchain's ideological roots emerged in Stewart Brand's van, in California during the 1960s. By making individual empowerment the center of his modern philosophy and providing the correct tools to achieve it, Brand started a powerful movement throughout the United States. It helped the DIY culture emerge to empower all individuals.

Later on, the cypherpunks made cryptography the newest means of empowerment, intending to free the people from the coercive state. Combining a strong ideological ambition with technical advances, the cypherpunks built the technological foundations of blockchain.

One finds these libertarian roots in blockchain, as the Bitcoin incident I describe above illustrates. Owing to the dangers that such an approach entails

---

[54]   Pieter Wuille (@pwuille), September 20, 2018, https://perma.cc/7TQJ-DYA7.

[55]   Awemany, "600 Microseconds," Medium, September 22, 2018, https://perma .cc/SB6G-J23J.

[56]   Angela Walch, "Deconstructing 'Decentralization': Exploring the Core Claim of Crypto Systems," in *Cryptoassets*, ed. Chris Brummer (Oxford University Press, 2019): 19.

by relying (too) heavily on good faith, part of the community may eventually move away from individual empowerment. Several blockchains will soon transfer power to (more) centralized organs and entities, despite its DNA, which I discuss in the coming chapter.

2. Blockchain's toolbox

1 FIRST, BLOCKCHAIN'S COMMONALITIES

To start my explanation about blockchain, I want to explore the commonalities between most of them, particularly the central role that encryption and immutability play. These two features explain why blockchain code creates trust, which is central to blockchain survival, since "virtually every commercial transaction has within itself an element of trust,"[1] in the words of Kenneth Arrow.

1.1 Encryption: It's All About the Code

One may define "encryption" as the process of converting information or data into code.[2] As we shall see, it proves essential in reaching a consensus (which creates trust) on blockchain while maintaining privacy.

1.1.1 Encryption as a path to integrity

Encryption is used not only in blockchain ecosystems, but all over cyberspace.[3] It is a cardinal point in blockchain ecosystems, as it enables "trust

---

[1] Kenneth Arrow, "Gifts and Exchanges," in *Altruism, Morality, and Economic Theory*, Edmund S. Phelps ed. (Russell Sage Foundation, 1975): 24.

[2] *See* "Cryptography is about power", Phillip Rogaway, "The Moral Character of Cryptographic Work," Cryptology ePrint Archive, Report 2015/1162 (2015): 11; and Julian Assange, "Conspiracy as governance," (2006), https://perma.cc/J29R-Q52M ("The universe believes in encryption").

[3] Discussing the importance of encryption, *see* Niels Ferguson, Bruce Schneier and Tadayoshi Kohno, *Cryptography Engineering: Design Principles and Practical Applications* (Wiley, 2011): 5. Generally, explaining that cryptography was originally used by governments and then moved on to the general public, *see* Catalina Goanta and Marieke Hopman, "Cryptocommunities as Legal Orders," Internet Policy Review 9 (2020); Phil Champagne, *The Book Of Satoshi: The Collected Writings Of Bitcoin Creator Satoshi Nakamoto* (Publishing LLC, 2014): 136 ("Satoshi Nakamoto November 25, 2009, 06:17:23 p.m.: The possibility to be anonymous or pseudonymous relies on you not revealing any identifying information about yourself in connection with the bitcoin addresses you use. If you post your bitcoin address on the web, then you're associating that address and any transactions with it with the name you

in code," and ultimately, the certification of authenticity without traditional intermediaries. Satoshi Nakamoto wanted Bitcoin, the most famous use of blockchain to this day, to be based on "cryptographic proof instead of trust;"[4] but, on the contrary, I argue that blockchain generates trust because it is based on cryptographic proof.[5] Indeed, "encryption is just a bunch of math, and math has no agency."[6] It forces all blockchain participants to equally engage their resources in the network, which creates trust.

Each blockchain transaction must be verified before being validated. The verification process simply ensures that both addresses are valid, and that the buyer's account holds the required amount of Bitcoin at the time of the transaction. The goal is merely to avoid double spending (and, for that reason, the verification process is central to the blockchain value). Accordingly, if a Bitcoin is transferred in exchange for the sale of a car, the verification process does not check whether that car actually ends up in the new buyer's hands.

These verification costs are voluntarily made high – thanks to cryptography – in order to prevent ill-intentioned users from intervening at low costs and validating double spending.[7] When a blockchain uses a Proof of Work mechanism, miners compete to solve a cryptographic puzzle (I provide a more detailed explanation later on in this chapter). That process requires significant computational power, which consumes electricity. Related costs create a strong disincentive to validating transactions with double spending as, if detected, they would be invalidated and the miner's reward would be lost.

---

posted under. If you posted under a handle that you haven't associated with your real identity, then you're still pseudonymous."); *see* also Don Tapscott and Alex Tapscott, *A Blockchain Revolution: How The Technology Behind Bitcoin Is Changing Money, Business, And The World* (Penguin Books, 2016): 94 ("Satoshi installed no identity requirement for the network layer itself, meaning that no one had to provide a name, e-mail address, or any other personal data in order to download and use the bitcoin software.")

4 Satoshi Nakamoto, "Bitcoin: A Peer-to-Peer Electronic Cash System" (2008), https://perma.cc/TGE8-H4DQ.

5 For a great analysis of trust in blockchain, *see* Kevin Werbach, *The Blockchain and the New Architecture of Trust* (MIT Press, 2018).

6 Bruce Schneier: *Data and Goliath: The Hidden Battles to Collect Your Data and Control Your World* (W.W. Norton & Company, 2015): 131.

7 Prateek Goorha, "The Return of 'The Nature of the Firm': The Role of the Blockchain," The Journal of the British Blockchain Association 1, no. 1 (2018): 71. Also, Floris F. Seuren, "Exploring the Applicability of Blockchain in Lowering Transaction Costs in the Commercial Real Estate Due Diligence Process: A Case Study Research" (2018), https://perma.cc/KH9W-QPLP.

1.1.2   Encryption as a key to identity

Blockchain encryption also serves another purpose at a more individual level: it enables users to interact without revealing their real space identity while certifying transactions.

One must consider the functioning of private and public keys to understand why that is. Notably, a private key is only in the possession of a private individual. It is not stored on a central server,[8] meaning that each user must take care not to lose it.[9] The public key is reciprocal (what one key does, the other one can undo) and publicly available.

First, let me explain the functioning of these keys outside blockchain. To this end, let us first look at the sender's side. She or he will be running the data she or he wishes to send (e.g., a picture) through a hash function (e.g., MD5 or SHA-256). This process will result in a hash value (a numeric value) identifying the data. The sender will then encrypt that hash value using her or his private key. This encryption will result in a new encrypted hash, called the signature. Ultimately, she or he will send the original data along with that signature. Then, the receiver will decrypt the signature using the sender's public key, which will result in a hash. In parallel, the receiver will also run the original data into the hash function used by the sender. She or he will obtain another hash. Should the two hashes be equal, this will prove the validity of the signature, as only the sender's public key can undo the encryption.

Now, in the context of blockchain, the sender generally uses a blockchain wallet that automatically generates and stores her or his private key. When sending the data (or token) on the chain, the blockchain software will sign the transaction with the sender's private key. This signature will indicate to the entire blockchain community that the sender has the authority to send that data or token. Indeed, decrypting the signature with that user's public key will certify that she or he (the owner of the data or token) is behind the transaction.

To this day, converting a public key into a private key is impossible for practical reasons, because of the computational power this requires. It is also

---

[8]   That is, if the user has not created a blockchain identity thanks to a third-party custodial service storing a copy of its private key. Discussing this *see* Vitalik Buterin, "On Collusion" (April 3, 2019), https://perma.cc/FE58-ZVJY.

[9]   That is, if the blockchain user is not using an intermediary to create and access her or his wallet. Documenting the many stories of Bitcoin wallet holders who have tried to recover old computers thrown in public dumps in a bid to retrieve their private keys, *see* Daniel Phillips and Stephen Graves, "How to Get a Bitcoin Address," Decrypt, September 21, 2020, https://perma.cc/KD4G-4QP3 (discussing different ways to store private keys). Also, Planet Money, "Bitcoin Losers (Classic)," January 1, 2021, https://perma.cc/RX3T-YUSJ. Finally, *see* Nathaniel Popper, "Lost passwords lock millionaires out of their Bitcoin fortunes," The New York Times, January 12, 2021, https://perma.cc/YZ7R-VC5G.

difficult to link public keys to the physical entities that control them. That being said, advances in big data analysis could, theoretically, undermine the anonymity offered by blockchains.[10] For instance, analyzing all of the transactions carried out by one user could help identify her or his real space identity.[11] Although a blockchain is not "telling who the parties are,"[12] the entire blockchain "tape"[13] – which includes the timestamp and quantum of individual trades – is made public to create trust in its integrity.[14] Tracking services are developed on the basis of that metadata, but they suffer from several drawbacks.[15] First, even if governments will use them, they will not be easily accessible to most individual users, since they ask for sophisticated techniques. That's an important point rarely raised when discussing the limits of pseudonymity. Second, they seem to work only on a few blockchains (for the time being)[16] and where the transaction volume is high.

In the end, anonymity is a continuous game of cat and mouse – technologies that protect real space identities are constantly evolving. For instance, Monero uses a technique called "ring signatures." The technique groups

[10]   Andrew Hayward, "US Government is Getting Serious about Tracking Crypto," Decrypt, July 15, 2020, https://perma.cc/9UN7-ZRA2 (discussing how U.S. agencies are developing cryptocurrency tracing tools). Also, U.S. Department of Justice, "Department of Justice Seizes $2.3 Million in Cryptocurrency Paid to the Ransomware Extortionists Darkside," Justice News, June 7, 2021, https://perma.cc/424P-BU3B; and Jeff Benson, "US Recovers Bitcoin Paid to Colonial Pipeline Hackers," Decrypt, June 7, 2021, https://perma.cc/WFT7-CPF2.

[11]   Exploring how to do this, *see* Yi Sun and Yan Zhang, "Privacy in Cryptocurrencies," Medium, October 25, 2018, https://perma.cc/WPP8-4VK8; Michael Kaplan, "I accidentally threw away $60M worth of Bitcoin," New York Post, May 26, 2018, https://perma.cc/U6XT-29ZF.

[12]   Satoshi Nakamoto, "Bitcoin: A Peer-to-Peer Electronic Cash System" (2008): 6.

[13]   *Id.*

[14]   Primavera De Filippi, "The Interplay Between Decentralization and Privacy: The Case of Blockchain Technologies," Journal of Peer Production, no. 7 (2016): 10 ("Although the content of communications can be encrypted so that it can only be accessed by the persons to whom it was actually addressed (e.g., by relying on end-to-end encryption), the metadata related to these communications (i.e., who is talking to whom, for how long, and what is the type of transaction in which they participate) needs to be visible to a majority of network's nodes. While this is not an inherent requirement of any decentralized system, it is, in practice, the most common implementation of these systems").

[15]   Discussing these services, *see* Steven Goldfeder, Harry Kalodner, Dillon Reisman and Arvind Narayanan, "When the Cookie Meets the Blockchain: Privacy Risks of Web Payments via Cryptocurrencies" (2017) (showing "how third-party web trackers can deanonymize users of cryptocurrencies.")

[16]   For an overview of how different blockchains ensure privacy, *see* Yi Sun and Yan Zhang, "Privacy in Cryptocurrencies," Medium, October 25, 2018, https://perma .cc/WPP8-4VK8.

dummy cryptographic signatures with at least one actual key. This prevents outside observers from identifying the "true" public keys that are being used in each transaction.[17] Monero furthermore combines this with ring confidential transactions and one-time stealth wallet addresses, which recently led the chief scientist of crypto-analytic firm Elliptic to say that he does not "expect to see blockchain monitoring-based compliance tools to appear for Monero any time soon, if ever."[18] Zcash is using "zero-knowledge proofs," a technique for conveying information (e.g., identifiers) from a prover to a verifier without revealing it.[19] Concerns that predict the end of pseudonymity should, therefore, be nuanced.[20] Third, non-transacting blockchain participants – such as the core developers – remain greatly protected, as most deanonymization services work on the basis of past transactions.[21]

One may observe two conflicting approaches to anonymity in the block-chain sphere. One involves working with governments in developing legally compliant blockchains where public institutions have powers to intervene.[22] The other consists of developing fully encrypted systems – these can go so

---

[17] "Ring Signature," Monero, https://perma.cc/WGU2-V8L2.
[18] Timothy Lloyd, "Blueleaks: How the FBI tracks Bitcoin Laundering on the Dark Web," Decrypt, July 7, 2020, https://perma.cc/XB2M-6VQL.
[19] "What are zk-SNARKs?," ZCash, https://perma.cc/3RJU-LMVZ ("Zero-knowledge proofs allow one party (the prover) to prove to another (the verifier) that a statement is true, without revealing any information beyond the validity of the statement itself.")
[20] *See*, for instance, this example of a transaction in which more than $1 billion was moved, while still being protected by pseudonymity; Liam Frost, "The Most Secretive Bitcoin Wallet just Moved nearly $1 billion," Decrypt, June 30, 2020, https://perma.cc/55A5-K29P.
[21] Even with the Bitcoin blockchain, see Colin Harper, "An Old Trick could Solve Bitcoin's Privacy Problem," Decrypt, May 31, 2020, (describing CoinSwap, a service that allows "two or more parties to swap coins between each other without publishing the real recipient's address to the blockchain"). Also, Mathew Di Salvo, "Crypto Users Apathetic About Privacy," Decrypt, September 2, 2020, https://perma.cc/A6HA-MTQ3 (describing CoinJoin, a service that allows users to "mix their Bitcoins together to hide transaction history"). In October 2020, the U.S. Department of Justice created a Cyber-Digital Task Force to study these new techniques, *see* Office of Public Affairs, "Attorney General William P. Barr Announces Publication of Cryptocurrency Enforcement Framework," United States Department of Justice, October 8, 2020, https://perma.cc/YZ5M-77E7. Also, *Report of the Attorney General's Cyber Digital Task Force: Cryptocurrency Enforcement Framework*, prepared by United States Department of Justice (Washington, DC, 2020), https://perma.cc/DQN3-56AV.
[22] IBM Institute for Business Value, "Building Trust in Government: Exploring the Potential of Blockchains" (2017): 1, https://perma.cc/C8J3-TPNQ ("IBM Institute for Business Value surveyed 200 government leaders in 16 countries on their experiences and expectations with blockchains"). In fact, cyber-forensics could also be used to identify criminals. *See* John Bohannon, "Why Criminals Can't Hide Behind Bitcoin," Science, March 9, 2016, https://perma.cc/5S9S-68WK.

far as hiding the number of transactions in which a particular user takes part.[23] To paraphrase Peter Steiner's famous cartoon: with the proper adjustments, nobody knows if you're a good or bad dog on a blockchain.[24] In this case, cryptographic techniques "preserve individual privacy in decentralized architectures."[25] This is further discussed in Chapter 7.

For the time being, let us agree that, because transactions are encoded,[26] the real-space identity of (most) blockchain users is protected by pseudonymity as long as they don't convert their tokens using an exchange which actually requires proof of identity.[27] Indeed, if a user converts her or his Bitcoin into euros using an exchange for which she or he has to provide an ID, her or his pseudonymity on the blockchain will be instantly tied to her or his real-life identity. But some exchanges operating outside Europe do not require such proof.

On top of preserving personal identities, blockchain encryption also protects the nature and purpose of each transaction.[28] Users on either side of the transaction interact with one another using peer-to-peer transmission, with communication occurring directly between them instead of being routed through a central point. The upshot is that, in general, only the existence of

---

[23] One of the notable projects is MimbleWimble. Bitcoin is working to make all amounts encrypted. For an explanation, *see* Don Tapscott and Alex Tapscott, *A Blockchain Revolution: How The Technology Behind Bitcoin Is Changing Money, Business, And The World* (Penguin Books, 2016): 459 (quoting an interview with Stephen Pair that occurred on June 11, 2015) ("The biggest threat to bitcoin is that it becomes so heavily regulated at some point that a competitor that's more private and more anonymous shows up and everybody switches to that").

[24] Peter Steiner, "On the Internet, Nobody Knows You're a Dog," New Yorker, July 5, 1993, https://perma.cc/AC52-4U2L.

[25] Primavera De Filippi, "The Interplay Between Decentralization and Privacy: The Case of Blockchain Technologies," Journal of Peer Production, no. 7 (2016): 1.

[26] Kevin Werbach, *The Blockchain and The New Architecture of Trust* (MIT Press, 2018): 45.

[27] Discussing that, *see* Daniel Phillips, "Report: 99.9% of Bitcoin Transactions Don't Go to the Darknet," Decrypt, January 29, 2020, https://perma.cc/8MJJ-3WKE. On the subject, please note that the Ethereum Foundation is advising its users to "buy ETH peer-to-peer" to gain control over the tokens. By contrast, "[e]xchanges are businesses that let you buy crypto using traditional currencies. They have custody over any ETH you buy until you send it to a wallet you control," *see* Ethereum Foundation, Decentralized exchanges (DEXs), May 26, 2021, https://perma.cc/Q34P-JVZ2.

[28] Robert P. Murphy and Silas Barta, *Understanding Bitcoin: The Liberty Lover's Guide to the Mechanics and Economics of Cryptocurrencies* (2017): 52 ("[I]t's possible to hide the 'meaning' of a transaction (to the extent that it's connected to people's identities) from everyone except the two parties to it. In contrast, conventional banking requires that these third parties be able to look up the real owner of an account and 'connect the dots' regarding who transferred what to whom").

a transaction is visible to outsiders; but the identity of the participants, and the nature and purpose of the transactions, remain hidden.[29]

While quantum computing could significantly alter this state of affairs, it remains a distant threat.[30] For the time being, the more significant limit to the principles of pseudonymity and privacy is the interest that blockchain users may have in disclosing information. For instance, when a blockchain user is proving possession of a physical good by providing the courts with a proof of transfer, the correspondence between her or his real-life identity and her or his blockchain identity is automatically established. Finally, it is important to note that, although the vast majority blockchains are encrypted, nothing prevents users from creating a blockchain where access is contingent on verification of the real space identity. To some extent, this is the case for private blockchains that are all about creating transactional infrastructures between already known and pre-approved participants – for example, companies operating in a specific industry.

1.2   Immutability: It's the Code, Again

1.2.1   Explanations

Blockchain is immutable because it is both decentralized and distributed. The decentralization of blockchain determines who controls it, while its distribution designates the location. The graph in Figure 2.1 is commonly used to represent these two concepts.

Blockchain is decentralized since no single user controls the information or data on the blockchain.[31] The power to alter the blockchain is equally shared among all of its users; this is why it has no choke points. As a result, changing one copy of the ledger has no impact on the rest of the blockchain. Put simply, no single user retains the power to alter the information contained in other

---

[29] *See* generally Gary C. Kessler, "An Overview of Cryptography," June 13, 2019, https://perma.cc/6F6R-2N87. Regarding what forensic blockchain services can achieve, *see* for instance James Smith, "Elliptic And Financial Privacy," March 4, 2019, https://perma.cc/B494-X5GP (a service used for "preventing, detecting, and pursuing criminal activity in cryptocurrencies"). Generally speaking, such services are mostly used to "combat financial crime, and do not allow it to be used for marketing, business intelligence, or any other purpose," *id.*

[30] Aleksey K. Fedorov, Evgeniy O. Kiktenko and Alexander I. Lvovsky, "Quantum Computers Put Blockchain Security at Risk," Nature 563, no. 7732 (2018): 465, 466 ("A quantum computer is a physical system harnessing quantum effects to perform computation").

[31] It, of course, creates trust, but also raises issues, *see* Daniel Phillips, "Someone Just Made a $2.6 million Mistake on Ethereum," Decrypt, June 10, 2020, https://perma .cc/B3WX-9B6T.

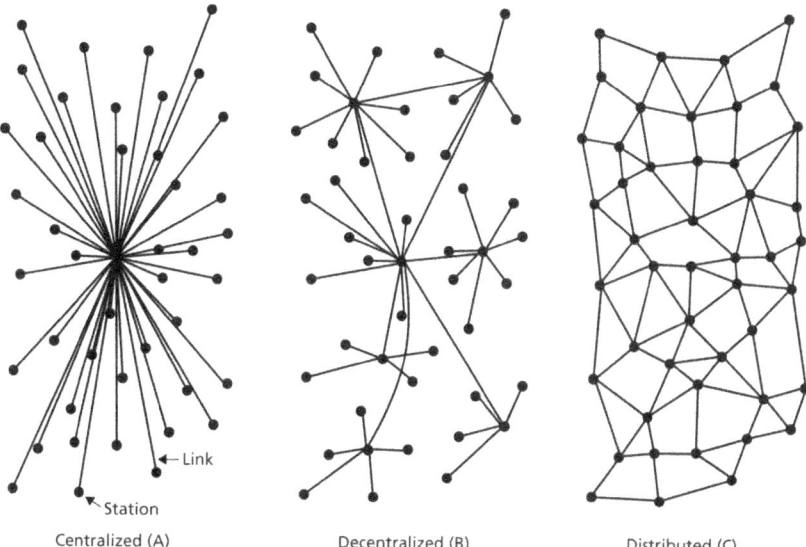

Centralized (A)   Decentralized (B)   Distributed (C)

Note: Re: distribution *see* Paul Baran, "On Distributed Communications Networks," IEEE
Transactions on Communications 12, no. 1 (1964).

Figure 2.1   Centralization vs. decentralization vs. distribution

users' copies. This inalterability applies to blockchain developers, courts and
other forms of public intervention.[32] It also means that the negative effects of
one person's reckless behavior are limited because only that person's copy of
the blockchain will be affected and thus invalidated.[33]

Blockchain is also distributed because its functioning mechanisms and data
are located across many computers through the network. Contrary to centralized systems, where core developers maintain control over these elements, they
are equally distributed between all the nodes in the network in the blockchain
space. Blockchain thus creates trust by granting equal access to the full ledger.

---

[32]   Because decentralization leads to immutability, which also limits blockchain
developers in altering applications, some are arguing for progressive decentralization,
where they would retain the ability to modify specific parameters for a limited period,
see Arthur Camara, "Why Progressive Decentralization is Blockchain's Best Hope,"
Medium, February 6, 2019, https://perma.cc/4UAC-DHYV.
[33]   Ross Mauri, "Three Features of Blockchain that Help Prevent Fraud," IBM,
September 19, 2017, https://perma.cc/DYM4-BA2J.

The distribution of power is cemented by a set of procedures, called the protocol.[34] Once the protocol is established, it is not possible to deviate from it unless decided by most users, who can then create a copy of the blockchain functioning with new rules. This is referred to as a "fork." From the outset, it is important to note that forking does impair the immutability principle.[35] The original (pre-forked) copy of a forked blockchain remains intact. For now, let me simply stress that blockchain reliance on a protocol is said to solve the "Byzantine Generals Problem,"[36] according to which computer systems cannot reach consensus without relying on a central authority.[37] In short, blockchain distribution eliminates the need to trust a single entity.

In this regard, the difference between blockchains and tech giants is blatant. Let us take social media as an example. Facebook not only controls the information of each user, but is also the only entity to have a full copy of the network data. It can grant access to selected users, withdraw that access, alter the data and so on. Facebook is neither decentralized nor distributed; it is centralized.

---

[34] Chris Dannen, *Introducing Ethereum and Solidity: Foundations of Cryptocurrency and Blockchain Programming for Beginners* (Apress, 2017): 3 ("[A] protocol is a system of rules that describes how a computer (and its programmer) can connect to, participate in, and transmit information over a system or network. These instructions define code syntax and semantics that the system expects. Protocols can involve hardware, software, and plain-language instructions."); *see* also Bryant Nielson, "Review of the 6 Major Blockchain Protocols," Richtopia, March 21, 2017, http://perma.cc/LA89 -TPLR.

[35] Paul Vigna and Michael J. Casey, *The Truth Machine: The Blockchain and The Future of Everything* (St. Martin's Press, 2018); 64 ("Blockchain technology doesn't remove the need for trust. In fact, if anything it's an enabler of more trustful relations. What it does do is widen the perimeter of trust."); *see* Sinclair Davidson, Primavera De Filippi and Jason Potts, "Economics of Blockchain," (2016) (arguing that blockchain is a "kind of spontaneous order produced by the market by people acting within the rules of the law of property, tort and contract").

[36] Phil Champagne, *The Book of Satoshi: The Collected Writings of Bitcoin Creator Satoshi Nakamoto* (e53 Publishing, LLC, 2014): 77 ("Satoshi Nakamoto Thu, 13 Nov 2008 19:34:250800: The proof-of-work chain is a solution to the Byzantine Generals' Problem.") For an explanation of the Byzantine Generals Problem, *see* Leslie Lamport et al., "The Byzantine Generals Problem," ACM Transactions on Programming Languages and Systems 4, no. 3 (1982): 382 ("This situation can be expressed abstractly in terms of a group of generals of the Byzantine army camped with their troops around an enemy city. Communicating only by messenger, the generals must agree upon a common battle plan. However, one or more of them may be traitors who will try to confuse the others. The problem is to find an algorithm to ensure that the loyal generals will reach agreement.")

[37] Aaron Wright and Primavera De Filippi, "Decentralized Blockchain Technology and the Rise of Lex Cryptographia" (2015).

On the contrary, blockchain-based social media services, such as Steemit,[38] generally cannot prevent one user from accessing the service or alter the data posted (as it is spread across various nodes). Furthermore, Steemit governance requires a majority of votes among the participants, as opposed to Facebook, whose board can decide on new governance mechanisms overnight. Considering that the first reason why people are not using Facebook is that they do not trust the company (in how it handles data),[39] one can easily understand how central blockchain's characteristics are to giving it value. Blockchain seeks to ensure predictability to remedy that trust issue; it attracts users by providing certainty about how the system will react to specific behaviors.[40] That being said, if trust in governance mechanisms were all that mattered, Steemit would now dominate Facebook. I will come back to that competition between blockchain (a "counter-trend" to centralization, as Mark Zuckerberg called it)[41] and non-blockchain products and services in Chapter 15.

Now, let us take a closer look at how blockchain immutability works in practice when it comes to the data it contains. As I said, blockchain is decentralized and distributed thanks to code. Transactions are put into blocks (here represented as "set of transactions"), and each block contains a header with the previous block's identification (its "hash value"). The hash value is made public, which helps the traceability of transactions and assets that blockchains contain. Generally speaking, the header also contains a cryptographic commitment (a Merkle tree), different types of mining data (depending on the consensus algorithm – such as the "nounce" to be found in case of a Proof of Work blockchain) and a timestamp.

One cannot double spend the same asset as a result, with the corollary that blockchain makes each digital object truly unique. This creates fundamental implications for property, as blockchain allows for the reintroduction of scarcity in cyberspace. Because what is scarce is more precious than what is not, one could surely argue that blockchain will introduce a new paradigm in the

---

[38] A social media running on top of the Steem blockchain functioning with Proof of Stake as the consensus protocol.
[39] *See* Casey Newton, "The Verge Tech Survey 2020: How People Feel about Apple, Google, Facebook, and More," The Verge, March 2, 2020, https://perma.cc/957Q-EDF2 (46 per cent of respondents declared that trust was the primary reason why they do not use Facebook).
[40] *See* Balázs Bodó, "Mediated Trust: A Theoretical Framework to Address the Trustworthiness of Technological Trust Mediators," New Media & Society (2020): 12 (explaining that blockchains seek to create trust by producing "confidence by hard-coding rules into the system" to ensure predictability).
[41] *See* Financial Times, "Facebook's Blockchain Experiment Raises Eyebrows," Financial Times, May 15, 2018, https://perma.cc/TS4F-F6KF.

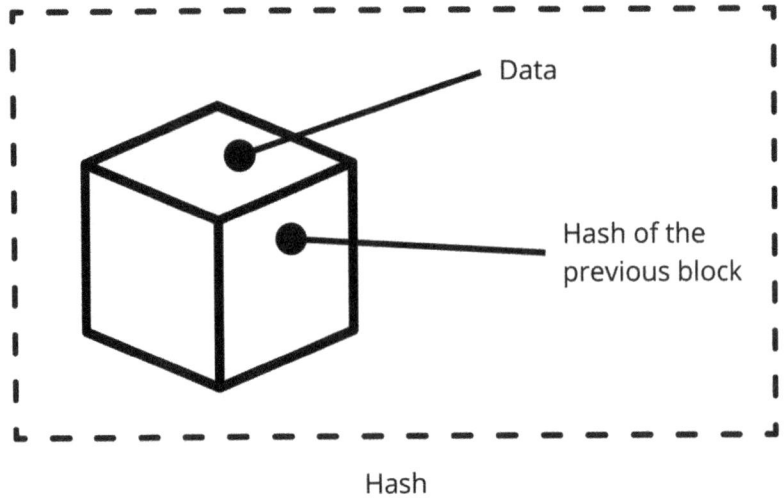

Hash

Figure 2.2   Content of a block

field of property law. But that's a different subject you will have to wait until Chapter 15 to learn more about.

The hash value is generated automatically by the blockchain software. Changing information within a block automatically changes it. If one modifies any piece of information in a block, a new identity is indeed assigned. Figure 2.3 presents an example in which substituting a "+" for a "vs." results in a completely different hash value.

Figure 2.3   Hashing outcome

Thus, should one blockchain participant modify one transaction in block #1, that block would get assigned a new identity. This would create a mismatch with the original identity of that block #1 initially recorded into block #2.[42] One would then need to recalculate all the subsequent blocks' hash values to re-validate the entire chain. And one would need to do so before the addition of a new block. Indeed, the protocol of most proof-of-work blockchains (such as Bitcoin) validates the chain with the most chain work (i.e., computational work) put into it. Should anyone want to change blockchain history, they would need to out-compete the computational power put in by all the miners and have the majority of them agree to the changed history. Doing so – i.e., a 51% attack – would be costly (for example, in electricity, should the blockchain operate under Proof of Work) and could be impossible in practice (should the blockchain have enough miners) with public permissionless blockchains. For that reason, hacking blockchains is possible when they are used and maintained by only a handful of users; but it is not when there are over several hundred users (this would require computing power that we do not have to this day).

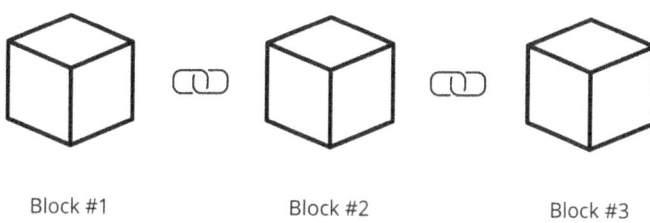

Block #1   Block #2   Block #3

Figure 2.4   A chain of blocks

It follows that blockchain presents its users with a trustful copy of the entire ledger history. As we will see in Chapter 6, providing blockchain users with such information is part of what sets apart blockchain from markets.

1.2.2   Unstoppable

Blockchain's immutability has consequences that go beyond the creation of an unalterable database.[43] Namely, when blockchain is used to "organize" the

---

[42]   A successful modification of the chain would then imply re-hashing the new version of the block one want to modify and, subsequently, re-hashing the entire chain of blocks.

[43]   I won't discuss the psychological pressure it creates; for that, *see* Arthur Camara, "Why Progressive Decentralization is Blockchain's Best Hope," Medium, February 6, 2019, https://perma.cc/4UAC-DHYV (explaining that "[t]he pressures of immortal

future through smart contracts, it makes the latter unstoppable as, once again, all the information (here, a smart contract) put on the blockchain is immutable and cannot be erased (here, cannot be stopped).[44]

"Smart contracts"[45] – defined as "a computerized transaction protocol that executes the terms of a contract"[46] – are programmed and automated transactions on a blockchain. They are "contract[s] built into the code."[47] With smart contracts, blockchain users ensure that a set of transactions will be automatically triggered if certain pre-defined conditions are met. Once these potential transactions are put on the blockchain, they cannot be modified or stopped – that is, unless a back door has been implemented to allow designated users to intervene,[48] and as long as the blockchain on which they are implemented is maintained.[49] Vitalik Buterin recently regretted adopting the term "smart con-

---

code paralyze developers: you can tinker in a test environment forever, but there will always be real-world variables you can't anticipate. Covering your eyes and hitting launch is no way to make breakthroughs. It's more likely to produce breakdowns").

[44] Rhys Lindmark, "#CryptoEthics Concepts: Decentralization-Enabled Unstoppable Code," Rhys Lindmark, July 8, 2018, https://perma.cc/VNR2-94KM.

[45] Lennart Ante, "Smart Contracts on the Blockchain—A Bibliometric Analysis and Review," BRL Working Paper Series No. 10 (2020).

[46] Nick Szabo, "Smart Contracts," University of Amsterdam, https://perma.cc/5NF3-R6N3.

[47] Report of the Joint Economic Committee Congress of the United States on the 2018 Economic Report of the President. Report 115-596, prepared by the House of Representatives (Washington, DC, 2018): 210. One could nonetheless underline that not all smart contracts are contracts in the legal sense. For a discussion of smart contracts' legality, *see* Thibault Schrepel, "Smart Contracts and the Digital Single Market Through the Lens of a 'Law + Technology' Approach," European Commission (2021).

[48] *See* George Samman and David Freuden, "DAO: A Decentralized Governance Layer For The Internet Of Value," Monsterplay, May 20, 2020: 11, https://perma.cc/47EX-GDZH (e.g., explaining that most decentralized finance smart contracts have "an admin key" that can be used for "killing" these contracts, "while others have a pause function or a master key to stop and making it difficult from the onset to decentralize"). Discussing other technical solutions to stop smart contracts, *see* Thibault Schrepel, "Smart Contracts and the Digital Single Market Through the Lens of a 'Law + Technology' Approach," European Commission (2021).

[49] *See* Vitalik Buterin, "Engineering Security Through Coordination Problems," Vitalik Buterin's website, May 8, 2017, https://perma.cc/G2PC-W4LN ("all clients and applications that depend on the original digital token will break, users will need to update their clients to switch to the new digital token, and smart contracts with no capacity to look to the outside world and *see* that they need to update will break entirely"). Tornado Cash, "Tornado.cash Is Finally Trustless!" Medium, May 20, 2020, https://perma.cc/S943-CXM2 ("no one can modify the smart contracts and the protocol is decentralized and unstoppable, as long as Ethereum isn't changed or taken down").

tracts," saying that "persistent scripts" would have been more appropriate.[50] I share this view.

To conclude on immutability, I want to underline that not all blockchains are necessarily immutable. That characteristic must be decided, and further maintained by vote. A small part of the Ethereum community, for example, is pushing for a reversal of illegal transactions, therefore refusing to enforce blockchain's quasi-absolute immutability.[51] This has already been done in the famous "DAO incident," but some are pushing to eliminate it as a default blockchain characteristic.[52] Although immutability is part of what gives blockchain value, and narrowing it could have unpredictable consequences, several blockchains will most likely take that chance in the coming years.

One last thing should be mentioned in this regard. When users want to revoke a transaction and stop it, a majority of them must enforce that decision. Put differently, blockchains' exceptions are applicable only when they emerge from a movement. This has significant implications in terms of regulation, which are discussed in Part 3.

2   AND NOW… SOME IDIOSYNCRASIES

Despite running on common characteristics, blockchain ecosystems compete against each other to provide their users with useful features.[53] Whether they are public or private, permissionless or permissioned, whether they rely on Proof of Work or another consensus protocol, blockchains can adopt distinct forms. These are critical for the purpose of antitrust analysis.

2.1   Public, Private, Permissionless or Permissioned

Access to a blockchain defines whether it is public or private. When a blockchain is public, anyone can access it. On the contrary, authorization is needed to access private blockchains. On top of blockchain's public or private nature, writing permissions on the ledger define whether a blockchain is permissioned

---

[50]   Vitalik Buterin, (@VitalikButerin), October 13, 2018, https://perma.cc/5S4R -RTMU.

[51]   *See* Vlad Zamfir, "'Code is Not Law' and Immutability Postponed," Cryptonomist, March 10, 2020.

[52]   *See* Nathaniel Popper, "A Hacking of More Than $50 Million Dashes Hopes in the World of Virtual Currency," The New York Times, June 17, 2016, https://perma.cc/ W5FU-P5SG.

[53]   *See* Garriga "Blockchain and Cryptocurrencies: A Classification and Comparison of Architecture Drivers" (2020): 5 (explaining that blockchains could be sorted out using seven key architecture features: cost, consistency, functionality and functional extensibility, performance and scalability, security, decentralization and privacy).

or permissionless. When anyone can write on the blockchain (validate blocks), it is permissionless. The blockchain is permissioned when only specific users can write on it. Therefore, public blockchains can be permissionless or permissioned; while private blockchains are, by definition, always permissioned. Some refuse to call them blockchains for their lack of openness, as this is contrary to blockchain core ideology – an argument that I find more and more convincing.[54]

More specifically, there is no access control in public permissionless blockchains. They are faithful to the original idea of Satoshi Nakamoto and, before that, to the cypherpunk and open-source movements.[55] Generally speaking, if you hear someone discussing "blockchain" without giving the specifics, chances are that person is referring to public permissionless ones. That certainly applies to this book. As for private blockchains, they usually take one of two different forms. The first form is where the blockchain is run by a single entity setting up the protocol and running it. The second is called "consortium blockchain," where a pre-selected set of nodes controls the consensus. All consortium blockchains operate under a group's leadership instead of a single entity.

Some of these characteristics will likely pique the interest of readers with a background in antitrust law. To a first approximation, private blockchains increase the likelihood of antitrust claims, such as refusals to deal, self-preferencing or pricing issues. However, it is important not to jump to conclusions. As explained later in this book, while some blockchains are indeed more problematic than others when it comes to antitrust enforcement, this does not mean that public blockchains raise no concerns, or that private blockchains should be held *per se* illegal.

2.2   Blockchain's Consensus

Blockchains can be further classified by the way they achieve consensus – that is, the agreement under which a blockchain operates. It materializes

---

[54] Defending that point of view, *see* Marija, "Is Blockchain Illegal?," Privacy Company, July 22, 2019, https://perma.cc/E68P-EN7N. I would rather qualify private blockchains as distributed ledger technologies with semi-decentralized systems. After all, one would not call the "Internet" a network for sharing information within one organization only. One would call that... an "Intranet."

[55] Eric Hughes, "A Cypherpunk's Manifesto," Activism, March 9, 1993, http://perma.cc/R9BK-VWZ5; *see also* Timothy May, "The Cyphernomicon," Nakamoto Institute, September 10, 1994, http://perma.cc/9D9P-USPS. More generally, *see* Jack Goldsmith and Tim Wu, *Who Controls the Internet? Illusions of a Borderless World* (Oxford University Press, 2006): 29.

in a code (run by the blockchain core software) that governs the transfer of value between nodes (any devices connected to the blockchain). As we shall see, whoever controls the consensus thus controls the incentive structure of a blockchain.[56] That is true for both private and public blockchains; and in both instances, the consensus ensures blockchain's integrity.

Generally, there is no mining activity on private blockchains. They run on a consensus that typically gives one or several participants the power to control transactions.[57] For that reason, some have argued that private blockchains are better equipped to prevent illegal activities than public ones, as pre-selected participants are in charge of verifying that the logic governing transactions is well respected.[58]

As we speak, most public blockchains (e.g., Bitcoin and Ethereum) use Proof of Work to achieve consensus. Here, miners (users involved in the process of mining, such as described below) compete to add a set of transactions – recorded in a block – to the chain by racing to solve a cryptographic puzzle in order to find a random number (called the "nounce").[59] Solving it requires "burning" actual resources (i.e., electricity as it requires a great deal of computing power), which of course raises environmental questions[60] and issues of scalability,[61] but which also creates a strong incentive to validate transactions properly. Indeed, the first miner to solve the puzzle and find the nounce is granted the right to validate the transaction and is rewarded with transaction fees and newly minted tokens. Thanks to Bitcoin, this is currently the world's most used consensus mechanism.[62] It is also described

---

[56] For more on coercive actions on blockchain, *see* Thibault Schrepel, "Collusion by Blockchain and Smart Contracts," Harvard Journal of Law and Technology 33, no. 1 (2019).

[57] Dulguun Batmunkh, "Private Blockchain Consensus Mechanisms," Medium, November 23, 2018, https://perma.cc/D9MA-QQVF.

[58] *See*, for instance, "Libra White Paper," Libra.org, https://perma.cc/5U7N-U78H. Libra has since become Diem.

[59] *See* Thibault Schrepel, "Is Blockchain the Death of Antitrust Law? The Blockchain Antitrust Paradox," Georgetown Law Technology Review 3, no. 2 (2019): 281, 292.

[60] *Contra* Vladimir Jelisavcic, "Bitcoin Uses a Lot of Energy, But Gold Mining Uses More," LongHash, September 13, 2018, https://perma.cc/QV8E-GVYW. Also, Albert Wenger, "Climate and Crypto," Continuations, March 20, 2021, https://perma.cc/39NR-9BQA. That said, electricity consumption remains an important subject. The numerous reactions following Elon Musk's May 2021 tweets on the subject reflected the concern in the space.

[61] *See* Connor Blenkinsop, "Blockchain's Scaling Problem, Explained," CoinTelegraph, August 22, 2018, https://perma.cc/PXZ4-J9XM.

[62] *See* Andrew Tar, "Proof-of-Work, Explained," CoinTelegraph, January 17, 2018, https://perma.cc/2TCU-XJVZ.

as the "safest" when it comes to ensuring blockchain integrity, and it has the advantage of allowing a relatively random distribution of block validation operations, at least in theory.

One of the most popular alternatives is the Proof of Stake mechanism, which is now being implemented on the Ethereum chain. Here, a user's chances to validate blocks increase with the number of tokens the user owns and the duration of possession. The idea is that the more a user has tokens, the more she or he has stakes in the game and will therefore verify transactions properly. A user with 200 tokens is thus twice as likely to be selected than another user with 100 tokens. There is no coin creation (mining) in Proof of Stake, so validators are exclusively rewarded with transaction fees.

Once a block is created, it must be committed to the blockchain. Different systems can be used: some involve a random group of signers, while others require a majority of all the signers.[63] Steemit and EOS, for instance, use delegated Proof of Stake, in which token holders vote for representatives who validate blocks.[64] In the case of Ethereum 2.0, blocks will be validated only if they receive enough attestations by validators.[65] This process is called "forging," or "minting."

Other protocols are also in sight. They include Proof of Activity, a combination of Proof of Work and Proof of Stake.[66] First, miners race to solve a cryptographic puzzle. The formed blocks do not contain any transactions, but act as a template. The system then switches to Proof of Stake. A randomly selected group of validators sign the new block, knowing that validators with more tokens are more likely to be chosen. The fees are then split between the miner and the validators who signed off on the block.

Proof of Burn is also used in blockchain ecosystems. Here, users "burn" coins or tokens by sending them to an address where they are irretrievable.[67]

---

[63]   Amy Castor, "A (Short) Guide to Blockchain Consensus Protocols," CoinDesk, March 4, 2017, www.coindesk.com/short-guide-blockchain-consensus-protocols ("In Tendermint, for example, every node in the system has to sign off on a block until a majority vote is reached, while in other systems, a random group of signers is chosen.")

[64]   Katie Roman, "Understanding EOS and Delegated Proof of Stake," Steemit, March 5, 2018, https://perma.cc/T72P-RU3C.

[65]   Ethereum 2.0 will allow up to 100 000 transactions per second, *see* Greg Thomson, "Ethereum 2.0 Will Walk and 'Roll' For Two Years Before It Can Run," Decrypt, July 1, 2020, https://perma.cc/U7NZ-UXW2.

[66]   Iddo Bentov et al., "Proof of Activity: Extending Bitcoin's Proof of Work Via Proof of Stake," Performance Evaluation Review (2014): 2.

[67]   Xiwei Xu et al., "A Taxonomy of Blockchain-Based Systems for Architecture Design," 2017 IEEE International Conference on Software Architecture (2017): 243, 251.

The more coins or tokens a user sends, the more likely the user will be selected to mine new blocks. The integrity of this consensus mechanism is, therefore, in the hands of its most influential users. The same goes for Proof of Capacity, where hard drive space is key.[68] Here, the probability of mining the next block – and earning a reward – increases with the user's hard drive capacity. Again, the system's integrity may rest entirely in the hands of those with the most resources.

Finally, it is worth mentioning Proof of Elapsed Time, where the algorithm uses a trusted execution environment to ensure that blocks get produced in a random lottery fashion, with no work coming from the node.[69] Participants are assigned a random amount of time to wait, and the first to complete the waiting time gets to commit the next block.

The upshot is that each of these consensus mechanisms attempts to strike the right balance between the network's security and scalability. And new mechanisms are constantly being developed to achieve that goal. In all likelihood, tomorrow's most commonly used protocol has yet to be created.

3   CHAPTER SUMMARY

This chapter started by exploring the numerous commonalities that exist between blockchains. The most notable of these is encryption, which protects the integrity of the blockchain ecosystem. Blockchain takes advantage of the costs involved in encryption to protect the entire network. This is akin to Jigoro Kano's view on Judo (Japanese for "the gentle way"): using the opponent's strength against her or him. Here, blockchain uses encryption costs to prevent greater ones (those coming from non-integrity). Encryption also protects users' and transactions' identity, which – as I will explore in Parts 2 and 3 of this book – offers new transactional possibilities, but creates enforcement issues.

We also analyzed blockchain's immutability, which stems from its decentralization and distribution. The absence of central and vertical control over the data which is located over the entire network creates trust in the system. This prevents bad actors from altering information relating to past transactions and enables users to create self-enforcing agreements. Blockchain's users bind themselves to their present will, constraining their future ability to behave.

---

[68]   Shihab S. Hazari and Qusay H. Mahmoud, "Comparative Evaluation of Consensus Mechanisms in Cryptocurrencies," Internet Technology Letters (2019): 1, 3.
[69]   *See* Brian Curran, "What is Proof of Elapsed Time Consensus? (PoET) Complete Beginner's Guide," Blockonomi, September 11, 2018, https://perma.cc/53EB-EJ5W.

The second section looked at the numerous differences that exist between blockchains. It explained the implications of these technical divergences. Figure 2.5 neatly summarizes these important differences. As one will see, blockchain can thus take numerous forms by combining them differently. This creates a dynamic environment in which blockchains compete with each other. I explore that organic competition in the next chapter.

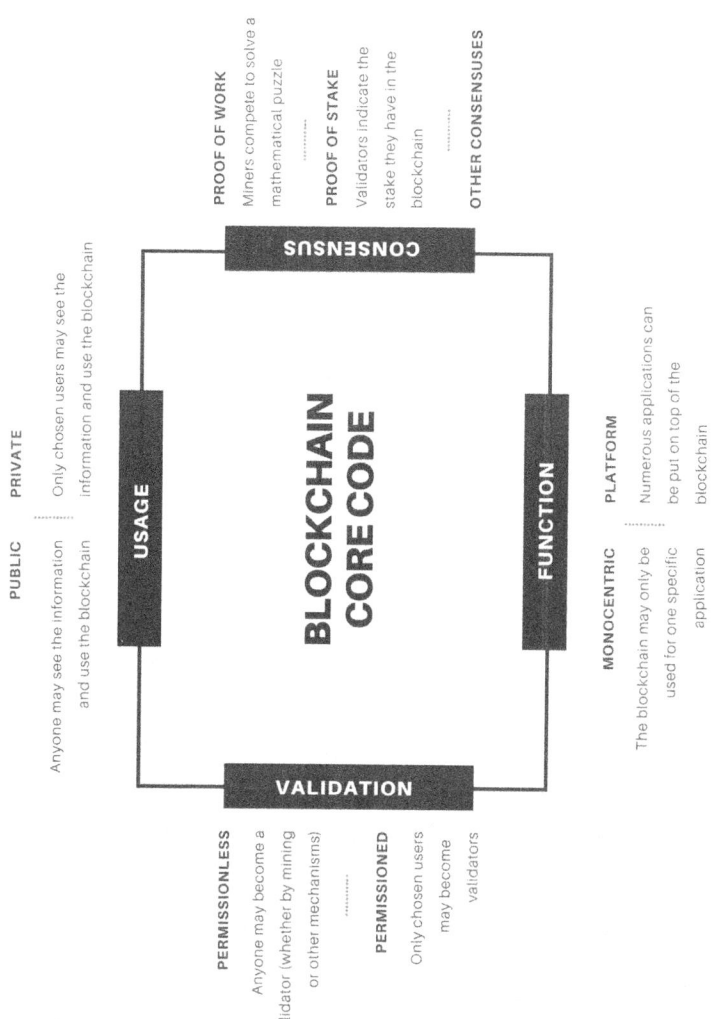

Figure 2.5   An overview of blockchain technicalities

3. Blockchain and Darwin

1   FIRST, DARWIN

In spite of the fundamental character of his literature, the transposition of Darwin's work to modern economies does not explain how new technologies appear. The answer to this enigma can be found in the work of W. Brian Arthur, who explained that new technologies result from unexpected combinations.[1] Blockchain, a combination of the technologies I mentioned in the first chapter, is very much a combinatorial technology. That being said, Darwin's findings do explain how living organisms (e.g., technologies) evolve and survive. They are thus crucial for understanding how blockchain – now that it exists – could develop.

Darwin started *The Origin of Species* by explaining that survival is more ferocious between different varieties of the same species than between different species.[2] Indeed, varieties consume the same food and are exposed to the same dangers, so the struggle for survival directly depends on the actions of others. As a result, only the species that are capable of adapting survive. Of course, one sees "nothing of these slow changes in progress."[3] Mutations happen over time, creating what Darwin calls natural selection. But natural selection is prevented when species grow in an environment protected by barriers. One may indeed observe fewer variations because the need to "diverge in structure, habits, and constitution"[4] to survive among other species tends to be significantly reduced. Since "we are much too ignorant in regard to the whole economy of any one organic being to say what slight modifications would be of importance or not,"[5] these barriers end up putting the species at risk.

---

[1]   *See* W. Brian Arthur, *The Nature of Technology: What It Is and How It Evolves* (Free Press, 2009).
[2]   Charles Darwin, *On the Origin of Species* (John Murray of Albemarle Street, 1859): 52.
[3]   *Id.* at 84.
[4]   *Id.* at 128.
[5]   *Id.* at 195.

Variations cause organisms to change themselves to "economize in every part."[6] As a result, a characteristic that is useful in one specific environment can become detrimental when the organism is moved to another.[7] On the contrary, the lack of a certain characteristic in a new environment may also cause the species to disappear. In the end, "natural selection acts solely by and for the good of each."[8] It is a strictly utilitarian process, without morality.[9] The strongest species and varieties live, and the weakest die.[10]

So, what is the lesson for blockchain? One must distinguish between two periods. The first period is one of natural selection between blockchain varieties. Before they compete with centralized applications, blockchain varieties undergo different mutations that could prove useful for that later stage of competition. These mutations occur at a time when blockchain is not protected by immutable barriers, whether natural or regulatory. They cannot be engineered; "no man can predict"[11] which characteristics will lead specific varieties to prevail.

The second stage is that of maturity. The most efficient blockchain varieties will logically thrive and, as a result, they will gradually enter the territory of centralized applications. The blockchain environment will then change. Competition between these two species – decentralized and centralized ones – will be engaged, and certain characteristics of blockchain will prove central to its survival. If several of these characteristics have been eliminated artificially before blockchain's varieties have reached maturity, their chance of survival will be significantly affected. For example, removing blockchain's immutability could cause the elimination of a key differentiating feature, compared to centralized applications where a few individuals control data. This is the danger of evolutionary systems involving human beings capable of changing trajectories voluntarily, which animals cannot do.[12] Manufacturing evolution is a perilous game.

---

[6] *Id.* at 147.

[7] *Id.* at 172.

[8] *Id.* at 201.

[9] *Id.* at 199.

[10] *Id.* at 244. Also, stressing that "natural selection acts by life and death." *Id.* at 194.

[11] *Id.* at 126.

[12] George Soros, "Fallibility, Reflexivity, and the Human Uncertainty Principle," Journal of Economic Methodology 20, no. 4 (2013): 319 (explaining that the main distinction "between natural and social science consists of the presence or absence of thinking participants who have a will of their own").

2   BLOCKCHAIN'S MULTIPLE USES

Blockchain's unique characteristics give rise to numerous use cases. Before exploring them, it is important to note that only platform blockchains can be used for different purposes, while monocentric blockchains are tied to one specific use.

2.1   Monocentric and Platform Blockchains

Not all blockchains allow software to run on top of the constitutional layer. Monocentric blockchains permit only one application. The Bitcoin blockchain is a good example, even if several initiatives have been announced to make it more versatile.[13] To this day, the Bitcoin blockchain is almost exclusively used for the Bitcoin cryptocurrency. This is due to the fact that its programming language cannot easily be exploited for other uses. Some are also questioning the willingness of Bitcoin miners to devote computing power to other types of transactions. This type of blockchain gets its entire value from the application for which it was created.[14]

Platform blockchains allow an unlimited number of applications to be added on top of layer 1. Ethereum is a great example of a platform blockchain, as anyone can upload a program onto the constitutional layer and leave it to self-execute. This freedom primarily exists because it uses Solidity as a programming language,[15] "allowing anyone to write smart contracts, and decentralized applications where they can create their own arbitrary rules for

---

[13]   "Bitcoin to Get Smart Contracts," Trustnodes, August 7, 2019, https://perma.cc/85HR-9BWF; Alyssa Hertig, "Pieter Wuille Unveils 'Miniscript,' A New Smart Contract Language for Bitcoin," CoinDesk, August 20, 2019, https://perma.cc/97D4-BYH9.

[14]   *See* Paul Vigna and Michael J. Casey, *The Truth Machine: The Blockchain and The Future of Everything* (St. Martin's Press, 2018): 99 ("How do tokens work? Just as Bitcoin's protocol steers users and participants into certain actions that serve the community's interest—in its case, creating a secure, reliable ledger that all can trust—the programs that run tokens incorporate incentives and constraints that encourage certain pro-social behavior. A new concept—token economics—is emerging. It encapsulates the idea that we can embed into these 'programmable' forms of money a way to steer communities toward desired common outcomes. Tokens might help us solve the Tragedy of the Commons. In other words, they could be a big deal.")

[15]   Carla L. Reyes, "If Rockefeller Were a Coder," George Washington Law Review 87, no. 373 (2019): 386 ("The Ethereum protocol supports its own coding language, Solidity, intended to enable software developers to write complex smart contracts more simply. Furthermore, Ethereum contracts are stateful and Turing-complete—they have 'memory that they will remember the next time they are called and ... they can have loops.'")

ownership, transaction formats, and state transition functions."[16] Here, the blockchain code can be described as a "fat protocol," "since the success of the application layer drives further speculation at the protocol layer."[17] Inversely, should a blockchain layer 1 encounter difficulties (or concentration problems), this would create a disincentive to use it.

As far as antitrust enforcement is concerned, it is easy to see how platform blockchains are prone to more infringements, as power at the fat protocol level can be more or less easily leveraged against other layers (depending on block-chain characteristics). I will return to this later in the book. One should not conclude, however, that monocentric blockchains are immune from antitrust issues. As we will see, market definition might be easier, leading to quicker antitrust enforcement activities.

2.2   Blockchain 1.0, 2.0 and 3.0

One can use blockchain for several distinct purposes, so let me propose a rudimentary nomenclature. For that purpose, I adopt a slightly modified version of the one offered by Melanie Swan in 2015, according to which one can distinguish between three categories of blockchain applications. The first (blockchain 1.0) is cryptocurrency, where blockchain tokens are used as coins.[18] The second (blockchain 2.0) is smart contracts. Here, blockchains are executing automated transactions between users.[19] The third (blockchain 3.0) encompasses all other blockchain uses, including peer-to-peer ridesharing, social media, online research and more.[20] In fact, blockchain 3.0 includes alternatives to the products and services that are generally described as the "sharing economy."

---

[16]   Ethereum, "A Next-Generation Smart Contract and Decentralized Application Platform," GitHub, https://perma.cc/G72K-YUVJ.

[17]   Joel Monegro, "Fat Protocols," Union Square Ventures, August 8, 2016, https://perma.cc/KGS6-7HLN.

[18]   Melanie Swan, *Blockchain: Blueprint for A New Economy* (O'Reilly Media, 2015): 1–8.

[19]   "A smart contract is a set of promises, specified in digital form, includ-ing protocols within which the parties perform on these promises." Nick Szabo, "Smart Contracts," University of Amsterdam, https://perma.cc/5NF3-R6N3. Ethereum, "A Next-Generation Smart Contract and Decentralized Application Platform," GitHub, https://perma.cc/G72K-YUVJ (describing smart contracts as "complex applications involving having digital assets being directly controlled by a piece of code implement-ing arbitrary rules.") For an overview of how smart contracts work, *see* Kevin Werbach and Nicolas Cornell, "Contracts Ex Machina," Duke Law Journal 67, no. 2 (2017): 319.

[20]   *See* Melanie Swan, *Blockchain: Blueprint for A New Economy* (O'Reilly Media, 2015): 29–70.

When it comes to antitrust, each type of blockchain comes with unique challenges. Blockchain 1.0 competes with states' currencies; it may lead to the disruption of their prerogatives. This alone will likely lead to heavy scrutiny from antitrust agencies, such as the antitrust investigation introduced by the European Commission against Diem – initially called Libra – Facebook's cryptocurrency.[21] Blockchain 2.0 applications, as we shall see in Chapter 9, may be used for setting up antitrust practices, as smart contracts create trust between participants – which is central to their willingness to engage in transactions (including illegal ones). Lastly, blockchain 3.0 comes with some challenges similar to those encountered with centralized platforms.

Here goes the general overview that I will explore further on. If one thing, Darwin teaches us that competition is utilitarian, meaning that only the end result matters for the varieties and species submitted to it. At times, it may imply anti-competitive practices. But for now, I want to focus on the competition between all these different blockchain types and analyze the procompetitive dynamism created between them.

3   A DARWINIAN ENVIRONMENT

The current blockchain ecosystem is highly dynamic. Varieties compete with each other through a combination of ideological orientations and business objectives that translate into technical characteristics.[22] Several trends are emerging from that competition. Projects are being built on top of others, creating a true Darwinian environment. Let us take a closer look.

3.1   A Dynamic Ecosystem

One can measure the dynamism of the blockchain ecosystem in many ways. Generally, two forces may encourage the adoption of a new technology: a top-down "institutional" force and a bottom-up "civilian" force. Regarding the first, consulting firm PwC found in 2018 that 84 percent of 600 surveyed executives from 15 territories said they were involved in blockchain experi-

---

[21]   Thibault Schrepel, "Libra: A Concentrate of Blockchain Antitrust," Michigan Law Review Online 118, no. 160 (2020).
[22]   Jeffery Atik and George Gerro, "Hard Forks on the Bitcoin Blockchain: Reversible Exit, Continuing Voice," Stanford Journal of Blockchain Law & Policy 1 (2018): 35 ("Exit, for miners at least, is reversible at low cost. The post-fork history seems to demonstrate that some miners simply mined the more profitable blockchain. Other miners remained on the same network for political reasons.")

mentation.[23] And while it is nearly impossible to list all the institutions that are already using it, a few big names spring to mind. They include the likes of Facebook, Wal-Mart, Amazon, PayPal, Bank of America, Microsoft, Google, HTC, IBM, ING, Intel, JP Morgan, the U.S. Commodity Futures Trading Commission, the Chicago Mercantile Exchange, Stanford University, Harvard University, Visa, Samsung, Tesla, Mastercard, Comcast and Fidelity.[24] For example, Wal-Mart is working with IBM on using blockchain to increase supply chain transparency by tracing food.[25] Microsoft has been developing blockchain products to allow its customers to reduce fraud and verify transactions.[26] Samsung is now offering access to its Samsung Blockchain Wallet to connect customers "to a world of decentralized apps."[27] Amazon offers more than 70 blockchain services to its customers,[28] and uses blockchain to allow all supply chain participants to access real-time supply chain data.[29] PayPal is allowing cryptocurrency trading for all its users.[30] Pfizer is tracking drugs from manufacturing to pharmacies using MediLedger.[31] Comcast uses it to offer a new targeted ads platform.[32] Boeing is selling airline parts on Honeywell,

---

[23] PwC, "Blockchain Is Here. What's Your Next Move?," https://perma.cc/TSJ9 -UKHQ.

[24] David Allessie, Maciej Sobolewski and Lorenzino Vaccar, "Blockchain for digital government," Publication Office of the European Union (2019): 14. For more, *see*, for instance, Michael del Castillo, "Blockchain 50: Billion Dollar Babies," Forbes, https://perma.cc/P7SU-DYUU; and Andrew Singer, "2019's Top 10 Institutional Actors in Crypto," Cointelegraph, February 1, 2020, https://perma.cc/QU4U-HZ73.

[25] The Leadership Network, "How Walmart used blockchain to increase supply chain transparency," The Leadership Network, January 22, 2020, https://perma.cc/ NH97-YAYS.

[26] Microsoft Azure, "Blockchain Technology and Applications," https://perma.cc/ D8B5-YQXG.

[27] Samsung, "Samsung Blockchain, Simple and Trust Proven," https://perma.cc/ 33G6-GGHG.

[28] Amazon Web Services, "Blockchain on AWS: Enterprise Blockchain Made Real," https://perma.cc/3NKA-PLQM.

[29] Dan Berthiaume, "Report: New Amazon Blockchain Solution Targets Product Authenticity," Chain Store Age, April 6, 2020, https://perma.cc/M55Q-FEKL.

[30] Robert Stevens, "PayPal Launches Cryptocurrency Trading for All US Users," Decrypt, November 12, 2020, https://perma.cc/84CE-XZU4.

[31] Gertrude Chavez-Dreyfuss, "Companies in Pharmaceutical Supply Chain Develop System to Track Counterfeit Drugs," Reuters, February 21, 2020, https:// perma.cc/E4RY-FTMQ.

[32] Jeff Baumgartner, "How Comcast Will Use Blockchain Tech for Targeted Ads," Light Reading, January 24, 2019, https://perma.cc/7NHU-ASAK.

a blockchain-based marketplace, for over $1 billion.[33] Hardly a single week passes without major announcements in the field.

Then there are also Canada, Mexico, the United States, Argentina, Austria, Denmark, Estonia, Georgia, Ireland, Italy, Latvia, Lithuania, Luxembourg, Malta, the Netherlands, Slovenia, Spain, Sweden, Switzerland, Ukraine, the United Kingdom, Ethiopia, Kenya, Liberia, Mauritius, Nigeria, Rwanda, South Africa, Sierra Leone, Tanzania, Uganda, Zambia, China, Hong Kong, India, Malaysia, Singapore, South Korea, Thailand, the United Arab Emirates and Australia.[34] These governments are using blockchain to facilitate the transparent administration of government contracts and public procurement procedures; transmit secure messages; implement and secure digital identity management; store health data; manage the land registry system; verify academic credentials; and soon, run their own cryptocurrencies.[35]

Regarding the "civilian" force, more than 1 billion transactions were recorded on public blockchains in 2019 alone, for a total exceeding 3 billion transactions in ten years.[36] That number sounds impressive, but let me note that Visa alone records 150 million transactions every day.[37] As for developers, over 7000 were active in 2019. But again, this must be put into perspective against the 6 million Android developers.[38] The same goes for the existence of over 7000 blockchain companies listed by Crunchbase.[39] There is thus much room for growth.

One can also measure blockchain dynamism from the inside, as opposed to merely analyzing adoption trends. Proof of Work continues to store the most value as far as protocols are concerned. The distribution of market capitalization by consensus algorithm showed an overwhelming 86.7 percent for Proof of Work in 2019.[40] The Ethereum Foundation has, however, started its migra-

---

[33] Michael del Castillo, "Honeywell Is Now Tracking $1 Billion In Boeing Parts on A Blockchain," Forbes, March 7, 2020, https://perma.cc/HBG2-KHCC.

[34] Lesa Moné, "Which Governments Are Using Blockchain Right Now?" ConsenSys, November 18, 2019, https://perma.cc/9H2M-UF3V.

[35] *See* Kevin Helms, "China's Digital Currency Has Been Used in 3 Million Transactions Worth Over a Billion Yuan So Far," Bitcoin, January 1, 2021, https://perma.cc/CK4G-BQV8; EU Blockchain Forum, "New Thematic Report: Central Bank Digital Currencies and a Euro for the Future," June 5, 2021, https://perma.cc/8UC6-TWZC; "Digital Dollar," Coindesk, https://perma.cc/TJN6-5HL8.

[36] Pogorzelski, "*Plus de 3 Milliards de Transactions Bitcoin et Crypto Réalisées en 10 Ans*" Cryptonaute, February 25, 2020, https://perma.cc/7LRE-MRVS.

[37] State of Adoption, "Report 2019/2020" (2020): 9, https://perma.cc/PZA9-X92Y.

[38] *Id.* at 8.

[39] Crunchbase, Blockchain Companies, May 26, 2021, https://perma.cc/KBF5-KKWX.

[40] State of Adoption, "Report 2019/2020" (2020): 28, https://perma.cc/PZA9-X92Y.

tion to Proof of Stake. Phase 0 of Ethereum 2.0 was launched in December 2020, while phases 1 and 2 will continue until 2022.[41]

Lastly, the distribution of investments is also a good indicator of where the blockchain ecosystem is headed. In 2019, finance protocols and applications (e.g., decentralized finance (DeFi), exchanges, fintech) generated the most venture returns.[42] In early 2020, DeFi contracts passed $12 billion (i.e., referring to the total value locked in DeFi), while several DeFi tokens have appreciated by 4000 percent this year alone. This has led to the creation of many blockchain remittance companies.[43] Last, the interest in decentralized autonomous organizations (DAOs) has also grown significantly since an incident in 2016 when hackers stole $50 million by exploiting software vulnerability. Over 1000 DAOs were created in 2019 alone.[44] I will come back to those in due course.

3.2   Today's Players

At the time of writing this chapter, at the end of 2020, two blockchains appear to stand out over 4000:[45] Bitcoin and Ethereum. As far as Bitcoin is concerned, the numbers are astronomical. Since publication of Satoshi Nakamoto's paper in October 2008 and the first transaction on January 12, 2009, Bitcoin passed the milestone of 500 million transactions in February 2020.[46] Just over 450 000 unique addresses were used on that blockchain during that same month.[47] In 2019, the total number of transactions per day was between 300 000 and 400 000.[48]

---

[41]   *See* Rene Millman, "What is Ethereum 2.0 and Why Does It Matter?" Decrypt, December 1, 2020, https://perma.cc/MEV8-WP57 (explaining these three different phases).

[42]   State of Adoption, "Report 2019/2020," (2020): 7, https://perma.cc/PZA9 -X92Y.

[43]   *See* Blockdata, "Remittance Market & Blockchain Technology," (2019), https:// perma.cc/4VVZ-K8UX.

[44]   State of Adoption, "Report 2019/2020," (2020): 143, https://perma.cc/PZA9 -X92Y.

[45]   *See* CoinMarketCap, "All Cryptocurrencies," CoinMarketCap, https://perma.cc/ PGE2-S46S (listing 4166 active coins and tokens as of January 5, 2021).

[46]   "Total Number of Transactions," Blockchain.com, https://perma.cc/ZB5X -CPHL.

[47]   "Unique Addresses Used," Blockchain.com, https://perma.cc/DJQ7-VWKZ.

[48]   "Confirmed Transactions Per Day," Blockchain.com, https://perma.cc/45X6 -Z6VF.

Ethereum has also grown significantly. As of April 2020,[49] over 700 million transactions had been recorded on the Ethereum chain since its launch in August 2015.[50] In 2020, it also surpassed the $1 trillion mark in settlements.[51] Each day of 2019, the number of transactions executed fluctuated between 400 000 and 1 million.[52] The Ethereum blockchain had 88 million unique addresses in February 2020. That same month, over 800 000 smart contracts were created, and 41 million automated transactions were concluded.[53] Token adoption and awareness are also on the rise.[54]

Many other projects have attracted significant investments. EOS, a blockchain development platform, raised $4.1 billion in 2018.[55] Figure, a fintech player leveraging blockchain for debt financing, raised almost $1.2 billion at the end of 2019.[56] Blockchain and semiconductor company Bitmain had raised more than $1.5 billion by the end of 2018.[57] The Telegram Open Network, a peer-to-peer distributed storage and hosting system, raised $850 million through an initial coin offering (ICO);[58] while stock brokerage application Robinhood had raised more than $850 million by the end of 2019.[59] Wait, there's more. Digital currency exchange Coinbase raised over $500 million by the end of 2018;[60] while Bakkt, a regulated Bitcoin futures and custody exchange, was approaching $500 million at the beginning of 2020.[61] Also,

---

[49] "Ethereum Total Transaction Count Chart," Blockchair.com, https://perma.cc/SDL2-XZG2.

[50] "Ethereum Transaction Hash (Txhash) Details, Ethereum (ETH) Blockchain Explorer," Etherscan, https://perma.cc/63H6-A8PT.

[51] Michael McSweeney, "Charting Ethereum's Five-Year Journey by the Numbers," The Block, July 30, 2020, https://perma.cc/P2PE-KRKT.

[52] "Total Number of Transactions Per Day," Etherchain.org, https://perma.cc/9K4A-Y2UC.

[53] "Ethereum by the Numbers—February 2020," ConsenSys, March 2, 2020, https://perma.cc/UY9E-ZDCL.

[54] According to the Financial Conduct Authority (FCA), 3.86 percent of the British general population owned cryptocurrencies in 2020, *see* Rebecca English et al., "Research Note, Cryptoasset Consumer Research 2020," Financial Conduct Authority, June 30, 2020: 5, https://perma.cc/XSS8-5EUW. The FCA also noticed an "increase in the percentage of those being aware of cryptocurrencies from 42% to 73% of adults," *id.*

[55] "EOS," Blockdata, https://perma.cc/72JB-9A83.

[56] "Figure," Blockdata, https://perma.cc/4TLQ-D3DR.

[57] "Bitmain," Blockdata, https://perma.cc/65FP-CE7W.

[58] "Telegram Open Network," Blockdata, https://perma.cc/9LSH-86U6.

[59] "Robinhood (Crypto)," Blockdata, https://perma.cc/T3GC-8HUF.

[60] "Coinbase," Blockdata, https://perma.cc/D7CW-HFZF.

[61] "Bakkt," Blockdata, https://perma.cc/3F2X-VG92. According to the FCA, 63 percent of tokens owner were using Coinbase in 2020, 15 percent Binance and 10 percent Kraken, *see* Rebecca English et al., "Research Note, Cryptoasset con-

Noku, an all-in-one custom blockchain platform, raised over 300 million in 2018.[62] Others – such as Kraken,[63] a bitcoin and cryptocurrency trading platform; BitFury,[64] a hardware and blockchain development solution; and Tron, a blockchain development platform for content sharing[65] – each raised over $100 million.

3.3   What's Next? The Crystal Ball

As the saying goes, "Prediction is hard, especially when it's about the future."[66] Drawing a portrait of what future blockchain ecosystems will look like is a perilous exercise, but I will try nonetheless: blockchain will evolve to the point of competing with non-blockchain products and services. Centralized firms will slow it down, capturing part of its value by recentralizing it artificially. But the value created by decentralized blockchains at layer 1 will nonetheless end up transforming part of the world's economic transactions.

Numerous institutions are also making predictions. The World Economic Forum predicts that 10 percent of global gross domestic product (GDP) will be stored on blockchain by 2027.[67] Bain & Company has predicted in a study that by 2026, distributed ledger technology and blockchain will increase the volume of global trade by $1.1 trillion from $16 trillion today – a 6.9 percent increase.[68] PwC's estimates are slightly higher: it attributes a $1.76 trillion impact to blockchain, representing 1.4 percent of the world's total GDP.[69] Lastly, Gartner prophesizes that blockchain will create $3.1 trillion worth of business value by 2030.[70]

---

sumer research 2020," Financial Conduct Authority, June 30, 2020, www.fca.org.uk/ publication/research/research-note-cryptoasset-consumer-research-2020.pdf, 19.

[62] "Noku," Blockdata, https://perma.cc/T3E8-UE96.

[63] "Kraken," Blockdata, https://perma.cc/CPV5-FNB6.

[64] "BitFury," Blockdata, https://perma.cc/H4YQ-A9ZU.

[65] "TRON," Blockdata, https://perma.cc/CP2F-KW5V.

[66] A sentence variously attributed to physicist Niels Bohr and baseball player Yogi Berra.

[67] World Economic Forum, "Deep Shift: Technology Tipping Points and Societal Impact" (2015): 24.

[68] "Blockchain Could Increase Global Trade Volumes by $1.1 trillion by 2026, Off the Current Base of $16 trillion," Bain, October 22, 2018, https://perma.cc/Z8DX -C3KY.

[69] Lujan Odera, "Blockchain Technology Is Set to Grow the Global GDP by $1.76 Trillion In the Next Decade: PwC Report," Bitcoin Exchange Guide, October 13, 2020, https://perma.cc/NP4B-LPKN.

[70] "Forecast: Blockchain Business Value, Worldwide, 2017—2030," Gartner, March 2, 2017, https://perma.cc/ATK2-3YHW.

Prediction growth often amounts to reading tea leaves. What matters here is not the exact numbers, but the idea that blockchain could enable new transactions on top of transforming existing ones. One must seek to understand why that is. Gartner provides us with what I find a convincing explanation of blockchain adoption.

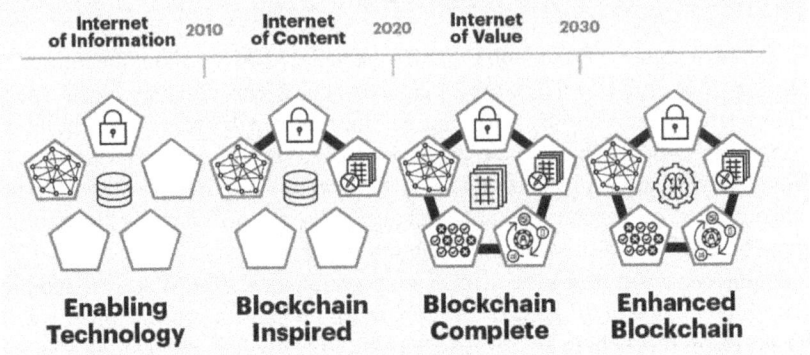

Source: Based on Kasey Panetta, "The 4 Phases of the Gartner Blockchain Spectrum," Gartner, October 14, 2019, https://perma.cc/HY96-9UKF.

Figure 3.1   *Stages of blockchain adoption – Gartner: 2019*

According to the company, the 2000s were the "information age," allowing market players to disseminate their offline content on the Internet. Technological advances such as improved Internet speed led to the "content society." But blockchain is different; it is a transactional technology. Should it ever impact society at large, it will transform the way we interact with each other (eliminating various intermediaries).

How exactly blockchain will achieve that remains to be seen. In fact, the technology is undergoing an evolutionary process that is accelerated by its capacity to fork. There will be (most likely) no eureka moments (i.e., "killer app") in its development, but rather a sequence of incremental changes in a more or less consistent and chaotic direction.[71]

In the end, these technical evolutions will influence the financial support blockchain will receive. For that reason, I am not quite sure (to say the least)

---

[71]   Discussing chaotic evolutions, see James Gleick, *Chaos: Making a New Science* (Vintage Books, 1996).

that one can prophesy exactly when blockchain will move from one phase to the other, but Gartner's logical steps seem to make sense.

The company describes the years 2020–2022 as the "trough of disillusionment," following the craze of the 2010s (Phase 1).[72] It further predicts that the decade we are just entering will be one of "large focus investments" (Phase 2); followed by global and large-scale value-add solutions between 2027–2030 (Phase 3).[73] And eventually, the 2030s could be the years of blockbuster ecosystems coupled with other technologies such as artificial intelligence and the Internet of Things (I will explain how blockchain could help these technologies in Chapter 15). That is, if blockchain and law become allies.

4   CHAPTER SUMMARY AND BEYOND

In this chapter, I have first discussed Darwin's findings. In *The Origin of Species*, he observed that competition occurs between varieties of the same species before moving on to competition between different species. Transposed to digital technologies and ecosystems, this means that competition first happens between blockchain's applications before moving between blockchain and non-blockchain applications.

With that in mind, I then explored blockchain ecosystems and verify the Darwinian hypothesis in the field. I showed that blockchain can be monocentric or platforms, depending on whether apps and services can function on top of them. I then distinguished between three different types of uses: blockchain 1.0 for cryptocurrencies, blockchain 2.0 for smart contracts and blockchain 3.0 for all other decentralized applications.

The next part of the chapter discussed how fast blockchain could challenge incumbent platforms. I started by exploring blockchain's increasingly fast adoption by both large institutional players and civilians. I discussed how the technology is being used and how it compares to non-blockchain services. Guessing what could happen in the coming years – always a dangerous exercise – I went back to Darwin's theory of evolution, explaining that looking for blockchain's killer app is probably a mistake; and, in any case, that anticipating the day (or week, or month, or year) when it will appear is even more doubtful.

---

[72] *See* "Blockchain Technology Spectrum: A Gartner Theme Insight Report," Gartner (2018): 10. Following a survey of 1386 senior executives in a dozen countries, more than 50 percent of respondents said that "blockchain technology has become a critical priority for their organizations in 2019—a 10-point increase over last year," "Deloitte's 2019 Global Blockchain Survey," Deloitte (2019): 3.

[73] "Blockchain-Based Transformation: A Gartner Trend Insight Report," Gartner: 7.

In the following chapter, I address the elephant in the room: what are most blockchains competing against, and what characteristics might enable them to survive against non-blockchain applications? In short, I discuss the reason(s) behind the blockchain craze and show that blockchains compete by translating ideology into technical advancements.

4.   Decentralization?

1   DECENTRALIZATION(S)

The subject of decentralization has long been discussed in political literature. However, it has a distinct meaning in the blockchain space, where it is seen as a way to create efficiency. In this chapter, I introduce a new analytical framework for evaluating decentralization in this context.

1.1   Multiple Features

The virtues of decentralization have been debated for centuries – most famously by thinkers like Alexis de Tocqueville, Pierre Joseph Proudhon, Frédéric Bastiat and Friedrich Hayek.

Tocqueville is known for his book *Democracy in America* (1835), whose vision is praised to this day. Tocqueville stressed that he could not imagine that a "nation could live or, above all, prosper without strong governmental centralization."[1] On the contrary, Proudhon pointed out that centralized states "crushed all freedom,"[2] as centralization leads to the "disarmament of a nation for the benefit of its government."[3] Following this logic, he underlined that the "salvation of the people" required decentralization, "for it saves them both from the tyranny of their leaders and from their own folly by dividing them."[4] Both authors also discussed decentralization from the perspective of individual

---

[1]   Alexis de Tocqueville, *Democracy in America* (1835, Laffont, 2012): 146, 154 ("Centralization succeeds without difficulty in imparting a steady appearance to everyday affairs; in skillfully dictating the details of social order; in suppressing slight disturbances and small transgressions; in maintaining society in a status quo which is not exactly either decadence or progress; in keeping a kind of administrative somnolence in the social body that administrators customarily call good order and public tranquility. In a word, it excels at preventing, not at doing.")
[2]   Pierre-Joseph Proudhon, *Du Principe Federatif et de la Necessite de Reconstituer Le Parti de la Revolution* (Kessinger Publishing, 2010): 71.
[3]   *Id.* at 103.
[4]   *Id.* at 101.

freedoms, leading them to opposite conclusions.[5] These debates neatly illustrate the spectrum of arguments that have been made regarding the virtues of decentralization (or lack thereof).

Bastiat and Hayek were more interested in the dynamics of economic systems. The former emphasized that decentralization is to be preferred over centralization because relying on the state for economic prosperity is "a fertile source of calamities and revolutions."[6] The latter pointed out that "the competitive system is the only system designed to minimize the power exercised by man over man."[7] One may infer two general features of decentralization from their early work.

The first relates to the democratic nature of decentralized systems. They allow for coordination without vertical hierarchy,[8] as the absence of a strong central authority makes exclusion more difficult.[9] Of course, the tyranny of the majority may oppress dissenting voices, but that tyranny may seem more bearable than the tyranny of the few. This explains why the growth of decentralized systems is more inclusive than that of centralized ones.[10]

The second feature of decentralized systems relates to the power and impact of decision making. In principle, decentralized systems allow for more informed decision making than centralized ones, as they empower individuals to protect their own interests. The upside is that this overcomes the fact that not all knowledge can be communicated to a centralized system that would act

---

[5]   Tocqueville favored centralized institutions, while Proudhon preferred decentralized ones.

[6]   *See* Frédéric Bastiat, *Sophismes Economiques* (Institut Coppet, 2015): 33. Bastiat was talking about "*une force irrésistible de décentralisation*" ("an irresistible power of decentralization"). According to Nathan Schneider, "Decentralization: An Incomplete Ambition," Journal of Cultural Economy 12, no. 4 (2019): 265, 267 ("The earliest reference to decentralization cited in the Oxford English Dictionary dates to 1846, in Popular Fallacies Regarding General Interests, translated from a treatise by the French laissez-faire economist Frédéric Bastiat.")

[7]   Friedrich Hayek, *The Road to Serfdom* (IEA, 2005): 41.

[8]   Yochai Benkler, *The Wealth of Networks* (Yale University Press, 2006): 62.

[9]   Discussing this point, *see* Philip E. Agre, "P2P and the Promise of Internet Equality," Communication of the ACM 46, no. 2 (2003): 39.

[10]   Sibylle Stossberg and Hansjörg Blöchliger, "Fiscal Decentralization and Income Inequality: Empirical Evidence from OECD Countries," Jahrbücher für Nationalökonomie und Statistik 237, no. 3 (2017): 225.

upon it.[11] The drawback is that the decision taken at a decentralized level may ignore information held by others.[12]

In any case, the impact of erroneous decisions is lower in decentralized systems than centralized ones, as in theory they tend to affect only those who have taken the decision. In Nicholas Nassim Taleb's words,[13] these systems "love mistakes," and allow more experimentation than centralized ones. Conversely, adverse decisions in a centralized system impact the entire system.[14]

The vast majority of cyber-communities promote decentralization across all cyberspace levels, often indirectly praising one of these two features.[15] Blockchain results from that desire.[16] That being said, pursuing this sole

---

[11] Friedrich A. Hayek, "The Use of Knowledge in Society," The American Economic Review 35, no. 4 (1945): 519, 524 ("The ultimate decisions must be left to the people who are familiar with these circumstances, who know directly of the relevant changes and of the resources immediately available to meet them. We cannot expect that this problem will be solved by first communicating all this knowledge to a central board which, after integrating all knowledge, issues its orders. We must solve it by some form of decentralization").

[12] *Id.* at 524.

[13] Nassim Nicholas Taleb, *Antifragile: Things That Gain from Disorder* (Random House Trade, 2014): 21.

[14] Alessandra Arcuri and Giuseppe Dari-Mattiacci, "Centralization versus Decentralization as a Risk–Return Trade-Off," The Journal of Law & Economics 53 (2010): 359 ("This paper characterizes the choice between centralization and decentralization as a risk-return trade-off and examines it in a model that integrates ideas from committee decision-making and portfolio theories. Centralization, by pooling expertise, rarely yields erroneous decisions; however, when it fails, the consequences are global. In contrast, in a decentralized system, erroneous decisions are more frequent, but their consequences are locally confined.")

[15] For a sub-distinction within this community, *see* Philip E. Agre, "Cyberspace as American Culture, 11 Science as Culture," Science as Culture 11, no. 2 (2002): 171, 185 ("[T]he libertarian left and the libertarian right both invest hopes for decentralization in the technology, one group identifying the Internet with democracy and the other group identifying it with markets. There remains a non-libertarian left, just barely, for which the Internet is purely an instrument of capitalist domination, and a non-libertarian right, now ascendant, for which the Internet is purely a vector of moral decay.")

[16] As we have shown, blockchain has libertarian roots. Not surprisingly, several famous libertarian thinkers were in favor of decentralization. For instance, Murray Rothbard defended the idea according to which every state should "be allowed to secede from the nation, every sub-state from the state, every neighborhood from the city, and, logically, every individual or group from the neighborhood," *see* Murray Rothbard, "Libertarian Forum," May 1969. As he further argued: "If it were in any way possible to grant this right of self-determination to every individual person, it would have to be done," *see* Murray Murray Rothbard, In *Liberalism* (Germany: 1927). This is the objective of blockchain communities. Robert Nozick defended a similar idea, arguing for a minimal state acting as a "night watchman" and letting its citizens

objective is not enough to ensure blockchain development and prosperity. For that, blockchain relies on increasing participants' own (financial) interest. The system is indeed designed to maximize their welfare while pursuing the overall objective of decentralization. I will come back to that in Chapter 7, but here I want to emphasize the importance of considering each blockchain participant's personal interest. The same applies to other technologies and management systems, which are also emerging to pursue the same goal of decentralization. Their capacity to benefit their participants at the individual level will determine their ability to achieve this objective. That applies to non-blockchain distributed ledger technologies and Solid – the technology promoted by Tim Berners-Lee (often described as the inventor of the World Wide Web).[17]

1.2   One Objective

Decentralized systems offer unique features, but what are they good for? The answer depends on the system being studied. One may wish to decentralize a political system to revive civic engagement; another may wish to decentralize corporate governance to make a company more inclusive.

Blockchain harnesses the power of decentralization to enable the emergence of a more efficient transactional infrastructure.[18] Let me return to the words of Satoshi Nakamoto for corroboration. When introducing his Bitcoin white paper, she/he/they/it explained that "[d]igital signatures provide part of the solution" for sending information "without going through a financial institution," yet "the main benefits are lost if a trusted third party is still required to prevent double-spending." For that precise reason, Nakamoto proposed "a solution to the double-spending problem using a peer-to-peer network."[19] The intention is solutionist: there are costs, and one must find a way to reduce

---

build concomitantly the different types of societies in which they want to live, *see* Thibault Schrepel, "Anarchy, State, and Blockchain Utopia: Rule of Law versus Lex Cryptographia," in *General Principles and Digitalisation* (Hart Publishing, 2020): 367. As we will see later on, other thinkers on the "left side" of the political debate were also in favor of decentralization, making it a non-partisan concept.

[17]   13D Research, "Why Decentralization Could Prove the Most Disruptive Tech Megatrend of the Next Decade," Medium, October 17, 2018, https://perma.cc/HRW2 -W5VS; Berkman Klein Center, "The Future of the Decentralized Web," Medium, July 31, 2019, https://perma.cc/MB9D-KBZG.

[18]   The search for efficiency, in fact, is a common trait to most technologies; on that, *see* Aldous Huxley, "Foreword" in *Brave New World* (1932, HarperCollins, 1994) ("In an age of advanced technology, inefficiency is the sin against the Holy Ghost.")

[19]   *See* Satoshi Nakamoto, *Bitcoin: A Peer-To-Peer Electronic Cash System* (2008): 1.

them. Blockchain is described as the ideal candidate, as it "requires minimal structure," being "robust in its unstructured simplicity."[20] The two features of decentralized systems – that is, coordination without vertical hierarchies and the reduction of an individual's decision making impact – are used to increase monetary exchange efficiency.

Ethereum has built on this foundation to develop a blockchain that enables more complex applications.[21] Its ambition is to allow "users to create any of the systems … and many others that we have not yet imagined, simply by writing up the logic in a few lines of code."[22] Vitalik Buterin, Ethereum co-founder, declares in the blockchain white paper:

> The intent of Ethereum is to create an alternative protocol for building decentralized applications, providing a different set of tradeoffs that we believe will be very useful for a large class of decentralized applications, with particular emphasis on situations where rapid development time, security for small and rarely used applications, and the ability of different applications to very efficiently interact.[23]

Ethereum praises the simplicity of the project by pointing out that: "A bare-bones version of Namecoin can be written in two lines of code, and other protocols like currencies and reputation systems can be built in under twenty." Blockchain's unique features – such as simplicity, universality, modularity, agility and non-discrimination – all create efficiencies redirected toward creating a new institutional technology.

Efficiency is a noble aim. Efficiency makes human flourishing possible by creating wealth[24] – a prerequisite for its distribution and the creation of a better society for the greatest number.[25]

Unfortunately, decentralization and efficiency sometimes cut in opposite directions. Outside of the blockchain sphere, it is not unusual for centralized

---

[20]   *Id.* at 8.
[21]   Overall, the Ethereum White Paper mentions the word "efficient" eight times and the word "inefficient" five times, https://perma.cc/ZTR8-8PUF.
[22]   Ethereum, "A Next-Generation Smart Contract and Decentralized Application Platform," GitHub, https://perma.cc/G72K-YUVJ.
[23]   Vitalik Buterin, "Ethereum White Paper," Ethereum, last modified December 9, 2020, https://perma.cc/M6FU-NVTY.
[24]   Steven Pinker, *Enlightenment Now* (Penguin Books Limited, 2018) (Chapter 8, explaining that the enlightened economy, by using machines toward better efficiency, helps in reducing poverty).
[25]   Kenneth G. Elzinga, "Goals of Antitrust: Other Than Competition and Efficiency, What Else Counts," University of Pennsylvania Law Review 125, no. 6 (1976): 1191, 1193 ("Once it is perceived that efficiency and equity are not mutually exclusive domains, and that both are susceptible to economic analysis, the nature of their relation-ship becomes the pertinent inquiry.")

systems to be more efficient than decentralized ones, as centralization allows for a reduction in many transaction costs. Given this, it is important to ask whether decentralization is cost effective in this context. The situation is different for blockchain, as the technology generates efficiency *because* of decentralization. That will prove essential when it comes to antitrust law, as we shall see.

1.3   A Comprehensive Theory of Decentralization

Blockchain communities often see decentralization as the best path to efficiently enable transactions and social interactions. However, one still needs to agree on what decentralization means and how it can be achieved – doing so proves to be the only way to assess if blockchain achieves this aim and how the law could help. Giving decentralization a proper definition is challenging.[26] This chapter attempts to address this difficulty; at the very least, it introduces the reader to what I mean by "decentralization" throughout the book.

Let me start with a proper definition: "decentralization" is a dynamic and multi-level concept that measures the autonomy enjoyed by a given subject in determining its competence. Now, let me unpack that definition.

By "competence," I mean the ability to determine the spheres of action within which a given individual can decide. In centralized systems, one can take action only if another subject has been granted the right to do so. Central systems may be horizontal (when the individual attributing competence is on the same layer) or vertical (when the individual attributing competence is on an upper layer). Systems in which one can decide without being formally granted the right to do so are decentralized,[27] both horizontally and vertically.

The concept of decentralization is also dynamic, meaning that one must consider the time factor. On a scale ranging from absolute autonomy to total determinism, the degree of decentralization should capture more than an instant. It needs to be analyzed over time; a system is not decentralized (or centralized) when it just presents certain momentary features. Evaluating decentralization requires one first to analyze the different factors leading to it,

---

[26]   Nathan Schneider, "Decentralization: An Incomplete Ambition," Journal of Cultural Economy 12, no. 4 (2019): 265. Already, Alexis de Tocqueville, *Democracy in America* (Laffont, 2012): 153 ("Centralization is a word repeated constantly today, and, in general, no one tries to clarify its meaning").

[27]   For example, Article 5 of the Treaty of Lisbon provides that the Union shall act only within the limits of the powers conferred upon it by the Member States in the Treaties in order to achieve the objectives set out in those Treaties. Any competence not attributed to the Union in the Treaties belongs to the Member States.

and second to understand how these different forces interplay with each other over the medium and long run.

And the concept is multi-level. One must analyze the extent to which the (de)centralization of one layer leads to the (de)centralization of an upper layer. Sometimes, different layers are tightly related, and the decentralization of one layer will lead to decentralization or the centralization of another one. Other times, layers do not show a causal link. Overall, a system is fully decentralized only when all layers are significantly decentralized. When this is not the case, and when moving one layer toward decentralization leads another toward more centralization, choices should be made regarding which one should be preferred.

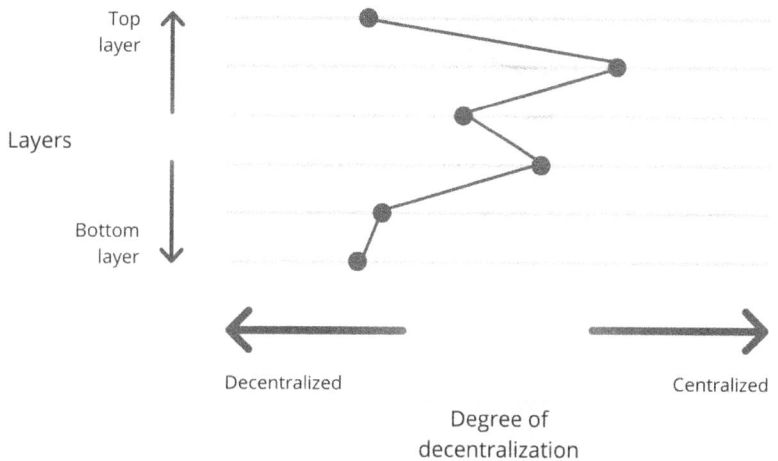

Figure 4.1   Representation of one ecosystem decentralization

Several questions arise from the chart in Figure 4.1.

First, how are the dots positioned on each layer? The answer depends on the subject being analyzed, but it always results from various constraints. With blockchain, Vitalik Buterin has pointed out that defining the degree of decentralization includes three axes.[28] The first is architectural decentralization, which represents how many computers the system comprises. The second is political decentralization, which represents how many individuals

---

[28]   Vitalik Buterin, "The Meaning of Decentralization," Medium, February 6, 2017, https://perma.cc/6FP5-9L8Z.

or organizations control these computers. The third is logical decentralization. In Buterin's view: "Blockchains are politically decentralized (no one controls them) and architecturally decentralized (no infrastructural central point of failure), but they are logically centralized (there is one commonly agreed state and the system behaves like a single computer)."[29] I will return to this later; but for the time being, let us keep in mind that each of the dots representing the degree of decentralization of one layer results from these different forces.

Second, what is the effect generated by one dot's motion on the upper and lower layers? One should distinguish three hypotheses falling under what I would call "complex decentralization."[30]

One, there might be no strong correlation between a layer and those that surround it. When this is the case, one should abandon efforts that seek to decentralize one layer in order to affect another. Two, there might be a robust correlation between the different layers. In such a scenario, one should analyze whether pushing one layer further toward decentralization (even the slightest) has acceptable consequences for the other layers. Three, one might observe only a mild correlation between the different layers. Here, it is necessary to analyze which types of (extreme) efforts would be required to push another layer toward more decentralization and whether the consequences are acceptable.

Third, where are decisions regarding the appropriate level of decentralization taking place? Here again, the answer depends on the subject. Legal structures (e.g., states or international unions) are typically top-down. Decisions regarding decentralization are primarily made at the upper level and are centralized by nature. Blockchain's structure is bottom-up: decentralization is generally embedded in lower layers. Where it exists, decentralization emerges rather than being decided.

Finally – and this brings me to the core of our subject – how can decentralization be achieved? Can the law help achieve this aim; and if so, under what conditions and with what drawbacks? Answering this question involves two separate interrogations. First, is the law a legitimate means of decentralizing a particular layer? Second, if this is the case, is the law effective at achieving this end? I tackle these issues in the following chapters.

---

[29] *Id.*
[30] Here relying on complexity theory, *see* W. Brian Arthur, *Complexity and the Economy* (Oxford University Press, 2014).

2 BLOCKCHAIN'S DECENTRALIZATION

I have just shown that decentralization is a dynamic and multi-level concept. In this section, I apply this finding to the blockchain sphere and analyze its implications. This leads me to study each layer of a blockchain and examine whether participants are free to determine their competence.

2.1 Layers and Interactions

Blockchain's overall governance is more horizontal than that of firms (as I will discuss later); nevertheless, its architecture comprises several layers. And each of these layers can be more or less decentralized. Let us investigate this together.

The first level is the "real space." While blockchain is undoubtedly a digital technology, it is made up of different components that exist in the material world. To cite but one example, the Chinese government's control over the Internet shows that power in the real space has an important impact on digital ecosystems. Accordingly, the separation between the real space and cyberspace, as proposed by the cypherpunks, has important limitations that should not be neglected.[31]

The second level is cyberspace and, more specifically, the Internet.[32] Blockchain exists only thanks to the Internet, as the technology is based on Transmission Control Protocol and Internet Protocol. Whoever controls the Internet can ultimately affect blockchain. The Internet Corporation for Assigned Names and Numbers, and the Internet Engineering Task Force, for example, could exert a decisive influence on blockchain if they wanted to. To date, these international bodies have been great in their neutrality – also because they have limited power. For that reason, barring a significant departure from the status quo, there appears to be little link between the (de)centralization of the Internet (as a technology) and that of blockchain. But this could change.

The third level is the "blockchain" layer or, put differently, the ledger (database). Often referred to as the "layer 1" (from a blockchain-based perspective),

---

[31] This is shown by the fact that governments are decreasing Internet freedom for the tenth year in a row (deliberately spreading false information to manipulate citizens, enforcing censorship and internet shutdowns…), as is shown by Freedom House, *see* Adrian Shahbaz and Allie Funk, "The Pandemic's Digital Shadow," Freedom House (2020), https://perma.cc/4JNE-A9AD.

[32] For a distinction between cyberspace and the Internet, *see* Lawrence Lessig, *Code: And Other Laws of Cyberspace*, Version 2 (Basic Books, 2006): 9 ("Though built on top of the Internet, cyberspace is a richer experience").

it contains the data that shows the current state of the blockchain, combining all transactions coming from higher layers.[33] The link between the (de)centralization of the third and fourth levels depends on whether the blockchain is public or private.[34] When a blockchain is public, anyone can explore the entire third level. It is wide open. But when a blockchain is private, only selected users can view it and, by definition, build its infrastructure and governance. In that regard, the third layer may play an essential role in attributing blockchain participants' competence at higher levels.

The fourth level is the blockchain infrastructure. I refer to this as the blockchain "constitutional level," as it has a defining impact on the higher levels, therefore defining the "rules of the game."[35] This level comprises the client's core code(s) that run on top of the third level.[36] It governs all transactions. This fourth level also contains what is often referred to as the "layer 2" (i.e., technical solutions increasing blockchain scalability, such as Bitcoin Lightning).[37] By determining whether a blockchain is permissionless or permissioned, this fourth level also plays a crucial role in distributing specific skills. In permissionless infrastructures, any user can participate in the consensus and thus ensure the blockchain's integrity; while in permissioned infrastructures, only selected users can do so. The decentralization of that fourth level is thus a precondition for the decentralization of higher levels.[38]

---

[33]   Bitcoin and Bitcoin Cash are two "layer 1" examples.

[34]   *See* Chapter 2, explaining the difference between public and private blockchains.

[35]   It is called the bottom layer because it "provides formal network participants with ultimate decision-making authority regarding what software application to run or whether to update the software application with new versions that exist. Due to the strong positive network effects experienced by public blockchain networks, the decision of each of the formal participants is influenced by their perception of other formal network participants' likely choices." Raina S. Haque, Rodrigo Seira Silva-Herzog, Brent A. Plummer and Nelson M. Rosario, "A Blockchain Development and Fiduciary Duty," Stanford Journal of Blockchain Law & Policy 2, no. 2 (2019): 140, 158.

[36]   For instance, Bitcoin Core (fourth level) is the main client running on top of the Bitcoin blockchain (third level). Bitcoin Unlimited (fourth level) is one of the main clients running of top of the Bitcoin Cash blockchain (third level).

[37]   Vitalik Buterin called it the "ultimate deciding layer," *see* Vitalik Buterin, "Notes on Blockchain Governance," Vitalik Buterin's website, December 17, 2017, https://perma.cc/34AB-ZL62.

[38]   Primavera De Filippi, "Blockchain Technology and Decentralized Governance: The Pitfalls of a Trustless Dream," *Decentralized Thriving: Governance and Community on the Web 3.0* (2019): 7 ("While it is, indeed, difficult to deploy a distributed governance system on top of a centralized infrastructure—because the party who controls the infrastructure inherits the power to influence the system—at the same time, a decentralized infrastructure does not necessarily entails a decentralized governance structure.")

The fifth level is the blockchain governance mechanism. It results from all the constraints imposed on the blockchain's participants when they interact among themselves. While the "blockchain" and "constitutional" layers may have architectural limits that exert a strong constraint over the governance of this fifth level, economic, political and logical considerations are also important.[39] Contrary to popular belief, the link between this level and the sixth level (blockchain applications) is not necessarily strong. For example, the centralization of blockchain miners does not rhyme with the centralization of blockchain uses. One should not attach too much importance to potential centralized outcomes on the fifth level when analyzing lower and higher levels. I will come back to this point.

The sixth level is comprised of blockchain applications. As I have explained, three types of applications can be distinguished: cryptocurrency (blockchain 1.0), smart contracts (blockchain 2.0) and the decentralized version of any kind of program a computer can run (blockchain 3.0). The lower levels partially determine the degree of (de)centralization at this sixth level. For one, monocentric blockchains are centered around one application only. Although platform blockchains permit different uses, they can nonetheless restrict the ability to run some applications on top of them, notably for compatibility reasons.

The seventh level is comprised of blockchain users. Its degree of (de)centralization depends on concepts that will be familiar to antitrust-savvy readers, such as network effects, lock-in and switching costs. Decentralization at this level is affected by design choices at the lower levels, and vice versa (if users cluster around a few applications, this will have the effect of centralizing the sixth level). It is also a function of first-mover advantage, the utility provided by each blockchain application and other market characteristics. One should note that ensuring the seventh level's decentralization is not the aim of blockchain or antitrust law, since it is not inversely correlated with users' welfare. Indeed, should a blockchain application prove more useful or better designed

---

[39] Vitalik Buterin, "The Meaning of Decentralization," Medium, February 6, 2017, https://perma.cc/6FP5-9L8Z ("Blockchains are politically decentralized (no one controls them) and architecturally decentralized (no infrastructural central point of failure) but they are logically centralized (there is one commonly agreed state and the system behaves like a single computer).") These three elements are important, *see*, for example, Napster which had a centralized logic, according to Philip E. Agre, "P2P and the Promise of Internet Equality," Communication of the ACM 46, no. 2 (2003): 42 ("Napster had a fatal flaw: although it afforded P2P sharing of music files, its centralized directory made it susceptible to legal attack.") Underlining the need to aggregate different parameters in order to assess decentralization, *see* Angela Walch, "Deconstructing 'Decentralization': Exploring the Core Claim of Crypto Systems," in *Cryptoassets*, ed. Chris Brummer (Oxford University Press, 2019): 24.

than others, all users would benefit from using it. It would create a network effect, increasing the utility they can derive from this application.[40]

One can represent these levels as illustrated in Figure 4.2. These levels should be analyzed together, as should competing blockchain ecosystems (i.e., a set of levels). In other words, there is significant and dynamic competition within each of these levels, between each of them and between separate ecosystems. This could be represented as an eighth level, as illustrated in Figure 4.3.

Finally, these blockchain ecosystems collaborate and compete with other technologies, services and applications, whether decentralized or centralized. I will study this dynamic in Part 3 of the book; but Figure 4.4 presents a representation of the entire landscape – this can be thought of as a ninth and final level.

3   HOW TO PROCEED FURTHER

I studied the decentralization of each level in terms not of participants' numbers (i.e., rivalry), but of each participant's capacity to determine its competence. Blockchain decentralization is a question of decision making processes rather than particular outcomes. Indeed, focusing on the latter would lead to a structuralist vision of blockchain, according to which one should prevent all centralized outcomes for its sake (e.g., applications with over X million users). As Vitalik Buterin underlines in a video we did together:

> blockchain communities also have centralization when it results in providing very valuable services (such as companies that are building projects, exchanges, people running layer 2 transaction systems of different kinds, companies providing wallets). Sometimes you find centralized actors because they deserve to succeed.[41]

I will come back to that idea later.

I should make two further observations at this stage regarding the degree of blockchain's decentralization. First, studies of decentralization should always specify which level is being discussed. I will endeavor to proceed accordingly, while keeping in mind that (de)centralization at one level may impact others. In fact, analyzing correlations with higher levels comes naturally,[42] but one must

---

[40]   *See* Thibault Schrepel and Vitalik Buterin, "Blockchain Code as Antitrust," Berkeley Technology Law Journal (2021).
[41]   Thibault Schrepel and Vitalik Buterin, "Blockchain Code as Antitrust," YouTube, published July 16, 2020, 12:37, https://perma.cc/A6VH-VJJR.
[42]   Philip E. Agre, "P2P and the Promise of Internet Equality," Communication of the ACM 46, no. 2 (2003): 40 ("At least sometimes, then, centralization on one layer is a precondition for decentralization on the layers above it").

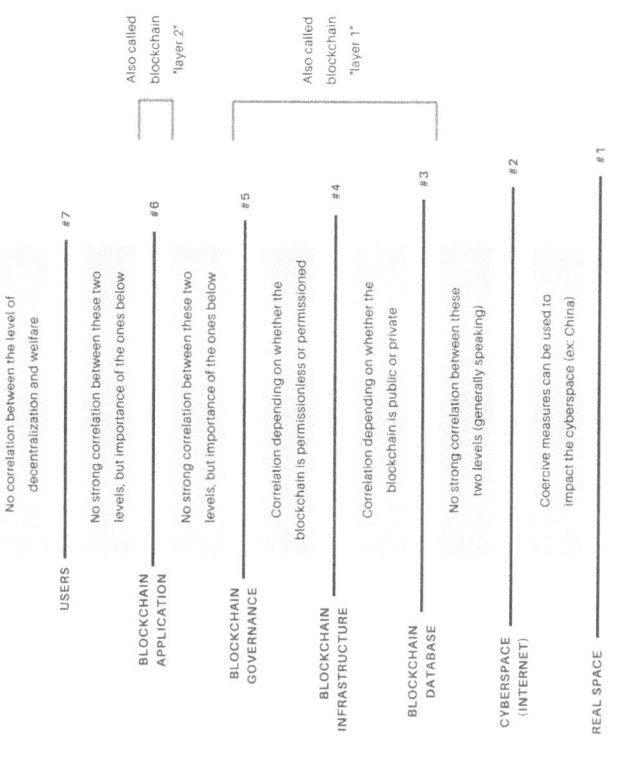

Figure 4.2   A view of blockchain layers

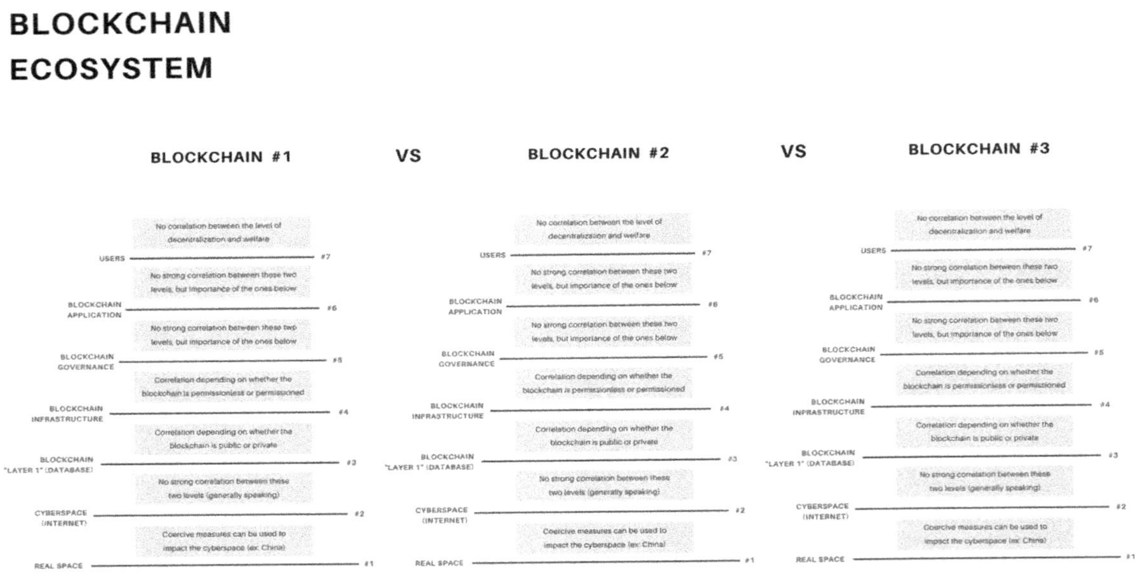

Figure 4.3   A view of the blockchain ecosystem

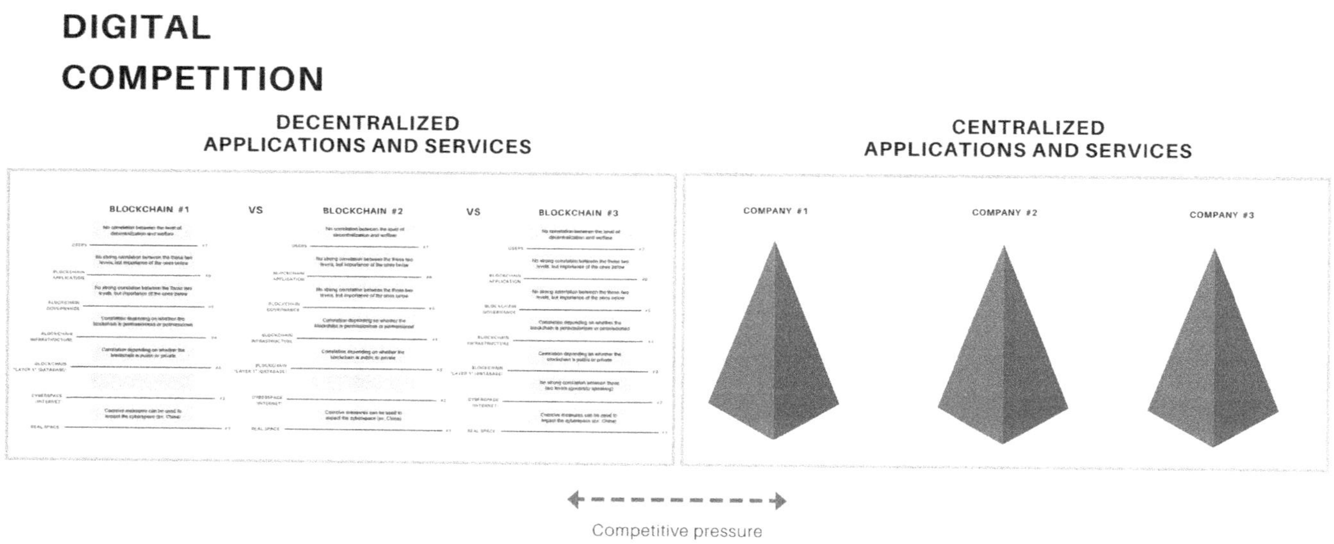

Figure 4.4   A view of blockchain cooperation and competition with the outside world

not forget that it may also affect lower levels. For example, when a blockchain is forked – that is, duplicated by a group of users to make it function based on new rules (see Chapter 8) – the centralization of the fifth level (blockchain governance) can lead to the creation of a new group of participants within the fourth level, and possibly even the third. This complex interplay makes it difficult to predict how given decisions will affect the (de)centralization of blockchain ecosystems.

Second, I want to recall that the present book is concerned with the interaction between blockchain and antitrust law. Thus, the study of decentralization aims to ascertain whether anti-competitive practices may artificially centralize blockchain ecosystems and thus reduce their efficiency and consumer welfare. Some might legitimately ask whether other objectives, such as protecting less efficient players, fit in this picture. But let us first agree on the means that are necessary to maximize decentralization before turning to these other considerations.

4   CHAPTER SUMMARY AND BEYOND

In this chapter, I have explained that the concept of "decentralization" – that is, the autonomy enjoyed by a given subject in defining its competence – is a multi-faceted concept with a rich history.

Although decentralization and efficiency are often opposed, the opposite is true in the blockchain space. With that in mind, I analyzed the degree to which blockchain is indeed decentralized. This required a dynamic and multi-level analysis: dynamic because blockchain ecosystems are rapidly evolving; and multi-level since these ecosystems have multiple interrelated layers. On that basis, the chapter discussed each layer of a blockchain ecosystem, and explained their interactions.

One may now question whether antitrust law can contribute to the overall decentralization of blockchain ecosystems, and if blockchain decentralization can help antitrust achieve its objective. Antitrust has been referred to as the Magna Carta of the free enterprise system[43] and, for that reason, the law of all economic transactions. It plays a central role in decentralizing the economy, including in the crypto space.

---

[43]   *United States v. Topco Assocs. Inc.*, 405 U.S. 596, 610 (1972).

5. Comes antitrust: the paradox

1   DECENTRALIZATION IN ANTITRUST LAW

Antitrust law seeks to protect consumers by ensuring that every company retains the competence to make its own business decisions, thus distributing economic power and autonomy throughout the economy. As I shall explain, this should not be confused with the "decentralization as an outcome" advocated by the part of the doctrine. I propose that only the competitive process should be decentralized, as indeed antitrust law seeks to protect consumer welfare and centralized outcomes may benefit consumers very much. The same is true for blockchain, as I have already established.

1.1   The Original Intent

A search on Google Scholar brings up no fewer than 1310 articles with the keywords "history of the Sherman Act."[1] The subject has been almost endlessly debated, but I want to focus on antitrust's often-misunderstood overall objective of decentralization to ensure consumer welfare.

In 1888, both the Democratic and Republican Parties put forward a bill that would become the United States' first federal antitrust law.[2] A month after the election of President Benjamin Harrison, President Cleveland stressed in his last State of the Union to Congress that: "Corporations, which should be carefully restrained creatures of the law and the servants of the people, are fast becoming the people's masters."[3]

In this context, John Sherman – who unsuccessfully ran to become the Republican candidate – proposed introducing what ended up being the Sherman Act. He began his hearings before Congress, in March 1890, by underlining the following: "the combination of labor and capital in the form of a corporation … ought to be encouraged and protected as tending to cheapen

---

[1]   "History of the Sherman Act," Google Scholar, https://perma.cc/S5YW-W4TA.
[2]   Carl T. Bogus, "The New Road to Serfdom: The Curse of Bigness and the Failure of Antitrust," University of Michigan Journal of Law Reform 49, no. 1 (2015): 45.
[3]   "December 3, 1888: Fourth Annual Message," Miller Center (2016), https://perma.cc/2YGN-NZSW.

the cost of production."[4] Indeed, "[t]he good results of corporate power are shown in the vast development of our railroads and the enormous increase of business and production of all kinds."[5]

However, Sherman also stressed the failures of the competitive process at times, thus hurting consumers:

> This bill does not seek to cripple combinations of capital and labor, the formation of partnerships or of corporations, but only to prevent and control combinations made with a view to prevent competition, or for the restraint of trade, or to increase the profits of the producer at the cost of the consumer.[6]

He added:

> I do not wish to single out the Standard Oil Company, which is a great and powerful corporation, composed in great part of citizens of my own State, and some of the very best men I know of. Still, they are controlling and can control the market as absolutely as they choose to do it.[7]

Sherman was indeed worried about several companies' power "to prevent competition and to fix the price of any commodity"[8] because it leads them to "disregard the interest of the consumer."[9]

In short, Sherman's ambition was to fight back against what he and others perceived to be excessive use of economic power concentrated in the hands of a few firms to protect consumers – not for the sake of it; not to protect democracies;[10] not for political reasons;[11] not to protect small businesses.[12] The Sherman Act was dubbed the "Magna Carta of free enterprise."[13] The central

---

[4]   Congressional Record, prepared by the Senate (1890): 2457.
[5]   *Id.*
[6]   *Id.*
[7]   Congressional Record, prepared by the Senate (1890): 2570.
[8]   *Id.*
[9]   *Id.*
[10]   *United States Steel Corporation: Hearings Before the Committee on Investigation of United States Steel Corporation*, prepared by the House of Representatives (Washington, DC, 1912): 2862 (Statement of Mr. Justice Louis D. Brandeis); see Mr. Justice Brandeis, "Competition and Smallness: A Dilemma Re-Examined," Yale Law Journal 66, no. 69 (1956): 69.
[11]   *See* Lina M. Khan, "Amazon's Antitrust Paradox," The Yale Law Journal 126, no. 3 (2017): 742 ("By orienting antitrust toward material rather than political ends, both the neoclassical school and its critics effectively embraced concentration over competition").
[12]   *See* "Lina Khan: 'This isn't about antitrust. It's about values'," Financial Times, March 29, 2019, https://perma.cc/7FVT-CHF9.
[13]   *United States v. Topco Associates, Inc.*, 405 U.S. 596, (U.S., 1972).

idea was to preserve market players' ability to decide without having to follow the instructions of powerful economic entities, because consumers are better off when they can do so.[14]

The two sections of the Sherman Act reflect this ambition, making sure that no company can live "the quiet life."[15] Section 1 is intended to prevent companies from combining their resources to obtain coercive power over others and eventually to achieve artificial centralization of the market (i.e., which does not result from the competitive process). When entering into such illegal agreements, colluders forgo the ability to conduct their business independently. They thus exercise coercive pressure on other companies (e.g., by raising prices or artificially restricting output), and consumers. Similarly, Section 2 prevents a firm from abusing its market power by preventing other firms from acting freely or excluding them from the market. Here again, the Sherman Act seeks to prevent the artificial centralization of markets.

In short, antitrust law prohibits centralization when it does not result from competition on the merits. But when it does, antitrust rules support centralized outcomes, as they increase consumer welfare by allowing them to benefit from better products and services.[16] It certainly does not embody a structuralist vision that would forbid all manifestations of market power – a "Curse of Bigness" type of argument.

The case law has been consistent in that regard, with the major exception of a few cases, including *Brown Shoe* before the Supreme Court. I will explore it

---

[14] This centralized power concerns both economic and political power, *see* Richard C. Schragger, "Decentralization and Development," Virginia Law Review 96, no. 8 (2010): 1851, 1852.

[15] John Hicks, "Annual Survey of Economic Theory: The Theory of Monopoly," Econometrica 3, no. 1 (1935): 8.

[16] *See,* for instance, *Verizon v. Trinko*, 540 U.S. 398, 407–08 (2004); *Leegin Creative Leather Products, Inc. v. PSKS, Inc.*, 551 U.S. 877 127 S. Ct. 2705, 168 L. Ed. 2d 623, 2705, 2722-2724 (2007); *Brooke Group Ltd. v. Brown & Williamson Tobacco Corp.*, 509 U.S. 209, 22–24 (1993). This appears clearly in the case of merger control, *see,* for instance, *Brown Shoe Co., Inc. v. United States*, 370 U.S. 294 (1962) (in this case, the court acknowledged cost savings in the creation of a large national shoe chain with integrated manufacturing operations, by conceding that some of the post-merger results would be beneficial to consumers). Also, *FTC v. Procter & Gamble Co.*, 386 U.S. 568 (1967) ("Economies achieved by one firm may stimulate matching innovation by others, the very essence of competition. They always allow the total output to be delivered to the consumer with an expenditure of fewer resources"). Lastly, *see United States v. Long Island Jewish Medical Center*, 983 F. Supp. 121, 148–49 (E.D.N.Y. 1997) ("the 'efficiencies' gained in this merger will ultimately result in benefits to the consumers").

next. For now, let me simply underline that antitrust law is not anti-monopoly.[17] Some scholars and judges have argued that it should be, including Justice Brandeis;[18] but these claims only appeared in the 1930s.[19]

1.2   Not *Brown Shoe*!

So far, I have discussed the Sherman Act's original intention and explained that most of the case law has stayed consistent with it. One could nonetheless question whether new objectives should be assigned to antitrust law, including the objective of becoming anti-monopoly (anti-centralized market outcome).

In *United States v. Columbia Steel Co.* (1948), the United States Supreme Court held that: "Industrial power should be decentralized. It should be scattered into many hands, so that the fortunes of the people will not be dependent on the whim or caprice, the political prejudices, the emotional stability of a few self-appointed men."[20] By stating so, the decision openly departed from the Sherman Act's original intention. *Brown Shoe* (1962) came a few years later, embodying the same vision: decentralization as an outcome, not as a mean toward other objectives (e.g., consumer welfare).

In that 1962 ruling, Chief Justice Warren spoke for the Court about the "desirability of retaining 'local control' over industry and the protection of small businesses."[21] Justice Warren further added that: "Congress appreciated that occasional higher costs and prices might result from the maintenance of fragmented industries and markets. It resolved these competing considerations in favor of decentralization. We must give effect to that decision."[22]

Robert Bork wrote two years later that "no matter how many times you read it," the decision holds that "although mergers are not rendered unlawful

---

[17]   The Neo-Brandeisians claim that it is. They are not the first, *see* David Millon, "The Sherman Act and the Balance of Power," Southern California Law Review 61 (1988): 1220 (arguing that the Sherman Act comes from an anti-monopoly tradition).

[18]   *See Liggett Co. v. Lee*, 288 U.S. at 580 (Brandeis J., dissenting).

[19]   The thesis of the political end of the Sherman Act appeared in the 1930s, *see* Thierry Kirat and Frédéric Marty, "The Late Emerging Consensus Among American Economists on Antitrust Laws in The Second New Deal," CIRANO Working Papers (2019): 29. For a translation in case law, *see*, for example, *United States v. Columbia Steel Co.*, 334 U.S. 495, (U.S., 1948), or *Northern Pacific R. Co. v. United States*, 356 U.S. 1 (U.S., 1958) (the court sought to "provid[e] an environment conducive to the preservation of our democratic political and social institutions"). For a context setting, *see* Robert Pitofsky, "Political Content of Antitrust," University of Pennsylvania Law Review 127, no. 4 (1979): 1051.

[20]   *United States v. Columbia Steel Co.* 334 U.S. 495, 536 (U.S., 1948).

[21]   *Brown Shoe Co., Inc. v. United States*, 370 U.S. 294 (U.S., 1962).

[22]   *Id.* at 344.

by the mere fact that small independent stores may be adversely affected, we must recognize that mergers are unlawful when small independent stores may be adversely affected."[23] He called the decision "the worst antitrust essay ever written."[24]

That decision was, in fact, the Supreme Court's first opportunity to interpret the Celler–Kefauver Act of 1950 – sometimes referred to as the Anti-Merger Act[25] – which amended Section 7 of the Clayton Act. In introducing the bill to the House, Representative Emanuel Celler observed that the small business community was the victim of "mammoth corporations," further described as "evils."[26] This gave the Department of Justice Antitrust Division the power to block asset acquisitions and acquisitions of non-direct competitors.[27] Put differently, the Division obtained power to forbid mergers and acquisitions between firms operating on distinct relevant markets.

The *Brown Shoe* decision resulted from the same intention: a merger may be prohibited for structural reasons, even if such prohibition ultimately leads to increased consumer prices. As the Court pointed out: "Of course, some of the results of large integrated or chain operations are beneficial to consumers. Their expansion is not rendered unlawful by the mere fact that small independent stores may be adversely affected."[28]

In a nutshell, the Court preferred a decentralized outcome over efficiency, as a matter of principle.[29] The decision sought to protect life forms – here, small

---

[23]   Robert H. Bork and Ward S. Bowman Jr., "The Crisis in Antitrust," Columbia Law Review 65, no. 3 (1965): 363.

[24]   Robert Bork, *The Antitrust Paradox: A Policy at War with Itself* (Basic Books Inc., 1978): 210.

[25]   Herbert Hovenkamp, "Distributive Justice and the Antitrust Laws," George Washington Law Review 51, no. 1 (1982): 23, 24. Noting the economic purpose of the Celler–Kefauver Act, *see* Eleanor M. Fox, "Modernization of antitrust: A New Equilibrium," Cornell Law Review 66, no. 6 (1980): 1151–53 (underlining three concerns, namely, "distrust of power, concern for consumers, and commitment to opportunity for entrepreneurs").

[26]   Congressional Record, prepared by the Senate (1949): 11.486. For a historical context, *see* Herbert Hovenkamp, "Distributive Justice and the Antitrust Laws," George Washington Law Review 51, no. 1 (1982): 24.

[27]   For a more positive opinion on the decision, *see* Eleanor M. Fox, "Antitrust, Economics, and Bias," Antitrust 2, no. 6 (1988): 7 (recalling the major goals of Section 7 of the Clayton Act: "to preserve diversity and pluralism, to decentralize power, and probably, but less explicitly, to prevent exploitation of consumers").

[28]   *Brown Shoe v. United States*, 370 U.S. 294, 344 (U.S., 1962).

[29]   William Kovacic notes that the *Brown Shoe* decision involved an assessment of "political and social values", *see* William E. Kovacic, "The Antitrust Paradox Revisited: Robert Bork and the Transformation of Modern Antitrust Policy," Wayne Law Review 36 (1990): 1439.

businesses – rather than maximizing consumer welfare.[30] Not surprisingly, *Brown Shoe* is commonly cited by the Neo-Brandeisian movement's proponents. They point out that modern antitrust has erroneously ignored *Brown Shoe*'s principles,[31] and that the time has come to reinstate them.[32] They argue for the protection of specific market structures – for decentralized outcomes. But in the absence of empirical studies establishing a systemic correlation between decentralized outcomes and innovation, or decentralized outcomes and the protection of democracy, one must question whether generalizing *Brown Shoe* is a good idea.[33] This type of reasoning is indeed proven to decrease consumer welfare while its benefits – other than electoral – remain undocumented.[34]

To the contrary, my objective with this book is to advocate for ensuring competition as a discovery procedure (in the sense of Friedrich Hayek – that is, the decentralization of economic opportunities leading to the emergence

---

[30] On the basis of this decision, *see FTC v. Procter & Gamble Co.*, 386 U.S. 568, 580 (U.S., 1967) ("Possible economies cannot be used as a defense to illegality. Congress was aware that some mergers which lessen competition may also result in economies but it struck the balance in favor of protecting competition. *See Brown Shoe Co. v. United States* (1962), *supra*, at 344.")

[31] Explaining how US courts have departed from the *Brown Shoe* decision, *see* Herbert Hovenkamp, "Markets in Merger Analysis," Antitrust Bulletin 57, no. 887 (2012).

[32] Such demands have never really disappeared. *See* Robert Earl Stemmons, "Adoption and Confusion of Microeconomic Theory and Policy in Antitrust Law," Missouri Law Review 51 (1986): 239. They are now presented in a more attractive light, but remain basically the same. *See* Lina M. Khan, "Amazon's Antitrust Paradox," The Yale Law Journal 126, no. 3 (2017): 718. Similarly, Tim Wu, "The Utah Statement: Reviving Antimonopoly Traditions for the Era of Big Tech: A new framework for holding private power to account," One Zero, November 18, 2019, https://perma.cc/5GD5-8C45 ("The broad structural concerns expressed by Congress in its enactment of the 1950 Anti-Merger Act, including due concern for the economic and political dangers of excessive industrial concentration, should drive enforcement of Section 7 of the Clayton Act"). Lastly, C. Paul Rogers, "Why Do Bad Antitrust Decisions Sometimes Make Good Law? The Alcoa and Brown Shoe Examples," SMU Law Review 72, no. 1 (2018).

[33] *See* Richard J. Gilbert, *Innovation Matters: Competition Policy for the High-Technology Economy* (The MIT Press, 2020): 117 (showing the absence of consensus in the economic literature when it comes to the link between innovation, competition and industry structures). Discussing the relationships between monopoly power and democratic principles, *see* Daniel A. Crane, "Fascism and Monopoly," Michigan Law Review 118, no. 7 (2020).

[34] Herbert Hovenkamp, "Is Antitrust's Consumer Welfare Principle Imperiled?" *Journal of Corporation Law* 45, no. 1 (2019) (underlining that Neo-Brandesians rejects the efficiency model to the benefit of small businesses, even though it leads to higher prices).

of efficient outcomes). This does not involve engineering specific market structures, but rather protecting dynamic competition by way of decentralizing decision-making so that agents can behave freely. It is about protecting a process, not achieving a specific result.

1.3   The European Side

A different yet similar logic (and history) exists in Europe. Article 3 of the Rome Treaty provides: "[T]he activities of the Community shall include, as provided in this Treaty and in accordance with the timetable set out therein: … the institution of a system ensuring that competition in the common market is not distorted."[35] The protocol on the internal market and competition, which is annexed to the Treaty on the European Union and the Treaty on the Functioning of the European Union (TFEU), restates the importance of "ensuring that competition is not distorted."[36] And, according to the TFEU, competition *is* distorted when companies collude (Article 101) or abuse their dominant positions (Article 102). In parallel, anticompetitive mergers are caught by the E.C. Merger Regulation 139/2004 of 20 January 2004.

All these behaviors and practices lead firms to reduce or eliminate the ability of other agents to engage freely in business activities: Article 101 TFEU prevents companies from colluding (because this deprives competitors and consumers of their capacity to act freely); Article 102 TFEU prevents firms from compelling their competitors to behave in a certain way. Concentrations are also prohibited when consolidated market power may hinder the competitive process, mainly due to coordinated or non-coordinated effects.[37] All these behaviors lead to artificial forms of centralization and ultimately hurt consumers by reducing innovation, driving prices up or even preventing the emergence of the European single market.

As is the case in the United States, European institutions ultimately seek to protect the competitive process. The European Commission puts it in its guidance on the application of Article 82 of the E.C. Treaty (now Article 102 TFEU) that "what really matters is protecting an effective competitive

---

[35]   European Union, "Treaty Establishing the European Community" (Consolidated Version), Rome Treaty, March 25, 1957, art. 3.
[36]   European Union, "The Treaty on the European Union, Protocol (No. 27) on the Internal Market and Competition, 2008," *Official Journal* C 83 (2008).
[37]   Coordinated effects occur when, as a result of the merger, it will become easier for the remaining entities on the market to coordinate. Non-coordinated effects occur when, as a result of the merger, the new entity will be in a better position to exercise (abuse) market power.

process and not simply protecting competitors."[38] The goal is thus to ensure the autonomy of all firms, which in turn should benefit consumers.[39] The Court of Justice of the European Union has constantly recalled this principle.[40] Accordingly, European courts and agencies have routinely affirmed that centralization should be deemed legal when it results from the competitive process's free play.[41]

2   THE SPECTER OF NEUTRALIZATION

I hope to have convinced readers that antitrust law and blockchain contribute to similar, if not identical, objectives (i.e., preserving agents' ability to act freely in the market, which entails the decentralization of decision-making processes).[42] For that reason, one might expect that both communities would work hand in hand to achieve decentralization. And yet, despite pursuing a common goal, blockchain and antitrust may end up canceling each other out. Here's why.

2.1   One Goal, Two Methods

Blockchain seeks the decentralization of decision making by eliminating inter-mediaries, while antitrust aims to achieve it by eliminating anticompetitive practices. They converge toward the same objective. That said, one should not be candid about how easy it will be to make them cooperate.

First, the Sherman Act is concerned with trusts[43] – hence the name "anti-trust". Since there is no trustee in the sense of a third-party fiduciary in

---

[38]   European Commission, "Guidance on the Commission's enforcement priorities in applying Article 82 of the EC Treaty to abusive exclusionary conduct by dominant undertakings," Communication from the Commission C45/02 (2009).

[39]   References to consumers appear in Article 101(3), Article 102 paragraph b, and EC Merger Regulation Article 2.

[40]   See, for example, judgment of 27 March 2012 – *Post Danmark A/S v. Konkurrencerådet*, C-209/10 EU:C:2012:172 (CJEU. 2012): para 175.

[41]   *See Post Danmark*, para 1 ("it is in no way the purpose of Article 102 TFEU to prevent an undertaking from acquiring, on its own merits, the dominant position on a market. Nor does that provision seek to ensure that competitors less efficient than the undertaking with the dominant position should remain on the market."). Similarly, *see Intel Corp. Inc. v. European Commission*, Case C-413/14 P ECLI:EU:C:2017:632 (CJEU. 2017): point 8.

[42]   This is a peculiarity of the relationship between antitrust law and blockchain. This technology, for example, does not always pursue the same objective as privacy law.

[43]   *See* Wayne D. Collins, "Trusts and the Origins of Antitrust Legislation," Fordham Law Review 81, no. 5 (2013): 2279, 2280.

blockchain's first layers, the target of antitrust laws is absent.[44] Blockchain may thus undermine the *raison d'être* of antitrust law, which will trigger epidermal reactions.

Furthermore, blockchain and antitrust may at times attack each other. Blockchain may be used to implement anticompetitive practices and be enforcement resistant, while antitrust may reinforce the role of intermediaries in the economy (by protecting them from different forms of anticompetitive exclusions) and label various blockchain behaviors as anticompetitive – regardless of the overall usefulness of these blockchain features.

In fact, antitrust law and blockchain ecosystems seek decentralization at two different levels. Antitrust law prohibits certain categories of conduct, creating tensions with tech communities without focusing much on digital architectures. Blockchain, on the contrary, seeks to decentralize by providing its users with a specific digital architecture. It does not prohibit (anticompetitive) practices where code allows. This creates tensions between them, as I show in Part 2 of this book. Their cooperation will require the identification of ways to deal with these mutual provocations, as I will explain in Part 3.

As things stand, both of these communities exhibit what Veblen called "trained incapacity" – the difficulty to think beyond a set of constraints and assumptions. Policymakers tend to believe that the law should be the most important constraint organizing our lives. For that reason, legal rules are often applied without looking for ways to coordinate with other constraints, including digital architectures.[45] In the meantime, blockchain communities tend to view legal enforcement as an adversary, and not as an ally. As John Perry Barlow stated in 1996: "I ask you of the past to leave us alone. You are not welcome among us. You have no sovereignty where we gather." After all, the law liberates, but it also implies illegality, lawsuits, liability assignment and sanctions. The antitrust and blockchain communities will gain from overcoming these biases.

---

[44] *See* Melanie Swan, *Blockchain: Blueprint for A New Economy* (O'Reilly Media, 2015): 69 (observing that "blockchain is a technology for decentralization. ... blockchain technology could help achieve what some commentators are calling the promise of 'Internet 3.0,' a re-architecting of the Net to assert the core objective of decentralization that inspired many of the early online pioneers who built the Internet 1.0.") *See also* Sinclair Davidson et al., "Disrupting Governance: The New Institutional Economics of Distributed Ledger Technology" (2016) (describing distributed ledger technology as "new institutional technology of governance that competes with other economic institutions of capitalism, namely firms, markets, networks, and even governments.")

[45] One has never read a court decision explaining how (digital) architectures may complement the rule of law, or even how antitrust law will impact these architectures at a general level.

2.2   The (Long) Road Ahead

If we want antitrust and blockchain to collaborate on a long-term basis, we need to talk about the problems that their cooperation will encounter along the way. The challenge before us is intricate.[46] On the one hand, it is a matter of getting legal minds to recognize that technology can help achieve objectives that the law cannot achieve on its own. There are three reasons for this.

First, blockchain provides a technical approach to the subject. It serves as a framework for decentralizing the economy by default, while antitrust mostly applies *ex post* by correcting past behaviors.[47]

Second, antitrust agencies' detection rate remains low, meaning that illegal behavior often goes unpunished.[48] And enforcement is costly, which makes it impossible to pursue all potentially illegal practices. This is particularly problematic in a world where illegal practices can be implemented through coding that quietly and immediately affects billions of users. Also, the rule of law is (unfortunately) inapplicable in some places. This is the case when the state bypasses legal constraints,[49] and when jurisdictions are mutually unfriendly and do not enforce foreign laws.[50] For example, enforcement of U.S. court judgments abroad can prove especially difficult in light of divergent rules on

---

[46]   Thibault Schrepel and Vitalik Buterin, "Blockchain Code as Antitrust," Berkeley Technology Law Journal (2021).

[47]   *Ex ante* regulations, such as the Digital Markets Act, are limited in scope. They only target a few practices and do not play the role of infrastructure.

[48]   *See* Emmanuel Combe, Constance Monnier and Renaud Legal, "Cartels: The Probability of Getting Caught in the European Union," Bruges European Economic Research Papers (2008).

[49]   "WJP Rule of Law Index 2020," World Justice Project, https://perma.cc/Y98Z -D2NE (showing that the rule of law is continuing a negative slide worldwide for the third year in a row).

[50]   *See* Yaad Rotem, "The Problem of Selective or Sporadic Recognition: 4 New Economic Rationale for the Law of Foreign Country Judgments," Chicago Journal of International Law 10, no. 2 (2010): 505, 508 (highlighting that China's courts rarely recognize foreign judgments, despite Chinese law formally entertaining the possibility of doing so); see also Brandon B. Danford, "The Enforcement of Foreign Money Judgments in the United States and Europe: How Can We Achieve a Comprehensive Treaty," The Review of Litigation 23 (2004): 381, 417 (suggesting that, in the absence of a judgments treaty with the U.S., foreign nations have no incentive to enforce U.S. judgments in their own courts and will often choose not to do so).

jurisdiction, requirements for special service of process, reciprocity and some foreign countries' public policy concerns,[51] including in Europe.[52]

Finally, antitrust law is complex and cannot be fully mastered by all companies – the compliance costs are high and many firms unwittingly infringe the law. Blockchains could therefore supplement antitrust by creating an architecture that leads to fewer anticompetitive practices.

On the other hand, blockchain communities would gain from working with (not against) antitrust law enforcers. That is because antitrust would eliminate practices that artificially centralize blockchain ecosystems and that blockchain architecture cannot stop or prevent. I will analyze them in Part 2. Doing so would also provide legal certainty, thus fostering investments and benefiting all the actors involved in commercial activities that rely on blockchain.

For these reasons, one should think of antitrust and blockchain as allies – not enemies – as they both seek the same objective, while presenting complementary strengths and defects. Doing so would lead policymakers to promote and implement a new "law + technology" approach that recognizes that the benefits of cooperation outweigh those of one-off confrontations. A game theorist would represent that approach as illustrated in Figure 5.1.

That bigger picture should guide every one of our actions in the field, including how we deal with mutual aggressions. After all, no great player has ever won a game of Go without conceding a few territories.

3   CHAPTER SUMMARY AND BEYOND

In this chapter, I first discussed decentralization in the context of antitrust law. I showed that antitrust law's objective has always been to free markets from economic coercion. In other words, it protects consumers by ensuring the decentralization of market players' decision making. The Sherman Act translates that objective, and so does the TFEU.

Despite having a similar objective, I explained that blockchain and antitrust do not automatically benefit from one another – their cooperation must be willingly enacted. Mainly, there are situations in which the law cannot be (fully)

---

[51]   *See* Yuliya Zeynalova, "The Law on Recognition and Enforcement of Foreign Judgments: Is It Broken and How Do We Fix It?" Berkeley Journal of International Law 31, no. 1 (2013): 150–51 (indicating that the enforcement of U.S. court judgments abroad can prove especially difficult in light of divergent rules on jurisdiction, requirements for special service of process, reciprocity and some foreign countries' public policy concerns).

[52]   Samuel P. Baumgartner, "How Well Do U.S. Judgments Fare in Europe?" George Washington International Law Review 40, no. 1 (2008) (suggesting that U.S. judgments face significant enforcement obstacles in Europe).

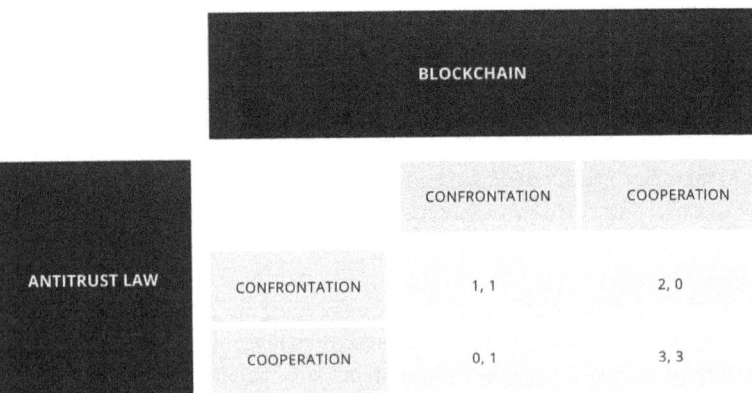

Figure 5.1   A game for decentralization

enforced. That is true when technology (such as blockchain) prevents legal enforcement and when the rule of law is not actionable (because one country is disregarding it, or because two jurisdictions are unfriendly). In other situations, the law interferes with technology developments; it creates a different type of tension.

That absence of mutual assistance between blockchain and the law would be problematic at two levels. First, it would be troublesome because blockchain could achieve decentralization in areas where the law does not apply. And second, by increasing the number of transactions executed, blockchain will simultaneously increase the number of anticompetitive practices that take place. Antitrust will thus be needed to eliminate these practices.

This latter point – how blockchain may (be used to) violate antitrust – is the subject of Part 2 of this book. When entering it, let us keep in mind that the "big picture" (the mutually beneficial nature of the cooperation between antitrust and blockchain) must inform how we deal with the "small one" (areas of tension between them). Failure to do so would lead to a lose-lose situation.

PART 2 – BEST FRENEMIES?

The second part of this book is dedicated to artificial centralization – namely, anticompetitive behaviors that take place on blockchains or are facilitated by them. I contend that studying these practices is essential to make blockchain and antitrust law function as allies; indeed, no sustainable cooperation is possible without addressing (and preparing for) the situations in which mutual aggressions will occur.

To this end, I first analyze the extent to which antitrust laws are currently applicable to blockchains. I show that the theory of the firm is central to modern antitrust (Chapter 6) and that it cannot be transposed to all blockchains. For that reason, I propose a new approach – dubbed "the theory of granularity"– which allows for the creation of a legal fiction, placing blockchain's activities (back) under the rule of law (Chapter 7). I explain that implementing that approach would benefit all the players in the blockchain ecosystem. This would clear the way for law enforcers to apply the rule of law and, in turn, would help eliminate the most harmful practices and encourage investments.

Once the question of *applicability* has been cleared up, I turn to how antitrust law could be *applied* to anticompetitive practices. To this end, I begin by looking at collusive practices, whether they concern the blockchain itself (Chapter 8) or make use of the blockchain to affect the "real space" (Chapter 9). I explain that these practices tend to centralize decision making power and thus contribute to the "artificial" centralization of different levels of blockchain ecosystems and the economy.

Part 2 closes by examining abuses of market power. I first show that the analysis of market power on blockchain raises several difficulties, and I offer suggestions to overcome them (Chapter 10). I then analyze the practices that may result from such power and show that they are heterogeneous (Chapter 11). I draw a risk map. Finally, I conclude by studying different forms of blockchain concentration (Chapter 12). I draw a distinction between hostile and mutually agreed concentrations and explain how these may recentralize blockchain.

6.   The theory of the firm

1   LEGAL FICTIONS

The concept of "legal fiction" is central to all legal systems, although regulation and court decisions refer to it only infrequently. I first explain its meaning by taking a brief detour through... trees and forests. I then show why it is useful for the present study.

1.1   Trees as a Legal Fiction

Christopher D. Stone is a law professor in the United States. In 1965, after a stint at the University of Chicago,[1] he joined the University of Southern California Law School, where he taught several subjects, including public international law and property law. One day in the fall of 1971, as he was nearing the end of a class, he asked his students the following question: "What would a radically different law-driven consciousness look like?" As he walked out of the classroom, down the corridor to his office, he wondered why he had asked such a strange thing. "How could a tree have rights," after all? Days went by, and still he continued to wonder. He soon became convinced that the answer to his question should be positive and decided to make it known.

In October that same year, he got in touch with the *Southern California Law Review*'s editor in chief. The Supreme Court had taken up a case, *Sierra Club v. Morton*, that touched upon his question. Although Stone did not think he would be able to publish his article before the case went to trial, he hoped that Justice William O. Douglas – who had agreed to write the preface to a symposium issue of the *Review* – would at least see the draft of his article. His strategy paid off. Although the Supreme Court decision did not follow his thesis, Justice Douglas wrote a dissent in which he held that: "Contemporary public concern for protecting nature's ecological equilibrium should lead to the conferral of standing upon environmental objects to sue for their own pres-

---

[1]   Christopher D. Stone, USC Gould, https://perma.cc/HZW3-CJDL.

ervation. See Should Trees Have Standing?"[2] In 1974, Stone published a book
in which he developed his theory further.

1.2   The Concept of Legal Fiction

Christopher Stone's book is a pillar of modern thinking on the subject. Of
course, the argument concerning what is a legal person – or a legal object to
which rights are attributed – did not originate in the 1970s. Since medieval
times, scholars have considered what rights should be attributed to corporations[3] – a debate they centered on the question of legal fictions. A "legal
fiction" is presumably defined as a fact created by courts or legislation to help
legal ruling.[4] Stone poses three conditions for the creation of a new one:

> They are, first, that the thing can institute legal actions at its behest, second, that in
> determining the granting of legal relief, the court must take injury to it into account;
> and, third, that relief must run to the benefit of it.[5]

A company meets these criteria. Legal systems have recognized them as
a legal fiction for hundreds of years.[6] Corporations are, in the words of John
Sherman, "artificial person[s] without fear of death, without a soul to save or
body to punish;"[7] and yet they are at the center of our modern economies. Not
only has the law "been able to exploit to its advantage and to maximize for
its needs" the fact that corporations are persons; but also, they can file legal
actions, suffer from damages and benefit from relief. One can find traces of
that recognition in the Rolls of British Parliament in 1444: "they [the Master
and Brethren of the Hospital] by that same name mowe be persones able to
purchase Londez and Tenementz of all manere persones." Here, the Hospital
was recognized as a legal fiction.

---

[2]   *Sierra Club v. Morton*, 405 U.S. 727, 742 (1972).
[3]   Christopher D. Stone, *Should Trees Have Standing? Law, Morality, and the
Environment* (Oxford University Press, 2010): 2.
[4]   Morris R. Cohen, *Law and the Social Order* (Harcourt, Brace & Company,
1933); 126 ("[L]egal fictions are useful in thus mitigating or absorbing the shock of
innovation, they work havoc in the form of intellectual confusion").
[5]   Christopher D. Stone, *Should Trees Have Standing? Law, Morality, and the
Environment* (Oxford University Press, 2010): 4.
[6]   Stanford A. Schane, "Corporation is a Person: The Language of a Legal Fiction,"
Tulsa Law Review 61, no. 563 (1987) ("The edification of the corporation to the status
of person is one of the most enduring institutions of the law and one of the most widely
accepted legal fictions").
[7]   Congressional Record, prepared by the Senate (1890): 2457.

As for the process of establishing legal fictions – once the criteria are known to be met – three methods have been used,[8] whether by the courts (in common law) or by the legislature (in civil law). The first is by assertion, where one thing is declared to be true. For instance, one may say that corporations are persons. The second is by assumption – more specifically, by an irrefutable presumption that may morph into a legal fiction. For instance, one may say that corporations are presumed to be persons. The third is by deeming. Here, X is deemed to be Y, which creates a disconnect between the reality before deeming the fact, and after.

1.3   Legal Fiction and Blockchain

If legal fictions are so convenient, why not create a multitude of them? The first objection is the necessity to agree on the desirability of the objective they ought to achieve. When courts use legal fictions to deny minorities their fundamental rights, the objective is achieved, but society does not come out better.[9] The second objection relates to the balance of power. Bentham called legal fictions "the stealing of legislative power" when courts create them. The third objection relates to the difficulty of creating a coherent legal system. Companies are legal persons, and although they can be charged with criminal activity, these crimes are committed by physical entities (persons). One must therefore put in place adequate measures to ensure that any illegal activity by a firm can be put to an end (that its perpetrators cease to act). The fourth and final objection concerns the systematization of the law. The creation of legal fictions leads to the elimination of case-by-case analysis, at least partially. For instance, a firm will always be a legal person. That may create difficulties because it entails giving the firm all the fundamental rights given to us, humans.

On the other hand, creating legal fictions significantly improves legal certainty. First, this applies to the entities directly concerned, which as legal fictions may bring actions under their own name and can thus be compensated for any damage they might unjustly suffer. It also creates legal certainty for all those who interact with these legal fictions, as trading partners can indeed bring legal actions against them. It helps when legal fictions rather than individuals benefit from illegal practices and cases where several individuals are responsible for a behavior. In short, although the creation of legal fictions is an

---

8   Eben Moglen, "Legal Fictions and Common Law Legal Theory: Some Historical Reflections," Tel-Aviv University Studies in Law 10, no. 33 (1989).
9   Legal fictions have been used to prevent minorities from being recognized as "peoples."

exercise that requires precision, it unlocks a range of potential interactions that can greatly benefit society.

I intend to explain that creating a new legal fiction for blockchains is essential to their decentralization. I have argued that decentralization is the capacity of subjects to determine their competence. That requires recognizing their legal existence before transferring such capacity. Doing so will also allow them to introduce proper legal actions and prevent illegal behaviors being turned against them.

2   THE FIRM IN ANTITRUST

Antitrust's most common legal fiction is the firm. That legal fiction has developed little since the 1930s and Ronald Coase's work. For that reason, one may wish to understand its premises to get a grasp of modern antitrust law.

2.1   The Theory of the Firm

The economic literature regarding the emergence of firms emphasizes the importance of transaction costs and the ability to reduce them thanks to top-down control. To this day, that theory has provided the bedrock for modern microeconomic analysis.

2.1.1   Highlights of Ronald Coase's article
In 1937, when he was 21 years old, Ronald Coase published "The Nature of the Firm."[10] It contains no mathematics and is just 20 pages long, but it remains one of the most-cited publications in economic theory today.[11] One can hardly overstate its impact.[12]

---

[10]   Ronald H. Coase, "The Nature of the Firm," Economica 4 (1937): 386.

[11]   Google Scholar counts about 45 000 citations, although the paper "had little or no influence for thirty or forty years," according to Ronald H. Coase, "The Nature of the Firm: Influence," Journal of Law, Economics & Organization 4, no. 1 (1988): 33. Explaining how Judge Bork helped rediscover Ronald Coase's article, *see* Alan J. Meese, "Robert Bork's Forgotten Role in The Transaction Cost Revolution," Antitrust Law Journal 79, no. 3 (2014). The Swedish Academy eventually called it Ronald Coase's "first major study," *see* "The Sveriges Riksbank Prize in Economic Sciences in Memory of Alfred Nobel 1991," NobelPrize.org, August 29, 2019, https://perma.cc/LUK3-HAAZ.

[12]   This is all the more true since the article's findings are still valid. Indeed, as Ronald H. Coase explained himself, the firm has not changed since then, *see* Russ Roberts, "Coase on Externalities, the Firm, and the State of Economics," EconTalk.org, August 30, 2019, https://perma.cc/SVJ7-9WWA.

In it, Coase sought to answer the following question: if markets are efficient, why do firms emerge? Coase responded simply and elegantly, stressing that firms make it easier to organize certain exchanges. Coase introduced the concept of transaction costs without naming it – referring to all the expenses the parties must incur to complete a transaction – and explained that firms exist to minimize these costs.[13] Indeed, a transaction involves different costs – the costs of finding economic agents on the market, negotiating, drafting a contract and so on. By internalizing these various externalities, firms reduce the cost of economic transactions. Firms were thus seen as an institutional device for the first time.[14] Coase opened the firm "black box."[15]

He then explained why firms reduce these costs. His explanations came down to the power of command and control.[16] Firms are hierarchically organized: orders and directions are given from the top and trickle down the hierarchy. This reduces the scope for costly opportunistic behavior that might otherwise make transaction unprofitable. Put differently, the reduction of these costs is often achieved by collaboration between employees, while market participants outside the firm are compelled to compete.

In Coase's words, "in place of the complicated market structure with exchange transactions is substituted the entrepreneur-co-ordinator, who directs production."[17] Reductions of costs follow, as "by forming an organisation and allowing some authority (an 'entrepreneur') to direct the resources, certain marketing costs are saved."[18] Coase thus defines the "firm" as "the system of relationships which comes into existence when the direction of resources is dependent on an entrepreneur."[19] On the contrary, this kind of efficiency is

---

[13]   Ronald Coase did not specifically name "transaction costs" as such; in fact, the term was first introduced by Carl J. Dahlman, "The Problem of Externality," The Journal of Law & Economics 22, no. 1 (1979): 141.

[14]   "Boudreaux on Coase," EconTalk.org, October 28, 2013, https://perma.cc/2T9V-AK63 .

[15]   *See* Oliver E. Williamson, "Opening the Black Box of Firm and Market Organization: Antitrust," in *The Modern Firm, Corporate Governance, And Investment*, eds. Per-Olof Bjuggren and Denis C. Mueller (Edward Elgar Publishing Ltd., 2009): 11, 33.

[16]   According to the *Cambridge English Dictionary*, "command and control" refers to "a situation in which managers tell employees everything that they should do, rather than allowing them to decide some things for themselves," *see* the *Cambridge English Dictionary*, s.v. "Command and Control."

[17]   Ronald H. Coase, "The Nature of the Firm," Economica 4 (1937): 388.

[18]   *Id.* at 392.

[19]   *Id.* at 394. An alternative theory claims that the firm does not exert more power over its employees than over independent contractors, *see* Armen Alchian and Harold Demsetz, "Production, Information Costs, and Economic Organization," The American Economic Review 62, no. 5 (1972): 777.

not found in the market, where free economic agents compete under emergent orders. One can thus define the boundary between the firm and the market: where control stops, the firm's perimeter stops.

Coase particularly emphasized the firm's ability to deal with contingencies during the performance of a contract. While firms manage long-term relationships, the market mainly permits short-term contracts based on the price mechanism.[20] Thus, Coase argued, "it seems improbable that a firm would emerge without the existence of uncertainty"[21] in the market. This assumption is based on the theory of incomplete contracts, according to which the contracting parties cannot anticipate all the situations that may arise during their contract's performance.[22] The firm helps in creating a way to settle disputes, which as a result reduces all the upfront costs related to the management of potential conflicts. Here again, Coase put the firm's ability to exercise control at the center of his demonstration. He was awarded the 1991 Nobel Prize in Economics for "his discovery and clarification of the significance of transaction costs and property rights for the economy's institutional structure and functioning."[23]

2.1.2 Coase's impact

Coase's article put transaction costs at the center of modern economics, making them "the ultimate unit of microeconomic analysis."[24] Although Coase complained in 1988 that the concept was "largely absent from current

---

[20] Ronald H. Coase, "The Nature of the Firm," Economica 4 (1937): 391–92 (arguing that a firm is likely to emerge in those cases "where a very short term contract would be unsatisfactory"); *id.* at 389 (arguing that the distinguishing mark of the firm is the supersession of the price mechanism); also *id.* at 390 (explaining that the main reason why it is profitable to establish a firm is that using the price mechanism has a cost).

[21] *Id.* at 392.

[22] *See* generally Oliver Hart and John Moore, "Incomplete Contracts and Renegotiation," Econometrica 56, no. 4 (1988): 755–85.

[23] "The Sveriges Riksbank Prize in Economic Sciences in Memory of Alfred Nobel 1991," NobelPrize.org, https://perma.cc/65EN-ASUU.

[24] Oliver E. Williamson, *Markets And Hierarchies: Analysis And Antitrust Implications* (Free Press, 1975): 20. For a broader perspective, *see* Richard A. Posner, "Nobel Laureate: Ronald Coase and Methodology," The Journal of Economic Perspectives 7, no. 4 (1993): 195, 206 (arguing that Ronald Coase rejected a place for formal theory in economics). Finally, underlining the fact that Ronald Coase has established the continuing legitimacy of the neoclassical model, *see* Herbert J. Hovenkamp, "The Antitrust Movement and the Rise of Industrial Organization," University of Iowa Legal Studies Research Paper 09-34 (2009): 105, 121.

economic theory,"[25] it has transformed the perception of the firm from a production function into a governance structure.[26]

This transformation of economic thinking heavily influenced Oliver
Williamson, among many others.[27] He researched the optimal design of firms[28]
and helped to open the firm "black box" even further, putting the firm's
"control instruments"[29] and the "means by which to infuse order"[30] at the
center of his analysis. Williamson was awarded the Nobel Prize in Economics
in 2009.

Alternative theories to those of Coase have also developed. For instance,
incentive theory portrays the firm as an incentive system that uses various
instruments combining authority, ownership and compensation to ensure

---

[25]   Ronald H. Coase, *The Firm, the Market, and the Law* (University of Chicago
Press, 1988): 6.

[26]   Scott E. Masten, "About Oliver E. Williamson," *in Firms, Markets, and
Hierarchies: The Transaction Cost Perspective*, eds. Glenn R. Carroll and David J.
Teece (Edward Elgar Publishing Ltd., 1999): 42.

[27]   *Id.* at 38. Williamson was awarded the Nobel Prize in 2009 "for his analysis of
economic governance, especially the boundaries of the firm," "The Sveriges Riksbank
Prize in Economic Sciences in Memory of Alfred Nobel 2009," NobelPrize.org,
https://perma.cc/S7FK-SVZ3. Underlining the importance of transaction costs in antitrust analyses, *see* Dennis W. Carlton, "Transaction Costs and Competition Policy,"
International Journal of Industrial Organization 73 (2020). One could also underline
the importance of the work of Armen Alchian and Harold Demsetz, who have linked
the issue of transaction costs to the definition and specification of property rights, *see*
Armen Alchian and Harold Demsetz, "Production, Information Costs, and Economic
Organization," The American Economic Review 62, no. 2 (1972); also, Benjamin
Klein and Andres V. Lerner, "The Firm in Economics and Antitrust Law," Issues in
Competition Law and Policy 1 (2008): 249.

[28]   Oliver E. Williamson, *Markets And Hierarchies: Analysis And Antitrust
Implications* (Free Press, 1975): 117 (analyzing transaction costs within the firm);
Scott E. Masten, "About Oliver E. Williamson," in *Firms, Markets, and Hierarchies:
The Transaction Cost Perspective,* eds. Glenn R. Carroll and David J. Teece (Edward
Elgar Publishing Ltd., 1999): 48. Generally speaking, discussing Williamson's indirect
contribution to the field of corporate law, *see* Roberta Romano, "Corporate Law and
Corporate Governance," Industrial and Corporate Change 5, no. 3 (1996): 277; Oliver
E. Williamson, "The Economics of Internal Organization: Exit and Voice in Relation
to Markets and Hierarchies," The American Economic Review 66, no. 2 (1976): 369
(arguing that internal firms structure matters in assessing the properties of administrative organization).

[29]   Oliver E. Williamson, "The Vertical Integration of Production: Market Failure
Considerations," The American Economic Review 61, no. 2 (1971): 112, 113.

[30]   Oliver E. Williamson, "Opening the Black Box of Firm and Market Organization:
Antitrust," in *The Modern Firm, Corporate Governance, And Investment*, eds. Per-Olof
Bjuggren and Denis C. Mueller (Edward Elgar Publishing Ltd., 2009): 34; Oliver
E. Williamson, "The Theory of the Firm as Governance Structure: From Choice to
Contract," The Journal of Economic Perspective 16, no. 3 (2002): 180.

that all employees contribute their best to the firm's interests.[31] The theory holds that firms must adopt institutional arrangements that ensure survival by aligning these incentives. They are thus a nexus of written and unwritten contracts between different economic actors in which each contractual relationship is an agency relationship, whose optimal configuration must be discovered. According to the proponents of this theory, there is no difference in nature between firms and the market. Both are said to depend on contractual relationships that do not imply any exercise of authority or control. As I will explain, none of these alternative theories is currently being used in antitrust and competition law.[32]

2.2   A Pillar of Modern Antitrust

Although Coase's theory was developed in the 1930s, modern antitrust is still constructed on the basis of this theory and has not adapted to changes in the nature of firms. Why is that? One may find a satisfying explanation in the fact that the nature of economic hierarchies has changed little to this day. Even the apparition of online platforms and aggregators has not changed the structure consisting of minimizing transaction costs thanks to vertical power. In a nutshell, Coase's theory is here to stay. As a matter of fact, and as we are about to see, all modern antitrust case laws and regulations are based on the above-mentioned article, whether in the United States or Europe. More specifically, Coase's theory helps point out where control is being exercised and, therefore, where the firm's boundaries are. Antitrust and competition law applies to all entities defined accordingly.

2.2.1   The firm's boundaries in antitrust and competition law
The Sherman Act in the United States and the TFEU in Europe are both the subject of extensive case law. The vast majority of the jurisprudence is not concerned with the question of the firm – that is, the person that is the subject of antitrust and competition law. The firm's structure has transformed very little since the introduction of these two texts; it has become more complex, but has not changed in nature.[33] For that reason, litigation generally involves

---

[31]   Developing on these instruments, *see* Bengt Holmström and Paul Milgrom, "The Firm as an Incentive System," The American Economic Review 84, no. 4 (1994): 972–91. Michael C. Jensen is at the origin of this alternative theory of the firm, *see* Michael C. Jensen, "Theory of the Firm: Managerial Behavior, Agency Costs and Ownership Structure," Journal of Financial Economics 3, no. 4 (1976): 78.

[32]   In fact, that theory had been expressly rejected by courts.

[33]   See Ian Bogost, "So Much for the Decentralized Internet," The Atlantic, July 26, 2020, https://perma.cc/Z75A-4J9E (explaining that centralized platforms very much

other issues subject to further disagreement. Nevertheless, blockchain's emergence forces us to reassess the definition of a "firm," to analyze whether decentralized groups can be captured by antitrust law as currently conceived or if blockchains should be captured through another theory.

In the United States, antitrust provisions apply to all "persons"[34] affecting trade and commerce by unlawful restraints and monopolies.[35] According to Section 7 of the Sherman Act:

> the word 'person,' or 'persons,' wherever used in sections 1 to 7 of this title shall be deemed to include corporations and associations existing under or authorized by the laws of either the United States, the laws of any of the Territories, the laws of any State, or the laws of any foreign country.[36]

The text does not further define the term "person"; it simply establishes exemption regimes for which antitrust is not applicable – mainly concerning federal government agencies and instrumentalities.[37]

The case law is more informative. In *Copperweld*,[38] the Supreme Court stressed that although "[n]othing in the literal meaning of [the Sherman Act] excludes coordinated conduct among officers or employees of the same company,"[39] there is "general agreement that § 1 is not violated by the internally coordinated conduct of a corporation and one of its unincorporated divisions." On that basis, the Court held that "there can be little doubt that the operations of a corporate enterprise organized into divisions must be judged as the conduct of a single actor," therefore exempting these operations from Section 1 of the Sherman Act.

---

embody the "command-and-control model"). Also, Erik Brynjolfsson et al., "Does Information Technology Lead to Smaller Firms?" Management Science 40, no. 12 (1994) (exploring the vertical boundaries of the firm and underlining changes in size, but not in the way control is exercised).

[34]   *See* Sherman Antitrust Act, 15 U.S.C. § 7 (1890).

[35]   *See* "S. 1, An Act to protect trade and commerce against unlawful restraints and monopolies (Sherman Antitrust Act), May 13, 1890," U.S. Capitol Visitor Center, https://perma.cc/8L5X-4FD5.

[36]   *See* Sherman Antitrust Act, 15 U.S.C. § 7 (1890).

[37]   *See* Eleanor Fox and Deborah Healey, "When the State Harms Competition—the Role for Antitrust and Competition Law," 13-11 NYU Law & Economics Research Paper Series (2014): 769, 784.

[38]   *Copperweld Corp. et al. v. Independence Tube Corp.* 467 U.S. 752 (1984).

[39]   Indeed, Section 8 of the Sherman Act underlines that "the word 'person', or 'persons', wherever used in this act shall be deemed to include corporations and associations existing under or authorized by the laws of either the United States, the laws of any of the Territories, the laws of any State, or the laws of any foreign country."

The Supreme Court was dealing with possible intra-group collusion for the first time with this decision.[40] One can only guess what would have been its reasoning before Coase's article (1937). The fact remains that *Copperweld* follows a Coasian logic:[41] the firm uses vertical control to save transaction costs; antitrust law must recognize the fact and exempt from Section 1 of the Sherman Act all agreements between two legal entities bound by such a control relationship.[42] In the words of the Supreme Court:

> The intra-enterprise conspiracy doctrine looks to the form of an enterprise's structure and ignores the reality. Antitrust liability should not depend on whether a corporate subunit is organized as an unincorporated division or a wholly-owned subsidiary. A corporation has complete power to maintain a wholly-owned subsidiary in either form. The economic, legal, or other considerations that lead corporate management to choose one structure over the other are not relevant to whether the enterprise's conduct seriously threatens competition.

In the end, "courts must examine whether the conduct in question deprives the marketplace of the independent sources of economic control that competition assumes" "when making a single-entity determination."[43] Only when "general

---

[40] Underlining that "this Court has not previously addressed the question," *Copperweld Corp. v. Independence Tube Corp.,* 467 U.S. 752 (1984).

[41] Rudolph J.R. Peritz, *Competition Policy in America: History, Rhetoric, Law* (Oxford University Press, 1996): 356; *see* also Benjamin Klein and Andres V. Lerner, "The Firm in Economics and Antitrust Law," Issues in Competition Law and Policy 1 (2008): 252 (calling *Copperweld* "consistent with Ronald Coase's theory of the firm").

[42] The presumption according to which the components of the firm "act to maximize the firm's profits" does not hold in rare cases when "the intrafirm agreements may simply be a formalistic shell for ongoing concerted action," *see American Needle Inc. v. National Football League,* 130 S.Ct. 2201, 2215 (U.S., 2010), citing *Topco Associates, Inc.,* 405 U.S., at 609; *United States v. Sealy,* 388 U.S. (U.S., 1967), at 352–54. In such cases, the two entities are then seen as two separate firms, as no control is being exercised.

[43] *American Needle Inc. v. National Football League,* 538 F.3d 736, 742 (7th Cir. 2008), confirmed on this by *American Needle, Inc. v. National Football League,* 560 U.S. 183 (2010) (focusing on "control a single aggregation of economic power"). It has been said in *Copperweld Corp. et al. v. Independence Tube Corp.,* 467 U.S. 752, 771 (U.S., 1984) that when one entity controls another, it is similar to "a multiple team of horses drawing a vehicle under the control of a single driver," and therefore, they form a single firm. Judge Easterbrook further called "silly" the fact of taking into consideration the sole interests of the parties without first analyzing control. In his view, "conflicts are [indeed] endemic in any multi stage firm," *see Chicago Prof'l Sports Ltd. P'ship v. NBA,* 95 F.3d 593 (7th Cir. 1996). Generally speaking, US courts hold parent companies liable for the behavior of their subsidiaries if: (1) the parent company itself was actively involved in the practice, or (2) the plaintiff managed to meet the requirements of corporate law to pierce the corporate veil of the subsidiary; on the subject, *see*

corporate actions are guided or determined" by "separate corporate conscious-
nesses" can two entities be seen as two separate firms in antitrust law.[44] One
must make no mistake about it: only control makes the firm and defines its
scope.[45]

In Europe, the theory of the firm as defined by Coase is also the basis of
modern competition law.[46] Article 1 of Protocol 22 to the European Economic
Area Agreement defines the "firm" as "any entity carrying out activities of
a commercial or economic nature," but the concept is not properly delimited
in the black letter of EU law. However, the case law defines "undertakings" as
"every entity engaged in an economic activity, regardless of the legal status of
the entity and the way in which it is financed."[47] The legal form of the entity
offering the economic activity does not matter.[48] In fact, as the CJEU made
clear in *Shell*, "undertakings" are economic units rather than legal units.[49]
Here again, the concept of undertaking takes Coase's path-breaking article as
a starting point.[50]

Carsten Koenig, "Comparing Parent Company Liability in EU and US Antitrust And
Competition Law," World Competition Law and Economic Review 69–100 41, no. 1
(2018): 69, 80 (stressing that holding parent companies liable is harder in the United
States than it is in Europe, notably because courts require proof that the control has been
exercised in practice, and do not simply rely on a theoretical control-based liability).

[44] *Copperweld*, 467 U.S. 752, 771 (1984).

[45] For instance, in *Copperweld*, 467 U.S. 752, 769 (1984), the Court focused its
analysis on the existence of "independent centers of decision making." It was confirmed in *American Needle, Inc. v. National Football League*, 560 U.S. 183 (U.S.,
2010).

[46] Florence Thépot, "The Firm in Antitrust and Competition Law," in *The
Interaction Between Competition Law and Corporate Governance* (Cambridge
University Press, 2019): 33.

[47] Case C-41/1990, *Klaus Höfner and Fritz Elser v Macrotron GmbH*, 1991
I-01979, para. 21. The term "undertaking" has been previously dealt with in Case
170/83, *Hydrotherm Gerätebau GmbH v. Compact del Dott. Ing. Mario Andreoli & C.
Sas.*, 1984 European Court Reports 1984-02999 para. 11.

[48] *AOK Bundesverband; Bundesverband der Betriebskrankenkassen;
Bundesverband der Innungskrankenkassen; Bundesverband der Landwirtschafts
Krankenkassen; Verband der Angestelltenkrankenkassen eV; Verband der
Arbeiter-Ersatzkassen; Bnndesknappschaft; See-Krankenkasse v. Ichthyol Company
Cordes; Mundipharma GmbH; Go ädeke Share Company; Intersan*, Joined Cases
C-264/01, C-306/01, C-354/01 and C-355/01I, ECR I-2493, Opinion of AG Jacobs
(ECJ, 2003): para. 25.

[49] *See Shell v. Commission*, Case T-11/89, European Court Reports: II-884 (CFI,
1992): para. 311. Ronald Coase was the first to explain that economic units exist thanks
to control, with the aim of reducing transaction costs.

[50] Wouter P.J. Wils, "The Undertaking as Subject of E.C. Competition Law and the
Imputation of Infringements to Natural or Legal Persons," European Law Review 25,
no. 2 (2000): 99, 102.

That definition of the "firm" is still incomplete, as it does not define its boundaries. For instance, in *Imperial Chemical Industries*, the CJEU ruled that the degree to which it carried out "the instructions given" by a company was essential in analyzing the independence of a subsidiary; and that "where a subsidiary does not enjoy real autonomy in determining its course of action in the market," the prohibitions set out in Article 101 of the TFEU were inapplicable.[51] The CJEU further held in *Akzo Nobel* that "the actual exercise of decisive influence"[52] defines firm limits in competition law; and that "it is sufficient for the Commission to prove that the subsidiary is wholly owned by the parent company to presume that the parent exercises a decisive influence over the commercial policy of the subsidiary."[53] In the end, a firm encompasses all the elements over which control is exercised, as in the United States.[54] For instance, in *Hydrotherm*, the CJEU found that a natural person, a limited

---

[51] *Imperial Chemical Industries Ltd. v. Commission of the European Communities*, Case 48/69, European Court Reports: 1972 619 (ECJ, 1972): paras. 133–34. *See* also *Viho Europe BV v. Commission of the European Communities*, Case C-73/95 P, European Court Reports: 1996 I-5457 (ECJ, 1996), in which the CJEU held that control can be inferred from subsidiaries not enjoying "real autonomy in determining their course of action in the market, but carry out the instructions issued to them by the parent company controlling them." *Viho Europe BV v. Commission of the European Communities*, Case C-73/95 P, European Court Reports: 1996 I-5457 (ECJ, 1996): para. 16; *Centrafarm BV and Adriaan De Peijper v. Sterling Drug Inc.*, Case 15/74, European Court Reports: 1974 1147 (ECJ, 1974); *Centrafarm BV and Adriaan De Peijper v. Winthrop BV*, Case 16/74, 1974 ECR 1183 (1974): para. 32; Case 30/87, *Corinne Bodson v. Pompes Funebres des Regions Liberees SA*, European Court Reports: 1988 2479 (ECJ, 1988): para. 19; *Ahmed Saeed Flugreisen and Others v Zentrale zur Bekaempfung Unlauteren Wettbewerbs*, Case 66/86, European Court Reports: 1989 803 (ECJ, 1989): para. 35; *Béguelin Import Co v. SAGL Import Export*, Case 22/71, European Court Reports: 1971 949 (ECJ, 1971): para. 8.
[52] *Akzo Nobel and Others v. Commission*, C-516/15 P, EU:C:2017:314, (ECJ, 2017): para. 55.
[53] *Id.* at para. 61. Indeed, the European Commission may analyze shareholdings or other factual elements. Studying who is supporting financial risks is one of them, *see J.C.J. Wouters and Others v. Algemene Raad van de Nederlandse Orde van Advocaten*, Case C—309/99, European Court Reports: 2002 1577 (ECJ, 2002), para. 48; *see* also Florence Thépot, "The Firm in Antitrust and Competition Law," in *The Interaction Between Competition Law and Corporate Governance* (Cambridge University Press, 2019): 37.
[54] In *Hydrotherm Gerätebau GmbH v. Compact del Dott. Ing. Mario Andreoli & C. Sas.*, Case 170/83, European Court Reports 1984-02999 (ECJ, 1984), the CJEU found that when legal entities have "identical interests and [are] controlled by the same natural person," they form "a single economic entity," *Hydrotherm Gerätebau GmbH v Compact del Dott. Ing. Mario Andreoli & C. Sas.*, Case 170/83, European Court Reports 1984-02999 (ECJ, 1984): para. 11. Despite this confusing wording, here again, the CJEU ended up analyzing the control exercised as the sole determinant of economic

partnership and another undertaking made up a single economic unit when they were all controlled by the same natural person.[55] That logic derives from Coase's "The Nature of the Firm."[56]

2.2.2   The firm as a pillar of antitrust and competition law

The definition of the firm's boundaries helps in three fundamental steps of antitrust and competition law: (1) determining whether the law should apply; (2) assessing practices; and (3) and assigning liability.

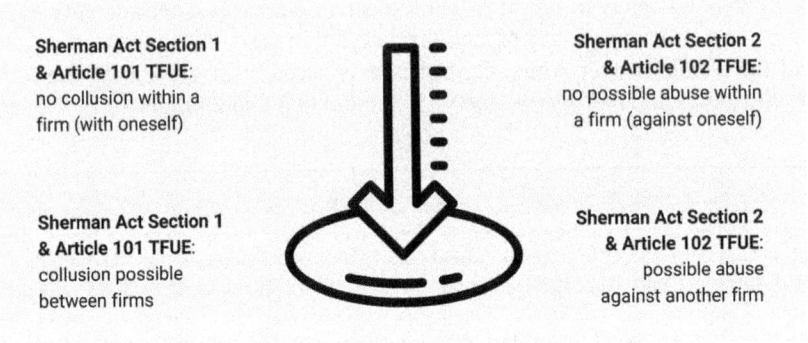

Sherman Act Section 1 & Article 101 TFUE: no collusion within a firm (with oneself)

Sherman Act Section 2 & Article 102 TFUE: no possible abuse within a firm (against oneself)

Sherman Act Section 1 & Article 101 TFUE: collusion possible between firms

Sherman Act Section 2 & Article 102 TFUE: possible abuse against another firm

Figure 6.1   Visualizing the firm's centrality in antitrust law

First, establishing the firm's boundaries helps determine the extent to which antitrust and competition law applies. U.S. antitrust law provides several exemptions to different types of entities, which require both the identification of the firm and an understanding of its activities. European competition law applies only to undertakings that carry out an economic activity. Once again, it is then necessary to identify the firm's boundaries to determine the activities carried out.

---

interests, *see* Ioannis Lianos, Valentine Korah and Paolo Siciliani, *Competition Law: Analysis, Cases, & Materials* (Oxford University Press, 2019): 329.

[55] *Hydrotherm Gerätebau GmbH v. Compact del Dott. Ing. Mario Andreoli & C. Sas.*, Case 170/83, European Court Reports 1984-02999 (ECJ, 1984): para. 12.

[56] Benjamin Klein and Andres V. Lerner, "The Firm in Economics and Antitrust Law," Issues in Competition Law and Policy 1 (2008): 266. Also, discussing the case law showing how central the element of "control" is, *see* Alison Jones, Brenda Sufrin and Niamh Dunne, *EU Competition Law: Text, Cases, and Materials* (Oxford University Press 7th, 2019): 157. *See*, for instance, *Jean Claude Becu et al.*, C-22/98, European Court Reports 1999 I-05665, (ECJ, 1999): paras. 89–91, in which the CJEU held that dock workers, performing work under the direction of their employers, were to be incorporated into the undertaking concerned.

Second, establishing the firm's boundaries is essential when agencies assess the legality of business practices.[57] In terms of collusion, U.S. and European courts have recognized that two legal entities that are part of the same economic unit – that is, the same firm – cannot be held guilty of collusion, as one cannot agree with oneself.[58] Antitrust prohibits several forms of cooperation outside the firm, while it always permits cooperation within the firm. The logic is similar in terms of monopolization and abuse of a dominant position. As a company cannot abuse its market power against itself, abuses of power are illegal only when they affect other firms. Above all, defining the boundaries of firms is essential to analyze market power (and thus whether Section 2 of the Sherman Act or Article 102 of the TFEU is applicable to a given case) and the ability to engage in anticompetitive practices. Control indeed confers the firm with the power to implement practices – including the ability to raise prices, which is often central in antitrust cases.

Finally, identifying the boundaries of firms is essential to assign liability.[59] Liability for anticompetitive practices rests with the parent company that ulti-

---

[57] Frank H. Easterbrook, "Allocating Antitrust Decisionmaking Tasks," Georgetown Law Journal 76, no. 305 (1987): 305, 314 (doubting the ability of courts to evaluate practices, even in light of transaction costs). Also, underlining that transaction costs economics "assumes away the critical question of who transacts with whom," but that "the question of who can trade is at least as important as the question of the terms of trading," *see* Herbert J. Hovenkamp, "Harvard, Chicago, and Transaction Cost Economics in Antitrust Analysis," Antitrust Bulletin 55, no. 3 (2010): 626.

[58] In the United States, *see*, for instance, *Zachair v. Driggs* 141 F 3d 1162 (4th Circ., 1998); *Copperweld Corp. et al. v. Independence Tube Corp.*, 467 U.S 752, 769, 767–72 (U.S., 1984); for an analysis, Herbert J. Hovenkamp, *Federal Antitrust Policy, The Law of Competition and its Practice* (West Academic Publishing, 2015): 246; also Spencer Weber Waller, "Corporate Governance and Competition Policy," George Mason Law Review 18, no. 4 (2011): 833, 841. In Europe, *see*, for instance, *Viho Europe BV v. Commission of the European Communities*, Case C-73/95 P, European Court Reports: 1996 I-5457 (ECJ, 1996); Case 170/83, *Hydrotherm Gerätebau GmbH v. Compact del Dott. Ing. Mario Andreoli & C. Sas.*, Case 170/83, European Court Reports: 1984-02999 (ECJ, 1984): paras. 11, 22; *Bundeskartellamt v. Volkswagen and VAG Leasing GmbH*, European Court Reports: Case C-266/93, 1995 I-3477 (ECJ, 1995); for an analysis, *see* Alison Jones, "The Boundaries of an Undertaking in EU Antitrust and Competition Law," European Competition Journal 8, no. 2 (2012): 301, 308.

[59] *Aalborg Portland and Others v. Commission*, Case C-204/00 P, European Court Reports: 2004 I-123, Opinion of AG Ruiz-Jarabo Colomerpara, (ECJ, 2004): para. 68.

mately controls other entities if such control has been exercised.[60] This logic stems from the classic distinction between ownership and control.[61]

It is safe to assume that antitrust law will capture the activities of blockchain participants at their individual level.[62] For example, one could imagine that a miner is considered a company on his own; after all, miners are operating an economic activity. Nevertheless, analyzing whether the entire blockchain layer 1 could be deemed a firm for the purpose of antitrust law is essential if agencies are to understand and apprehend anticompetitive practices that are carried out beyond the simple framework of the individual. For example, suppose a blockchain is implementing practices to exclude another blockchain from the market. In that case, one will want to punish these practices rather than each individual action leading to the entire scheme. I will return to these practices in the coming chapters.

In other words, defining the firm's boundaries is a necessary step in understanding competitive dynamics, in analyzing practices and eventually, in assigning antitrust liability to the blockchain when, as an entity, it seeks to achieve survival through anticompetitive ways. It is thus essential to carefully consider the elements that are taken into account when defining "firms" under antitrust law. I showed that in the United States, as in Europe, only one element matters: control. This reasoning is problematic when it comes to blockchain.

---

[60]   In the United States, *see In re Digital Music Antitrust Litigation*, 812 F. Supp. 2d 390 (S.D.N.Y., 2011) (rejecting "a joint liability theory to put entire corporate families on the hook for antitrust violations"); *Cupp v. Alberto-Culver USA, Inc.*, 310 F. Supp. 2d 963 (W.D. Tenn., 2004) (holding that the mere existence of a corporate relationship does not implicate a parent in its subsidiary's actions). In Europe, *see Villeroy & Boch AG v. European Commission*, Case C-625/13, Reports of Cases before the Court of Justice and the Court of First Instance 1 (ECJ, 2017): para. 146; *Evonik Degussa GmbH and AlzChem AG v. European Commission*, Case C-155/14 P, Reports of Cases before the Court of Justice and the Court of First Instance 1 (ECJ, 2016): para. 27; *Comm'n and Others v. Versalis and Others*, Joined Cases C-93/ 13 P & C-123/13 P, Reports of Cases before the Court of Justice and the Court of First Instance 1 (ECJ, 2015): para. 40. For an analysis, *see* Alison Jones, "The Boundaries of an Undertaking in EU Antitrust and Competition Law," European Competition Journal 8, no. 2 (2012): 328–31.

[61]   Discussing the distinction, *see* Spencer Weber Waller, "Corporate Governance and Competition Policy," George Mason Law Review 18, no. 4 (2011): 833, 835.

[62]   When antitrust and competition law is applied to individuals, the capacity to reveal their real-life identities becomes crucial, *see* Thibault Schrepel, "Is Blockchain the Death of Antitrust Law? The Blockchain Antitrust Paradox," Georgetown Law Technology Review 3, no. 2 (2019): 322.

3   NEW INSTITUTIONAL CHALLENGES

I have established that antitrust law is built on the theory of the firm, as defined by Ronald Coase. I must now analyze whether the first layer of a blockchain can be considered a firm (in the antitrust sense), or whether it is a new transactional institution. To this end, I show that blockchain introduces an alternative way to transact: one that ultimately escapes antitrust oversight because it does not involve any clear power of command and control.

3.1   Coase vs. Blockchain

Blockchain layer 1 is a transactional institution competing with firms and markets. It can indeed be used in a unique way to reduce specific transaction costs, which can make it attractive. And it may also encourage new transactions thanks to its singular characteristics. All these elements come into play when analyzing the importance of blockchain as an institution.

3.1.1   Blockchain is not a firm

In Coase's theory of the firm, transaction costs explain which exchanges occur within or outside the firm. Blockchain could help expand the firm's scope by reducing certain transaction costs, such as those that are currently necessary to ensure the proper execution of a transaction – the use of smart contracts is one example.

But the unique characteristics of blockchain open up new opportunities for transactions. First, blockchain can be used outside the firm to save on certain transaction costs.[63] Such reductions may occur for small and large transactions by lowering search costs, contracting costs and coordination costs, among others.[64] Regarding small-scale activities, blockchain may help transact without a central authority, since it creates an architectural trust between the parties.[65] It may therefore open new perspectives for small businesses. When

---

[63]   *See* Max Raskin, "The Law and Legality of Smart Contracts," Georgetown Law Technology Review 1, no. 2 (2017): 304, 305, 336 (opposing blockchain "radicals" with those arguing that smart contracts help in reducing the firm's transaction costs). Also, Christian Catalini, "The Firm as a Nexus of Smart Contracts? How Blockchain and Cryptocurrencies Can Transform the Digital Economy," Yale Journal on Regulation: Notice & Comment, June 7, 2017, https://perma.cc/KM4Y-963N.

[64]   Don Tapscott and Alex Tapscott, *Blockchain Revolution: How the Technology Behind Bitcoin Is Changing Money, Business, and the World* (Penguin Books, 2016): 95–101 (underlining that smart contracts could help corporate governance by providing pre-automated answers in case of conflict).

[65]   Clay Shirky, *Here Comes Everybody: The Power of Organizing Without Organizations* (Penguin Books, 2009): 41 (arguing that when there is a small

it comes to larger-scale activities, blockchain could cut the costs of having a central authority coordinating many transactions,[66] and could extend the boundaries of efficient contracting into what was once the firm's exclusive province.[67] For example, blockchain could also create transparent chain supply without having any entity coordinating the ledger. It already allows for cryptocurrencies without a single entity, ensuring there is no double spending and preserving ledger integrity.

Moreover, blockchain can allow for the creation of new types of transactions[68] by leading specific transaction costs not only to fall moderately, but to collapse.[69] That explains why, according to Bain, blockchain will increase the value of world's transactions by 6.9 percent. And blockchain can also permit loosely coordinated groups to operate transactions previously out of reach, even within the firm. For example, there are smart contracts automating the

---

decrease in transaction costs, "small companies become more effective, doing more business at lower cost than the same company does in a world of high transaction costs"); Catherine Mulligan, "Blockchain Will Kill the Traditional Firm," Imperial College Business School Blogs, October 16, 2017, https://perma.cc/VZ5M-LKWM; ConsenSysMedia, "Joe Lubin – Nature Of The Firm, v2.0 Keynote from EtherealNY #Blockchain Conference 2018," YouTube, published on May 13, 2018, https://perma .cc/H5WV-K7WK (arguing that "tokenizing everything will create fluid hyper efficient markets, and we will all be able to wrap ourselves in APIs and be very effective single elements").

[66]   Sinclair Davidson, Primavera de Fillippi et al., "Blockchains and the Economic Institutions of Capitalism," Journal of Institutional Economics 14, no. 4 (2018): 649. Also, Clay Shirky, *Here Comes Everybody: The Power of Organizing Without Organizations* (Penguin Books, 2009): 41 (arguing that management challenges grow faster than organizational size).

[67]   Tom Glocer, "Blockchain, Coase and the Theory of the Firm," Tom Glocer's blog, October 23, 2017, https://perma.cc/2UQ4-Z9JR.

[68]   Sinclair Davidson, Primavera de Fillippi et al., "Blockchains and the Economic Institutions of Capitalism," Journal of Institutional Economics 14, no. 4 (2018): 653–56 (arguing that the mass adoption of blockchain "may lead to an evolution of the economic institutions of capitalism itself"); Nick Tomaino, "The Slow Death of the Firm," Thecontrol.co, October 21, 2017, https://perma.cc/TC42-HD3G (arguing that blockchain helps in the creation of new products that could not be created by firms); Sid Venkateswaran, "Ronald Coase and the Nature of the Blockchain," Medium, December 18, 2017, https://perma.cc/F7NS-FDPC.

[69]   Clay Shirky, *Here Comes Everybody: The Power of Organizing Without Organizations* (Penguin Books, 2009): 44. James Hazard, Odysseas Sclavounis and Harald Stieber, "Are Transaction Costs Drivers of Financial Institutions? Contracts Made in Heaven, Hell, and the Cloud in Between," in *Banking Beyond Banks and Money*, eds. Paolo Tasca et al. (Springer, 2016).

payment of employees' salaries every 12 seconds and automatically maintained as long as the employees' obligations are met.[70]

Second, Williamson argues that firms help minimize opportunism that can arise when incomplete contracts are concluded – that is, contracts that fail to anticipate certain future states of the world. And indeed, the firm provides parties with a framework to find a solution[71] in the event of a litigious situation that has not been contractually framed. On the contrary, blockchain is immutable,[72] and in that regard, it does not facilitate the management of unforeseen circumstances. Some past research implies that economic agents should always prefer the firm to blockchain for that reason.[73] But in fact, blockchain manages opportunism in different ways – namely, by integrating market mechanisms into a closed and guaranteed payment system through cryptographic enforcement and execution.[74]

Furthermore, smart contracts can also help in managing unforeseen events. First, several smart contracts could be combined (one is called upon only if another one has been previously executed) to manage situations where cryptographic features are insufficient.[75] Second, ever-increasing computing power could eventually be used to create comprehensive smart contracts,

---

[70]   Vasilios Mavroudis et al., "Snappy: Fast On-chain Payments with Practical Collaterals," Paper, Network and Distributed Systems Security Symposium 2020, San Diego, CA, February 23, 2020.

[71]   Irving Wladawsky-Berger, "Blockchain and the Future of the Firm," WSJ Blog, September 29, 2017, https://perma.cc/ZDG7-6LRW.

[72]   Differently put, blockchain is generally seen as an economic world of complete contracts, while firms are a nexus of incomplete contracts. On that, *see* Sinclair Davidson, Primavera de Fillippi et al., "Blockchains and the Economic Institutions of Capitalism," Journal of Institutional Economics 14, no. 4 (2018): 641. On how the firms can help in managing incomplete contracts, *see* Oliver Hart and John Moore, "Property Rights and the Nature of the Firm," Journal of Political Economy 98, no. 6 (1990): 1119; Oliver E. Williamson, *The Economic Institutions of Capitalism* (Free Press, 1985): 32.

[73]   Oliver Hart, "An Economist's Perspective on the Theory of the Firm," Columbia Law Review 89, no. 7 (1989): 1757; *see* Sinclair Davidson, Primavera de Fillippi et al., "Blockchains and the Economic Institutions of Capitalism," Journal of Institutional Economics 14, no. 4 (2018): 641. After all, the actual execution of transactions is "a secondary part of life; the primary problem or function is deciding what to do and how to do it," *see* Frank H. Knight, *Risk, Uncertainty and Profit* (Hart, 1921): 267, 268.

[74]   Sinclair Davidson, Primavera de Fillippi et al., "Blockchains and the Economic Institutions of Capitalism," Journal of Institutional Economics 14, no. 4 (2018): 649–50.

[75]   For an explanation of a smart contract library, *see* Thibault Schrepel, "Collusion by Blockchain and Smart Contracts," Harvard Journal of Law and Technology 33, no. 1 (2019): 143.

capable of anticipating the outside world to a greater extent.[76] Third, while smart contracts' rigid rules may create a disconnect with the outside world, this outside world is increasingly governed by algorithmic rules, making it (more) predictable. In fact, this real-world is more and more connected to the digital world, with sensors and IoT, for example. Quantum computing will speed up this trend.[77] Smart contracts will, therefore, govern the actual world more easily in the coming years. And finally, one could ask the following question: why should contracts be perfectly complete? After all, they exist to govern and order the actual world, not to be just as complicated.[78]

As a result, to hold smart contracts' incompleteness as being an insurmountable limit is misinformed. It follows that blockchain differs from the firm, and that each of these entities enjoys a comparative advantage over certain types of transactions.

3.1.2   Blockchain is not a market

Blockchain layer 1 differs from the market in several ways related to the possibility of creating a "cryptographic stigmergy" – that is, allowing sizeable groups of individuals to interact with one another in a stable environment and without the need for trust.[79] This differentiates blockchains from markets because the latter usually require a trust-inducing mechanism between the parties to a transaction.[80] Blockchains provide an infrastructure making them more than mere market transactions implemented under a set of governing rules.

Blockchain also provides participants with more information than markets. First, blockchain provides users with more insight than just the price of products and services; for example, a user may access the history of transactions

---

[76]   Erik Brynjolfsson, *Machine, Platform, Crowd* (WW Norton and Co., 2018): 319 (discussing the increase in computing power).

[77]   In fact, if quantum computing were already available, it would be possible to code more nuanced smart contracts. Indeed, a qubit may contain more alternatives than a bit (0 or 1). On quantum computing and blockchain, *see* Amira Bou Guera, "How Will Quantum Computing Affect Blockchain?" Consensys, December 3, 2019, https://perma.cc/3ZJV-HM6C.

[78]   Edmund S. Phelps, *Mass Flourishing: How Grassroots Innovation Created Jobs, Challenge, and Change* (Princeton University Press, 2013): 206 (sketching the idea that contracts do not have to be complete).

[79]   Prateek Goorha, "The Return of 'The Nature of the Firm': The Role of the Blockchain," The Journal of the British Blockchain Association 1, no. 1 (2018): 73 (arguing that blockchain is based on the use of the price mechanism thanks to which coordination across the cryptographic space is made possible).

[80]   *Id.* at 72.

carried out by a future co-contractor.[81] Second, public permissionless block-chains are open access. This reduces the price of discovering the conditions for any transaction. Third, the concept of tokenization can help create an efficient marketplace because the platform is managed in perpetuity by decentralized nodes that are rewarded for their network maintenance efforts. Fourth, block-chain forces its users to accommodate the costs of verifying transactions (as I explained in Chapter 2).[82] In short, blockchain eliminates numerous transaction costs in traditional markets and replaces them with a system of small fees that create trust between parties (i.e., users' engagement in the costly activity of verifying transactions). This makes blockchain a tool that is both valuable and versatile.[83]

3.1.3 Blockchain as an institution

As far as transaction costs are concerned, blockchain's importance as a separate institution remains hard to quantify.[84] Indeed, blockchain does not completely eliminate transaction costs;[85] in fact, one may list additional ones associated with the use of smart contracts in four categories.[86] The first category is search

---

[81] *Id.*; Udo Pesch and Georgy Ishmaev, "Fictions and Frictions: Promises, Transaction Costs and the Innovation of Network Technologies," Social Studies of Science 49, no. 2 (2019): 264, 269.

[82] Prateek Goorha, "The Return of 'The Nature of the Firm': The Role of the Blockchain," The Journal of the British Blockchain Association 1, no. 1 (2018). Also, Floris F. Seuren, "Exploring the Applicability of Blockchain in Lowering Transaction Costs in the Commercial Real Estate Due Diligence Process: A Case Study Research," Semanticscholar.org (2018), https://perma.cc/KH9W-QPLP.

[83] Richie Etwaru, *Blockchain: Trust Companies: Every Company Is at Risk of Being Disrupted by a Trusted Version of Itself* (Dog Ear Publishing LLC., 2017): 185 (arguing that Coase did not consider the improvement to market efficiencies from increased trust in transactions). More broadly, *see* Qiao Wang, "Cryptonetworks and the Theory of the Firm," Token Daily, October 4, 2018, https://perma.cc/9ZUK-54QM (explaining that crypto networks differ from markets because they benefit from network effects); and Jesse Walden, "Past, Present, Future: From Co-ops to Cryptonetworks," Andreessen Horowitz (2019), https://perma.cc/349H-KUT2 (explaining that traditional platforms first collaborate with their users and end up competing with them, while blockchain platforms may sustain continued cooperation).

[84] Craig S. Wright, "Proof of Work as it Relates to the Theory of the Firm," (2017), https://perma.cc/A984-BE62 (contending that the distinction between blockchain and other institutional ways is narrower than one may expect, regardless of the protocol that is being implemented).

[85] Udo Pesch and Georgy Ishmaev, "Fictions and Frictions: Promises, Transaction Costs and the Innovation of Network Technologies," Social Studies of Science 49, no. 2 (2019): 271.

[86] Ben Garfinkel, "Recent Developments in Cryptography and Possible Long-Run Consequences," (2019): 92; Jeremy M. Sklaroff, "Smart Contracts and the Cost of Inflexibility," University of Pennsylvania Law Review 166 (2017): 297.

costs. These include the cost of verifying smart contract features, establishing confidence in smart property and learning about cryptographic tools. The second category is bargaining costs. These notably arise when economic agents draft contracts and translate them into computer code.[87] The third category concerns commitment costs that are engaged when paying fees to full nodes[88] or information services, protecting against coercion and theft of digital assets, and managing the risk of smart contracts failure. The fourth relates to enforcement costs – that is, the costs of ensuring contract execution once a smart contract has been called.

As a result, it might be that only a few transactions will be optimized via blockchain; for the rest, firms and markets will do. For now, no empirical analysis has compared the costs and features of implementing different types of transactions within these three institutions.[89] One can only refute the Coasian assumption according to which markets and firms are the only two "alternative methods of coordinating production" by stressing that the number of transactions implemented on blockchain continues to grow,[90] and that blockchain enables numerous novel transactions.[91] Blockchains do not merely reduce transaction costs; they also minimize the scope for opportunism and have certain characteristics that make them "unstoppable" (as I explained in Chapter 2).[92] The interplay of these features enables blockchains to open up so many new frontiers and become an institution on their own.[93]

---

[87]   Don Tapscott and Alex Tapscott, *Blockchain Revolution: How the Technology Behind Bitcoin Is Changing Money, Business, and the World* (Penguin Books, 2016): 103; Jeremy M. Sklaroff, "Smart Contracts and the Cost of Inflexibility," University of Pennsylvania Law Review 166 (2017): 298 (arguing that "the pressure to construct larger and longer-term agreements that can change flexibly in response to unpredictable events, will exist even in a world of smart contracts").

[88]   Full nodes are blockchain participants that store an entire copy of the blockchain ledger on their computers, for more, *see* Chapter 7.

[89]   *See* Sinclair Davidson, Primavera de Fillippi et al., "Blockchains and the Economic Institutions of Capitalism," Journal of Institutional Economics 14, no. 4 (2018): 640 (discussing the idea that blockchain is an institutional technology); also, Vitalik Buterin, "Visions, Part 1: The Value of Blockchain Technology," Ethereum Blog, April 12, 2015, https://perma.cc/BBF8-MK6U.

[90]   "Daily Bitcoin Transactions Have Increased by 57% Since the Beginning of 2019," Longhash, April 2, 2019, https://perma.cc/4ASC-C873.

[91]   Blockchain could increase global trade volumes by $1.1 trillion by 2026, *see* Bain, "Blockchain Could Increase Global Trade Volumes by $1.1 trillion by 2026, off the Current Base of $16 trillion," October 22, 2018, https://perma.cc/Z8DX-C3KY.

[92]   Thibault Schrepel, "Collusion by Blockchain and Smart Contracts," Harvard Journal of Law and Technology 33, no. 1 (2019): 120 (discussing the idea that blockchain code is unstoppable).

[93]   Similarly, *see* Catalina Goanta and Marieke Hopman, "Crypto Communities as Legal Orders," Internet Policy Review 9, no. 2 (2020): 15 (arguing that "an inter-

3.2   The Great Escape

So far, I have argued that blockchain layer 1 opens what can be thought of as a third transactional way. Given that, it is necessary to consider how antitrust law could apply to this unique institution. As I explain, public permissionless blockchains escape the theory of the firm due to the absence of command and control, and this may also be the case – to a lesser extent – for private consortium blockchains.

3.2.1   Public permissionless blockchains

3.2.1.1   Emergence and horizontality
Public permissionless blockchains are technological and economic realities – some would say spontaneous organizations.[94] They associate the price mechanism of markets with constitutional properties that are typically associated with nation states. The existence and survival of public permissionless blockchain do not depend on one individual, and the decisions of a few individuals cannot stop them.[95] In other words, such blockchains function thanks to emergent behavior rather than top-down planning.[96]

---

net platform such as the Silk Road may very well make up its own socio-legal order"). Also, see Brian Arthur, *Complexity and the Economy* (Oxford University Press, 2015), preface (describing an economy not as a container for its technology, but as an expression of it).

[94]   Sinclair Davidson, Primavera De Filippi and Jason Potts, "Economics of Blockchain," (2016). Also, Karl J. Friston and Christopher D. Frith, "Active Inference, Communication and Hermeneutics," 68 Cortex (2015): 129 (speaking to the notion of generalized synchrony as a universal phenomenon which this book applies to public permissionless blockchain).

[95]   *See* Jameson Lopp, "Who Controls Bitcoin Core?" Cypherpunk Cogitations, December 15, 2018, https://perma.cc/ET5E-JPB4 (arguing that "the definition (control) of Bitcoin the protocol is like the definition of a language ... No one is forced to agree with the definition of a given word in a dictionary, neither are they forced to agree with code in a given Bitcoin implementation by running it. ... No one controls Bitcoin. No one controls the focal point for Bitcoin development"). According to the Uniform Law Commission, "control means, when used in reference to a transaction or relationship involving virtual currency, the power to execute unilaterally or prevent indefinitely a virtual currency transaction," *see* Uniform Regulation of Virtual-Currency Business, prepared by the National Conference of Commissioners on Uniform State Laws (California, 2017): Act 102(3)(A).

[96]   ConsenSysMedia, "Joe Lubin – Nature Of The Firm, v2.0 Keynote from EtherealNY #Blockchain Conference 2018," YouTube, published on May 13, 2018, https://perma.cc/CB6T-R7E5 (arguing that "top-down command and control has taken us a long way as a society," but that "we can do much better" thanks to blockchain).

These characteristics of blockchain allow for stigmergic coordination: the type found in nature, where "certain species of animals—such as ants, termites, birds, etc.—create complex social structures that do not rely on any hierarchical structure."[97] Indeed, public permissionless blockchain governance relies on different incentives that do not include direct control or coercion. In other words, firms are essentially vertical structures, while blockchains are far more horizontal.[98] As a result, no single participant can exercise a controlling influence over the entire blockchain's management or policies.[99] And indeed, most of the blockchain community see "control as liability" and thus seek to avoid designing or updating blockchains in a way that would seize control over them.[100]

In short, public permissionless blockchains are emergent and horizontal entities. It follows that Ronald Coase's theory of the firm, which centers on direct top-down control to reduce transaction costs, cannot be transposed to blockchain. As John Hicks pointed out: "[T]here is, there can be, no economic theory which will do for us everything we want all the time."[101] By escaping the theory of the firm, blockchain ecosystems may fall beyond the oversight of antitrust enforcers.

It is thus necessary to assess the extent to which antitrust law can apply to blockchain. In other words, is it possible to apply antitrust law to entities that are not firms without creating a new legal fiction? In that regard, I have explained that antitrust can still capture blockchain activities at each participant's level. However, this will not suffice if and when antitrust agencies want to tackle anticompetitive practices at the infrastructure level.

One may then question whether there exists another legal fiction that could fill this void. For example, is the concept of association of undertakings helpful

---

[97]   *See* Sinclair Davidson, Primavera de Fillippi et al., "Blockchains and the Economic Institutions of Capitalism," Journal of Institutional Economics 14, no. 4 (2018): 641.

[98]   Several technologies (e.g., Backfeed) can introduce verticality into blockchain. On the subject, *see* Sinclair Davidson, Primavera de Fillippi et al., "Blockchains and the Economic Institutions of Capitalism," Journal of Institutional Economics 14, no. 4 (2018). This, however, remains the exception to the principle of horizontal governance in public blockchains.

[99]   Patrick Murck, "Who Controls the Blockchain?" Harvard Business Review, April 19, 2017: 1–2, https://perma.cc/EKK6-KWWT ("[B]lockchain networks rely on a decentralized infrastructure that can't be controlled by any one person or group ... No single party controls the data or the information.")

[100]   *See* Vitalik Buterin, "Control as Liability," Vitalik Buterin's website, May 9, 2019, https://perma.cc/KBZ2-MA9G.

[101]   John Hicks, *Classics and Moderns: Collected Essays on Economic Theory, Vol. III* (Basil Blackwell, 1983).

in this regard? As you may expect, the answer is negative. An association of undertakings is composed of different firms, each with a separate economic activity. As they come together within an association, antitrust creates a legal fiction to catch anticompetitive practices – mainly collusive agreements. Things are different for blockchains. First, not all participants have an economic activity; some have no turnover. Most importantly, even when these participants have an economic activity – such as mining – they all contribute to the same blockchain's survival.[102] They differ in that sense from associations of undertakings, which may reduce the incentive of separate economic entities (undertakings) to compete. Instead, miners and other blockchain participants collaborate within the same entity.

3.2.1.2 No control; no borders; no antitrust

The lack of command and control within blockchains creates two legal issues. First, the principle of individual liability implies that entities cannot be punished for practices over which they have no control. As a result, one may wonder how to attribute liability within blockchains layer 1 to all the practices happening within it.

Second, the absence of command-and-control results in a lack of well-defined borders. Public permissionless blockchains are at the disposal of whoever wants to access them; they are in the public domain – one does not need any authorization to consult them, exploit the information they contain, register information or conclude transactions.[103] They are there. As a result, their exact contours are extremely hard to define. It is thus difficult to assess the legality of practices (cooperation being mainly permitted within entities, and not outside of it) and their effects (antitrust and competition being concerned with the effects of practices outside the firm).[104]

---

[102] Corroborating this point, see Chris Pike and Antonio Capobianco, "Antitrust and the Trust Machine," OECD Blockchain Policy Series (2020): 8 (explaining that, for example, "validators would appear unlikely to be considered to be independent contractors (as for example is claimed in the case of ride-sharing platforms), since they follow strict protocols in the gig-work they do for the blockchain").

[103] Helen Eenmaa-Dimitrievaa and Maria José Schmidt-Kessen, "Creating Markets in No-Trust Environments: The Law and Economics of Smart Contracts," Computer Law and Security Review 35, no. 1 (2019): 69, 72 (calling public blockchains "a truly public space"); Mark A. Engelhardt, "Hitching Healthcare to the Chain: An Introduction to Blockchain Technology in the Healthcare Sector," Technology Innovation Management Review 7, no. 10 (2017): 22, 28.

[104] *See* section 2.

It thus appears that antitrust and competition law become mostly inapplicable to blockchain ecosystems.[105] The bigger a blockchain gets as a transactional institution, the bigger the problem will be. It is thus necessary to create a new legal fiction around blockchain layer 1 so that the law can be (re)applied.

3.2.2   Consortium (private) blockchains

In this section, I analyze the two most commonly used consortium (or private) blockchains to date: Corda and Hyperledger (Fabric). The lessons I draw can be generalized to all consortium blockchains. Before going into more detail, let me remind you once more that I am trying to establish whether one or more participants can exercise control over these blockchains and, in particular, over transactions. This control implies the capacity to influence or stop transactions and detect illegal ones beforehand. When this is the case, these blockchains can be categorized as firms for the purpose of antitrust enforcement.

3.2.2.1   Corda

Corda's architecture is built as follows: the global Corda Network supports the operation of any Business Network created on top of it.[106] The Corda Network provides users with stability between nodes, manages some basic technical aspects (e.g., oracles and tokens), gives agents an identity framework and notary services that prevent double spending. There is no general shared ledger on Corda: each node maintains its own database of the states (facts) it is aware of in a personal vault.

As far as Corda's governance is concerned, it is necessary to distinguish the Corda Network and the Business Network.[107] The Corda Network comprises four bodies. The Governing Board is the formal decision making authority of the Corda Foundation. The Technical Advisory Committee focuses on specific technical topics (e.g., changes to network parameters). The Governance Advisory Committee recommends actions to the Board on non-technical matters (including due diligence). Lastly, the Operator runs the day-to-day operations, such as managing membership, supervising the Network Notary and supporting the participants. The Operator charges the Foundation for these services.

---

[105] Geoffrey Moore, "The Nature of the Firm—75 Years Later," OpenMind (2014): 8, https://perma.cc/CY4G-WHE7 ("[T]he very structure of the firm is evolving … No doubt this will create a new generation of liability cases focused on determining the boundaries of accountability, and I do not envy the adjudicators of these cases as those boundaries are inherently fuzzy.")

[106] "Business networks," Corda Solutions Site Documentation.

[107] "Business networks (consortiums)," Corda Network's website, https://perma.cc/X4MY-4QJK.

The Business Network's governance comprises two bodies. The first is the Business Network Governor, in charge of defining and implementing the Network's strategic management and governance policies (e.g., membership, organizational structure, business processes and disputes).[108] The Governor also ensures that the Business Network complies with its legal and regulatory duties. The second is the Business Network Operator. It is responsible for the daily management of the Business Network. Importantly, it also designs and implements shared Corda applications (known as "CorDapp") for network members to transact. It manages nodes' membership, allowing them to join the Network.

3.2.2.2 Hyperledger

In terms of architecture, Hyperledger is an "umbrella" (or "greenhouse") for blockchains: it aims to facilitate the implementation of blockchain solutions by providing a background platform (i.e., a framework and tools) that creates interoperability between projects.

Hyperledger's governance stems from a few participants chosen by the entire community.[109] There are two elected bodies. The first is the Technical Steering Committee, composed of 11 elected contributors and maintainers that implement new tools and decide on technical matters.[110] The second is the Governing Board, which is in charge of non-technical governance. This includes approving Hyperledger's budget, managing business and marketing issues, updating the Code of Conduct and ensuring legal compliance.[111]

Several projects have been created to date on top of Hyperledger, one of them being Hyperledger Fabric. Initiated by IBM and Digital Assets to facilitate the deployment of blockchains for companies, it allows the latter to create their own "Networks." These Networks are background technical infrastructures that support blockchain services implemented and managed by their creators. Within these Networks, administrators may create consortia for participants to interact with one another. Transactions in Hyperledger Fabric take place and are recorded at the consortium level, not on the Network.

Participants wishing to transact secretly may create their own channels. Channels are separate ledgers of transactions. These private blockchains are

---

[108] "Governance structure," Corda Network's website, https://perma.cc/Z9D8-5HDF.

[109] The Linux Foundation, "ABCs of Open Governance," Hyperledger's website, September 6, 2017, https://perma.cc/U4LX-AFT8.

[110] The Linux Foundation, "Hyperledger Project Charter," Hyperledger's website, January 22, 2016: 4, https://perma.cc/4BET-ULB6.

[111] The Linux Foundation, "Hyperledger-Fabricdocs Documentation, Release Master," Hyperledger Fabric's website (2020): 3–4, https://perma.cc/3PUL-2QBS.

accessible only by selected participants and operate under different rules from those of the Network in which they are created.[112] When the Network updates its rules, the channel does not have to. Channel administrators may be different from the Network or consortia administrators, and Network administrators cannot enter channels if they are not invited.

3.2.2.3   *Analysis*

No participants of Corda or Hyperledger Fabric can monitor and control all the transactions within these networks. The capacity to analyze them is shallow because of the lack of oversight regarding the content of these transaction. Indeed, these consortium blockchains provide their participants with a specific infrastructure, but do not validate each transaction or require the reason for the transaction to be recorded. It follows that the firm's theoretical model cannot be transposed to these two blockchains, even if they do rely on a more "vertical" form of control than public permissionless blockchains.

   Generally, the extent to which private (consortium) blockchains allow multiple participants to exercise control must be studied on a case-by-case basis. They range from an almost firm-like model to one that is more similar to public permissionless blockchains.

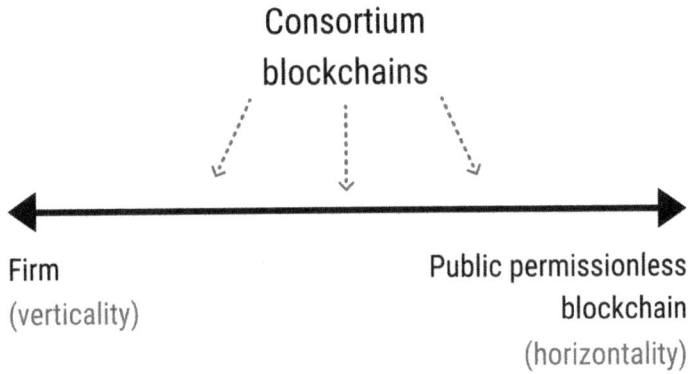

Figure 6.2   A scale of consortium blockchains

Corda and Hyperledger Fabric are in the middle, with Corda being slightly closer to a traditional firm. Private blockchains thus exist on a spectrum,

---

[112] The Linux Foundation, "Hyperledger-Fabricdocs Documentation, Release Master," Hyperledger Fabric's website, (2020): 75, https://perma.cc/3PUL-2QBS.

according to the nature of control that is exercised within them. The more "horizontal" the control is within these private blockchains, the closer they are to public permissionless ones. Also, the more horizontal, the more the role being played by each participant matters (as opposed to vertical structures, where only a few individuals at the top decide on the governance). It is thus necessary to carefully analyze the governance (the role played by each participant) and architecture of a blockchain to understand where it sits on this spectrum. This type of analysis will bring us closer to the granularity level that I will investigate in the next chapter.

And DAOs? One may wonder whether the firm's theory fully captures them.[113] DAOs are sets of rules (smart contracts) governing interactions without relying extensively on individuals.[114] Although they are typically not organized around executives or shareholders,[115] DAOs differ a lot in nature.[116] Here again, only a case-by-case analysis can reveal whether a form of vertical control is exercised within them. This analysis may be easier than it is for consortium blockchain. DAOs generally rely on a decentralized architecture for governance – the idea is to govern all transactions thanks to the protocol. Thus, depending on how DAOs set permissions to manage specific tasks, they will be more or less fully assimilable to the firm in the sense of antitrust law. Generally speaking, their governance is more horizontal than one may find within consortium blockchains, making them less similar to firms.

4   CHAPTER SUMMARY AND BEYOND

I have explained that legal fictions achieve specific objectives by granting rights to subjects and entities. Their creation is a strenuous exercise, and for this reason courts and legislatures are reluctant to design new ones. Antitrust law, for instance, has been based on the same legal fiction as was theorized the 1930s. Ronald Coase's early work defines the "firm" as a zone in which vertical control is exercised to reduce transaction costs.

---

[113] There is no consistent definition of DAOs. This article addresses DAOs and decentralized autonomous corporations jointly, as the distinction is more fluid. *See* Vitalik Buterin, "DAOs, DACs, Das and More: An Incomplete Terminology Guide," Ethereum Blog, May 6, 2014, https://perma.cc/FZ96-TKDT.

[114] *See* George Samman and David Freuden, "DAO: A Decentralized Governance": 4 (explaining that DAOs make "corporate" interactions "programmable for the first time").

[115] Philippe Honigman, "What is a DAO?" Hackernoon, July 4, 2019, https://perma.cc/88ES-24RQ.

[116] George Samman and David Freuden, "DAO: A Decentralized Governance": 3 ("DAOs are as diverse as humanity itself").

Over the last several decades, the theory of the firm as developed by Coase has become a crucial part of antitrust analysis. It is used to define entities to which antitrust laws apply and to characterize and assess anticompetitive practices. The creation of an "inside" and "outside" the firm thus guides both collusion and monopolization cases.

But one cannot transpose the theory of the firm to blockchain layer 1, as it does not feature the same vertical control. The absence of vertical control averts antitrust law, meaning that most of the behavior within that layer cannot be sanctioned. This is problematic for blockchain communities, as applying antitrust could benefit them by eliminating illegal practices. It is thus necessary to create a new legal fiction around that layer – Chapter 7 makes a proposal along those lines.

7. The theory of granularity

1 FIRST, MARKOV'S BLANKET

Andrei Andreyevich Markov was a Russian mathematician who died in 1922. Most of his work focused on the theory of stochastic process, which, in probability theory, is defined as a process involving the operation of chance. From this theory stems what Judea Pearl described in 1988 as the "Markov blanket," a subset of variables from which one may infer a random variable. Each Markov blanket is minimal, meaning that none of the variables can be removed without impacting the whole. It follows that each Markov set (e.g., a living organism) is made up of several elements, and that deleting one of them will change the set evolution.

Markov's sets explain why living things exist separately from others and develop in differentiated ways.[1] Without blankets, biological elements would dissipate, creating one big mass of information in which there were no distinct entities. The blanket is what separates us from what isn't us.

But a Markov blanket is only observational; it does not explain why these sets of information remain unified. This is where Karl Friston, a British theoretical neuroscientist teaching at the University College of London, comes in. According to Friston, each organism is composed of several overlapping Markov sets. And here is the core of his theory: each of these sets resists a tendency to dissolve to align the actual world with its predictions.[2] The best way for each set to achieve that result is to remain unified and act in such a way that the prediction comes true, which is minimizing "prediction error" or, as Friston says, minimizing free energy.

In this chapter, I will argue that blockchain's blanket is created by the blockchain nucleus's willingness to stand together to ensure survival. This chapter is inspired by Friston's free energy principle, which I realized only a few months

---

[1]   Judea Pearl, *Probabilistic Reasoning in Intelligent Systems: Networks of Plausible Inference* (Morgan Kaufmann Publishers, 1988).
[2]   Shaun Raviv, "The Genius Neuroscientist Who Might Hold the Key to True AI," Wired, November 13, 2018, https://perma.cc/9M44-45TG ("within us are blankets separating organs, which contain blankets separating cells, which contain blankets separating their organelles").

after I started working on it. Minimizing free energy explains why blockchain participants form a blanket by coming naturally together to ensure survival: it minimizes surprises. As Friston told me during our exchanges, "I concur with your sentiment that the nucleus would be subject to the same sorts of dynamics seen in other (non-vertical) forms of self-organisation," such as living organisms.

2   BLOCKCHAIN'S LEGAL FICTION

In this section, I introduce the theory of granularity and outline how it enables the application of antitrust law to blockchains. Transactional by nature, that theory aims to explain public permissionless blockchains beyond the simple cost reduction framework. It seeks to translate accurately the governing reality of such blockchains, creating for the purpose a new legal fiction that encapsulates blockchain without forcing it into inadequate boxes.

2.1   Dynamics of Blockchain Governance

The theory of granularity, to which one may want to provide a semantic explanation, frames blockchain governance as a new transactional institution. By doing so, it fills the gap created by the impossibility of applying the theory of the firm to public permissionless blockchains.

2.1.1   Semantic explanation

In "The Nature of the Firm", Ronald Coase distinguished between organizations and organisms.[3] While firms are organizations, blockchains are clusters of organisms that, by nature, are spontaneous. Their functioning must be analyzed and understood this way so that antitrust and competition law can be properly applied when necessary.

The present chapter introduces the theory of granularity for the purpose. Generally, the notion of granularity defines the size of the smallest element in a system – that is, an organism. Thus, this theory aims to analyze the role played by each component of a blockchain. Unlike the firm, where vertical control is exercised over its components, blockchains are made up of horizontal governance mechanisms. This reinforces the importance of each organism,

---

[3]   *See* Ronald H. Coase, "The Nature of the Firm," Economica 4 (1937): 387. Friedrich Hayek, to whom Ronald Coase refers, called organisms "an order which is not made by anybody but which forms itself," *see* Friedrich Hayek, *Kinds of Order in Society* (Liberty Fund, 2013).

as one cannot merely assume that they will follow one coordinated direction.[4] One must then study blockchain's smallest organisms, the role they play and their dynamism.[5] It is only by analyzing the granularity level that blockchain governance can be properly understood.[6]

2.1.2 Understanding blockchain governance

Blockchain is a space in which different forms of power are being exercised. However, unlike the firm, in which one exercises a power of command and control, I have explained that no single actor can entirely control a public permissionless blockchain.[7] As a result, multiple interests can compete within the same blockchain; they may even be opposed. Blockchain "contribute[s] to the realization of a number of individual objectives which no one knows in their totality."[8] For that reason, one must study the different types of power that are generally found within public permissionless blockchains to understand which interests may eventually prevail over others. In doing so, we should keep in mind that "people who think the purpose of blockchains is to completely expunge soft mushy human intuitions and feelings in favor of completely algorithmic governance (emphasis on 'completely') are absolutely crazy."[9]

I study blockchain power games by analyzing what I have described as the fifth blockchain level in Chapter 4: the governance layer. That level sits on top of more technical ones, and it appears to be central in defining the activities at the levels above. Furthermore, different constraints come into play in blockchain governance – namely, economic, political, logical, sociological, architectural and legal ones. Understanding how these constraints interact is a challenge; but it is essential in order to get a grip on who holds control over blockchain layer 1 and how that power is exercised over other participants.

---

[4] For an analysis of the role played by each blockchain participant, *see* section 2.1.2.
[5] David S. Evans, "Economic Aspects of Bitcoin and Other Decentralized Public-Ledger Currency Platforms," Coase-Sandor Institute for Law & Economics Working Paper No. 685 (2014) (explaining that the analysis of public ledger platforms is "much more complicated" than typical open project projects).
[6] When the granularity level is reached, it is impossible to break down the elements into smaller pieces.
[7] *See* Christian Catalini and Joshua S. Gans, "Some Simple Economics of the Blockchain," MIT Sloan Research Paper No. 5191-16 (2019): 16 (arguing that, in the blockchain, each participant "can theoretically shape its evolution in a way that is proportional to its stake in the platform – e.g. in terms of computing power, storage, labor or capital dedicated to it").
[8] Friedrich Hayek, *Law, Legislation and Liberty* (Routledge, 1973): 109.
[9] Vitalik Buterin, "Notes on Blockchain Governance," Vitalik Buterin's website, December 17, 2017, https://perma.cc/34AB-ZL62.

A distinction between all three categories of public permissionless block-chain participants is helpful in this regard – namely, between founders or core developers (I will often present them together for the sake of simplicity), users and miners. I show that although each blockchain has its specificities, the above-mentioned groups will use the same mechanisms to express their prefer-ences,[10] and will encounter the same limits if they act on their own. Eventually, their powers may suffer from four constraints that Lawrence Lessig described with his "pathetic dot theory": law, markets, social norms and architecture.[11]

As for private blockchains, I have explained that they mimic that structure to different degrees, depending on their original design. The closer they are to public permissionless blockchains, the less the theory of the firm will be transposable to them. The following developments then become relevant for public permissionless as well as private blockchains.

---

[10]   Jean Bacon et al., "Blockchain Demystified: A Technical and Legal Introduction to Distributed and Centralized Ledgers," Richmond Journal of Law & Technology 25, no. 1 (2018).

[11]   *See* Lawrence Lessig, *Code: And Other Laws of Cyberspace, Version 2.0* (Basic Books, 2006): 124 ("Norms constrain through the stigma that a community imposes; markets constrain through the price that they exact; architectures constrain through the physical burdens they impose, and law constrains through the punishment it threat-ens"). These constraints are "distinct, yet, they are plainly interdependent. Each can support or oppose the others," *see id.* at 123. Also, Primavera De Filippi, "Blockchain Technology and Decentralized Governance: The Pitfalls of a Trustless Dream," *Decentralized Thriving: Governance and Community on the Web 3.0* (2019) (for an application of these four constraints to blockchain).

2.1.2.1   The power of founders and core developers[12]

Blockchain founders and core developers are those who implement the original rules of a blockchain.[13] They design the code software and determine which
consensus protocol will be used.[14]

Although core developers work on the fourth level of blockchain – its infrastructure – they interact with other blockchain participants at the fifth level.
Indeed, one may stress that the blockchain architecture limits their power,
as they lose any form of direct control over other participants once they put
the blockchain online.[15] For most blockchains (but not all!),[16] founders and
core developers cannot unilaterally impose any changes[17] or control who may

---

[12]   Founders and core developers are here put in the same category, although one
may want to distinguish between them, as they are eventually in charge of the blockchain core code.

[13]   Vlad Zamfir, "Blockchain Governance 101," Goodaudience (blog), September
30, 2018, https://perma.cc/T4BY-NFE7. In short, core developers, also called "protocol developers," are to be differentiated from the developers building decentralized applications on top of the blockchain. Core developers are indeed "reviewing
the code, proposing conceptual changes to the code, reviewing changes proposed
by other coders, drafting new code and revising existing code, security-testing new
code, compiling code into new releases, and communicating about the project with
other developers, among others," according to Angela Walch, "In Code(rs) We Trust:
Software Developers as Fiduciaries in Public Blockchains," in *Techno-Social and
Legal Challenges* ed. Philipp Hacker, et al. (Oxford University Press, 2019): 9. *See*
also Hanna Halaburda and Christoph Mueller-Bloch, "Will We Realize Blockchain's
Promise of Decentralization?", Harvard Business Review, September 4, 2019, https://
perma.cc/PM6L-TT7H. Being in charge of the blockchain's original design gives them
the opportunity, of course, to design it in a way to exercise more or less influence over
the entire blockchain. For example, if core developers grant themselves the power to
validate each transaction, they will exercise more control over the blockchain than
under a Proof of Work mechanism.

[14]   *See* Michel Rauchs et al., *Distributed Ledger Technology Systems: A Conceptual
Framework* (Cambridge Center for Alternative Finance, 2018): 55 (describing the different forms of protocol design and calling them anarchic, hierarchical, federal, pluto-
cratic or democratic).

[15]   Primavera de Filippi and Greg Mcmullen, "Governance of Blockchain Systems:
Governance of and by Distributed Infrastructures," Blockchain Research Institute and
COALA (2018): 21; Raina S. Haque et al., "Blockchain Developers and Fiduciary
Duty: An Ill-Fitting Framework," CLS Blue Sky (blog), June 21, 2019, https://perma
.cc/WE5Q-QAGJ ("These developers are structurally unable to make decisions to
impose changes on participants in a network").

[16]   *See* Ying-Ying Hsieh et al., "The Internal and External Governance of
Blockchain-Based Organizations," in *Bitcoin and Beyond: Blockchains and Global
Governance*, ed. Malcolm Campbell-Verduyn (2017): 8–9.

[17]   In fact, founders and core developers may simply submit changes to the majority
of participants, *see* Raina S. Haque et al., "A Blockchain Development and Fiduciary
Duty," Stanford Journal of Blockchain Law & Policy 2, no. 2 (2019). One may suggest

propose protocol updates.[18] For instance, any Bitcoin Improvement Proposals must be voted upon, according to miners' computing power, before they get implemented.[19] Indeed,"[t]he nature of Bitcoin is such that once version 0.1 was released, the core design was set in stone for the rest of its lifetime,"[20] unless the majority agrees to change it.

---

that analyzing how core developers' proposals to update a blockchain protocol are being welcomed may prove useful in determining the degree of their power over other participants.

[18] On some blockchains, the core developers are the only ones with the power to actually propose core code updates to the network. This is the case with Bitcoin Core, in which "maintainers" "have commit access and are responsible for merging patches from contributors. They perform a janitorial role merging patches that the team agrees should be merged. They also act as a final check to ensure that patches are safe and in line with the project goals. The maintainers' role is by agreement of project contributors," *see* "About Bitcoin Core," https://perma.cc/U696-6Y2J. It can also be that only the core developers can send emergency message to all the nodes on the network to ask them to adopt updates, as is the case on the Bitcoin blockchain, Angela Walch, "In Code(rs) We Trust: Software Developers as Fiduciaries in Public Blockchains," in *Techno-Social and Legal Challenges* eds. Philipp Hacker, et al. (Oxford University Press, 2019): 4, 13; *see* also Arthur Gervais et al., "Is Bitcoin a Decentralized Currency?," IEEE Security & Privacy 12, no. 3 (2014), https://perma.cc/T6H7-AZ75. Nevertheless, Bitcoin core developers cannot impose these changes unilaterally, *see* Nick Tomaino, "The Governance of Blockchains," Medium, February 28, 2017, https://perma.cc/ MKW4-PHS7. The same is true for the Ethereum core developers, *see* Jean Bacon et al., "Blockchain Demystified: A Technical and Legal Introduction to Distributed and Centralized Ledgers," Richmond Journal of Law & Technology 25, no. 1 (2018): 35. In short, protocol developers are not delegated with power or authority by other participants. There exists no agency relationship between developers and other participants in the network. Protocol developers lack the ability to bind other network participant, and no other network participant has the power to control the voluntary actions of protocol developers. They have no power to speak authoritatively for the community as a whole. On that, *see* Raina S. Haque et al., "A Blockchain Development and Fiduciary Duty," Stanford Journal of Blockchain Law & Policy 2, no. 2 (2019): 139, 178. *See* Yessi Bello Perez, "The Controversies of Blockchain Governance and Rough Consensus," TNX, January 25, 2019, https://perma.cc/45W8-LXT7 (explaining that changes to the core code are submitted to nodes. They may vote to implement them, or to reject them). *See* also Sarah Azouvi et al., "Egalitarian Society or Benevolent Dictatorship: The State of Cryptocurrency Governance," 22nd International Conference on Financial Cryptography and Data Security (2018), https://perma.cc/S2GR-UJD5 (explaining that discussions regarding blockchain updates can nonetheless be centralized).

[19] "Only developers can design and communicate proposed changes. As such, the developers speak and are listened to. Every BIP is authored by a developer," Jeffery Atik and George Gerro, "Hard Forks on the Bitcoin Blockchain: Reversible Exit, Continuing Voice," Stanford Journal of Blockchain Law & Policy 1 (2018): 32.

[20] Satoshi Nakamoto, "Re: Transactions and Scripts: DUP HASH160 ... EQUALVERIFY CHECKSIG," Bitcointalk.org, June 17, 2010, https://perma.cc/37PA -79WC (he insisted: "If Bitcoin catches on in a big way, these are things we'll want to

The more participants are included in those voting procedures, the more decentralized that blockchain layer is.[21] The opposite is also true. For instance, Decred[22] and Tezos[23] are cryptocurrencies with more centralized governance systems. One of Tezos' principal characteristics is the ability to amend its consensus when necessary.[24] The presence of off-chain and side-chain governance mechanisms, usually controlled by developers, should also be closely studied.[25]

It remains that core developers do not control who can use the blockchain at the platform layer[26] or who can build applications on top of it.[27] That is because blockchain founders and core developers cannot impose changes on the blockchain code, interface, application, data or benefice.[28] Their main role

---

explore in the future, but they all had to be designed at the beginning to make sure they would be possible later").

[21] For an example of such a vote, *see* Yogita Khatri, "Zcash community votes to allocate 20% of network mining rewards to support development," The Block, January 29, 2020, https://perma.cc/ENA4-EG4M.

[22] *See* Decred, https://perma.cc/VWE7-97DT.

[23] L.M. Goodman, "Tezos — a self-amending crypto-ledger" (2014), https://perma .cc/978T-GZNJ.

[24] According to which "protocol can be amended to reflect virtually any blockchain based algorithm."

[25] *See* Vlad Zamfir, "Introducing Casper 'The Friendly Ghost'," *Ethereum* (blog), August 1, 2015, https://perma.cc/6A7Q-JMRX for a description of developments of "off-chain" and "sidechain" mechanisms. For a description of the need for these mechanisms, *see* Benito Arruñada and Luis Garicano, "Blockchain: The Birth of Decentralized Governance," Pompeu Fabra University, Economics and Business Working Paper 1608 (2018): 1.

[26] Only permissioned blockchains permit that to be done, *see* Hanna Halaburda and Christoph Mueller-Bloch, "Will We Realize Blockchain's Promise of Decentralization?" Harvard Business Review, September 4, 2019, https://perma.cc/PM6L-TT7H. As for permissionless blockchain, as Tapscott and Tapscott put it, "nothing passes through a central third party; nothing is stored on a central server," Don Tapscott and Alex Tapscott, *A Blockchain Revolution: How The Technology Behind Bitcoin Is Changing Money, Business, And The World* (Penguin Books, 2016): 35.

[27] Christian Catalini, "The Firm as a Nexus of Smart Contracts? How Blockchain and Cryptocurrencies Can Transform the Digital Economy," Yale Journal on Regulation: Notice & Comment, June 7, 2017, https://perma.cc/KM4Y-963N (arguing that "the token can bootstrap the development of an entire innovation ecosystem where anyone can build novel applications on top of the underlying protocol without requiring permission from a network operator or intermediary").

[28] Nick Tomaino, "The Slow Death of the Firm," The Control, October 21, 2017, https://perma.cc/H59E-WMZY. On Bitcoin, for instance, "developers who propose changes to the software can let the development team know. If it is a simple noncontroversial change then they will adopt it. If not, the developer is supposed to post the change and it will be adopted if there is a broad consensus in the community that it should be," *see* David S. Evans, "Economic Aspects of Bitcoin and Other Decentralized

is thus close to that of "advisors,"[29] but their influence is limited by blockchain participants' desire to maximize their own benefit, which may lead them, should they disagree with core developers, to refuse the implementation of new rules, to move to a rival ecosystem or to fork the blockchain.[30] Social norms further limit them because they may fear not being influential enough to prevent hard forks.

Hard forks result in backward-incompatible software updates. When they do not obtain a sufficiently broad consensus among miners,[31] hard forks cause the chain to split in two, permanently. Indeed, miners who do not follow the new block validation requirements will be unable to add their blocks to the latest version of the blockchain, as the core client will automatically reject them as non-compliant. Instead, a new chain of blocks will form, creating a split: two chains following different rules. These forks limit the core developers' willingness to act against the interests of other participants.[32] And core developers may also fear soft forks, although to a lesser degree. Soft forks happen when

---

Public-Ledger Currency Platforms," Coase-Sandor Institute for Law & Economics Working Paper No. 685 (2014): 1, 16. Also, Peder Østbye, "The Adequacy of Competition Policy for Cryptocurrency Markets" (2017), https://perma.cc/2DQ5-7PFU (stressing that the inability of blockchain's creators to alter the protocol or manipulate the transactions on the ledger is a key characteristic that should be taken into account in modeling competition law).

[29]   Don Tapscott and Alex Tapscott, *Blockchain Revolution: How the Technology Behind Bitcoin Is Changing Money, Business, and the World* (Penguin Books, 2016): 89; also, Raina S. Haque et al., "Blockchain Developers and Fiduciary Duty: An Ill-Fitting Framework," CLS Blue Sky (blog), June 21, 2019, https://perma.cc/WE5Q -QAGJ ("A protocol developers/s' ability to influence the welfare of the cryptocurrency holder – i.e., the value of the cryptocurrency – is therefore limited to proposing and advocating for a solution that the community may or may not adopt"). One may stress, nonetheless, that when these "advisors" are all working in the same space, they may collude to impose these changes more easily, *see* Vitalik Buterin, "The Meaning of Decentralization," Medium, February 6, 2017, https://perma.cc/6FP5-9L8Z.

[30]   Nick Tomaino, "The Slow Death of the Firm," The Control, October 21, 2017, https://perma.cc/H59E-WMZY. Generally, on the importance of product design as a way to control the use of the product, *see* Lawrence Lessig, *Code: And Other Laws of Cyberspace, Version 2.0* (Basic Books, 2006). This explains why, after the DAO Ethereum fork in 2015, Ethereum and Ethereum Classic have survived: miners have switched from one to the other, depending on the gains they could realize. For more on the major Ethereum forks, *see* Ashley Viens, "Mapping the Most Important Ethereum Forks," Visual Capitalist, November 26, 2019, https://perma.cc/5BT7-ASWF.

[31]   *See* TechCrunch, "Blockchain Governance with Vlad Zamfir (Ethereum Foundation) at Ethereum Meetup 2018," published on August 21, 2018, YouTube, https://perma.cc/QZG6-R6XN (explaining that when a decision is considered to be illegitimate because it does not follow the norms, there is a high risk of forking).

[32]   *See* Dirk A. Zetzsche, Ross P. Buckley and Douglas W. Arner, "The Distributed Liability of Distributed Ledgers: Legal Risks of Blockchain," University of Illinois

new rules are implemented, but when the blocks following the original rules are not rejected from the chain. These modifications are backward-compatible, accommodating miners who implement the change and those who do not.

Nevertheless, one should underline that these limits on core developers' power are linked to the decentralized nature of blockchain governance, which is not a necessary feature, but needs to be enacted.[33] New blockchains may appear in which greater power is given to the founders and core developers.[34] However, such blockchains will suffer from two inherent limits. First, the extent to which a (re)centralized blockchain could thrive remains to be seen.[35] Such blockchains could deplete trust by confining power in the hands of a few, thus disincentivizing users from joining them. Second, a (re)centralized blockchain could function less efficiently than a truly decentralized one, because all its participants would no longer be in a position to improve it. This lack of efficiency, even if it only concerned certain types of transactions, could hinder these blockchains – which probably explains why, to this day, they have not prospered.

2.1.2.2   The power of users[36]

On permissionless public blockchains, users propose new transactions. Anyone can become a user.[37] Users exercise substantial power over the blockchain, since their decision to use it (or not) is central to the blockchain's economic

---

Law Review (2018): 1361 (explaining that core developers may want to collaborate with other participants).

[33]   *See* Hanna Halaburda and Christoph Mueller-Bloch, "Will We Realize Blockchain's Promise of Decentralization?" Harvard Business Review, September 4, 2019, https://perma.cc/PM6L-TT7H.

[34]   For instance, one could imagine a blockchain in which the consensus mechanism could involve the blockchain foundation in the validation of all transactions.

[35]   *See* David Evans, "Economic Aspects of Bitcoin and Other Decentralized Public-Ledger Currency Platforms" (2013): 16.

[36]   *See* Zetzsche et al., *The Distributed Liability of Distributed Ledgers: Legal Risks of Blockchain* (2017): 1384.

[37]   *See* Jean Bacon et al., "Blockchain Demystified: A Technical and Legal Introduction to Distributed and Centralized Ledgers," Richmond Journal of Law & Technology 25, no. 1 (2018): 34.

and social value.[38] Their influence extends from influencing transaction fees[39] to providing additional value by developing and using applications running on top of the platform layer.[40] They can also force hard forks on the blockchain.[41] However, their power is limited by the fact they cannot (easily) exercise coordinated control, as their actions are highly decentralized and spontaneous.[42] This creates an architectural limit and makes their behavior primarily dependent on prices.[43]

---

[38] *See* Thibault Schrepel, "Is Blockchain the Death of Antitrust Law? The Blockchain Antitrust Paradox," Georgetown Law Technology Review 3, no. 2 (2019): 296 (studying network effects on public and private blockchains). Also, Mappo, "Blockchain Governance 101", Medium, January 14, 2019, https://perma.cc/2LB8 -32NV (explaining that users may indirectly hinder network effect by implementing unpopular decisions). Lastly, Vitalik Buterin, "The Limits to Blockchain Scalability," Vitalik Buterin's website May 23, 2021, https://perma.cc/6K2S-9455 ("The Ethereum blockchain has fully resolved consensus failures in ten hours; if your blockchain has only one client implementation, and you only need to deploy a code change to a few dozen nodes, coordinating a change to client code can be done much faster. The only reliable way to make this kind of coordinated social attack not effective is through passive defense from the one constituency that actually is decentralized: the users.")

[39] Hanna Halaburda and Christoph Mueller-Bloch, "Will We Realize Blockchain's Promise of Decentralization?" Harvard Business Review, September 4, 2019, https:// perma.cc/PM6L-TT7H.

[40] *See* Vitalik Buterin, "Notes on Blockchain Governance," Vitalik Buterin's website, December 17, 2017, https://perma.cc/ADP8-UCG4 (stressing that users' influence is limited by their potential lack of technical knowledge). Also, Balázs Bodó and Alexandra Giannopoulou, "The Logics of Technology Decentralization – The Case of Distributed Ledger Technologies," Amsterdam Law School Research Paper 2019-05 (2019): 1, 8 (developing the idea that core developers may use their technical skills to influence others). Lastly, see Vitalik Buterin, "The Most Important Scarce Resource is Legitimacy", Vitalik Buterin's website, March 23, 2021, https://perma.cc/FZH7-ZZSV (explaining that despite the importance of core developers and validators, users have an important role to play in the ecosystem: providing projects with legitimacy).

[41] Jake Frankenfield, "Hard Fork (Blockchain)," Investopedia, November 25, 2019, https://perma.cc/M9G2-7NVE.

[42] Vitalik Buterin, "The Meaning of Decentralization," Medium, February 6, 2017, https://perma.cc/6FP5-9L8Z. In the words of Vitalik Buterin, blockchain communities are "using coordination problems" to their advantage, preventing one group of users from taking over, *see* Vitalik Buterin, "Engineering Security Through Coordination Problems," Vitalik Buterin's website, May 8, 2017, https://perma.cc/C3U5-KE9S.

[43] *See* Lawrence Lessig, *Code: And Other Laws of Cyberspace, Version 2.0* (Basic Books, 2006).

2.1.2.3   The power of miners[44]

On permissionless public blockchains, miners validate transactions assembled into blocks. Any participant can become a miner.[45] Miners follow the rules encoded in the fourth blockchain level (e.g., the Bitcoin Core client).[46] They can comply with a different set of rules, but they will then waste computing power by producing an orphaned block, thus losing potential rewards. Following the main client's rules is miners' dominant strategy.[47]

If they coordinate their behavior, miners can influence a blockchain by realizing a 51 percent attack,[48] thus forcing a soft fork.[49] The risk is higher when miners are grouped into mining pools.[50] In such a scenario, the blockchain pro-

---

[44]   *See* Evans, *Economic Aspects of Bitcoin and Other Decentralized Public-Ledger Currency Platform*, 1–2 (explaining that "the open-source public ledger platforms require another class of participants—the laborers who perform transaction processing—that require pecuniary compensation as an integral element of the protocol." These laborers are called "miners" within the blockchain sphere).

[45]   *See* Jean Bacon et al., "Blockchain Demystified: A Technical and Legal Introduction to Distributed and Centralized Ledgers," Richmond Journal of Law & Technology 25, no. 1 (2018): 34.

[46]   Generally, it is said that "miners only have a limited role in the Bitcoin system, to secure the ordering of transactions, and they should NOT have the power to determine anything else, including block size limits and other block validity rules," on that *see* Vitalik Buterin, "Engineering Security Through Coordination Problems," Vitalik.ca, May 8, 2017, https://perma.cc/G2PC-W4LN.

[47]   It has been said, in fact, that "a miner's vote is better understood as its prediction of the collective stance of the broader miner community than as an expression of the voting miner's individual preference," *see* Jeffery Atik and George Gerro, "Hard Forks on the Bitcoin Blockchain: Reversible Exit, Continuing Voice," Stanford Journal of Blockchain Law & Policy 1 (2018): 27–28.

[48]   *See* Primavera De Filippi and Benjamin Loveluck, "The Invisible Politics of Bitcoin: Governance Crisis of a Decentralised Infrastructure," Internet Policy Review 5, no. 3 (2016): 10–11.

[49]   Vitalik Buterin, "The Meaning of Decentralization," Medium, February 6, 2017 (arguing that the risk is particularly high when there is a strong community spirit); Vitalik Buterin, "Engineering Security Through Coordination Problems," Vitalik Buterin's website, May 8, 2017, https://perma.cc/C3U5-KE9S (underlining that "it is theoretically possible for miners to switch 99% of their hashpower to a chain with new rules," but in practice "quite hard to do"). More generally, *see* Taylor Pearson, "The Blockchain Man," Ribbonfarm, October 10, 2017, https://perma.cc/76FC-EK42 (contending that "appeals to authority, and perhaps violence, will be replaced by forking. If you disagree with a decision, you can fork a new blockchain").

[50]   Mining pools may indeed facilitate collusion, for instance, if all miners are in the same space. Nonetheless, whether there is a mining pool does not shift the paradigm as, in any case, such pools only reflect the will of their members. On the subject, *see* Craig S. Wright, "Proof of Work as it Relates to the Theory of the Firm," (2017), https://perma.cc/A984-BE62. Generally, individual miners do not have enough computing power to mine a block in widely used blockchains successfully – hence the existence of mining

tocol is changed to loosen the rule-set enforced by full nodes.[51] Such a change occurs when enough hashing power, or energy expended to mine a cryptocurrency, is devoted to it.[52] The power of miners to start soft forks is nonetheless limited by both the blockchain's architecture[53] and social norms – they must convince blockchain participants operating as nodes to run the new version of the software.[54] Miners also suffer from market constraints, as initiating a soft fork may decrease the value of the tokens they own.[55] The price mechanism also guides their actions, creating a strong market-related constraint. Finally, even if a fork were created, the new community would have the strenuous task of convincing other users to join it.[56] For example, Bitcoin had been forked over 100 times at the time of writing. Over 30 of them are considered failures,

---

pools, *see* Philipp Hacker, "Corporate Governance for Complex Cryptocurrencies? A Framework for Stability and Decision Making in Blockchain-Based Organizations," in *Regulating Blockchain. Techno-Social and Legal Challenges*, ed. Philipp Hacker et al. (Oxford University Press, 2019): 32, https://perma.cc/DYZ2-THLJ. Miners may nonetheless, even at their individual level, prioritize transactions and exercise a form of power as such, *see* Nikhil Malik et al., "Why Bitcoin Will Fail to Scale?" (2019).

[51]   Full nodes are created where blockchain participants store an entire copy of the blockchain ledger on their computers, for more, *see* section 2.1.3. Underlining that "[t]here do exist non-mining full nodes," *see* Ethereum White Paper, 27.

[52]   Kristian Soltes, "The First Blockchain Antitrust Case. Or Is It?" Constantine Canon (Blog), May 29, 2019, https://perma.cc/RVB9-V96J.

[53]   *See* Ying-Ying Hsieh, Jean-Philippe Vergne and Sha Wang, "The Internal and External Governance of Blockchain-Based Organizations," in *Bitcoin and Beyond Cryptocurrencies, Blockchains, and Global Governance* (Routledge, 2019).

[54]   *See* Jean Bacon et al., "Blockchain Demystified: A Technical and Legal Introduction to Distributed and Centralized Ledgers," Richmond Journal of Law & Technology 25, no. 1 (2018): 37 (showing that there is no guarantee that nodes will agree to fork).

[55]   *See* Satoshi Nakamoto, "Bitcoin: A Peer-To-Peer Electronic Cash System," (2008), https://perma.cc/KJT5-KJ43. Also, Vlad Zamfir, "Blockchain Governance 101," Medium, September 30, 2018, https://perma.cc/D2VD-ZMMD (arguing that in the case of a fork, the trademark loses value).

[56]   John Light, "The Differences between a Hard Fork, a Soft Fork, and a Chain Split, and What They Mean for the Future of Bitcoin," Medium, September 25, 2017, https://perma.cc/ABQ3-GF7L. In the case of a soft fork, however, the blockchain remains compatible with previous versions despite the modification to its protocol, *see* Raina S. Haque et al., "A Blockchain Development and Fiduciary Duty," Stanford Journal of Blockchain Law & Policy, 2 (2019): 162 (new transactions and new blocks can still be processed on the blockchain, as long as they do not violate the new rules of the protocol). Also, Christian Ewerhart, "Finite Blockchain Games," Economics Letters 197 (2020) (showing that "adherence to conservative mining or to the longest-chain rule constitute pure-strategy Nash equilibria", which explains why miners will generally be tempted to disregard forks).

while another 29 projects are no longer capable of transacting. Among the remaining forks, just a few are considered valuable.[57]

2.1.3   The blockchain power game

This overall balance of power, common to all public permissionless block-chains, is the general analytical framework (as illustrated in Figure 7.1) within which to analyze whether one of these groups, on a case-by-case basis, has sufficient influence to qualify as control under antitrust or competition law.

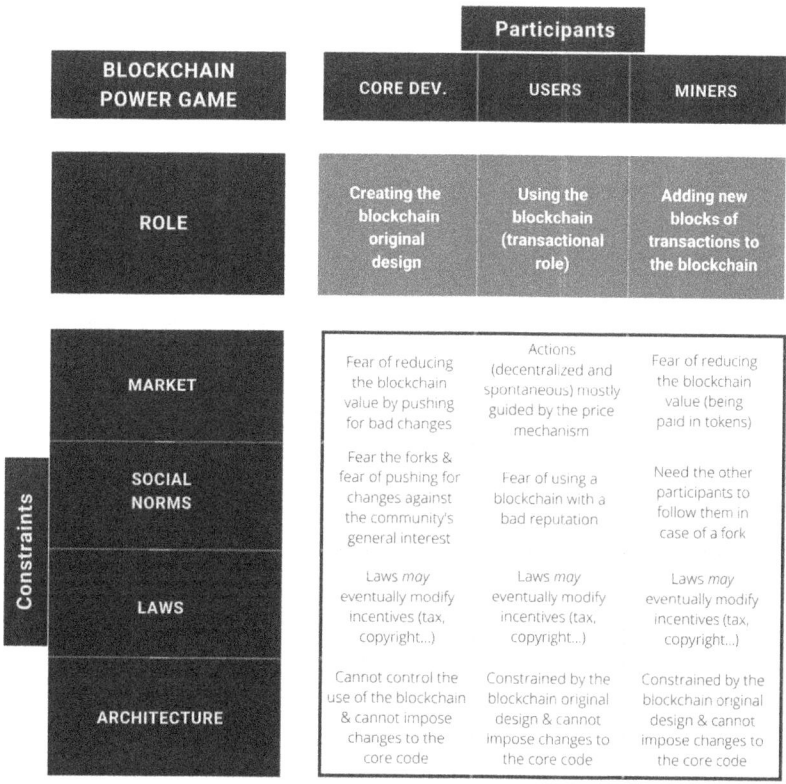

BLOCKCHAIN POWER GAME	Participants		
	CORE DEV.	USERS	MINERS
ROLE	Creating the blockchain original design	Using the blockchain (transactional role)	Adding new blocks of transactions to the blockchain
Constraints MARKET	Fear of reducing the blockchain value by pushing for bad changes	Actions (decentralized and spontaneous) mostly guided by the price mechanism	Fear of reducing the blockchain value (being paid in tokens)
SOCIAL NORMS	Fear the forks & fear of pushing for changes against the community's general interest	Fear of using a blockchain with a bad reputation	Need the other participants to follow them in case of a fork
LAWS	Laws *may* eventually modify incentives (tax, copyright...)	Laws *may* eventually modify incentives (tax, copyright...)	Laws *may* eventually modify incentives (tax, copyright...)
ARCHITECTURE	Cannot control the use of the blockchain & cannot impose changes to the core code	Constrained by the blockchain original design & cannot impose changes to the core code	Constrained by the blockchain original design & cannot impose changes to the core code

Figure 7.1   A representation of blockchain power game

---

[57]   See Buy Bitcoin Worldwide, "Failed Forks," Buy Bitcoin Worldwide, https://perma.cc/UX88-CDGN.

On top of all that, core developers, users and miners may also store a copy of the blockchain ledger. When doing so, their computers are labeled as light nodes if they store only a subset of the blockchain ledger and full nodes if they store a copy of the entire blockchain.[58]

Although these nodes are passive and cannot be designated as actors in the blockchain, they ensure its integrity. This role carries power. First, blockchain participants who are nodes may alter their copy of the blockchain.[59] Second, they may also (threaten to) validate blocks in which there is double spending.[60] Their job is indeed to prevent users from spending the same token twice by allowing miners to verify the proposed transaction against a list of previous unspent transaction outputs. They protect blockchains value. However, their power is mainly limited by the fact that they cannot either control or influence transactions.[61]

This is the blockchain power game. It is well balanced, and technical solutions (called "layer 2" solutions) are constantly provided to maintain that balance. But these solutions are insufficient to maintain balance when different groups of blockchain participants come together to escape these constraints to the detriment of the broader ecosystem. When this occurs, they are exercising control over the blockchain.

2.2   The Blockchain Nucleus

Thus far, the theory of granularity has allowed me to determine the different forms of power enjoyed by blockchain participants. I must now detail how to

---

[58]   *See* Bacon et al., "Demystified", 19.

[59]   Philipp Hacker, "Corporate Governance for Complex Cryptocurrencies? A Framework for Stability and Decision Making in Blockchain-Based Organizations," in *Regulating Blockchain. Techno-Social and Legal Challenges*, ed. Philipp Hacker et al. (Oxford University Press, 2019) (explaining that blockchain participants operating as nodes are confirming authenticity through consensus). *See* Patrick Waelbroek, "An Economic Analysis of Blockchains," CESifo Working Paper Series 6893 (2018): 22 (blockchain participants operating as nodes have voting power on changes in the communication protocol.) Lastly, *see* Felix Irresberger, "Coin Concentration of Proof-of-Stake Blockchains," Leeds University Business School Working Paper 19-04 (2019): 1, 3 (explaining that nodes with more coins have more voting power).

[60]   In such a scenario, blockchain participants operating as nodes would add these blocks to their local copy of the blockchain and broadcast them to other nodes on the network.

[61]   *See* Mengerian, "The Market for Consensus," Medium, December 27, 2016, https://perma.cc/X4RV-5BNP ("Nodes enforce block validity rules to attempt to stay in consensus with the other nodes on the network. Nodes enforce block validity rules to try to influence properties of Bitcoin as a system").

identify a legal fiction controlling the blockchain.[62] To this end, I explain what a blockchain nucleus is and then analyze its influence over other blockchain participants. I then describe how to define such a nucleus.

2.2.1 Usefulness and challenges

2.2.1.1 *The nucleus*

None of the three types of blockchain participants – core developers, users and miners – can impose their power on other groups to the point of taking complete control over the blockchain. Blockchains are indeed decentralized. They prevent the exercise of vertical power, and this differentiates them from firms in which a group, or sometimes even an individual, can control the other participants and "force them to collaborate," so to speak.

That being said, even with horizontal and decentralized governance, a group of participants may achieve a form of control over the blockchain by collaborating, by circumventing (some of) the constraints imposed on them,[63] and by changing them in the long run.[64]

I contend that such a coalition exists for each blockchain (at least, for the surviving ones),[65] and I call it the nucleus. The nucleus includes all the participants who have a personal interest (albeit transiently) to collaborate toward the same long-term goal: ensuring the blockchain's survival.[66] Its members do not

---

[62] The usefulness of antitrust and competition law is here presumed. Discussing antitrust legitimacy, *see* Oliver E. Williamson, "Allocative Efficiency and the Limits of Antitrust", The American Economic Review 59 (1969): 105, 116.

[63] There are several solutions that allow the nucleus to strengthen its influence – for example, quadratic voting, *see* Eric A. Posner and E. Glen Weyl, "Voting Squared: Quadratic Voting in Democratic Politics", Vanderbilt Law Review 68, no. 2 (2015): 441, 441, 446 ("everyone votes on proposals (in the case of referenda) or candidates by buying as many votes pro or con as they want. The price they pay is the square of the number of votes they buy … it give[s] proportional weight to people whose interests in a social outcome are stronger than those of other people").

[64] Returning to Lawrence Lessig's pathetic dot theory, I am here studying the extent to which the dot may change the constraints. More specifically, I am analyzing how interactions between dots (blockchain participants) are contributing to modifying their environment.

[65] *See* Vlad Zamfir, "Blockchain Governance 101," Goodaudience (blog), September 30, 2018, https://perma.cc/T4BY-NFE7 (for a blockchain to be successful, collaboration is needed).

[66] Within the firm, all participants have an interest in its survival. Within the blockchain, only those within the nucleus have a similar interest. The work of Karl Friston is helpful, by analogy, in understanding how organisms have an "interest" in staying together, *see* for instance Karl Friston et al., "Knowing One's Place: A Free-Energy Approach to Pattern Regulation", Journal of the Royal Society Interface 12 (2015): 1. A parallel may indeed be drawn between the principle of free energy, explaining how

compete as they are, together, trying to maintain and expand their blockchain. Their short-term interests may diverge from time to time[67] – for example, when two miners are racing to mine new blocks.[68] Still, they seek to ensure blockchain integrity and systematically promote the same blockchain instead of other ones.

2.2.1.2   Usefulness

Assessing which participants have joined forces and are thus part of the nucleus is essential to determine who ultimately controls the blockchain. Put differently, it leads to identifying the participants that can be held liable for a breach of antitrust law when it is shown that they have anticompetitively exerted their influence.[69] Identifying the nucleus amounts to creating a legal fiction to which the law can be applied, but also to which rights can be granted (see Figure 7.2).

The nucleus should indeed become a legal fiction that can be liable for anticompetitive practices, but also able to claim damages. In that regard, determining the nucleus size will prove central. It will prove useful in cases of anticompetitive practices directed at a blockchain nucleus. When a legal entity – whether a blockchain nucleus or a firm – infringes antitrust law and causes damages to another nucleus, the latter must have the means to introduce a legal action, stand by its rights and claim damages. Assigning liability and granting rights to blockchain ecosystems are thus two sides of the same coin.

---

biological systems maintain their order, and the blockchain nucleus, dealing with the question of how public permissionless blockchains maintain their existence. For further explanations on the idea of free energy and how cells stay together in the real space, *see* Shaun Raviv, "The Genius Neuroscientist Who Might Hold the Key to True AI," Wired, November 13, 2018, https://perma.cc/9M44-45TG.

[67]   Again, blockchain is not "a multiple team of horses drawing a vehicle under the control of a single driver," *see Copperweld Corp. et al. v. Independence Tube Corp.*, 467 US 752 (U.S.,1984). Horses (participants) may go any direction they want, except if they have an interest not to – that is, if they are part of the nucleus.

[68]   In fact, Satoshi Nakamoto suggested postponing competition for validating blocks under specific circumstances, *see* Satoshi Nakamoto, "Re: A Few Suggestions," Bitcointalk.org, December 12, 2009, https://perma.cc/JB2T-AQPT ("[w]e should have a gentleman's agreement to postpone the GPU arms race as long as we can for the good of the network").

[69]   In a sense, identifying the blockchain nucleus relates to the theory of incentives as developed by Bengt Holmström and Paul Milgrom, "The Firm as an Incentive System," The American Economic Review 84, no. 4 (1994): 972. The nucleus allows for anticipation of the extent to which the participants cooperate with each other, or conversely, compete with each other.

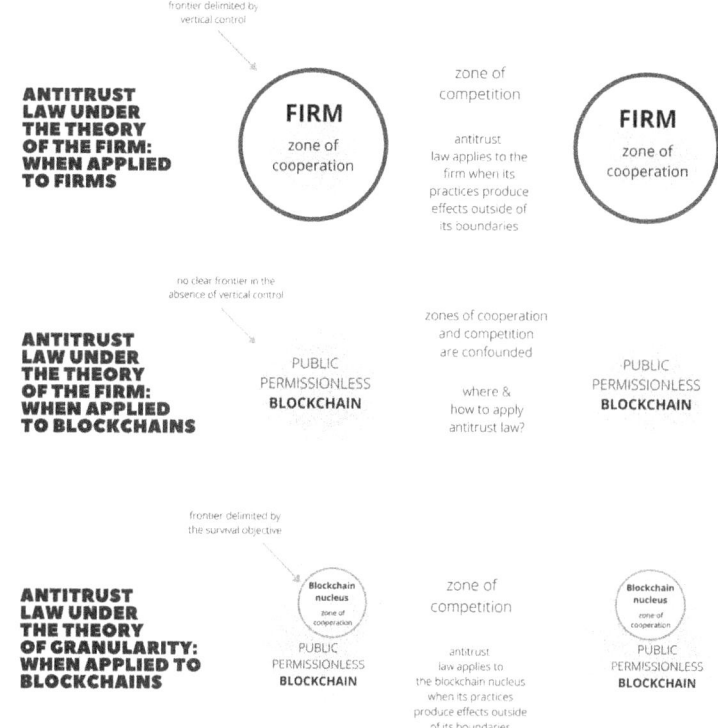

Figure 7.2   A representation of a blockchain nucleus

3   DEFINING THE NUCLEUS SIZE

Courts and antitrust agencies will face the task of determining the nucleus size. The further away a participant will be from the nucleus's center, the more difficult it will become to genuinely include her or him in the nucleus. With distance, it will prove harder to show that she or he could have influenced other participants' behavior. Only a case-by-case analysis can elucidate this question. This analysis should nevertheless be based on concrete and quantifiable frameworks to ensure legal certainty, limit legal errors and reduce regulatory costs. To this end, agencies should focus their investigation on economic agents' ability to exert a horizontal power of command and control. They should also consider their capacity to interfere with the blockchain's economic value and influence norms.[70]

Let me be more specific. The first element that should be factored in to determine which participants are part of the nucleus is the technical ability to exert a horizontal quasi-power of command and control. One must assess each blockchain's architectural characteristics to determine whether a few users may impose such decisions on others. The more a group of users can control others, the more they can single-handedly contribute to the block-chain's survival, and therefore be considered part of the nucleus. In fact, the original design of a blockchain can give one of the three groups of users more or less power. It can put them in charge of implementing the execution of transactions, designate them as miners or even enable them to change the design a blockchain's design unilaterally. Some blockchains might also use several mechanisms based on the platform layer to create governance (whether off-chain or side-chain).[71]

The second element is the ability of each participant to interfere with the blockchain's economic value.[72] When some users govern the pricing structures, the blockchain's attractiveness or economic incentives, they have indirect control over the blockchain. This ability can be assessed by looking at technical elements. For instance, the capacity to change the size of each block, which may alter the number and types of transactions, is a sign of control. The same goes for the power to propose modifications to the core code to attract new participants. Finally, the more a participant has invested in the blockchain, the more he has an incentive to control its economic value.[73] For that reason,

---

[70]   It may prove necessary to combine the analysis of these three different capacities to establish a body of corroborating evidence. Such methodology is often used in antitrust and competition law, *see*, for instance, *Knauf Gips v Commission*, C-407/08 P, European Court Reports: 2010 I-06375 (ECJ, 2010): para. 65; *Monsanto Co. v. Spray-Rite Service Corp.*, 465 US 752, 768 (U.S., 1984) (stating that circumstantial evidence that reasonably tends to prove that the parties had a conscious commitment to a common scheme designed to achieve an unlawful objective could be used).

[71]   On the subject, *see* Vlad Zamfir, "Blockchain Governance 101," Goodaudience (blog), September 30, 2018, https://perma.cc/T4BY-NFE7 (arguing against the idea that blockchain nodes should automatically upgrade when an on-chain governance process decides on an upgrade because "blockchain governance is too important for us to let a small handful of cryptocurrency whales make arbitrary decisions").

[72]   Our analysis here borrows from the theory of incentive systems developed about the firm by Michael C. Jensen, "Theory of the Firm: Managerial Behavior, Agency Costs and Ownership Structure," Journal of Financial Economics 3, no. 4 (1976): 78. That being said, it differs from Jensen's theory because it does not focus solely on contract (the law), but also on blockchain digital architecture, norms and market incentives.

[73]   For that reason, core developers tend to be closer to the nucleus than simple users. These investments can be of a financial nature, but can also be measured in terms

previous investments in a blockchain can show agencies where to look for the nucleus.

The third element is the ability to influence a blockchain's norms.[74] Here, "norms" are defined as the "constraints imposed not through the organized or centralized actions of a state, but through the many slight and sometimes forceful sanctions that members of a community impose on each other"[75] – that is, the unwritten rules that one often feels compelled to follow.[76] The more a participant can incentivize others to behave in a certain way – on pain of rejection from the community – the more they exercise control over the blockchain's general direction.[77] For example, when core developers can influence other participants into accepting all of the modifications they would like to apply to the core (e.g., by arguing about the necessity for technical upgrades, security failures, bugs…), they effectively pilot part of the blockchain.

4   THE THEORY OF GRANULARITY IN ACTION

The theory of granularity would enable agencies to identify a blockchain's nucleus. It would thus permit the creation of a legal fiction to which antitrust can be applied. In turn, this would impose new obligations upon blockchain participants while simultaneously giving them new means to challenge anti-competitive behavior. This theory would make it possible to analyze relevant markets and market power in antitrust proceedings. The theory of granularity

---

of time and trust devoted to the blockchain. For instance, a participant with numerous smart contracts running on a blockchain has a strong interest in its survival. For an explanation of why having invested (in something) in the past creates a strong incentive to keep on investing, in particular because of sunk costs and path dependence, *see* Hai R. Arkes and Catherine Blumer, "The Psychology of Sunk Costs," Organizational Behavior and Human Decision Processes 35 (1984): 124 (explaining that "the sunk cost effect is manifested in a greater tendency to continue an endeavor once an investment in money, effort, or time has been made.")

[74] *See* Vlad Zamfir, "Blockchain Governance 101," Goodaudience (blog), September 30, 2018, https://perma.cc/T4BY-NFE7 (discussing norms in blockchains).

[75] Lawrence Lessig, *Code: And Other Laws of Cyberspace, Version 2.0* (Basic Books, 2006): 340.

[76] *See* Vlad Zamfir, "Blockchain Governance 101," Goodaudience (blog), September 30, 2018, https://perma.cc/T4BY-NFE7 (blockchain governance is not merely an issue of design; it is also a result of politics). Also, Ying-Ying Hsieh et al., "The Internal and External Governance of Blockchain-Based Organizations," in *Bitcoin and Beyond: Blockchains and Global Governance*, ed. Malcolm Campbell-Verduyn (Routledge, 2017) (norms may also come from outside the blockchain – for instance, from media or general public interest).

[77] *See* Nigel Dodd, "The Social Life of Bitcoin," Sage Journal 10 (2017) (studying the influence of norms in the Bitcoin blockchain).

would also make it possible to impute anticompetitive practices to a given set of blockchain participants.

4.1   Market Analysis

Public permissionless blockchains are horizontal and decentralized. The absence of borders makes it very difficult to apply traditional competition policy tools to them – including market definition. In turn, this makes it almost impossible to determine whether a given participant can exert any market power. The theory of granularity could help antitrust agencies and courts to overcome both difficulties.

4.1.1   Relevant markets

Two-sided markets have been the object of numerous studies,[78] including a great deal about market definition.[79] At this point in time, and following the Supreme Court's *American Express* decision, courts and agencies often consider that there is a single market encompassing both sides of two-sided transaction markets – that is, those in which the two sides transact directly with one another through an intermediary.[80] In that case, the Supreme Court considered that both sides – merchants and cardholders – were part of the market for

---

[78]   The first article on the subject was Jean-Charles Rochet and Jean Tirole, "Platform Competition in Two-Sided Markets," Journal of the European Economic Association 1, (2003): 990. At the time of writing, it has been cited 4483 times according to Google Scholar, including 2400 times since January 1, 2015. *See* also Melvyn Weeks, "The Evolution and Design of Digital Economies" (2018): 27 (explaining that "economists and computer scientists are learning how to adapt the tools developed to build and understand the dynamics of centralised marketplaces" to decentralized markets).

[79]   *See* Lapo Filistrucchi et al., "Market Definition in Two-Sided Markets: Theory and Practice," Journal of Competition Law and Economics 10, no. 2, (2014): 293 (introducing a conceptual framework for defining relevant markets in two-sided markets). More generally, *see* Louis Kaplow, "Why (Ever) Define Markets?" Harvard Law Review 124, (2010): 81. For an answer, *see* Gregory J. Werden, "Why (Ever) Define Markets: An Answer to Professor Kaplow," Antitrust Law Journal 78 (2012): 729.

[80]   According to *Ohio v. American Express Co.*, 585 U.S. ___ 138 S. Ct. 2274, 201 L. Ed. 2d 678 (2018) ("The key feature of transaction platforms is that they cannot make a sale to one side of the platform without simultaneously making a sale to the other"). The Supreme Court held that they should be called "supplying only one product transactions" (internal citation omitted) for that reason, stressing that "[i]n two-sided transaction markets, only one market should be defined."

credit card transactions.[81] The European Commission, in its *Android* decision, confirmed the same principle.[82]

This has important implications when it comes to studying market power. Indeed, once they have identified the relevant product (or service) market, antitrust agencies usually study market power by identifying substitutes.[83] Such an analysis is made possible because centralized two-sided platforms or aggregators are often centered around one or a few products or services. For instance, Uber offers one easily identifiable service. Other transporters, such as Lyft, are part of the same relevant market.

The way agencies define the market is also crucial when it comes to analyzing potential anticompetitive effects. When they consider that two sides of the platform or aggregator are part of the same relevant market, anticompetitive effects on one side can be compensated by procompetitive effects on the other. Such logic cannot be applied when two sides of a platform or aggregator are considered two relevant markets.

With that logic in mind, one can see how defining relevant markets is more complex when it comes to public permissionless blockchains. As I explained in Chapter 3, one may distinguish between three major types of blockchain applications.[84] The first allows only one type of application – namely, cryptocurrencies. They compete with each other. Blockchain 2.0 permits the execution of smart contracts which can automate an almost infinite number of transactions. For that reason, all blockchain 2.0 platforms do not compete together, as they may automate transactions of a potentially very different nature. They cannot be easily shoehorned into a single product market. Finally, blockchain 3.0 makes it possible to do everything a computer can do, but in a decentralized and distributed fashion.[85] The creators of such blockchains have no control over which products and services will ultimately be offered. Thus, one cannot consider such blockchains as part of a single relevant market. For example, unlike smartphone or computer operating systems, blockchains 3.0 are not intended to work on pre-defined types of products (e.g., smart-

---

[81] *Id.*, "[t]ellingly, credit cards determine their market share by measuring the volume of transactions they have sold."

[82] "Google Android case" in *Google LLC. v. Commission*, Case AT.40099, C/2018/4761 (EC, 2018): para. 213, "for the definition of the relevant market, demand-side substitution constitutes the most immediate and effective disciplinary force on the suppliers of a given product."

[83] *Id.*, *see* also Jon Baker, *The Antitrust Paradigm: Restoring a Competitive Economy* (Harvard University Press, 2019): 185.

[84] Melanie Swan, *Blockchain: Blueprint for A New Economy* (O'Reilly Media, 2015): Preface, IX.

[85] *Id.*

phones). They can run wherever the Internet is available and they may even allow the subsequent development of operating systems.

As a result, public permissionless blockchains pose new challenges in terms of market definition that cannot be addressed by transposing the analyses of centralized two-sided platforms, as they are transactional infrastructures on top of which any types of products or services can be built freely. The theory of granularity, on the contrary, makes it possible to identify a blockchain nucleus and to provide both a theoretical and practical answer to these market definition issues.

Once the blockchain nucleus has been identified, one may define the types of activities around which it is built – that is, all activities ensuring the blockchain's survival. This makes it possible to identify substitutable blockchains (and centralized products or services) on the demand side. Blockchains may operate in several relevant markets, just as centralized platforms do. Focusing on the blockchain nucleus then allows us to delimit the geographical market (the area in which entities compete) by identifying all the substitutable products and services from the user's point of view.

4.1.2   Market power

For many years, academic articles have insisted on a disconnect between static legal analysis and the dynamic nature of digital markets.[86] Public permissionless blockchains exacerbate this problem because their borders are not as stable as those of firms. Public permissionless blockchains have no entry or exit door, freeing their participants to move from one blockchain to another. This flexibility should lead agencies to rethink how they analyze market power.[87]

The theory of granularity helps overcome this difficulty by grouping participants within a single legal fiction. Comparing the different nuclei in the same relevant market leads to establishing their market power. And of course, one will be required to keep in mind that entry barriers may be much lower in blockchain ecosystems than in more traditional markets. To be sure, some

---

[86]   For instance, *see* J. Gregory Sidak and David J. Teece, "Dynamic Competition in Antitrust Law," Journal of Competition Law & Economics 5, (2009): 581, 582 (underlining that antitrust and competition law has been static for several decades already); also Jan Krämer and Michael Wohlfarth, "Market Power, Regulatory Convergence, and the Role of Data in Digital Markets," Telecommunications Policy 42, no. 2 (2017): 154, 168 (underlining that, for instance, the dynamic nature of digital markets is *per se* in conflict with static approaches to define the relevant market); Michael O. Wise, "Antitrust's Newest New Learning Returns the Law to its Roots: Chaos and Adaptation as New Metaphors for Competition Policy," Antitrust Bulletin 40, no. 4 (1995).

[87]   Generally speaking, as has been stressed by Lawrence Lessig, "an unmovable, and unmoving, target of regulation, then, is a good start toward regulability," Lawrence Lessig, *Code: And Other Laws of Cyberspace, Version 2.0* (Basic Books, 2006): 139.

will remain, mostly for technical reasons (one will be required to learn about blockchain functioning and characteristics). Still, most of today's entry barriers will be removed, since access to dominant blockchains with significant market power will be open.

4.2   Anticompetitive Practices

The theory of granularity enables agencies to analyze the effects of practices by recreating an "inside" and "outside" (the nucleus), which is essential for antitrust analysis. Ultimately, it enables them to assign liability to the nucleus while also granting rights to its participants.

4.2.1   The assessment of practices
Firms decide internally to partake in collusive agreements or monopolization practices, but antitrust law is mostly concerned with such behavior's external effects.[88] That distinction between the effects inside and outside the firm guides the analysis of all potential practices. This prevents the application of antitrust law to public permissionless blockchains. The absence of clearly defined boundaries for such blockchains at the platform layer precludes a distinction between what is inside or outside. Analyzing practices within blockchain ecosystems becomes immensely complex for that reason.

The delimitation of a blockchain nucleus reintroduces the possibility of analyzing internal and external effects, since it recreates borders – namely, inside and outside the legal fiction. One can easily understand this through the example of collusion. As entities cannot collude with themselves, one needs to delimit their boundaries to analyze whether a collusive practice has occurred. In that regard, only agreements between two different nuclei should be worrisome. Agreements between blockchain participants outside of any nucleus, *de facto* lacking any ability to control, should not trigger antitrust concerns.

The same goes for monopolization and abuse of dominance cases. The theory of granularity makes it possible to define a legal fiction whose market power will be assessed in relation to others. In turn, this enables agencies to determine whether a legal fiction abused its power by analyzing the external effects of its behavior. This analysis is not possible when blockchains are seen only from a distance, because blurry decentralized entities in which no one exercises a power of command and control have no visible frontiers. The theory of granularity fixes that.

---

[88]   Thibault Schrepel, "Antitrust Conversations with Nobel Laureates," *Concurrentialiste Review* (2018): 14.

4.2.2   The assignment of liability

A firm controls its behavior on the market. That is true both for firms in their classic form and for firms that operate digital products and services. As Jean-Charles Rochet and Jean Tirole stressed in 2003, "platforms are controlled by competing entities, either profit-maximizing firms or not-for-profit associations."[89] This is because platforms such as Microsoft are matchmakers: they allow app developers to find consumers and vice versa. The same is true for aggregators such as Facebook, on top of which there is no app developing, but whose service is to collect a critical mass of users on one side to leverage access on the other.[90] They keep control of their practices, regardless of their business model.

Decentralized platforms are different because a few users cannot unilaterally decide on a strategy. For that reason, blockchains differ significantly from the model introduced by Rochet and Tirole, as practices emerge on them rather than being imposed.[91] The decentralized and horizontal nature of blockchain raises two important antitrust-related issues: characterizing anticompetitive practices and identifying the person(s) liable for them. The theory of granularity introduced in this chapter provides an answer to both.

I have shown that the behavior of participants in public permissionless blockchains may be influenced in three ways by the nucleus: (1) the technical ability to enjoy a restricted and horizontal quasi-power of command and control; (2) the ability to interfere with the blockchain's economic value; and (3) the ability to influence the blockchain's norms. As a result, the nucleus

---

[89]   Jean-Charles Rochet and Jean Tirole, "Platform Competition in Two-Sided Markets," Journal of the European Economic Association 1 (2003): 1000.

[90]   For further thoughts on the distinction, *see* "Platforms Versus Aggregators, What About Amazon? Walmart Buys Flipkart", Stratechery, May 10, 2018, https://perma.cc/E9T5-RB9E. Studying the implications of the distinction in antitrust law, *see* Thibault Schrepel, "Platforms or Aggregators: Implications for Digital Antitrust Law," Journal of European Competition Law & Practice 12 (2021): 1.

[91]   Blockchains are no "islands of conscious power," D.H. Robertson, *Control of Industry: Cambridge Economic Handbooks IV* (Nisbet, 1923): 385, coining the terms to describe firms. No overall conscious strategy can be imposed on blockchain. It is problematic to the extent that objective intent is usually inferred from the implementation of practices, which no longer seems possible here. Generally, on the role of intent in antitrust and competition law, *see* Marina Lao, "Aspen Skiing and Trinko: Antitrust Intent and Sacrifice", Antitrust Law Journal 73 (2005): 171, 208 (discussing the role of intent in the *Aspen Skiing* and *Trinko* cases); Nicolo Zingales, "Antitrust Intent in An Age of Algorithmic Nudging," Journal of Antitrust Enforcement 7 (2019): 386, 387 (proving the existence of a subjective intent is not required in antitrust and competition law, but proving objective intent is).

participants are to be held liable for all illegal conduct committed within the nucleus or the perimeter that it can control or influence to a great degree.[92]

Agencies and courts will have to decide on the width of that perimeter on a case-by-case basis.[93] By analogy with the American and European liability regimes for parent companies,[94] agencies will have to prove each time that the nucleus had the power to influence other participants, and that it actually exercised that influence.[95] However, the nucleus participants should not be held liable for practices committed outside of the perimeter they can influence.[96] This absence of liability is not problematic, because blockchain participants outside that perimeter are submitted to different constraints that deprive them of any power to coordinate their actions effectively to change the blockchain direction or abuse their power with that aim. The lack of control should logically lead to a lack of liability. For example, one occasional miner will not be included in a blockchain nucleus, but this should not be troubling as that miner cannot influence the blockchain (and infer or stop anticompetitive behaviors).

---

[92] One must distinguish between different degrees of distance with the nucleus – that is, different degrees of collaboration or competition with it. This is equivalent to analyzing one participant's ability to compete with other participants by moving away from the nucleus when desired. This capacity is a key criterion in antitrust and competition law for determining the extent to which economic agents are undertaking, *see Coöperatieve Vereniging Suiker Unie v. Commission*, Joined Cases 40–48, 50, 54–56, 111, 113 and 114–73, European Court Reports: 1975 1663 (ECJ, 1975): para. 173. The CJEU has frequently repeated this rule, *see*, for instance, *T-Mobile Netherlands BV, KPN Mobile NV, Orange Nederland NV and Vodafone Libertel NV v. Raad van bestuur van de Nederlandse Mededingingsautoriteit*, Case C-8/08, European Court Reports: ECLI:EU:C:2009:343 (ECJ, 2009): para. 32, *Allgemeine Elektrizitäts-Gesellschaft AEG-Telefunken AG v. Commission*, Case 107/82, European Court Reports: 1983 3151 (ECJ, 1983): para. 49. As such, the further a participant is from the nucleus, the less that nucleus will be able to control it.

[93] Some participants may indeed collaborate to ensure the blockchain survival in a majority of cases – they constitute the nucleus's nearby perimeter – while other participants may compete regularly with the nucleus, especially if they have a personal interest in the survival of another blockchain.

[94] *See* Carsten Koenig, "Comparing Parent Company Liability in EU and US Antitrust and Competition Law," World Competition 41, no. 01 (2018) (explaining that in the United States, courts rely less on assumptions to infer liability to parent companies than they do in Europe).

[95] *Alliance One International, Inc., formerly Standard Commercial Corp. and Others v. European Commission*, Case T-24/05, European Court Reports: 2010 II-05329 (ECJ, 2010).

[96] Vitalik Buterin, "Control as Liability", Vitalik Buterin's website, May 9, 2019, https://perma.cc/SR7C-9M43 ("every bit of control you have is a liability"). Liability in blockchain must stop where control stops.

Finally, for fine calculation, the nucleus will be subject to the same rules applied to firms. The turnover realized by the nucleus, based on all its transactions, will serve as a basis for calculating sanctions.[97]

5 A WIN-WIN THEORY

The creation of a legal fiction around blockchain nuclei will benefit both antitrust and blockchain communities. By facilitating the enforcement of the rule of law, blockchain participants will indeed be able to enforce antitrust laws or be sanctioned when infringing them.

5.1 A Win for Antitrust

The theory of granularity helps create a legal fiction for public permissionless blockchains and private ones (whose governance is not vertical). Surely, other legal fictions will be proposed in the coming years. Regardless of its name, creating a legal fiction is a prerequisite for applying the rule of law to blockchain layer 1. The ability to do so is crucial.

First, the creation of a legal fiction ensures that blockchains do not escape antitrust enforcement for theoretical reasons. This is a prerequisite before discussing the technical barriers to enforce antitrust against illegal practices (see the following chapters). Second, assigning liability to the right entity ensures that whoever controls blockchains will have a strong(er) incentive to comply with legal requirements. The urge to play by the rules is always stronger when one knows that the rules could actually be enforced. As such, antitrust will not only protect actors that lie outside of blockchain ecosystems; it will also protect those inside the blockchain who cannot stop the anticompetitive practices. Antitrust will free blockchain layer 1 from these practices.

5.2 A Win for Blockchain

Creating a distinct legal fiction centered on blockchains' nucleus will present an important step forward for related ecosystems.

First, the creation of such fiction will attribute rights to blockchains' nuclei. This will legitimize collaboration between blockchain participants in the nucleus that would otherwise have been prohibited. Indeed, I have explained

---

[97] *See*, for example, MK Manoylov, "Bitcoin Transaction Values and Fees Grew in 2020's Third Quarter," The Block, October 10, 2020, https://perma.cc/3GQK-8EWL (during the second quarter of 2020, "users transacted more than $225B, posting an average of $2.4B a day"). Even a small percentage of this value represents a very significant and dissuasive sum of money.

that antitrust law defines a legal fiction (e.g., the firm) and then applies only to the effects that occur outside of it. Decisions that produce an effect outside of the blockchain nucleus will be submitted to antitrust law. In contrast, decisions taken by the nucleus whose effects are purely internal to that entity will be exempt from antitrust scrutiny.[98]

Second, creating a legal fiction will increase legal certainty pertaining to the application of antitrust law and regulation. Decades of research suggest that doing so will encourage investments,[99] and will make entrepreneurs want to "embark" on the creation of innovative products and services.[100] Blockchain communities say so themselves: regulatory issues and accompanying legal uncertainty are the most important reasons preventing greater investment and adoption of blockchain technology.[101] The sooner a legal fiction is created, the better for the ecosystem. In its absence, one could imagine court decisions holding all blockchain participants liable for wrongdoings, even though most of them will not have the power to prevent these illegal practices.

Finally, the creation of a legal fiction will give the nucleus the right to institute legal actions and claim damages in cases of antitrust violation, whether caused by another nucleus or a non-blockchain entity. Going back to Christopher Stone's writing, blockchain's legal fictions will be able to institute legal actions in their name; courts will calculate injury to them, and relief will be run to their benefit. For example, one could imagine that a blockchain layer 1 (illegally) excluded from the market by another blockchain that engaged in predatory pricing could introduce a valid claim before the courts or antitrust agencies. In the following chapters, I will explain how this will play out when it comes to collusion and monopolization practices.

---

[98] *See* Carla L. Reyes, "If Rockefeller Were a Coder," George Washington Law Review 87, no. 373 (2019): 428.

[99] Avinash Dixit, "Entry and Exit Decisions Under Uncertainty," Journal of Political Economy 97, no. 3 (1989): 620; Robert S. Pindyck, "Irreversibility, Uncertainty, and Investment," Journal of Economic Literature 29 (1991): 1110; Avinash Dixit and Robert S. Pindyck, *Investment Under Uncertainty* (Princeton University Press 1994); Ricardo J. Caballero and Robert S. Pindyck, "Uncertainty, Investment, and Industry Evolution," International Economic Review 37, no. 3 (1996): 641; Nicholas Bloom et al., "Uncertainty and Investment Dynamics," The Review of Economic Studies 74, no. 2 (2007): 391.

[100] Edmund S. Phelps, *Mass Flourishing: How Grassroots Innovation Created Jobs, Challenge, and Change* (Princeton University Press, 2013): 206.

[101] See PwC, "PwC's Global Blockchain Survey 2018: Blockchain is Here. What's your Next Move?" (2018): 4, 11, https://perma.cc/PK33-RCD3 (48 per cent of survey respondents indicated that the lack of regulatory certainty is preventing the adoption of blockchain. This was ranked as the first reason).

For all these reasons, creating an antitrust-related legal fiction will be invaluable for blockchain ecosystems and, ultimately, for decentralization. It will protect them from illegal practices that could hinder blockchain's capacity to decentralize the economy. There is no doubt that centralized companies will multiply illegal behaviors toward blockchain ecosystems in the years to come, as we will see in the coming chapters. Being recognized as a legal entity will allow them to protect their interests and innovate toward decentralization.

6   CHAPTER SUMMARY AND BEYOND

In this chapter, I have used the theory of granularity to open the blockchain "black box." First, I have discussed blockchain governance and shown how the influence of different participants neutralize their position. As no blockchain participant can control the blockchain by itself – and ensure its survival – I have explained that a group of participants may want to come together to achieve common goals. By doing so, they free themselves from other participants' constraints and end up forming the blockchain nucleus.

The blockchain nucleus gives rise to an entity that should benefit from rights, but could also be held liable for illegal conducts. I have shown how this would work by analyzing relevant markets and market power, evaluating anticompetitive practices and assigning liability.

Now that I have discussed antitrust law's *applicability*, I move on to exploring the anticompetitive practices that could be implemented thanks to blockchains. That is, I explore the *application* of antitrust law to different forms of behavior that could take place within blockchain ecosystems. I start with collusive agreements and show that blockchain may actually help agents to implement (more) effective cartels.

8. Collusion on blockchain

1   WHERE WE'RE AT

Collusive agreements are consistently described as the antitrust infringement
that has the most severe impact on consumers. But recent academic discussions
regarding this topic appear to be missing the forest for the trees. Indeed, collusion enabled by algorithms (so-called "algorithmic collusion") has attracted
the lion's share of policymakers' attention. While this type of collusion may be
a threat, it is much less so than collusion enabled by blockchains.

1.1   The Basics of Collusion

The antitrust literature on monopolization and abuses of dominant positions is
highly polarized, as some authors dispute the harmful nature of such practices.[1]
There is no such debate in the literature dealing with collusive agreements. In
fact, "[n]o modern development in antitrust law is more striking than the global
acceptance of a norm that condemns cartels as the markets most dangerous
competitive vice."[2] Cartels are regularly described as "the supreme evil of
antitrust,"[3] a quasi-moralist assertion around which the academic community
seems to have found a point of agreement.[4]

   Collusive agreements (i.e., agreements and concerted practices, and cartels
and vertical agreements) make up the vast majority of the cases decided by
the Federal Trade Commission (FTC), the Department of Justice (DOJ), and
the European Commission, other than merger investigations. For instance, the

---

[1]   This has been especially true since the appearance of the Chicago School. *See*
generally Robert H. Bork, *The Antitrust Paradox: A Policy at War with Itself* (Basic
Books, 1978) (discussing the positive impact of monopolization practices on the
consumer).

[2]   William E. Kovacic, "The Value of Policy Diversification in Cartel Detection
and Deterrence", paper presented at OECD, "Roundtable on Ex Officio Cartel
Investigations and the Use of Screens to Detect Cartels," DAF/COMP(2013)27 (2013).

[3]   *Verizon Commc'ns v. Law Offices of Curtis V. Trinko*, 540 U.S. 398, 408 (2004).

[4]   For a critique of the moralization of antitrust and the use of words such as "evil,"
see Thibault Schrepel, "Antitrust Without Romance," N.Y.U. Journal of Law & Liberty
13, no. 2 (2020).

European Commission sanctioned zero abuses of dominance between 1991 and 2004,[5] focusing all of its attention on clearing up the jurisprudence related to collusion. As a result, collusive agreements on both North American and European soil have been the subject of extensive case law.[6]

1.2   Algorithmic Collusion

Recent academic research on collusive practices has focused heavily on the use of algorithms.[7] The publication of *Virtual Competition* in 2016 was a pivotal moment in that regard, as it sounded the alarm about algorithmic collusion.[8] The two authors argued that current antitrust doctrine was powerless in the face of collusion orchestrated by computer algorithms, sometimes assisted by artificial intelligence.[9] This led to a slim academic consensus that antitrust agencies should focus their efforts on this new "supreme evil." Yet asking for a substantial change in antitrust laws to tackle algorithmic collusion is misguided, for at least two reasons.

First, there is a lack of conclusive empirical studies documenting the phenomenon's frequency in the actual world. In other words, the occurrence of algorithmic collusion has not been documented in official publications coming from antitrust and competition agencies,[10] in any of the reports given to these agencies,[11] or in the Organisation for Economic Co-operation and

---

[5]   *See* Thibault Schrepel, *L'Innovation Prédatrice en Droit de la Concurrence* (Bruylant, 2018): 360.

[6]   *See* U.S. Dep't of Justice, Antitrust Div., "Workload Statistics FY 2009–2018," https://perma.cc/75A5-ADRY. Also, a study of federal antitrust class action cases filed between January 1, 2007 and December 31, 2009 shows that 80 percent of the cases asserted Section 1 claims, *see* William Kolasky, "Antitrust Litigation: What's Changed in Twenty-Five Years?" Antitrust 27, (2012): 9–10.

[7]   At the time of writing, Google Scholar lists 141 academic articles discussing "algorithmic collusion" since January 1, 2017. *See* "Search for Algorithmic Collusion," Google Scholar, https://perma.cc/RLM2-SS7F (search field for "algorithmic collusion").

[8]   Ariel Ezrachi and Maurice E. Stucke, *Virtual Competition: The Promise and Perils of the Algorithm-Driven Economy* (Harvard University Press, 2016).

[9]   Dealing, more generally, with the danger of AI, *see* Jamie Condliffe, "Elon Musk Implored Lawmakers to Prevent People from Building AI that Could Destroy Us All," MIT Technology Review, July 17, 2017, https://perma.cc/QF3K-9GUW.

[10]   *See* OECD, "Algorithms and Collusion—Note from the European Union," DAF/COMP/WD(2017)12 (2017): 12, https://perma.cc/Q8SS-6QRJ; Margrethe Vestager, Comm'r, Eur. Comm'n, Algorithms and Competition (March 16, 2017), https://perma.cc/YES2-4GMJ. *Bundeskartellamt* and *Autorité de la Concurrence*, "Algorithms and Competition," November, 2019 https://perma.cc/CD5K-GRYK.

[11]   *See*, for instance, Jacques Crémer et al., "Competition Policy for the Digital Era: Final Report, European Commission" (European Commission, February 2019), https://

Development's publications relating to collusion.[12] When looking at antitrust litigation brought in the United States and Europe, algorithmic collusion is virtually non-existent.[13] For that reason, the priority is first to quantify the phenomenon rather than drastically change antitrust and competition law.[14] The academic community must play its part; but for the time being, cases of collusion before antitrust agencies cover agreements between individuals, not algorithms.

Second, even if algorithmic collusion became a frequent practice, it would remain old wine in a new bottle. Such collusion is a more elegant way of implementing the same anticompetitive practices that have existed for centuries. Whether or not it relies on algorithms, the nature of anticompetitive collusion remains identical. Algorithmic collusion is at the origin of two problems: detection and liability assignment. In terms of detecting illegal practices, algorithms could enable faster implementation of agreements between companies, potentially for only a few seconds.[15] In terms of liability assignment, difficulties may arise when the algorithm whose initial order was to maximize the company's profits decides "on its own" to collude.[16]

---

perma.cc/RS4G-MVTR; UK Digital Competition Expert Panel, *Unlocking Digital Competition* (OGL, 2019), https://perma.cc/7GUU-6ABP.

[12] *See*, for instance, OECD, "Summary of Discussion of the Roundtable on Algorithms and Collusion," DAF/COMP/M(2017)1/ANN2/FINAL (2018), https://perma.cc/XX27-K7BJ.

[13] At the time of writing, a search on the WestLawNext search engine, using "adv: 'algorithms' AND 'Sherman Act § 1'", brought up only 13 cases; hardly any concerned actual algorithmic collusion, but rather non-algorithmic collusion in which one or two companies were using algorithms in their business model. A similar search, using "adv: 'algorithmic collusion'," brought up zero cases.

[14] For an emphasis on the need for such empirical work, *see* Thibault Schrepel, "Here's Why Algorithms Are Not (Really) a Thing," *Concurrentialiste*, May 15, 2017, https://perma.cc/4WA4-R76Y. For now, legal and economic papers dealing with the subject adopt an "experimental approach." *See*, for instance, Nan Zhou et al., "Algorithmic Collusion in Cournot Duopoly Market: Evidence from Experimental Economics" (2018).

[15] *See* Sam Schechner, "Why Do Gas Station Prices Constantly Change? Blame the Algorithm," Wall Street Journal, May 8, 2017, https://perma.cc/BD9J-Y5R3. Generally speaking, the main challenge posed by the digital economy to antitrust and competition agencies is that of speed. *See* Richard Posner, "Antitrust in the New Economy," Antitrust Law Journal 68 (2001): 925 ("[T]he enforcement agencies and the courts do not have adequate technical resources, and do not move fast enough, to cope effectively with a very complex business sector that changes very rapidly.")

[16] *See* OECD, "Algorithmic Collusion: Problems and Counter-Measures—Note from Ariel Ezrachi and Maurice E. Stucke," DAF/COMP/WD(2017)25 (2017): 25, 97, https://perma.cc/3EA9-RZR7 (explaining that algorithms may, with no human input, decide on implementing illegal practices to maximize profits).

Solutions to both of these problems are already starting to emerge. For instance, competition authorities are deploying algorithms to detect algorithmic collusion.[17] An algorithmic antitrust battle may not be far off. As for the assignment of liability, it could be attributed to the company that is using the algorithm, to the company that created it, to individuals, or to the algorithm itself. Assigning that liability is simply a matter of legal choice. To sum up, algorithmic collusion is not yet quantified; and even if it were, it would not raise fundamental problems for antitrust law.

Antitrust and competition agencies would be well advised to focus on their resources where consumer harm can already be quantified. Unfortunately, the publication bias that pushes part of the scientific community to publish about algorithmic collusion creates a headwind and leads authorities to misdirect these resources. In the meantime, the issue of collusion by blockchain becomes ever more pressing – not because it is quantified already, but, as I shall explain, because it threatens the very foundations of antitrust enforcement.

2   BLOCKCHAIN AS COLLUSION

In this section, I study if creating a blockchain between competitors could amount to an infringement of antitrust law. I distinguish between the creation of a public or private blockchain, as this leads to different conclusions.

2.1   Public Blockchains

Can the creation of a blockchain (in itself) qualify as a collusive agreement without further analyzing the information contained within it or the use made out of it? In both the United States and Europe, I show that a public blockchain's mere creation should not trigger antitrust or competition law interventions.[18]

In the United States, Section 1 of the Sherman Act states that: "Every contract, combination in the form of trust or otherwise, or conspiracy, in restraint of trade or commerce among the several States, or with foreign nations, is declared to be illegal."[19] The term "agreement" is not defined, but it is clear from the case law that an agreement does not need to be a formal written doc-

---

[17]   *See* Thibault Schrepel, "Computational Antitrust: An Introduction and Research Agenda," Stanford Journal of Computational Antitrust 1 (2021): 1. More generally, see the computational antitrust project at Stanford University.

[18]   Jones Day, "Blockchains and Antitrust: New Technology, Same Old Risks?" (2018): 1–2, https://perma.cc/S6GH-ERPY.

[19]   Sherman Antitrust Act, 15 U.S.C. § 1 (1890).

ument.[20] The United States Supreme Court held that companies enter into an illegal agreement when "the possibility of independent action" is excluded and when they exhibit "a conscious commitment to a common scheme."[21] Parties could meet these two criteria by agreeing to create and use a blockchain.

That being said, the exchange of public information is generally not considered an infringement of antitrust rules. In earlier decisions, the Supreme Court was concerned with such exchanges of public information, including "suggestions as to both future prices and production."[22] Following *United States v. United States Gypsum Co.*, in which the Supreme Court underlined that agreements to exchange information were evaluated under the rule of reason, the case law now focuses on actual evidence of anticompetitive harm.[23] And when information is publicly available, "the risk of its exchange between competitors seems low."[24] Because the plaintiff bears the initial burden of proof to show that the agreement to exchange information led to substantial anticompetitive effects in a relevant market, the mere creation of a blockchain is unlikely to be seen as illegal in the United States.[25]

In Europe, Article 101(1) of the TFEU provides that "all agreements between undertakings, decisions by associations of undertakings and concerted practices that may affect trade between Member States and which have as their object or effect the prevention, restriction or distortion of competition

---

[20] *See* George A. Hay, "The Meaning of 'Agreement' Under the Sherman Act: Thoughts from the 'Facilitating Practices' Experience," Review of Industrial Organization 16 (2000): 113.

[21] *Monsanto v. Spray-Rite Serv. Corp.*, 465 U.S. 752, 768 (U.S., 1984).

[22] *Am. Column & Lumber Co. v. United States*, 257 U.S. 377, 399 (U.S., 1921).

[23] *United States v. U.S. Gypsum Co.*, 438 U.S. 422, 438 (U.S., 1978).

[24] OECD, "Information Exchanges Between Competitors under Competition Law," DAF/COMP(2010)37 (2010): 296. In fact, "[c]ompetition does not become less free merely because the conduct of commercial operations becomes more intelligent through the free distribution of knowledge of all the essential factors entering into the commercial transaction." *Maple Flooring Mfrs. Ass'n. v. United States*, 268 U.S. 563, 583 (U.S., 1925). For a list of all criteria used to characterize an illegal exchange of information, *see* Spencer W. Waller, "Trade Associations, Information Exchange, and Cartels," Loyola Consumer Law Review 30, (2018): 206–207.

[25] A similar conclusion was reached in a case concerning a blockchain shipping consortium, allowing different entities to "cooperate with respect to the provision of data to a blockchain-enabled, global trade digitized solution that will enable shippers, authorities and other stakeholders to exchange information on supply chain events and documents and to collaborate with the Platform Providers on products to be offered on the Platform and the marketing of same." The Federal Maritime Commission has declined to challenge an agreement, *see* "Blockchain Shipping Consortium wins Maritime Antitrust Nod," Law 360, February 13, 2020, https://perma.cc/32Q4-ZRSF.

within the internal market" are prohibited.[26] On that basis, one might ask whether creating a blockchain could amount to an agreement, a decision by associations of undertakings or a concerted practice.

The jurisprudence holds that the proof of an agreement requires:

> the existence of the subjective element that characterizes the very concept of an agreement, that is to say, a concurrence of wills between economic operators on the implementation of a policy, the pursuit of an objective, or the adoption of a given line of conduct on the market.[27]

One could see the creation of a blockchain by several companies as an agreement: they are indeed expressing their joint intention to conduct themselves on the market according to the information that will be contained on the blockchain and to abide by the same protocol mechanism. However, not all agreements are illegal; it depends on their nature and effects. For that reason, there is little reason to believe that the mere creation of a blockchain would constitute an anticompetitive agreement under antitrust law.

The creation of a blockchain might also be framed as a decision by an association of undertakings. But only anticompetitive decisions emanating from these associations are actionable for competition law purposes. The question is whether the mere creation of a blockchain for anticompetitive purposes may lead to intervention. Although this is theoretically possible, only a closer examination of the association's nature and effects can provide definitive answers. One cannot conclude that the sole creation of a blockchain is therefore problematic on a general basis.

Last, could blockchain be seen as a concerted practice? According to European jurisprudence, concerted practices are characterized by the "coordination between undertakings which, without having reached the stage where an agreement properly so-called has been conducted, knowingly substitutes practical co-operation between them for the risks of competition."[28]

The CJEU further holds that Article 101 prevents direct or indirect contacts between such operators whose object or effect is to influence the conduct on the market of an actual or potential competitor.[29] Interestingly, the European General Court has considered that the unilateral disclosure of information

---

[26] Consolidated Version of the Treaty on the Functioning of the European Union art. 101(1), May 9, 2008, 2008 O.J. (C 115) 47, 88–89.

[27] *Bayer AG. v. Commission*, Case T-41/96, European Court Reports: 2000 II-3383 (CFI, 2000): para. 173.

[28] *Imperial Chemical Industries Ltd. v. Commission*, Case 48/69, European Court Reports: 1972 619 (ECJ, 1972): paras. 64–65.

[29] *Suiker Unie v. Commission*, Case C-40/73, European Court Reports: 1663 (1975): para. 174.

relevant to the market may constitute a concerted practice,[30] which is precisely what sharing information on a public blockchain entails. Public blockchains could also discourage companies – especially small ones – from offering different prices than competitors. As a result, provided that an anticompetitive object or effect is shown, creating a public blockchain could constitute a collusive practice in and of itself. But could such an object or effect be shown?

The Horizontal Guidelines provide that "in general, exchanges of genuinely public information are unlikely to constitute an infringement of Article 101."[31] The Guidelines further add that "genuinely public information is information that is generally equally accessible (in terms of access costs) to all competitors and customers"; and that "[f]or information to be genuinely public, obtaining it should not be more costly for customers and companies unaffiliated to the exchange system than for the companies exchanging the information."[32] This is exactly what blockchain does: it turns private information into genuinely public information. It makes markets more transparent, with all the pros and cons that entails.

European case law holds that public information sharing constitutes a cartel only when the information concerns future prices[33] or strategies.[34] The sharing

---

[30]   *Tate & Lyle plc v. Commission*, Joined Cases T-202/98, T-204/92 and T-207/98, European Court Reports: 2001 II-2040 (CFI, 2001): paras. 35, 54, 61.

[31]   Guidelines on the Applicability of Article 101 of the Treaty on the Functioning of the European Union to Horizontal Co-operation Agreements, para. 92, COM (2011) C 11/1 (January 14, 2011).

[32]   Makan Delrahim, "Never Break the Chain: Pursuing Antifragility in Antitrust Enforcement," the United States Department of Justice, August 27, 2020, https://perma .cc/NEZ8-WC5E ("Blockchain solutions might, for instance, facilitate sharing of competitively sensitive information. As Dr. Thibault Schrepel has observed, by virtue of its distributed ledger, the blockchain 'turns private information into genuinely public information.' It may be difficult (or impossible) to identify which actors are sharing what information because the blockchain is based on pseudonyms and largely anonymous transactions. This combination of factors could embolden competitors to share more competitively sensitive information through the blockchain than they would otherwise").

[33]   *See* generally *Cimenteries CBR v. Commission*, Joined Cases T-25/95, T-26/95, T-30/95, T-31/95, T-32/95, T-34/95, T-35/95, T-36/95, T-37/95, T-38/95, T-39/95, T-42/95, T-43/95, T-44/95, T-45/95, T-46/95, T-48/95, T-50/95, T-51/95, T-52/95, T-53/95, T-54/95, T-55/95, T-56/95, T-57/95, T-58/95, T-59/95, T-60/95, T-61/95, T-62/95, T-63/95, T-64/95, T-65/95, T-68/95, T-69/95, T-70/95, T-71/95, T-87/95, T-88/95, T-103/95 and T-104/95, European Court Reports: 2000 1531 (CFI, 2000); *Aalborg Portland A/S v. Commission*, Joined Cases C-204/00 P, C-205/00 P, C-211/00 P, C-213/00 P, C-217/00 P and C-219/00 P, European Court Reports: 2004 I-123 (ECJ, 2004).

[34]   *Guidelines on the Applicability of Article 101*, 92; *See Cimenteries CBR v. Commission*, Joined Cases T-25/95, T-26/95, T-30/95, T-31/95, T-32/95, T-34/95,

of actual prices constitutes a "market behavior which does not lessen each undertaking's uncertainty as to the future attitude of its competitors. At the time when each undertaking engages in such behavior, it cannot be sure of the future conduct of the others."[35] I have identified no jurisprudence sanctioning the mere act of publicly sharing actual prices because such practices do not restrict companies' freedom to determine their market behavior independently.[36] Indeed, the jurisprudence holds that shared data must be "ultimately aimed at reducing or eliminating uncertainty about the future pricing behavior of parties."[37] This reasoning is confirmed in the European Commission Guidelines on the applicability of Article 101 to horizontal cooperation agreements, which refer to information reducing "strategic uncertainty."[38] In short, the data must be of such a nature that the company cannot refrain from taking it into account when defining its market behavior.[39]

Evidently, the fact that public blockchains allow for information to be made public can encourage cartel creation.[40] But it also makes markets more fluid. For these reasons, it is unlikely to be considered anticompetitive. In fact, I contend that it should not be, as blockchain's open nature ultimately helps decentralize the economy. Luckily, it is up to the Commission to show that

---

T-35/95, T-36/95, T-37/95, T-38/95, T-39/95, T-42/95, T-43/95, T-44/95, T-45/95, T-46/95, T-48/95, T-50/95, T-51/95, T-52/95, T-53/95, T-54/95, T-55/95, T-56/95, T-57/95, T-58/95, T-59/95, T-60/95, T-61/95, T-62/95, T-63/95, T-64/95, T-65/95, T-68/95, T-69/95, T-70/95, T-71/95, T-87/95, T-88/95, T-103/95 and T-104/95, European Court Reports: 2000 II-00491 (CFI, 2000): para. 1531 (regarding price intention); *Aalborg Portland A/S v. Commission*, Joined Cases C-204/00 P, C-205/00 P, C-211/00 P, C-213/00 P, C-217/00 P and C-219/00 P, European Court Reports: 2004 I-123 (ECJ, 2004). With regard to natural capacity increases, *see* Commission Decision 72/474, 1972 O.J. (L 303/24); Commission Decision 84/405, 1984 O.J. (L 220/27) (regarding investment plans).

[35] *Ahlström Osakeyhtiö v. Commission*, Joined Cases C-89/85, C-104/85, C-114/85, C-116/85, C-117/85 and C-125–129/85, European Court Reports: 1996 I-1307 (ECJ, 1996) para. 64; *see also* OECD, *Information Exchanges Between Competitors*, 28, 29, 165. Furthermore, *see* generally OECD, "Unilateral Disclosure of Information with Anticompetitive Effects," DAF/COMP(2012)17 (2012): 20; *Atlantic Container Line v. Commission*, Cases T-191/98 and T-212–214/98, European Court Reports: 2003 II-3275 (CFI, 2003): para. 1154.

[36] Alison Jones, Brenda Sufrin and Niamh Dunne, *EU Competition Law: Text, Cases, and Materials* (Oxford University Press 7th, 2019): 903.

[37] Commission Decision COMP/39.188 of October 15, 2008, Relating to a Proceeding Under Article 81 of the EC Treaty, at 72, C(2008) 5955 final (2008).

[38] *See* Guidelines on the Applicability of Article 101, para. 61.

[39] Nicolas Petit, *Droit européen de la concurrence* (Lextenso, 2018): 628.

[40] Discussing this point, *see* Izabella Kaminska, "Exposing the 'if we call it a blockchain, perhaps it won't be deemed a cartel?' tactic," *Financial Times*, May 11, 2015, https://perma.cc/2U4S-JTGA.

the exchange of information is the only plausible explanation of subsequent behavior's parallelism.[41] Matching that burden is complex, even though the European Commission may apply the method of *faisceau d'indices* (bundle of indicators).[42] Indeed, similar prices or market behaviors may have numerous explanations other than collusion. Consequently, there is every reason to believe that a company sharing its current prices on a blockchain would not infringe Article 101 of the TFEU.

2.2   Private Blockchains

I now turn to private blockchains and examine whether their creation may amount to collusion. Here, one must question whether the conditions of access and use for private blockchains may be anticompetitive. These conditions are what differentiate private blockchains from public ones. The case law is clear in that matter: conditions of access can constitute an anticompetitive agreement. When the defendants have "market power or exclusive access to an element essential to effective competition,"[43] the blockchain's exclusion may constitute a concerted refusal to deal. It may also constitute market sharing if the colluders use the ledgers' information to adapt their strategy[44] (even if the information being shared is perfectly legal, but essential to operate on the market). In that regard, one may see the creation of a private blockchain as anticompetitive if its conditions of access have detrimental effects on competition.

Given this, antitrust agencies will scrutinize the creation and use of private blockchains closely. Indeed, public blockchains turn public information into private information, but private blockchains keep it private. The incentive to adapt business strategies based on private information is higher, as not all competitors can change their behaviors accordingly. Also, private blockchains would be more natural tools to share illegal information than public ones, as they are sheltered from the enforcers.

---

[41]   *See BPB Industries plc v. Commission*, Case T-65/89, European Court Reports: 1993 II-389 (CFI, 1993).

[42]   *See Dresdner Bank AG v. Commission*, Joined Cases T-44/02, T-54/02, T-56/02, T-60/02 and T-61/02, European Court Reports: 2006 II-3567 (CFI, 2006): paras. 64–67.

[43]   *See Northwest Wholesale Stationers, Inc. v. Pacific Stationery and Printing Co.*, 472 U.S. 284, 296 (U.S., 1985).

[44]   Here, the analysis concerns both the use and the creation of the blockchain itself.

Additionally, in Europe, exclusion from a blockchain may constitute an abuse of collective dominance,[45] which falls within Article 102 of the TFEU. This practice is found where collectively dominant firms enjoy some structural, contractual or economic link allowing them to coordinate their behavior and act as a collective entity.[46] One could see the decision to exclude users from a blockchain as an abuse of collective dominance. Although the case law punishing such abuses remains scarce,[47] it could be revived. In short, antitrust agencies will, in all likeliness, keep a close eye on the establishment, use and abuse of private blockchains.

3 COLLUSIVE AGREEMENTS REGARDING BLOCKCHAINS

Blockchains could give rise to various implementations of collusive behaviors. I classify them into two categories: the agreements that concern the operation of blockchains, on the one hand; and those that concern the modification of blockchains, on the other.

3.1 Blockchain Operation

I distinguish three fundamental types of decisions relating to the operation of blockchains: decisions concerning entry into these blockchains; decisions concerning their consensus mechanisms; and decisions concerning their fee and reward structures.

3.1.1 Entry

Public blockchains are accessible to everyone by default. Any user may also become a miner or validator (the terminology differs depending on the consensus mechanism that is used) on permissionless blockchains. Therefore, it would appear that no collusive decision can be made regarding the condi-

---

[45]   *See Laurent Piau v. Commission*, Case T-193/02, European Court Reports: 2005 II-209 (CFI, 2005): para. 118.

[46]   The ongoing debate regarding minority shareholdings should be mentioned here. *See* Einer Elhauge, "How Horizontal Shareholding Harms Our Economy— And Why Antitrust Law Can Fix It," Harvard Olin Center, Discussion Paper No. 982 (2018), (arguing that horizontal shareholdings harm the economy). But *see* Thomas A. Lambert and Michael E. Sykuta, "The Case for Doing Nothing About Institutional Investors' Common Ownership of Small Stakes in Competing Firms," University of Missouri School of Law Legal Studies Research Paper No. 2018-21 (2018); OECD, "Common Ownership by Institutional Investors and its Impact on Competition," DAF/ COMP(2017)1 (2017): 6.

[47]   *See* Nicolas Petit, *Droit européen de la concurrence* (Lextenso, 2018): 411.

tions that determine access to any of their functions. This is mostly true, but more attention needs to be paid to establishing these consensus mechanisms. Different consensus mechanisms can be put into place, and not all of them present the same degree of anticompetitive risk, as they do not require the same type of information.

Bitcoin, for example, distributes all transaction information to each user. This availability allows them to become miners by assessing the costs associated with the mining activity. This ensures a certain degree of decentralization, but it also facilitates potential collusive agreements by making these costs public.[48] To this extent, one might want to provide users access to only certain types of information. But when this is the case, only one group of users decides what information is available to others. Those users thus exercise power – knowledge is power, as they say. For that reason, there is a balance to be struck when it comes to distributing the right amount of information and creating the right incentives for miners to behave properly.

Private blockchains are also interesting in that regard. Gatekeepers can choose who can access what information, which creates opportunities and risks. On the one hand, these blockchains facilitate business secrecy[49] and privacy protection by removing some of the virtues of decentralization. But they also allow for the risks of cartel formation to be managed. For example, the Peruvian antitrust agency ruled in October 2020 that the creation of a joint venture between shipping companies and port operators would not be problematic (i.e., would not facilitate collusion) as, thanks to the use of a private blockchain to channel information, only the parties to a transaction would access relevant information.[50] On the other hand, private blockchain holders may organize the blockchain and manage it, allowing for governing collusion when they so desire.

Last, one may want to stress that access to other facilities outside the blockchain may also raise antitrust issues. Perhaps unsurprisingly, the first blockchain antitrust case concerned a third party.[51] In this case, filed in September 2018 to the U.S. District Court for the Northern District of California, the

---

[48] Cong and He, "Blockchain Disruption".

[49] *Id.* at 9.

[50] *Informe de aprobación*, prepared by Fiscalia Nacional Economica (Santiago, 2020): para. 54.

[51] For a complete analysis of that case, *see* Thibault Schrepel, "The first case of 'blockchain antitrust': Gallagher v. Bitcointalk.org," *Concurrentialiste*, May 28, 2020, https://perma.cc/W8RC-9EW9.

plaintiff claimed that the defendants – Bitcointalk.org, a Bitcoin developer, and the Bitcoin Foundation – were "operating an illegal monopoly." He explained:

> I have been a member of the website Bitcointalk.org since 2011 or 2012 when Bitcoin was $5 each. ... I was going to be creating cryptocurrency towns. The defendants, together, used ... Bitcointalk.org to deny me any ability to compete by banning me, and slandering my name even though I had 0 negative points in their reputation system.

According to the plaintiff, the practice amounted to "monopolizing the cryptocurrency technology on their website" – more specifically, to a violation of Section 1 of the Sherman Act. The case was eventually dismissed for procedural reasons, but it shows how facilities outside the actual blockchain can play an important role. For that reason, one may expect more cases of this nature to flourish in the coming years.[52]

Let me recall in that regard that coordinated refusals to deal are labeled as "boycotts" and are prohibited under Section 1 of the Sherman Act. Specifically, *NYNEX Corp. v. Discon* (1998) states that boycotts involving vertical schemes are subject to the rule of reason, while horizontal boycotts constitute *per se* violations of the Sherman Act (*Klor*, 1959). As for European competition law, the European Commission held in *Papiers peints de Belgique* (1974) that "collective boycott is traditionally considered one of the most serious infringements of the rules of competition, since it is aimed at eliminating a troublesome competitor. Such a boycott constitutes an intentional infringement of Article 85 (1)," now Article 101 of the TFEU. The principle has since been confirmed.[53] On top of that, refusals to deal can also be sanctioned under Section 2 of the Sherman Act and Article 102 of the TFEU. I will study that in Chapter 11.

---

[52]   *See,* for example, in Australia, Samuel Haig, "Lawyer to File Crypto Class-Action Seeking Billions From Social Media 'Cartel'," CoinTelegraph, August 12, 2020, https://perma.cc/SVU6-BJ77 (accusing Google, Facebook, Twitter and YouTube of implementing a cartel intended to prevent the "burgeoning cryptocurrency sector"). In the complaint, the plaintiff argued that: "The Respondents, by their announcement and implementation of bans on advertising of cryptocurrencies and related content, have given effect to provisions in contracts, and engaged in a concerted practice, that has the purpose and has had the effect of substantially lessening competition in cryptocurrency markets in contravention of section 45 of the Act", *see* Notice of Filing and Hearing, prepared by Federal Court of Australia (Sydney, NSW, July 14, 2020): para. 2.

[53]   *See Protimonopolný úrad Slovenskej republiky v. Slovenská sporiteľňa a.s.*, Case C-68/12, ECLI:EU:C:2013:71 (ECJ, 2013).

3.1.2   Consensus

Blockchain consensus is nothing less than a blockchain's primary rules of the game. By deciding how transactions can be validated, the consensus mechanism is at the core of blockchain's value and integrity. Miners have the most substantial influence on it because they are bound by it at an individual level and can change it by way of a fork.

Each miner's power is minimal on widely used blockchains where many transactions are recorded at any given time. The situation is different when miners are grouped into pools where the profit generated by the entire mining activity is shared according to each miner's hashing power.[54] The incentive to join such pools leads to rapid expansion. As a result, as of 2021, fewer than ten mining pools dominate Bitcoin, with just a handful validating more than 50 percent of all transactions on the Bitcoin blockchain.[55] Because these pool miners are often physically together, it is easy to see how they could coordinate their behavior.[56] Only a change in the blockchain's consensus mechanism may redistribute mining power.[57]

Although no consensus mechanism should be *per se* anticompetitive, some can facilitate the emergence of anticompetitive practices.[58] Let me illustrate this by discussing two of them. Using Proof of Work, miners compete to add a set of transactions gathered as a block in the chain by racing to solve a cryptographic puzzle.[59] The first to solve it gets to verify and validate the block and is rewarded by receiving a transaction fee and newly minted tokens. Thanks to Bitcoin, Proof of Work is currently the world's most used consensus mechanism.[60] It has the advantage of allowing a relatively random distribution of

---

[54]   *See* Kevin Werbach, *The Blockchain and the New Architecture of Trust* (MIT Press, 2018): 45.

[55]   *See* "Hashrate Distribution," BlockChain, https://perma.cc/4USA-DZP3.

[56]   For an example of miners coordinating their behavior through a pool, *see* Kristian Soltes, "The First Blockchain Antitrust Case. Or Is It?" Constantine Cannon, May 29, 2019, https://perma.cc/NG3X-S3LS.

[57]   Changing the consensus mechanism may undermine mining pools' power. For instance, several pools threatened to create hard forks during the Bitcoin block size controversy. *See* David Dinkins, "Satoshi's Best Kept Secret: Why is There a 1 MB Limit to Bitcoin Block Size," CoinTelegraph, September 19, 2017, https://perma.cc/6VWW -VF53.

[58]   Do miners and/or validators form a single economic entity? If that is the case, they are not separate undertakings and, as a consequence, there is no possible collusion between them. *See* Ioannis Lianos, "Blockchain Competition," CLES Research Paper 8/2018 (2018): 84.

[59]   Thibault Schrepel, "Is Blockchain the Death of Antitrust Law? The Blockchain Antitrust Paradox," Georgetown Law Technology Review 3, no. 2 (2019): 292.

[60]   *See* Andrew Tar, "Proof-of-Work, Explained," CoinTelegraph, January 17, 2018, https://perma.cc/2TCU-XJVZ.

block validation operations, but encounters scaling issues due to the power that mining requires and scaling issues.[61] Pools capture most of the mining activities, presenting concerns regarding potential collusion between them.[62] One could also imagine that the leaders of pools may sometimes want to coordinate their behavior. Thus, the Proof of Work consensus mechanism fails to protect Bitcoin and other blockchains from collusive agreements that could ultimately lead to a change in consensus.

Under Proof of Stake, soon to become Ethereum's consensus mechanism, each user's chance of validating blocks increases with the number of tokens that he owns. A user with 200 tokens will be twice as likely to be selected as another user with 100 tokens. There is no coin creation (mining) in Proof of Stake, so validators are typically rewarded in transaction fees. Once a block is created, it must be committed to the blockchain. Different systems are used: some choose a random group of signers,[63] while others require a majority. Overall, there is a risk that, by identifying the largest token holders, one could attempt to collude with them.[64] Nonetheless, it appears more complicated than identifying mining pools with the most significant hashing power under Proof of Work. Also, while someone could rent computing power and therefore become a powerful miner, the renting of tokens is more unlikely.

Overall, one point emerges from all this: the risk of collusion is high when miners or validators are big players, and especially when the community can identify them.[65] Blockchain participants may bribe them, or they may coordinate among themselves.[66] Conversely, the risk of collusive agreements is much lower when the miners and validators are chosen randomly. Of course,

---

[61]   *See* Vladimir Jelisavcic, "Bitcoin Uses a Lot of Energy, But Gold Mining Uses More," LongHash, September 13, 2018, https://perma.cc/QV8E-GVYW. Also, Connor Blenkinsop, "Blockchain's Scaling Problem, Explained," CoinTelegraph, August 22, 2018, https://perma.cc/PXZ4-J9XM.

[62]   For an overview of the distribution of hashrate among mining pools, *see* "State of Adoption, 2019/2020," (2020): 45, https://perma.cc/PZA9-X92Y.

[63]   Amy Castor, "A (Short) Guide to Blockchain Consensus Protocols," CoinDesk, March 4, 2017, https://perma.cc/ER9Q-824B ("In Tendermint, for example, every node in the system has to sign off on a block until a majority vote is reached, while in other systems, a random group of signers is chosen.")

[64]   Large mining pools are easily identifiable on the Ethereum blockchain. At the time of writing, they are Ethermine, Sparkpool, Nanopool and F2Pool_2. They represent more than 70 percent of the Ethereum mining activity, *see* Etherscan, https://etherscan.io.

[65]   For a description of the whale problem, *see* "Thought Bitcoin Had a Whale Problem? Ethereum is Much Worse," LongHash, August 27, 2018, https://perma.cc/7TZ2-VARV.

[66]   *See* Dylan Yaga et al., "Blockchain Technology Overview," NIST Interagency/Internal Report 8202 (2018): 25; *see also* Vitalik Buterin, "On Collusion," Vitalik

selecting them on a truly random basis may compromise the blockchain's integrity by entrusting power to potentially malevolent participants who have little to lose. Regulatory agencies will be required to consider that balance when studying new consensus mechanisms in the years to come.

3.1.3   Fees and rewards

Transaction fees are essential to the integrity of many blockchains. By creating a reward for miners, they encourage them to verify transactions correctly. Some blockchains do not use any fees and seek to ensure their integrity differently. The endgame is always to prevent double spending of the same token.

As far as the Bitcoin blockchain is concerned, transaction fees are a combination of a minimum fee directly related to the transaction's size and a bounty decided by each user to reward miners for validating their transaction faster.[67] With the Ethereum blockchain, the fees result from a similar system, using a so-called "gas" mechanism that allows for higher than minimum fees. By contrast, private blockchains rarely use transaction fees. Integrity is, in principle, ensured by a gatekeeper. For example, Hyperledger does not use fees; validation is reached "post consensus." The R3 Corda blockchain also works with a no-charge system, where each transaction is validated based on transaction uniqueness.

A question then arises: which mechanism presents the most anticompetitive risks? And can these fee structures be the manifestation of an anticompetitive practice? The answer is positive. Let us imagine that two blockchain nuclei agreed to change the rules for calculating transaction fees in another blockchain and attack that blockchain for the purpose (by devoting computational power). This would amount to a collusive agreement. The same would apply if two nuclei agreed together to change their own calculation rules in an identical fashion. In both cases, the decision would produce an effect outside a single blockchain. This explains why it could qualify as an anticompetitive practice.

Things are different should participants simply agree to change the rules for calculating the fees of a blockchain in which they participate. Here, regardless of the issues related to legal fictions, new rules affect all the participants. One could show the existence of an agreement leading to their implementation, but showing anticompetitive effects would prove difficult. Indeed, changing the rules implies validation by a majority of participants. One could think that they would refuse to implement new rules against their own interest. There is,

---

Buterin's website April 3, 2019, https://perma.cc/6RDF-RQWQ (detailing the risk of bribery on blockchain).

[67]   This is described as being "market-based" in the Ethereum white paper: 27, https://perma.cc/ZTR8-8PUF.

therefore, is a strong presumption that new rules will produce a positive effect for most of the community if they are implemented — therefore exempting them from antitrust scrutiny. In a nutshell, decisions that are internal to only one blockchain are simply neutral (or pro-competitive) business strategies.

3.2   Blockchain Modification

I distinguish three fundamental types of decisions related to the modification of blockchains: decisions that concern the core client; decisions to generate a fork; and decisions that affect the application level. Not all of them create a significant impact on other participants and blockchain layers. For example, the concentration of mining activities – often used as an example to show that blockchain is not decentralized[68] – does not significantly affect blockchain's use. It follows that these different types of potential collusion must be analyzed in the context of blockchain's entire ecosystem (with its different layers).

3.2.1   Core client and developers

As we have already seen, the client's code – running on top of the database layer – is key to blockchain's fourth level (infrastructure). Its design is essential because it allows for more or less coordination between the core developers. This is all the more important given that the developers working on the blockchain's core software are usually small groups with a great deal of power over the network, as I have previously explained. The Bitcoin Foundation[69] and the Ethereum Foundation[70] are two such groups. Their mission is to promote and ensure core client integrity. The same goes for private blockchains such as Hyperledger and R3, as they have corporate members that fund them and contribute to the code according to well-established governance structures.[71] In short, the number, interest and location of these developers are often concen-

---

[68]   For example, *see* Elon Musk, (@elonmusk), May 16, 2021, https://perma.cc/ HR2Z-VS8V ("Bitcoin is actually highly centralized, with supermajority controlled by handful of big mining (aka hashing) companies"). As we saw in Chapter 7 (with the "blockchain power game"), calling a blockchain centralized because the mining power is concentrated in the hands of a few is inaccurate, as miners cannot capture the entire decision-making process or size a power of command and control.

[69]   *See* the Bitcoin Foundation, https://perma.cc/S2UM-GWLU.

[70]   *See* Ethereum, https://perma.cc/2FC9-KWM8.

[71]   Kevin Werbach, *The Blockchain and the New Architecture of Trust* (MIT Press, 2018): 121. More generally, on governance and blockchain, *see* Don Tapscott and Alex Tapscott, "Realizing the Potential of Blockchain: A Multistakeholder Approach to the Stewardship of Blockchain and Cryptocurrencies," World Economic Forum (2017): 7.

trated, which often gives them the ability to steer changes.[72] However, these core developers (e.g., Bitcoin's and Ethereum's) are rarely granted the power to impose changes on the client. Thus, all modifications require a majority of these blockchains' participants.

Against this background, one should establish which agreements between core developers could amount to violations of antitrust law. First, they may propose changes whose effects are not directed inside the blockchain, but outside of it. They may, for example, want to change the code to create an agreement with another blockchain. In these situations, two legal fictions are involved. Here, antitrust law could be infringed, although one should mention that such modifications will improve blockchains in a majority of cases. Second, modifications can produce effects only within the blockchain. When the goal is to increase blockchain survival, one could consider that it benefits participants inside the blockchain. Antitrust law would thus not apply. Instead, when the modification is not intended to maximize blockchain survival, one could attribute it to participants outside the blockchain nucleus. It could then infringe antitrust law. Antitrust agencies will be tasked with identifying such agreements and their effects. That implies understanding how they can be implemented – from a technical perspective – and how coercive they are. And third, modifications can produce a "mixed-bag" effect, ensuring blockchain survival while creating a negative effect outside of it. Agencies will then be tasked to analyze whether this negative effect was strictly correlated to the chosen strategy for maximizing survival.[73]

When it comes to public blockchains, core developers can use different means to get in touch with miners and nodes regarding future changes to the blockchain. Bitcoin uses Bitcoin Improvement Proposals (BIPs), a mechanism that allows core developers to probe miners about technical changes.[74] The developers propose a modification and the miners express their agreement by raising "flags." The more computing power a miner has, the more flags they have at their disposal. A general position on the blockchain thus emerges and the modification can be adopted or rejected in this way.[75] Other times, BIPs

---

[72] *See* Aaron Van Wirdum, "MIT to Take Over Funding of Three Bitcoin Core Developers," CoinTelegraph, April 23, 2015, https://perma.cc/9SZV-JKMB.
[73] See Thibault Schrepel, "The Enhanced No Economic Sense Test: Experimenting with Predatory Innovation," New York University Journal of Intellectual Property & Entertainment Law 7, no. 2 (2018): 53 (explaining the need for agencies to analyze product, here blockchain, modifications).
[74] *See* Kyle Torpey, "BIP 9: Enabling Easier Changes and Upgrades to Bitcoin," Bitcoin Magazine, January 27, 2016, https://perma.cc/JVM7-N7FZ.
[75] *See* Jeffery Atik and George Gerro, "Hard Forks on the Bitcoin Blockchain: Reversible Exit, Continuing Voice," Stanford Journal of Blockchain Law & Policy 1 (2018): 28.

activate automatically thanks to the signaling of a majority of miners, with no "voting."[76]

Similarly, Ethereum uses Ethereum Improvement Proposals. Ethereum developers also use Ethereum requests for comments to discuss these proposals before putting them to a vote.[77] Here again, coordination is made possible between developers and anyone accessing the forum. Antitrust agencies will, without a doubt, monitor the exchanges allowed by these mechanisms. Last, let me underline that one can use all forms of communication available after real-life identities are identified. The "Awemany episode," which I described in Chapter 1, illustrates core developers' ability to make the right phone call to the relevant mining pools.

As for private blockchains, the risk of collusion regarding the core client is even greater. While no one can force participants to use a specific core client in public blockchains (economic incentives direct them toward a single one), things are different with private blockchains, where the gatekeeper can impose one client on all participants. Further, the gatekeeper retains the ability to amend the core client. It can implement a change, for example, after consultation with specific participants only. Where such power exists, one may easily see how unilateral interventions create control over the blockchain, which could ultimately prompt collusive agreements when a few blockchain participants are involved in deciding the change or unilateral conduct when only one participant is changing the consensus.

One recent case illustrates the anticompetitive potential of modifying one blockchain core code. In late 2019, four lawsuits were filed by crypto investors over alleged manipulation of the cryptocurrency Tether and the exchange Bitfinex. Consolidated in January 2020, these actions relied on an academic paper first published in 2018 by John M. Griffin (University of Texas at Austin) and Amin Shams (Ohio State University). They argued that Tether and Bitfinex had coordinated to manipulate the price of Bitcoin.[78]

According to the plaintiffs, Tether issued 2.8 billion tether tokens between 2017 and 2018 with the ambition to flood the Bitfinex exchange while falsely pretending that U.S. dollars fully backed its tokens (a stablecoin, i.e., a cryptocurrency designed to minimize volatility).[79] The defendants used this unbacked

---

[76]   *Id.* at 29.

[77]   "Ethereum Improvement Proposals," Ethereum, https://perma.cc/NXC5-CTTT.

[78]   John M. Griffin and Amin Shams, "Is Bitcoin Really Un-Tethered?," The Journal of Finance 75, no. 4 (2020).

[79]   *Leibowitz et al. v. iFinex et al.*, 1:19-cv-09236-KPF (S.D.N.Y. 2019): point 87 ("Until February 2019, Tether was saying on its website that all USDT (its token) were 'backed 1-1 by traditional currency held in our reserves. So 1 USDT is always equivalent to 1 USD'").

Tether ("USDT") to purchase Bitcoin, which led to artificial pricing in the cryptocurrency market, as it allowed Bitfinex and Tether to wrongfully "signal to the market that there was rapidly growing demand for cryptocurrencies."[80] The bubble eventually burst and $466 billion in value was lost in less than a month. The plaintiffs are asking for over $1.4 trillion in (treble) damages.

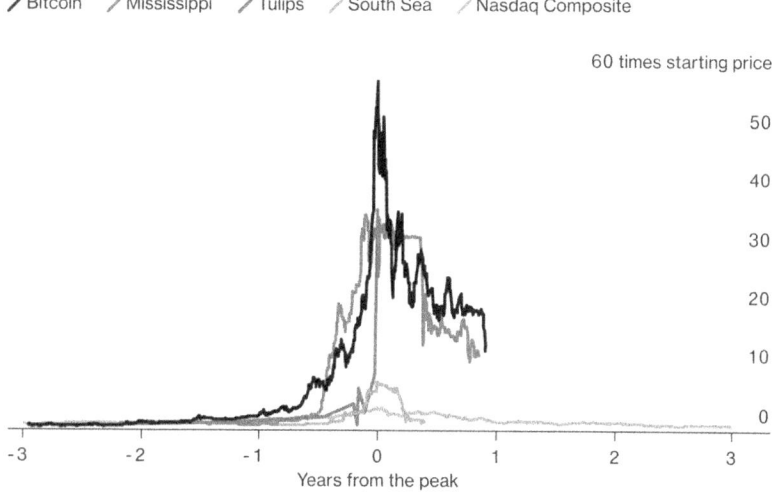

Source: Eric Lam et al., "Did Bitcoin Just Burst? How It Compares to History's Big Bubbles," Bloomberg, January 17, 2018, https://perma.cc/8XXD-RGGK.

Figure 8.1   Cryptocurrency bubble between 2017–18

The plaintiffs are introducing eight causes of action, one of which concerns antitrust laws and, more specifically, Section 2 of the Sherman Act. According to the plaintiffs, Tether controlled at the time "more than 80% of the market for stablecoins in the United States and the world. Tether therefore ha[d] monopoly power."[81] On that basis, the plaintiffs argue that the "issuance of unbacked USDT was designed to gain greater market share so Tether could eliminate stablecoin competition and maintain pricing control over the bitcoin and cryp-

---

[80] *Leibowitz v. iFinex*, Case 1:19-cv-09236-KPF: point 6. According to the plaintiff, "half the growth in the cryptocurrency market was driven by Bitfinex and Tether's manipulative scheme", *see Leibowitz v. iFinex*, Case 1:19-cv-09236-KPF: point 11.

[81] *Leibowitz v. iFinex*, Case 1:19-cv-09236-KPF: point 273.

tocurrency market."[82] This supposed monopolization practice "inflate[d] one of the largest bubbles in history."[83]

While the definition of the relevant market remains to be debated,[84] and the merits of the practices should be analyzed in the light of numerous (and contrary) proofs, one can already draw several lessons from this case.

The first lesson concerns the subject matter. The first blockchain antitrust cases – known to date[85] – all concern cryptocurrencies, showing that for now, the field is still very much focused on blockchain 1.0.[86] The second lesson concerns the ability to manipulate blockchain, or, at the very least, to influence its value. But one should nonetheless underline Tether's very particular infrastructure, allowing only a few users to decide among themselves the creation of new tokens. This indicates the necessity to study the "power game"[87] within each blockchain – which implies understanding the norms, the market, the law and the digital architecture on a case-by-case basis, and how interactions between blockchain participants may influence them.

The third lesson is the ability to apply antitrust law when the identities of blockchain participants are public, and when powerful analytical tools are used to detect potential practices. The academic article which led to this case studied "over 200 gigabytes of transactional data from over ten different sources."[88] Performing such an analysis requires specific methods and means. Future cases concerning blockchain 2.0 and 3.0 – where the identity of transactions is not strictly financial – will not only require even more sophisticated means, but will call for regulators to cooperate with blockchain communities to enforce the rule of law. The fourth and final lesson relates, once again, to the necessity to think of antitrust law and blockchain together. As one can see, and regardless of the merits of this particular case, blockchain is an infrastructure that does not prevent all (potential) anticompetitive practices by itself (regardless of the merits of that particular case). It needs antitrust law.

---

[82]   *Id.* at point 276.

[83]   *Id.* at point 107.

[84]   To follow the docket activity, *see In re Tether and Bitfinex Crypto Asset Litigation*, Case Number 1:19-cv-09236, in the U.S. District Court for the Southern District of New York.

[85]   *Gallagher v. Bitcointalk.org et al.*, 3:18-cv-05892-EMC (N.D. Cal. 2018); *United American Corp. v. Bitmain, Inc.*, 1:18-cv-25106-KMW (S.D. Fla. 2018); and *Leibowitz v. iFinex*, Case 1:19-cv-09236-KPF.

[86]   *See* Chapter 3.

[87]   *See* Chapter 7.

[88]   *Leibowitz v. iFinex*: point 128.

3.2.2 Forks

Not all modifications to the rules of a blockchain result in surviving forks. Some are adopted by the entire blockchain community, but a large majority are rejected. Forks are dangerous from an economic standpoint, as they can divide the value and usefulness of the blockchain. This is one important reason why blockchain communities want to avoid them, generally speaking. Only exceptionally will both chains become valuable in the long run – this is what happened with Bitcoin and Bitcoin Cash, or Ethereum and Ethereum Classic. In most situations, one of the two chains will be abandoned, along with all the transactions recorded on it.[89]

Authorities should pay close attention to forks resulting from an external group trying to weaken a blockchain. One can easily imagine a group of blockchain participants reducing the competitive pressure by forking a competing blockchain before abandoning it. Antitrust law will apply to these situations. Conversely, a fork that stems from a blockchain's own participants and proves to be genuinely viable cannot be qualified as an anticompetitive practice. It results from the desire of a portion of that blockchain community to ensure long-term survival by modifying the rules.

A recent case at the border of these two strategies helps understand the underlying logic. In *United American Corp. v. Bitmain*, the U.S. District Court for the Southern District of Florida had to decide on the legality of a fork from the Bitcoin Cash blockchain. What happened? In August 2018, a change was proposed to allow the blockchain to accept larger blocks, which had the advantage of speeding up the validation of transactions and facilitating the blockchain's scalability. Bitcoin.com mining pools supported this change. Another fraction of that blockchain – which included United American Corp. – opposed the move, pointing out that only a few miners would then have the necessary capacity to validate the new blocks (as they would require significantly more computing power).[90]

The change was implemented on November 15, 2018. Within minutes, Bitmain Technologies redirected its mining power toward the validation of

---

[89] The same goes for the reward, *see* Alyssa Hertig, "Why Are Miners Involved in Bitcoin Code Changes Anyway?," Coindesk, July 30, 2017, https://perma.cc/AZ3J-HZXB. In practice, "[t]he vast majority of forks are transitory-one breach is abandoned and the entire community re-aligns around the surviving branch, which then forms the canonical blockchain," *see* Jeffery Atik and George Gerro, "Hard Forks on the Bitcoin Blockchain: Reversible Exit, Continuing Voice," 29.

[90] Discussing how to balance these interests, *see* Vitalik Buterin, "The Limits to Blockchain Scalability," Vitalik Buterin's website May 23, 2021, https://perma.cc/6K2S-9455 (underlining that "[i]t's crucial for blockchain decentralization for regular users to be able to run a node").

blocks following the new rules. The objective, it seems, was to surpass United American Corp.'s mining power and thus to motivate a majority of users to join the new chain. It succeeded a few hours later and implemented a mechanism for "locking down" the blockchain immediately afterward.[91]

The plaintiff argued that Bitcoin.com had conspired illegally with Bitmain Technologies by renting its mining power to take over the blockchain.[92] The district court dismissed the initial complaint in February 2020, and in April 2021, found that because of the absence of evidence showing coordination between Bitcoin.com and Bitmain, Section 1 of the Sherman Act had not been violated.[93]

Supposing here that Bitcoin.com had indeed rented Bitmain Technologies' computing power, and conspired against United American Corp., the plaintiff would have had the burden of proving that the agreement had actually been implemented to harm the blockchain and reduce its chances of survival. Put another way, United American Corp. would have been required to show that the fork was made to benefit some users only. This would have been difficult to prove. In the absence, and because antitrust law does not protect competitors

---

[91] According to the plaintiff, "The decision by Sechet, Chancellor and Cox to 'lock down' the block chain after an arbitrary number of blocks close to the tip of the blockchain – through a mechanism referred to as 'checkpoints' and 'Deep Reorg Prevention' – will allow anyone with 51% hashing power to quickly cement control of the blockchain ledger. They would also cement control over future changes to Bitcoin Cash functionality as well as changes to the consensus rules. Combining this checkpoint power with the hashing power of Bitcoin ABC backers like Ver (through Bitcoin.com) and Wu (through Bitmain Technologies' mining pools, AntPool and BTC.com) amounts to centralization. Anyone who combines hashing power and checkpoints in this fashion will be able to override any consensus reached by the rest of the network, forcing others to conform or create an unwanted hard fork," *see* point 90 of the amended complaint.

[92] For Ethereum, a similar question would include renting "tokens" rather than computing power. On that, *see* Vitalik Buterin, "On Collusion," Vitalik Buterin's website, April 3, 2019, https://perma.cc/FE58-ZVJY ("there's an even cheaper attack than buying donuts (an attack that can be thought of as a kind of obfuscated bribe): renting them. If an attacker is already holding ETH, they can use it as collateral on a platform like Compound to take out a loan of some token, giving you the full right to use that token for whatever purpose including participating in votes.")

[93] *United American Corp. v. Bitmain, Inc.*, 1:18-cv-25106-KMW (S.D. Fla. 2021), Order Granting Defendants' Joint Motion to Dismiss First Amended Complaint ("As noted, defendants' allegedly unlawful conduct fits into neither a horizontal, vertical nor hub-and-spoke restraint of trade paradigm …". "After a painstaking review of the Complaint, the Court concludes that it lacks facts that create a reasonable expectation that discovery will reveal evidence of illegal agreement.") The final judgment was issued on April 7, 2021.

or economic agents, no infringement to Section 1 of the Sherman Act would have been found despite the proof of an agreement.[94]

In any case, this litigation helps understand why blockchain and antitrust must be thought of together and not in silos. For example, had the Court concluded on the basis of that case that all forks are illegal (because, after all, they are agreements reducing the original blockchains' value), this would have deprived blockchain communities of an essential feature: the possibility to exit the blockchain and compete with it. And, at times, forks are also essential to fix bugs in the blockchain core code (or improve it) and therefore make it a better infrastructure. In short, courts and agencies must keep in mind that, because blockchains are overall beneficial to consumers, practices within them must be analyzed with the intention to preserve the technology. *Per se* rules and other prohibitions related to blockchain's essential features should be avoided for that reason.

3.2.3   Applications

We have already seen that blockchain's ecosystems are built on different interrelated layers. For that reason, whoever wants to study blockchain's sixth level – that is, applications – must do so in the context of the entire ecosystem and its key characteristics. The famous "The DAO" incident neatly illustrates why looking at this broader picture is so important.

On June 17, 2016, someone discovered a vulnerability in the smart contract governing The DAO, a decentralized autonomous organization.[95] It had been exploited by one user who seized over 3.6 million Ether; but thanks to The DAO design, these tokens had been frozen for 28 days before being transferred permanently. A debate ensued within the Ethereum community regarding the creation of a blockchain fork in which one would modify the smart contract to retransfer all the stolen Ether before the deadline. A vast majority of the Ethereum community answered in the affirmative, allowing them to fork the blockchain successfully, and withdraw the funds.[96]

This episode is interesting insofar as a blockchain application – here a smart contract (blockchain 2.0) – has been modified at a lower level. This shows that blockchain's immutability also applies to that level. In The DAO case, block-chain participants had no choice but to (re)transfer the funds rather than cancel

---

[94]   The agreement would not have considered to restrain interstate or foreign trade, *see* 15 U.S.C. § 1. For a similar practice, *see* Yilun Chen, "Tron takeover? Steem community in uproar as crypto exchanges back reversal of blockchain governance soft fork," The Block, March 2, 2020, https://perma.cc/T5PM-L493.

[95]   The name is confusing. I am here discussing a specific DAO, called "The DAO."

[96]   *See* Luit Hollander, "History of Ethereum Hard Forks," Medium, May 4, 2020, https://perma.cc/6DEM-YCWJ.

the original transfer. To what extent can this constitute an illegal agreement? Here again, when the practice takes place within the nucleus to protect the blockchain, it escapes antitrust, as it results from a single entity. The situation is quite different when it results from the anticompetitive intention of a group of users who do not intend to ensure the blockchain's survival. In such cases, the practice is not implemented within the blockchain nucleus, and therefore is not protected by that legal fiction. This opens the door to antitrust enforcement.

4   CHAPTER SUMMARY AND BEYOND

In this chapter, I first examined whether the creation of a blockchain could, in itself, amount to a violation of antitrust laws. This seems unlikely as far as public permissionless blockchains are concerned. Conversely, the design of private blockchains could lead to the creation of an anticompetitive cartel, depending on the parameters.

I then analyzed the extent to which the running of blockchains could amount to anticompetitive collusion. More specifically, I examined practices regarding the operation or the modification of blockchains. I explained that the day-to-day operation of a blockchain might lead to coordination and raise antitrust issues. This coordination includes decisions about the entry into a blockchain, the consensus mechanism and the calculation of fees. When it comes to modifying a blockchain – changes to the core client, the implementation of a fork or practices impacting applications – I explained that courts and agencies should distinguish between internal and external practices. The former, which are implemented by the blockchain nucleus, should be deemed legal. The latter could infringe antitrust. The distinction between public and private blockchains has proven central to my analysis.

So far, I have analyzed practices that mainly affect blockchain ecosystems. In the next chapter, I turn to practices where blockchains are anticompetitively used in a way that directly impacts the "real space." Here, the distinction between public and private blockchains also proves to be crucial, but for a different reason: the governance it allows.

9. Collusion using blockchain

1   GETTING STARTED

Companies may want to use blockchain to set up collusive agreements concerning the "real space." While there are clear reasons why companies may want to do so, as opposed to using a non-blockchain medium, it appears even more beneficial for them to augment blockchain with smart contracts. By doing so, they can indeed govern their agreements while benefiting from blockchain's core characteristics, such as immutability.

1.1   No Smart Contract

Companies may use blockchain to enter into collusive agreements.[1] By so doing, their intention might be to ensure the visibility and traceability of any shared information in order to organize their collusion more efficiently. In that respect, public and private blockchains offer distinct advantages.

When the blockchain is public, companies can ensure that they have access to all information listed in the same place, with no user hiding anything from others.[2] For example, all the colluders may use a blockchain to share the price of their products. Doing so would reinforce their trust, as it would provide them with a constant flow of immutable information, accessible at all times. That being said, companies may also fear that sharing information on public blockchains will make it easier for enforcers to detect their agreements (though

---

[1]   *See* Hitoshi Matsushima, "Blockchain Disables Real-World Governance," Kyoto University, Institute of Economic Research Working Papers 1017 (2019): 2 ("once a blockchain becomes available, agents can execute agreements regardless of their legality and without help from trusted intermediaries"). Let us note here that setting up a collusion on blockchain does not necessitate in-depth technical knowledge of the technology. Multiple services are offered to companies to help them design a blockchain or use an existing one, *see* generally "Substrate," Parity, https://perma.cc/2WMU -2SMG. It can be assumed that blockchain will be used for collusive agreements of a significant size rather than for agreements with little impact on the market.

[2]   Lin William Cong and Zhiguo He, "Blockchain Disruption and Smart Contracts" (2017): 20 ("greater information distribution may foster collusion which hurts competition").

the information could be encrypted). It will be interesting to see how this plays out and the extent to which public blockchains will be used to support collusive behavior.

When a blockchain is private, all the companies involved in a collusive agreement get exclusive and secure access to the information. This feature can help strengthen cohesion between them, as it leads to a lower detection risk.[3] Private blockchains also allow the information to be certified before being published, which once again creates a considerable advantage over physical agreements or digital media other than blockchain. And, similarly to public blockchains, the immutability of information published on private blockchains could reinforce the colluders' trust in each other. For that reason, private blockchains appear to constitute a great medium for organizing collusive practices.

1.2   Smart Contract!

As we have already seen, smart contracts are potential transactions recorded in a blockchain and automatically executed if and when several conditions are met.[4] For example, they can be used for the automatic unlocking of an apartment door rented on Airbnb when the fee is sent to the owner's account. They can be implemented to create an agreement between companies whose governance follows a combination of smart contracts. But they might also encompass illegal agreements. On top of using a blockchain to collude, companies may set up smart contracts to automate the agreement and make it more predictable and transparent between them.

With a public blockchain, smart contracts can be implemented so that the information published on the blockchain serves as a parameter for the agreement that will be adjusted accordingly. For instance, a smart contract could automate transfers between colluders and make side payments. It could also set a collusive price for sharing markets.

With a private blockchain, smart contracts may serve the same purpose as public blockchains – that is, governing the relationship between users. They may also be used to govern the agreement's framework by deciding what information is published and who has access to it (which can be changed at any moment in time). Private blockchains allow the most sophisticated level

---

[3]   The Law Society and Tech London Advocates, "Blockchain: Legal and Regulatory Guidance Report," The Law Society, September 7, 2020: 57, https://perma .cc/3HUN-J62G (discussing the exchange of sensible information in the context of private blockchains).

[4]   For an overview of smart contracts' functioning *see* Thibault Schrepel, "Smart Contracts and the Digital Single Market Through the Lens of a 'Law + Technology' Approach," European Commission (2021).

of governance. They would thus be an ideal tool to implement collusive agreements.

Whether they rely on public or private blockchains, smart contracts fundamentally alter the nature of collusion. There are two reasons for this. First, blockchain-based collusion is cooperative. Because these smart contracts are coded directly into the blockchain, their immutability may strengthen collusion's stability by forcing certain behaviors (as long as they concern online actions, such as making a payment). Second, they make collusion genuinely dynamic. This characteristic is worrying, as one can easily implement smart contracts without technical knowledge.[5]

I will explore these reasons in the next section. For now, let me simply mention that smart contracts may use common libraries and be combined.[6] In other words, the execution of one smart contract could be conditioned to another. This ultimately enables colluders to maintain complex governance mechanisms.[7] In short, they have the potential to make collusion efficient, robust and hard to detect.

2　　LIVING UP: THE DOUBLE EFFECT

Cartel stability depends on economic and social elements. Indeed, collusion succeeds when participants have more to gain from cooperation than deviation (the "economic perspective" of cartel stability). Colluders must also trust that none of them will denounce the others by applying for leniency (the "social perspective" of cartel stability).[8] These two perspectives complement one

---

[5]　Multiple services offer to convert plain language into smart contracts. *See*, for example, OpenLaw, "OpenLaw," https://perma.cc/C42U-J7PL. Other services, enabling "no-code" programming, allow the creation of blockchain applications without writing a single line of code, *see*, for example, Oasis Labs, "Blockchain & Data Privacy," XDocs, https://perma.cc/54VK-HGMV; Xooa, https://perma.cc/ 4AQ9-GHUF; Kaleido, "Zapier," https://perma.cc/WN8D-S5MH; Julian, "Building a No-Code Blockchain App with IBM Blockchain Platform and Joget on OpenShift," Joget Blog: Joget Open Source Low Code Application Platform News and Updates (blog), February 25, 2020, https://perma.cc/XHZ9-S5DW. On the subject, *see* Michael Tuijp, "No-Code Blockchain Integration: The Future of Business-to-Blockchain?" Medium (blog), July 11, 2020, https://perma.cc/HHT3-7JQ4.

[6]　*See* generally "Contracts: Libraries," Solidity, https://perma.cc/CVZ2-ZJY9.

[7]　*See* "Interactions Between Smart Contracts with Solidity," Zupzup, https://perma .cc/XW9V-F89T (detailing different ways to link smart contracts).

[8]　For an explanation of the economic perspective, *see* Robert C. Marshall and Leslie M. Marx, *The Economics of Collusion: Cartels and Bidding Rings* (MIT Press, 2012): 108. For an explanation of the social perspective, *see* J.D. Jaspers, "Managing Cartels: How Cartel Participants Create Stability in the Absence of Law," European Journal on Criminal Policy and Research 23 (2017): 319, 322.

another; indeed, colluders have no interest in leaving the agreement (and denouncing it) if the illicit gains are high while the risk of detection is low.

Blockchains can be helpful on both fronts. For a start, blockchain provides colluders with more information than they get using another medium—I call this the "visibility effect." At the same time, blockchains also ensure that agreements are opaque to outsiders, such as non-colluding competitors and agencies—I call this the "opacity effect."

2.1   The "Visibility Effect"

Blockchains provide transparency to their participants. Colluders may monitor each other's market behavior more easily inside the blockchain than outside of it. As a result, blockchains prevent the ability to deviate secretly. This strengthens trust between colluders or, at least, the confidence they have in the information on which the collusion is based. Blockchains may also correct deviation by imposing targeted sanctions.

2.1.1   Preventing deviant behaviors

2.1.1.1   More stability
Blockchain may automate governance and therefore prevent deviation. To understand why this is crucial to colluders, one must first analyze the conditions that make collusion sustainable.

Because anticompetitive agreements are illegal, colluders cannot deploy legally binding contracts to ensure their implementation. As a result, the strategy of their co-conspirators is highly unpredictable. They act in their own interests, making the stability of agreements highly dependent on each party's benefits. Thus, collusion is said to be non-cooperative;[9] it follows that the ability to observe each other's actions and interact frequently is crucial for stability. "Trust begins where prediction ends."[10]

Blockchain helps in that regard. By granting firms access to an extensive amount of information, public blockchains enhance the ability to observe other colluders' practices. The nature of information stays fundamentally the same. Still, blockchain gathers all information in the same place and ensures its immutability. This proves helpful to colluders—for example, one company

---

[9]   Louis Kaplow, *Competition Policy and Price Fixing* (Princeton University Press, 2013): 177 ("the fundamental distinction between cooperative and noncooperative games is that cooperative games allow binding agreements while noncooperative games do not.")

[10]   J. David Lewis and Andrew Weigert, "Trust as a Social Reality," *Social Forces* 63, no. 4 (1985): 967, 976.

cannot modify the ledger to hide a deviation from the cartel. Blockchain visibility also prevents deviation because the risk of detection by other colluders is high.[11] Of course, the ability to detect cheating is not the only determinant of the cartel's duration,[12] and blockchains will not make cartels indefinite. Still, one may expect collusive agreements to become more stable thanks to the easier identification of deviations.

On top of that, smart contracts may ensure the execution of agreements between participants. For instance, firms could automatically record all transactions and detect unusual transactional flows by any of the colluders, such as a deviation from the collusive price. They could also regulate the price that colluders charge, and smart contracts can allow an automatic distribution of earnings according to pre-defined criteria. Their theoretical immutability is important in that regard:[13] they have the potential to strengthen the economic and social stability of collusion. Higher (illegal) gains can therefore be achieved.[14]

In a sense, smart contracts help to transform collusion into a cooperative game.[15] The importance of the medium in which the game is played (here blockchain) is often underestimated, yet it is very important in our case. Considering that about half of collusive agreements end because of internal conflicts between their members,[16] and that those conflicts mostly arise after deviation by a colluder, one should not underplay the importance of blockchain as a medium.

---

[11] Margaret C. Levenstein and Valerie Y. Suslow, "What Determines Cartel Success?" Journal of Economic Literature 44, no. 1 (2006): 67, 69.

[12] Although it is an important one, *see* D.K. Osborne, "Cartel Problems," The American Economic Review 66, no. 5 (1976): 835; see also Nicolas Petit, *Droit européen de la concurrence* (Lextenso, 2018): 245.

[13] *See infra* Appendix 1.

[14] *See* Christopher R. Leslie, "Antitrust Amnesty, Game Theory, and Cartel Stability," Journal of Corporation Law 31 (2006): 462 ("When players utilizing trusting strategies are paired up, they solve the prisoner's dilemma in experiments and achieve greater gains than those using distrusting strategies."); James P. Gahagan and James T. Tedeschi, "Strategy and the Credibility of Promises in the Prisoner's Dilemma Game," Journal of Conflict Resolution 12, no. 2 (1968): 224, 226; David M. Messick et al., "Individual Adaptations and Structural Change as Solutions to Social Dilemmas," Journal of Personality and Social Psychology 44, no. 2 (1983): 294.

[15] Expressed in terms of game theory, the study of mathematical models for projecting scenarios between players.

[16] *See* Margaret C. Levenstein and Valerie Y. Suslow, "What Determines Cartel Success?" Journal of Economic Literature 44, no. 1 (2006): 43, 75–76.

2.1.1.2   Limits

Despite the previous developments, one should not expect blockchain to help the cartelization of the entire economy. Collusion using the technology will, indeed, encounter several limits.

The first relates to the quasi-absence of human intervention in smart contracts' execution, making them highly inflexible. This creates difficulties for colluders willing to adapt to market fluctuations and other unforeseen events during collusion.[17] It forces colluders to insert some flexibility into their agreements' governance by permitting human intervention while trying to maintain blockchain's immutable features.

Practically, it will require them to design smart "smart contracts" – including narrowly defined clauses for colluders to intervene. Blockchain participants could also use decentralized applications (D-Apps). Any software could be turned into a D-App and be inserted into a smart contract, creating an almost infinite number of possibilities for antitrust and competition law infringements.[18] The result is that blockchain-based collusion is immutable by nature, which builds trust; but is also adaptable, since D-Apps give colluders flexibility to bring external forces to the very same contract. It allows machines (D-Apps) or physical persons to change the collusion trajectory while maintaining its initial existence. Implementing D-Apps, however, requires technical expertise.

The alternative will be for colluders to encode only part of their agreement on the blockchain and leave the rest to legal contracts.[19] Such proceedings may prove attractive for parties that wish to avoid smart contracts' inherent limitations. But in so doing, the parties would lose the assurance that the agreement would be properly executed because it would be (partially) de-automated.

---

[17] Notably, it removes smart contracts from the domain of judicial oversight, including mutual mistake, illegality, capacity, consideration, fraud and duress. *See* Kevin Werbach, *The Blockchain and the New Architecture of Trust* (MIT Press, 2018): 126.

[18] For a more detailed explanation of how the D-Apps function, *see* "Chainlink: Linking Smart Contracts with Real-World Applications," State of the Dapps, September 4, 2019, https://perma.cc/BQ5S-DT99.

[19] In fact, "[s]everal groups are building solutions using the mutual hashing of smart and legal contracts, including a subgroup of the R3 consortium led by the British bank Barclays, the Monax Burrow software now part of the Hyperledger open source project, and OpenLaw." *See* Kevin Werbach, "Trust, But Verify: Why the Blockchain Needs the Law," Berkeley Technology Law Journal 33 (2018): 489, 544. "Legal contract" is here defined as a "program that runs on the brain of a lawyer," *see* Tim Ferriss, "Nick Szabo Interview," in The Tim Ferriss Show (Podcast), YouTube, published on June 4, 2017, https://perma.cc/Y7Z5-72PY.

They would then engage in the complicated art of maintaining a fair balance between all participants' interests in the long run.

A second major limit to the stability of collusion using blockchains relates to the use of oracles. When the conditions for triggering smart contracts refer to the information contained within the blockchain, no particular issue of trust arises. For instance, if one designs a smart contract that transfers a token when its value goes over a certain amount, the entire operation can be easily automated. Conversely, when smart contracts refer to information coming from the outside world, an issue appears as to whether one should trust the accuracy of the information documented. For example, if a smart contract is triggered when an aircraft is over an hour late, sending compensation to all passengers, how can one ensure the delay will be properly recorded within the blockchain?

The algorithm or device used to find the information in the real space and document it within the blockchain is called an "oracle." Oracles are essential to many smart contracts. They reintroduce trust issues because they introduce a single point of failure that can have practical consequences for the stability of the collusion or any type of agreement. For that reason, part of the blockchain community is working toward fixing that issue. Different initiatives are underway; but first, it is important to explain the differences between varieties of oracles, as they each raise specific issues.

Some oracles are physical or tangible devices that measure real-world values, such as temperature or whether a shipment has arrived safely (using chips). Other oracles are intangible and comprise only code. That said, one must make a further distinction between single node oracles and a distributed network of oracles.[20] The first relies on one source of information, while the second combines several oracles to create an average of the information they communicate.[21]

One may logically expect collusive smart contracts to rely mostly on intangible single node oracles. These are highly centralized by nature – which creates a trust issue.[22] Their centralization is also problematic from an antitrust

---

[20] Ekin Tuna, "Design Considerations: Centralized and Decentralized Oracles," Medium, June 5, 2019, https://perma.cc/YGA4-LYHC. For an overview of oracles' functioning *see* Thibault Schrepel, "Smart Contracts and the Digital Single Market Through the Lens of a 'Law + Technology' Approach," European Commission (2021).

[21] Mike Orcutt, "Blockchain Smart Contracts are Finally Good for Something in the Real World," MIT Technology Review, November 19, 2018, https://perma .cc/6HPN-FSPD. Also, World Economic Forum, "Bridging the Governance Gap: Interoperability for Blockchain and Legacy Systems: White Paper," World Economic Forum, December 9, 2020: 16, https://perma.cc/W5RM-L843 (insisting on the necessity to build an oracle network that operates across blockchain environments).

[22] As such, they may be used for collusive purposes; on that, *see* Lin William Cong and Zhiguo He, "Blockchain Disruption and Smart Contracts," Review of Financial

perspective, as agencies could see the use of the same oracle by several competitors as anticompetitive.[23]

Several proposals are in development to solve that issue of centralization and reliance. For example, one could use intangible distributed oracles.[24] Oracles could also apply a voting game that motivates users to validate the correct data.[25] Vitalik Buterin offered one of the first proposals for a trusted data feed by introducing the SchellingCoin.[26] Other solutions will be put forward; but for now, oracles are a thorn in the side of colluders.

For that reason, one may wonder whether smart contracts will rely on genies instead of oracles. An oracle is a question-answering machine, while a genie is a command-executing system.[27] After receiving a high-level command, the genie seeks to follow the spirit rather than the letter of that command.[28] It overcomes the issue of documenting the outside world into the blockchain; the genie works by extrapolating distances to bridge the gap between the two. But of course, genies and other AI-related solutions come with issues in terms of design and subsequent control.

2.1.2   Correcting deviation

Besides preventing deviations, blockchain and smart contracts can be used to punish them. Specifically, the sale of a product at a different price than that agreed upon by colluders could be automatically recorded and punished by smart contracts. These smart contracts could be automated on the basis of several conditions combined (e.g., duration, spread with the collusive price). They would play a part in reinforcing collusion; indeed, the threat of automated and targeted punishments de-incentivizes deviations. After all, "one of the greatest curbs on crime is not the cruelty of punishments, but their infal-

---

Studies (2017): 1754, 1781 (explaining that shared oracle services may provide the possibility of tacit collusion).

[23]   Similarly, *see "Eturas" UAB and Others v Lietuvos Respublikos konkurencijos taryba*, Case C-74/14, ECLI:EU:C:2016:42 (ECJ, 2016) (discussing the anticompetitiveness of two companies using a "uniform booking method").

[24]   Nick Bostrom, *Superintelligence: Paths, Dangers, Strategies* (Oxford University Press, 2014): 179.

[25]   John Adler, Ryan Berryhill and Andreas Veneris, "Astraea: A decentralized Blockchain Oracle," 2018 IEEE International Conference on Internet of Things (2018), https://perma.cc/A6C3-GFDH.

[26]   Vitalik Buterin, "SchellingCoin: A Minimal-Trust Universal Data Feed," Ethereum (blog), March 28, 2014, https://perma.cc/9Z99-DPKF.

[27]   Nick Bostrom, *Superintelligence: Paths, Dangers, Strategies* (Oxford University Press, 2014): 181.

[28]   *Id.* at 191.

libility ... The certainty of punishment, even if moderate, will always make a stronger impression."[29]

We know from empirical work that intentional deviation must be visibly and effectively punished for collusion to persist.[30] The threat of returning to a competitive situation may deter such behavior,[31] but ideally, the punishment must be directed only at the deviation.[32] Blockchain could help colluders in that regard. One way would be to request an initial payment of tokens to participate in the agreement and then automatically regulate their distribution based on the party's compliance.[33] But of course, this would require a rather large monetary sum that could be picked up during annual audits. More simply, one could adjust the blockchain's participation fees according to each colluder's past behaviors or expectations, making it more expensive for certain members to be part of, or deviate from, the agreement.

Unintentional deviation is usually not as problematic for the cartel's stability, as long as it does not occur too often and deviations are compensated in a way that preserves each colluder's interests. Blockchain and smart contracts make that possible, as they can be used to ensure a fair balance by redistributing any extra profits made by a deviation between all colluders. Here again, they improve the stability of collusive agreements.

Whether the deviation is intentional or not, smart contracts should indeed compensate for the gains made by a deviating member to avoid the possibility of lucrative infringement (which occurs when the benefits are higher than the punishment). This economic element of cartel stability depends on the perceived and actual profits that result from cheating compared with the likelihood of punishment by other colluders.[34] By increasing the detection of

---

[29] Cesare Beccaria, *On Crimes and Punishments*, trans. David Young (Hackett Publishing Co., 1986): 58.

[30] *See* Daniel Orr and Paul W. MacAvoy, "Price Strategies to Promote Cartel Stability," Economica 32, no. 126 (1965): 186.

[31] Robert C. Marshall and Leslie M. Marx, *The Economics of Collusion: Cartels and Bidding Rings* (MIT Press, 2012): 136. *See* also Ian Ayres, "How Cartels Punish: A Structural Theory of Self-Enforcing Collusion," Columbia Law Review 87 (1987): 295, 302. Deviance regarding the pricing structure is especially problematic in terms of cartel survival, *see* Robert C. Marshall and Leslie M. Marx, *The Economics of Collusion: Cartels and Bidding Rings* (MIT Press, 2019): 106. For that reason, smart contracts may be directed against such practices before others.

[32] Robert C. Marshall and Leslie M. Marx, *The Economics of Collusion: Cartels and Bidding Rings* (MIT Press, 2019): 137.

[33] *See* Vitalik Buterin, "Decentralizing Everything," YouTube, published on September 18, 2017, https://perma.cc/4Q5K-TLH2 (discussing this mechanism).

[34] J.D. Jaspers, "Managing Cartels: How Cartel Participants Create Stability in the Absence of Law," European Journal on Criminal Policy and Research 23, (2017): 319, 321–22 ("[C]artels invest more in means to prevent cheating than to resort to ex post

deviation and the potential accuracy of sentences, blockchain will raise the costs of misbehaving and make collusive agreements more stable.

2.2   The "Opacity Effect"

Despite creating a strong "visibility effect," blockchain generates a concomitant "opacity effect;" it does not make information available to everyone – and especially not to competitors and agencies. Blockchain increases members' trust in one another because it protects them from being detected, which has great implications for agencies' investigations.

2.2.1   Detection

2.2.1.1   *Stability*

As I have shown, public and private blockchains provide users with different opacity settings. Public blockchains are freely accessible, and all the information they contain is part of the public domain. Anyone can access it without even "entering" the blockchain.[35] One needs no membership or authorization. For example, the history of all Bitcoin transactions is open to all, regardless of whether one is a Bitcoin owner. Private blockchains have opposite features. Information stored on private blockchains is available only to its users and can be channeled to just some of them.[36] Both types of blockchain, however, generate a "visibility effect" (among colluders) while producing an "opacity effect" (among non-colluders).

This double effect exists on public blockchains because all transactions are hashed through cryptographic functions,[37] and because users' identities are protected by pseudonymity. For instance, only the sending and receiving

---

punishments, which are costly."). More generally, see Richard J. Gilbert, *Innovation Matters: Competition Policy for the High-Technology Economy* (MIT Press, 2020): 117.

[35]   *See* Dylan Yaga et al., "Blockchain Technology Overview," NIST Interagency/Internal Report 8202 (2018): 44.

[36]   *See* Kevin Werbach, *The Blockchain and the New Architecture of Trust* (MIT Press, 2018): 96 ("[Private blockchain] generally provide[s] granular controls on who can *see* and manage information on the ledger ... A permissioned distributed ledger system grants control over access. It may also grant parties different levels of visibility into transactions compared to the fully transparent approach of public blockchain systems.")

[37]   *See id.* at 45 ("Converting a file into a hash is easy but going from the hash back to the original file is virtually impossible except through massive trial and error.") Generally speaking, hashing is the process of taking an input (information on the blockchain) and turning it into a cryptographic output.

Bitcoin addresses, the Bitcoin amount and a timestamp appear on the Bitcoin blockchain.[38] On Ethereum, one may identify whether the transaction results from a smart contract (as this information shows), but the agreement's terms remain secret.[39] More specifically, the source code of the smart contract itself (e.g., the Solidity code for Ethereum's smart contracts) is generally not stored on the blockchain.[40] Only the compiled bytecode is stored on it, so that the Virtual Machine can execute the smart contract when it is being called. One cannot convert that bytecode back into the original programming language without missing information. A meticulous translation could give a sense of what the smart contract is all about, but that is about it.[41]

As a result, analyzing the transactions made by one user can prove useful for discerning a pattern, but the transaction's exact nature remains mostly secret. The opacity effect is even more substantial with private blockchains because their existence may be kept secret, and their entry subject to specific conditions and approval.

Blockchain thus protects colluders from detection by antitrust and competition authorities. As I discussed in Chapter 2, the protection is not foolproof, but is definitely greater than that which exists outside of blockchain ecosystems. And when the fear of exposure is partially or entirely dispelled, it reinforces the mutual trust that colluders have.

---

[38] Jean Bacon et al., "Blockchain Demystified," Queen Mary School of Law Legal Studies Research Paper No. 268/2017 (2018): 41.

[39] *See,* for instance, Etherscan, https://etherscan.io/tx/0x9bd7d73bce1c3a 420093c7f82e150874136968df1ca418faf23aead4c5e3a8f4 (indicating "Contract 0xdd4c48c0b24039969fc16d1cdf626eab821d3384 Gitcoin Grants: Tornado.cash").

[40] Yi Zhou, Deepak Kumar, Surya Bakshi, Joshua Mason, Andrew Miller and Michael Bailey, "Erays: Reverse Engineering Ethereum's Opaque Smart Contracts," in 27th Security Symposium 18 (2018) (showing that 77.3 percent of smart contracts have not released public source codes and remain opaque even after using a decompiler). For a counter-example, *see* Ethereum (ETH) Blockchain Explorer, Etherscan https://etherscan.io/address/0xeb17adcc8cf24d2d6813f50f647b613df01014a2#code.

[41] Solutions are being developed to better protect privacy by hiding the content of smart contracts even when decompilers are being used, *see* Ahmed Kosba, Andrew Miller, Elaine Shi, Zikai Wen and Charalampos Papamanthou, "Hawk: The Blockchain Model of Cryptography and Privacy-Preserving Smart Contracts," in Proceedings of 2016 IEEE Symposium on Security and Privacy (2016); also, Xiwei Xu, Cesare Pautasso, Liming Zhu, Qinghua Lu and Ingo Weber Xu, "A Pattern Collection for Blockchain-based Applications," EuroPLoP'18: Proceedings of the 23rd European Conference on Pattern Languages of Programs 3 (2018). Showing how GPT-3 and other APIs could help translate smart contracts, *see* Thibault Schrepel, "Smart Contracts and the Digital Single Market Through the Lens of a 'Law + Technology' Approach," European Commission (2021).

This shield provided by blockchain is critical in terms of collusion longevity, as "a rise in the probability of detection and conviction causes the immediate collapse of the least stable cartels."[42] Antitrust agencies seek to create a prisoner's dilemma in which each player shares the same dominant strategy: to report the agreement. This outcome can be achieved only if one can detect the collusion. Because of blockchain's protection, it becomes harder for antitrust agencies to create an incentive to deviate – the overall level of stability increases. To be sure, detection by antitrust agencies is not the only way collusion can end. On top of the economic returns from deviation, or the collusion simply losing its financial value (because of changes in the market), leniency procedures and complaints from outside the agreement are two significant causes. Nevertheless, empirical studies show that collusive agreements have a shorter duration when antitrust authorities expand enforcement efforts toward detecting them.[43]

2.2.1.2   Type

On top of affecting cartel stability, the opacity effect will affect the types of agreements that colluders agree upon. The increase in trust thanks to blockchain will lead to more aggressive collusion. If the detection risk is high, colluders should, in their best interests, set up an agreement that deviates only slightly from the competitive price.[44] But where the detection risk is low, colluders should deviate substantially from the competitive price.[45] Anticartel enforcement influences firms' behavior,[46] and when it disappears, one can expect behaviors to change.

In a nutshell, blockchain helps cartel stability because of the double effect, and it also changes the nature of the agreement. I remain curious to see whether companies will massively use blockchain to set up illegal agreements. For one thing, blockchain is often presented as a "big open book," immutable by nature. Companies may fear using it for that reason, despite the opacity effect. They may also be wary of using blockchain for such a purpose because immutability does not allow for much flexibility. That, however, remains to be seen.

---

[42]   Joseph E. Harrington, Jr., *The Theory of Collusion and Competition Policy* (MIT Press, 2017): 27.

[43]   *See*, for example, Margaret C. Levenstein and Valerie Y. Suslow, "Breaking Up Is Hard to Do: Determinants of Cartel Duration," The Journal of Law & Economics 54, no. 2 (2011): 455.

[44]   George J. Stigler, "A Theory of Oligopoly," Journal of Political Economy 72, no. 1 (1964): 44, 46

[45]   Although a high collusive price could also raise each firm's individual incentive to deviate.

[46]   *See* Michael Kent Block et al., "The Deterrent Effect of Antitrust Enforcement," Journal of Political Economy, 89, no. 3 (1981): 429, 434.

Human's tendency to be overconfident—that "everything will go according to the plan"[47]—remains a strong driver of behavior. Companies could (will?) very well use blockchain precisely because it is immutable and allows them to enforce their original intentions. I leave this analysis to behavioralists.

2.2.2 Agencies' investigations

The opacity effect does not entirely prevent antitrust agencies from detecting collusion. Two methods can be used to identify such agreements: one reactive, the other proactive (*ex officio*).[48]

The reactive method mainly consists of using complaints, whistleblowers, grand juries, informants, search warrants, dawn raids and leniency applicants, which blockchain cannot prevent.[49] Still, by reinforcing trust between colluders (social perspective), this method might prove less efficient in the coming years than it is today. I study why that is in the following pages. But for now, the focus on agency investigations leads me to consider the proactive method, which translates into market surveillance, industry monitoring and screening. It is the method that is the most affected by the "opacity effect."

Proactive methods aim to identify anticompetitive effects visible outside of the blockchain. There are two sub-types of approaches to the proactive detection of collusive agreements: one structural and the other behavioral.[50] The structural approach involves screening specific markets to identify collusive agreements. Typically, an antitrust authority decides on the industry to screen and determines whether it exhibits characteristics that make the firms inclined to collude. The behavioral approach flags firms' behaviors or market outcomes to detect any patterns of collusive agreements.[51] Both types eventually rely on market-based evidence from pricing patterns.[52]

---

[47]   *See* Ulrike Malmendier and Timothy Taylor, "On the Verges of Overconfidence," Journal of Economic Perspectives 29 (2015): 3 (explaining that humans tend to be over-confident).

[48]   *See* Nicolas Petit, *Droit européen de la concurrence* (2nd ed. 2018, kaka): 693; *see* also OECD, "Ex Officio Cartel Investigations and the Use of Screens to Detect Cartels," DAF/COMP(2013)27 (2013): 87–88.

[49]   *See* OECD, "Ex Officio Cartel Investigations and the Use of Screens to Detect Cartels," DAF/COMP(2013)27 (2013): 92–93.

[50]   *Id.* at 20.

[51]   Joseph E. Harrington, Jr., "Detecting Cartels," in *Handbook of Antitrust Economics*, ed. Paolo Buccirossi (MIT Press, 2008): 213.

[52]   *See* Louis Kaplow, *Competition Policy and Price Fixing* (Princeton University Press, 2013): 259 ("Certain pricing patterns may indicate successful oligopolistic coordination or a breakdown that implies its prior existence.") For a list of these patterns, *see* OECD, "Ex Officio Cartel Investigations and the Use of Screens to Detect Cartels," DAF/COMP(2013)27 (2013):28.

Considering that, in the words of Richard Posner, "[e]conomically significant collusion should leave some visible traces,"[53] blockchain does not necessarily help companies when it comes to these proactive methods. Collusion
impacting prices to end consumers will remain visible to everyone's eyes;
here, the medium is not relevant. Things are different for collusion regarding
business-to-business prices (between companies in the production chain).
These prices are often not publicly available, and blockchain will complicate
the investigation of antitrust agencies by encrypting most of the relevant information. Only a more collaborative "law + technology" approach may avert this
outcome, as I will explore in Part 3.

3   EVERYTHING COMES TO AN END

While blockchain is conducive to collusive agreements, it can also precipitate
their downfall when smart contracts automate the exit from collusion. In the
end, blockchain strengthens the cohesion of colluders, and it speeds up collusion unfolding after the first dissension appears. One should therefore expect
the number of leniency applications to decrease as they typically result from
ailing cartels.

3.1   Smart Ending

Smart contracts may be used to exit collusive agreements, whether to force the
exclusion of a colluder deviating from the cartel or for a company to manage
its own exit. One might organize these automated exits following several
pre-established rules, ultimately leading to extra challenges for antitrust
agencies.

3.1.1   Forcing exclusion
Smart contracts are useful to prevent co-conspirators from deviating. As soon
as a conspirator is caught selling its products below the agreed price, she or he
can be automatically ejected from the agreement. If all the colluders know this
mechanism, it will strengthen their incentive to comply.

In practical terms, none of the colluders has the power to exclude each other
from a public blockchain. Smart contracts' governance could, however, organize exclusion from the agreement running on top of such a blockchain. As far
as private blockchains are concerned, the exclusion may be total or partial.
Colluders deviating from the cartel could be excluded entirely from the block-

---

[53]   Richard A. Posner, "Oligopoly and the Antitrust Laws: A Suggested Approach,"
Stanford Law Review 21 (1968): 1562, 1587.

chain or only from certain functions, such as adding or validating information and reading part of the blockchain.

Finally, empirical evidence suggests that the stability of collusion is endangered after sanctions are imposed against deviations.[54] That is why colluders generally invest in detection tools, which help prevent deviation and maintain the agreement.[55] Colluders will then be required to set these sanctions at an appropriate level. On the one hand, implementing smart contracts makes it possible to dissuade deviant behaviors and manage collusive agreements. On the other hand, punishments should not be too strict or too frequent. In short, despite the help of blockchain, running collusive agreements remains a complex endeavor.

3.1.2   Exiting

Parties can also use smart contracts to exit collusive agreements, whether this is automatic (as soon as one identifies specific deviant behaviors) or on-demand.

Theoretically, smart contracts will speed up the dissolution of collusive agreements when they start to falter. Such a situation occurs when colluders suspect that an antitrust agency may detect the collusion (causing "death by antitrust"), or when there is a strong disagreement between colluders (leading to a "natural death," which the blockchain alone cannot prevent). By facilitating the identification of deviation, blockchain is a means of speeding up its dissolution when it turns sour.

Nonetheless, one may question whether companies will use smart contracts to exit an illegal agreement while leaving evidence of the collusion behind or if they will first try to hide their past behaviors. Of course, users' identities are protected by pseudonymity,[56] and most information regarding their transactions is encrypted. But colluders can do more – namely, use different technics

---

[54]   *See* Margaret C. Levenstein and Valerie Y. Suslow, "Breaking Up Is Hard to Do: Determinants of Cartel Duration," The Journal of Law & Economics 54, no. 2 (2011): 455.

[55]   J.D. Jaspers, "Managing Cartels: How Cartel Participants Create Stability in the Absence of Law," European Journal on Criminal Policy and Research 23, (2017): 319, 322 ("[C]artels invest more in means to prevent cheating than to resort to ex post punishments, which are costly.")

[56]   *See* Kevin Werbach, *The Blockchain and the New Architecture of Trust* (MIT Press, 2018): 179 ("The supposed anonymity of the blockchain is also not an absolute bar against legal enforcement. Firms such as Elliptic and Chainalysis work with law enforcement agencies to track down criminals by analyzing cryptocurrency transaction patterns.") There is a (never-ending?) race. It remains uncertain which of the developers or tracking companies will win it – if either one ever does. Ethereum, which is working on incorporating quantum resistance into its design, shows that the barriers created by blockchain are getting higher.

to overcome immutability. A first set of solutions consists of bypassing immutability, thereby creating a technical workaround without impacting it. For example, colluders could simply store the hash of the data on the blockchain while storing the actual data elsewhere. Alternatively, they could delete the encryption key before leaving the blockchain. As previously explained, this will prevent the retrieval of the data.

A second set of solutions consists of impacting immutability.[57] This could be done using a chameleon hash function.[58] Here, trusted users (e.g., the colluders) access a trapdoor key to change the information while maintaining chain integrity.[59]Alternatively, colluders could use mutable blockchains recording various possible versions of transactions or flexible memory blockchains that enable changes while preserving the integrity of hash values.[60] Should they want to change the version of their transactions before exiting the blockchain, they could then use meta-transactions.[61] Another solution consists of using

---

[57] For a description of these technics, *see* Thibault Schrepel, "Smart Contracts and the Digital Single Market Through the Lens of a 'Law + Technology' Approach," European Commission (2021). Generally, *see* Giuseppe Ateniese, Bernardo Magri, Daniele Venturi and Ewerton Andrade, "Redactable blockchain – or – Rewriting history in Bitcoin and friends," IEEE European Symposium on Security and Privacy 1, no. 1 (2017).

[58] Eugenia Politou, Fran Casino, Efthimios Alepis and Constantinos Patsakis, "Blockchain Mutability: Challenges and Proposed Solutions," IEEE Transactions on Emerging Topics in Computing 10, no. 1 (2019): 9 ("A chameleon hash is a cryptographic hash function that contains a trapdoor, and the knowledge of this trapdoor allows collisions to be generated efficiently"); Ashritha Kondapally, M. Sindhu and K.V. Lakshmy, "Redactable Blockchain using Enhanced Chameleon Hash Function," International Conference on Advanced Computing and Communication Systems 5, no. 1 (2019); Ke Huang, Xiaosong Zhang, Yi Mu, Fatemeh Rezaeibagha, Xiaojiang Du and Nadra Guizani, "Achieving Intelligent Trust-Layer for Internet-of-Things via Self-Redactable Blockchain," IEEE Transactions on Industrial Informatics 16, no. 4 (2019); Giuseppe Ateniese, Bernardo Magri, Daniele Venturi and Ewerton Andrade, "Redactable blockchain – or – Rewriting history in Bitcoin and friends," IEEE European Symposium on Security and Privacy 1, no. 1 (2017); lastly, *see* Gideon Greenspan, "The Blockchain Immutability Myth," MultiChain, May 4, 2017, https://perma.cc/A6BD-9V3K.

[59] Jan Camenisch, David Derler, Stephan Krenn, Henrich C. Pohls, Kai Samelin and Daniel Slamanig, "Chameleon-hashes with ephemeral trapdoors," IACR International Workshop on Public Key Cryptography 20, no. 1 (2017).

[60] Ali Dorri, Salil S. Kanhere and Raja Jurdak, "MOF-BC: A memory optimized and flexible blockchain for large scale networks," Future Generation Computer Systems 92, no. 1 (2019).

[61] Politou Eugenia, Fran Casino, Efthimios Alepis and Constantinos Patsakis, "Blockchain Mutability: Challenges and Proposed Solutions," IEEE Transactions on Emerging Topics in Computing 10, no. 1 (2019): 10.

a data structure that allows blockchain users to retract information without changing the hash value of recorded blocks.[62]

Of course, these solutions are technical and would have to be implemented from the moment the collusion is created. Colluders will not do so in most cases. But either way, establishing the link between the data found on the blockchain and the collusive practices will remain a challenge for agencies.[63] That said, fears are (sometimes) irrational, and companies may still be reluctant to colluder on a public permissionless blockchain.

The same goes for private blockchains although it is well known that the owner may have the right to override, edit and delete information.[64] The colluders will thus have to convince her or him (the owner) to remove the incriminating information before they terminate their agreement. If all colluders agree to delete the information, this will be easier to perform than if they were using a public blockchain. And because it is easier to obtain a voting majority on small private blockchains—where all the participants may be colluders—than on large and public ones, private blockchains appear to be a better medium for colluders.

3.2   Leniency 2.0

Blockchain, coupled with smart contracts, may cause a decrease in the number of leniency applications. This is not necessarily as problematic as it seems, considering that smart contracts can also put an end to illegal practices.

3.2.1   Blockchain and leniency

Studying the impact of blockchain on leniency applications requires consideration of three elements.

---

[62]   Richard D. Kuhn, "A Data Structure for Integrity Protection with Erasure Capability," NIST Cybersecurity White Paper 1, no. 1 (2018).

[63]   Dawn raids are unannounced inspections conducted by antitrust agencies at companies' premises with the goal of finding incriminating evidence.

[64]   *See* Christian Catalini and Catherine Tucker, "Antitrust and Costless Verification: An Optimistic and a Pessimistic View of the Implications of Blockchain Technology," MIT Sloan Research Paper 5523-18 (2018): 11 ("[P]ermissioned blockchains are not necessarily immutable, and key participants could technically collude to rewrite the log of transactions before discovery takes place."); *see* also Dylan Yaga et al., "Blockchain Technology Overview," NIST Interagency/Internal Report 8202 (2018) : 34 ("For permissionless blockchain networks, the adoption of a longer, alternate chain of blocks could be the result of a form of attack known as a 51% attack.") For an explanation of the hard fork made by Ethereum, *see* Karen Yeung, "Regulation by Blockchain: The Emerging Battle for Supremacy between the Code of Law and Code as Law," Modern Law Review 82 (2019): 234.

The first relates to the current trends in leniency applications in both Europe and the United States. Introduced in 1978 by the DOJ[65] and in 1996 by the European Commission,[66] the leniency procedure enables colluders to self-report their illegal behavior and hand over evidence in exchange for (partial) immunity from legal sanctions. It is critical to ensure the detection, investigation and prosecution of hard-core cartels and other types of collusion. Over the years, leniency has become the "most effective tool in the fight against cartels."[67] The DOJ also stated that: "The Program (and its counterpart for individual leniency applicants) has been an incredible success in deterring and detecting antitrust crimes."[68] It is the "most important investigative tool for detecting cartel activity."[69]

Still, several studies estimate the annual probability that a cartel would be detected, conditional on being detected, at 13–17 percent.[70] This low detection rate proves that leniency procedures are not sufficient in and of themselves. On top of that, the number of leniency applications fell by half in Europe between 2014 and 2016.[71] One can observe the same trend in the United States.[72] This shows that the leniency procedure faces important challenges. Blockchain will not make things any easier.

---

[65]   OECD, "Leniency for Subsequent Applicants," DAF/COMP(2012)25 (2012): 9 ("In 1978 the US Department of Justice (US DoJ) adopted its first Corporate Leniency Policy in an attempt to overcome these limitations and enhance deterrence.")

[66]   *Id.* at 10 ("In 1996, the European Commission (EC) adopted its first Leniency Notice.")

[67]   *Id.* at 18. In Europe, "leniency policy covers purely administrative liability of companies and does not extend to individuals." *Id.* at 29. This is different in the United States. According to the European Commission, "the leniency policy proves very successful," *see* "Cartels: Leniency," European Commission: Competition, https://perma .cc/ZM33-KWUF.

[68]   "Silver Anniversary: The Antitrust Division's Leniency Program Turns 25," U.S. Department of Justice, April 10, 2018, https://perma.cc/9Q8B-QVBB.

[69]   OECD, "Leniency for Subsequent Applicants," DAF/COMP(2012)25 (2012): 152.

[70]   For the United States, *see* Peter G. Bryant and Edwin Eckard, "Price Fixing: The Probability of Getting Caught," The Review of Economics and Statistics 73, no. 3 (1991): 531. For Europe, *see* Emmanuel Combe, Constance Monnier and Renaud Legal, "Cartels: The Probability of Getting Caught in the European Union," Bruges European Economic Research Papers (2008).

[71]   *See* Johan Ysewyn and Siobhan Kahmann, "The Decline and Fall of the Leniency Programme in Europe," Concurrences Review, 1-2018 (2018): 44, 45 ("In 2014 there were 46 leniency applications, which dropped to 32 applications in 2015, and finally only 24 applications have been registered in 2016.")

[72]   *See* Charles McConnell, "Type A Leniency Applications Down, US DOJ Official Says," Global Competition Review, June 15, 2018, https://perma.cc/88UH -XEZA.

The second element concerns the technical difficulties created by block-chain, as it will complexify the work of antitrust agencies. First, blockchain protects users' identities. That is all the more so with public blockchains, where there is no need for the creator of a blockchain to approve users. Second, the transactions recorded on the blockchain are encoded and cannot be decrypted by anyone other than the parties to a transaction. This encryption also protects colluders by preventing agencies from tracing the history of their collusion. Third, even if users' identity and purpose of their transactions were known, the deletion of the data contained therein by agencies would remain quite challenging (to say the least).[73] In this respect, perhaps the exit of com-panies with the automatic destruction of information by smart contracts would be preferable to a leniency application with no subsequent possibility of elimi-nating the collusive agreement, or at least, the information illegally published.

The third element is linked to the fact that, besides its technical characteris-tics, blockchain enables colluders to manage the risk of detection. In turn, this should reduce the number of leniency applications. Most of these procedures are indeed started by colluders who fear being discovered. Technology helps in that regard. This is all the more true with private blockchains, as they can be set up so that only specific users can access the entire blockchain. This will limit their ability to hand over incriminating information to antitrust agencies. As a result, when choosing between leniency and an exit through smart con-tract,[74] there is every reason to believe that blockchain would, at least partially, overshadow leniency applications.

How worrying is all this? At first sight, the expected decrease in the number of leniency applications may seem problematic, as antitrust agen-cies rely heavily on them to detect collusive agreements.[75] According to the Organisation for Economic Co-operation and Development (OECD), the per-centage of cartel cases detected through leniency applications is reported in the survey to range between 45 and 55 percent for countries such as Canada, Chile, Germany, Korea and New Zealand, and over 85 percent for the European

---

[73]   Once again, immutability can be undermined only with the approval of a major-ity of blockchain users, unless proper mechanisms have been implemented from the start.

[74]   Evgenia Motchenkova, "Effects of Leniency Programs on Cartel Stability," Tilburg University Center Discussion Paper, 2004-98 (2004): 1.

[75]   *Id.* at 22; *see* OECD, "Ex Officio Cartel Investigations and the Use of Screens to Detect Cartels," DAF/COMP(2013)27 (2013): 9, 108 (noting that "in some jurisdic-tions leniency programme cases have 'crowded out' efforts to expose cartels by other means," but also stating that although competition authorities tend to deny it, "[i]n the recent past the majority of the Commission's cartel cases have originated from leni-ency. At the same time, the Commission has continued pursuing cases also on ex officio basis.")

Union.[76] In the United States, more than 90 percent of the penalties imposed by the DOJ in recent years are linked to investigations assisted by leniency applicants.[77] This report shows a reactive policy by antitrust agencies. It also signals to companies that a well-designed collusive agreement that frames and rectifies disagreements has a good chance of (extended) survival.[78]

By undermining leniency programs' effectiveness, blockchain will force competition agencies to become proactive again, failing which companies will have a growing sense of impunity from antitrust and competition law. Only a strengthening of proactive detection will increase the risk of punishment and force companies to seek leniency again.[79]

3.2.2   A (almost) similar end

In its Notice on Immunity from fines and the reduction of fines in cartel cases, the European Commission argues that leniency programs exist to detect and end illegal collusive agreements.[80] The European Commission stresses that "by their very nature, secret collusive agreements are often difficult to detect and investigate," and that rewarding undertakings that are willing to put an end to their participation is in the community's best interest.[81] The United States shares a similar view, where leniency programs are seen as a "prompt and effective" means to stop companies from further participation in collusive agreements.[82]

---

[76] "Answer to Parliamentary Questions E-0890/09, E-0891/09, & E-0892/09," European Parliament, April 2, 2009, https://perma.cc/K4WZ-LX9P (stating that before the European Commission, 46 out of 52 cartel decisions (88 percent) from 2002 through 2008 were triggered by a leniency application).

[77] Michael Saller, "Challenges and Co-Ordination of Leniency Programmes – Background Note by the Secretariat," OECD Working Party No. 3 On Co-Operation and Enforcement, DAF/COMP/WP3(2018)1 (2008): 6.

[78] *See* Hans Wolfgang Friederiszick and Frank P. Maier-Rigaud, "Triggering Inspections Ex Officio: Moving Beyond a Passive EU Cartel Policy," Journal of Competition Law and Economics 4, no. 1 (2008): 89. Margaret C. Levenstein and Valerie Y. Suslow, "What Determines Cartel Success?" Journal of Economic Literature 44, no. 1 (2006): 71.

[79] *See id.* at 5.

[80] In theory, the leniency application is open only to horizontal cartels and leaves out the exchange of information. European Commission, "Commission Notice on Immunity from Fines and Reduction of Fines in Cartel Cases, O.J. 2006/C 298/11," Official Journal of the European Union (2006).

[81] *Id.* at 17.

[82] *See* U.S. Department of Justice, Antitrust Div., "Frequently Asked Questions About the Antitrust Division's Leniency Program and Model Leniency Letters" (2017), https://perma.cc/C2K3-7UNB.

Smart contracts can achieve the same end. By discouraging firms from cheating on cartels, by automating punishments and by giving a means to exit the agreement under predetermined conditions, one may expect that the number of leniency applications will drop.[83] But this decrease is not necessarily as problematic as it seems.

I have explained that an increase in the number of "natural" deaths is expected thanks to smart contracts. This tendency to move away from self-reporting and toward the self-regulation of collusive agreements operating on blockchain could eventually manifest itself in two ways: by making collusive agreements robust during their existence with very few deviant behaviors, and by making their disappearance sudden. Put differently, one can expect an increase in the number of collusive agreements along with an increase in their profitability, but not necessarily in their duration.

Therefore, the partial demise of leniency proceedings should not be a significant concern for stopping illegal behavior.[84] In fact, one could point out that blockchain will lead to a faster dissolution of collusive agreements than leniency programs currently do. Studies suggest that leniency helps detect unprofitable and poorly designed collusive agreements; in short, those that are about to collapse anyway. Blockchain will do the same, but potentially more rapidly.

But of course, there is a difference between ending collusion thanks to smart contracts or leniency – an important one. Without public sanctions being imposed by an antitrust agency, private enforcement will be hindered. This will deter affected parties from recouping the damages they have suffered. It follows that smart contracts will impact the chain that enables damages to be compensated – especially in Europe, where private enforcement follows public enforcement more commonly than in the United States.

4   CHAPTER SUMMARY AND BEYOND

In this chapter, I have explained that blockchain is the rainforest of tomorrow's collusive agreements: full of original life forms and alternative possibilities. Blockchain gives rise to unidentified creatures and dangerous species. This is all the more true if companies use smart contracts to increase collusive

---

[83]   Indeed, if "the possibility for a deviator to apply for leniency increases the payoff of cheating, thus making collusion more difficult to sustain," quite the contrary is also true. *See* Wouter P.J. Wils, "Leniency in Antitrust Enforcement: Theory and Practice," World Competition Law & Economic Review 30, no. 1 (2007): 25.

[84]   On the contrary, European follow-on enforcement, which requires first a decision coming from a public agency to introduce a subsequent trial, will likely disappear in such scenarios without being replaced by any blockchain mechanism.

Table 9.1   Smart contracts in the context of collusion

Trust by smart contracts	At the creation of collusive agreements	During the life of collusive agreements	Causing the death of collusive agreements
Type of smart contract	What: smart contracts ensuring the efficiency of traditional collusion (i.e., whose effects are manifested outside of the blockchain) Objective: collusion using the blockchain as a trustful medium and smart contract as a governance tool	What: smart contracts preventing deviant behaviors Objective: to ensure trust between colluders by automating transactions and publishing trustworthy information What: smart contracts correcting deviant behaviors Objective: to impose targeted punishments as compensation for the deviation and to recreate trust between colluders	What: smart contracts forcing one deviant colluder to exit the blockchain Objective: to eject a deviant colluder (when the deviation cannot be forgiven) to recreate a trustful environment What: smart contracts allowing one colluder to exit the blockchain at will Objective: to create trust between colluders by providing them an exit gate (prevent entrapment)

agreements' stability. Illegal practices then become visible to colluders while ensuring their opacity to non-colluders. As a result, collusion becomes more robust because deviation is easier to detect, but it (perhaps paradoxically) ends more abruptly. One could sum up these findings as outlined in Table 9.1

Collusive agreements using blockchain will significantly affect the real space. First, they will increase artificial centralization by increasing colluders' ability to go unchallenged. Second, they will constrain non-colluding companies facing such cartels. For these reasons, antitrust law enforcement must become proactive in eliminating collusions and re-establishing decentralization. Otherwise, participants will not be able to compete under a classic Darwinian process. So, here again, the law could be the ally of blockchain communities. I will discuss how this could happen in Part 3; but before I do, I want to explore monopolization and abuses of dominant positions, as blockchains may also lead to this type of behaviors.

10. Blockchain power

1 MARKET DEFINITION

The methodology for defining relevant markets in antitrust law has evolved little over the last couple of years. Blockchain challenges it at its core. One may hope for the development of a more technology-centric approach in response.

1.1 Where We're At

The concept of market power is central to antitrust law, whether in the United States or Europe. To evaluate it, one must first define the relevant market – that is, the market on which companies are said to compete. To this end, courts and agencies identify the products and services that are substitutes, starting the analysis from the entity being investigated to reach a general understanding of the market in question. This entails defining two elements: one material, the other geographical.

In the United States, the relevant product market consists "of a group of substitute products".[1] The geographical market definition refers to the location within which one can show customers' willingness or ability to substitute one product for another. The same goes for suppliers' willingness or ability to serve some customers.[2]

In an article entitled "Why (Ever) Define Markets?," Louis Kaplow argued that "the market definition process is incoherent as a matter of basic economic principles and hence should be abandoned entirely."[3] The author held that defining the market was "impossible without first formulating a best estimate of market power," and that it was "rendering further analysis pointless and possibly leading to erroneous outcomes." Although this has been the most cited

---

[1] "Horizontal Merger Guidelines," the US Department of Justice, August 9, 2010, https://perma.cc/6MYT-6SMK.

[2] *Id.* at 4.f.

[3] Louis Kaplow, "Why (Ever) Define Markets?" Harvard Law Review 124, (2010).

antitrust article of the 2010s,[4] one may underline how much market definition has stayed the same.

The method for defining the relevant market is similar in Europe. The materiality of market definition relates to the identification of a relevant product market. According to the *Continental Can* case:

> the definition of the relevant market is of essential significance, for the possibilities of competition can only be judged in relation to those characteristics of the products in question by virtue of which those products are particularly apt to satisfy an inelastic need and are only to a limited extent interchangeable with other products.[5]

The geographical market is the area within which products and services compete. And following *United Brands*:

> the opportunities for competition under article [102] of the treaty must be considered having regard to the particular features of the product in question and with reference to a clearly defined geographic area in which it is marketed and where the conditions of competition are sufficiently homogeneous for the effect of the economic power of the undertaking concerned to be able to be evaluated.[6]

Defining these two parameters is a prerequisite to analyzing the substitutability of products and services within the perimeter.[7] The method has remained constant for decades[8] and, in practice, the CJUE rarely overrules the European Commission on the definition of relevant markets.[9] The Commission announced its intention to revise its Notice on market definition in January 2020.[10]

---

[4]   According to HeinOnline citations count.

[5]   *Europemballage Corporation and Continental Can Company Inc. v. Commission*, Case 6-72, European Court Reports: 1973 -00215 (ECJ, 1973): para. 14.

[6]   *United Brands Company and United Brands Continentaal BV v. Commission*, Case 27/76, European Court Reports: 1978 -00207 (ECJ, 1978): para. 11.

[7]   For the demand substitution, the "small but significant and non-transitory increase in price" test is commonly used. The supply substitution may also be taken into account, according to the Commission Notice, when "its effects are equivalent to those of demand substitution in terms of effectiveness and immediacy," para. 20.

[8]   There are a few exceptions, such as the *Servier* case in *Servier SAS and Others v. Commission*, Case T-691/14, ECLI:EU:T:2018:922 (ECJ, 2018).

[9]   Miguel Sousa Ferro, "Judicial Review: Do European Courts Care About Market Definition?" Journal of European Competition Law & Practice 6, no. 6 (2015).

[10]   European Commission, "Competition: Public Consultations," European Commission, https://perma.cc/NVJ7-YS9N.

1.2   Blockchain Challenges

1.2.1   Relevant markets

Defining the relevant product markets requires antitrust agencies to identify the layer of the blockchain that is impacted by an anticompetitive practice. When it concerns the blockchain infrastructure, agencies should study whether the blockchain is monocentric or acts as a platform (as I explained in Chapter 3). Monocentric blockchains can be used for one application only – Bitcoin is a great example. The product market follows.

Platform blockchains are more challenging. When they are public permissionless, they can be used simultaneously in a wide variety of applications. Here, the theory of granularity is helpful to define which activity is at the heart of the survival strategy. The relevant product market follows that core activity. When they are private, they restrict their general access and governance functions. That simplifies market definition, as they usually go in one easily identifiable direction. In fact, it is not uncommon to see private blockchains operating in one specific market. That being said, several of them have more general ambitions. This is the case with Hyperledger and Corda. Here again, one must analyze the activities from which they derive income and compare their importance to other entities.

The analysis is logically easier at the application level (described as the sixth level of the blockchain in Chapter 4). In fact, it resembles the one conducted outside blockchain: one may simply study the extent to which that application competes with others.

The geographical market definition follows the product market. Depending on the product or service identified as being relevant, agencies will have to assess consumers' willingness to substitute it to other products and services located within a limited perimeter. In that regard, blockchain does not differ from centralized digital products and services.[11]

1.2.2   A law + technology approach

Once the relevant product or service has been identified, one should analyze the characteristics of each blockchain. Some of these characteristics appear decisive in the adoption of specific blockchain products and services. For example, a public blockchain that serves primarily to register property titles may enjoy a strong reputation because of its immutability. The same goes for an application that lists the supply of diamonds, where trust in the information is essential. When this is the case, blockchain does not compete with other

---

[11]   *See*, for instance, the Google decisions published by the European Commission.

products and services: it is on its own market.[12] Conversely, where blockchain characteristics do not primarily explain why it is used, it tends to compete with similar products or services offered by centralized undertakings.

One point needs to be discussed in that regard. In recent years, antitrust agencies have shown a tendency to focus on companies' business models to segment markets. This pattern is particularly visible in the decisions of the European Commission. For example, the Commission held in its *Google Android* decision that Google did not compete with Apple in the demand-side market for smartphone because, among other things, Apple's iOS was not licensed to third-party original equipment manufacturers.[13] That market definition sits inconsistently with unambiguous survey evidence showing that since Android's entry, many consumers contemplate both ecosystems on equal footing in their purchasing decisions, despite their distinct business models.[14]

Generally, business models should not play such a significant role in antitrust agencies' market definitions on the user side. Instead, focusing on end-user adoption rather than contractual arrangements seems to be a more realistic way to define relevant markets on the demand-side. Blockchain applications may compete with centralized firms' products and services, depending on the importance of blockchain characteristics in driving adoption.[15]

---

[12]   Recognizing that blockchain may create new segments within the relevant markets, *see Décision n° 19-DCC-259 du 18 décembre 2019 relative à la prise de contrôle exclusif de la société Softeam par le groupe La Poste*, prepared by *Autorité de la Concurrence* (Paris, 2019): point 16.

[13]   *Google LLC. v. Commission*, Case AT.40099, C/2018/4761 (EC, 2018): para 218.

[14]   For instance, *see* Chance Miller, "These are the Top Reasons Users Switch from Android to IoS, According to a New Survey," 9to5mac, August 23, 2018, https://perma .cc/2HYD-9PV3 ("According to a survey of 2,500 U.S. consumers, some 29 percent had switched mobile operating systems. 11 percent of those switchers went from iOS to Android, while the other 18 percent went from Android to iOS"); Abhin Mahipal, "Survey: 3 in 10 Android Users Would Consider Upgrading to iPhone 12," Sellcell, October 5, 2020, https://perma.cc/UDD5-AWMX ("In the last survey, we asked more than 2500 iPhone users whether they intend to upgrade to the upcoming iPhone 12, and four in 10 said they would").

[15]   Discussing the matter, *see Affaire M.9619 – CDC/EDF/ENGIE/La Poste: Décision de la Commission en application de l'article 6(1)(b) du règlement (CE) n°139/2004 du Conseil et de l'article 57 de l'accord sur l'Espace économique européen*, prepared by the European Commission (Brussels, 2020): point 52 (underlining that "the responses to the market survey are nuanced with respect to a distinction between different automated solutions. A majority of certification providers consider that a distinction should be made between the use of algorithms, barcodes or blockchain technology") [translated from French]. Analyzing the matter, *see* Antoine Babinet and David Dubois, "'Archipels' Case: EU's First Merger Control Analysis of a Private Blockchain Consortium," Journal of European Competition Law & Practice (2021).

Of course, understanding adoption also requires agencies to be forward-looking – that is, to anticipate future states (and uses) of a technology. Here, one cannot overlook the importance of code as it defines actual use-cases of a technology, but also its dynamic capability. For example, Ethereum uses Solidity, a Turing-complete language. It means that anything computable can be computed using that language (the reason why Ethereum is called the "world's computer"). Ethereum's dynamic capability is, therefore, higher than that of Bitcoin, whose primary language, C++, is not Turing-complete. For that reason, antitrust agencies' ability to understand and analyze blockchain code will be essential to the definition of markets and the capture of their dynamism.

2   MARKET POWER

The way market power is defined in antitrust cases has been questioned numerous times in the last couple of years. It remains focused on market shares. This creates an issue for blockchain layer 1, since the calculation of market shares involves comparing blockchains by means of values expressed in their own tokens.

2.1   Where We're At

Once the market is defined, antitrust agencies must assess whether the entity under investigation enjoys any market power, being typically defined as "the power to control prices or exclude competition."[16] However, since measuring that power is often difficult, antitrust agencies use an indirect method. The logic is as follows:

- The relevant market is the playing field.
- All companies in that field are players.
- Players are to be compared to one another.

The smaller the field, the fewer the players on it and the more powerful they necessarily are. But that method for determining market power is questiona-

---

[16] *See United State v. El du Pont de Nemours*, 351 US 377, 76 S. Ct. 994 (U.S., 1956). *See* also "the ability profitably to maintain prices above competitive levels for a significant period of time," Horizontal "Merger Guidelines," US Department of Justice, April 8, 1997, https://perma.cc/E92F-DJ6J.

ble.[17] Typically, antitrust agencies use market shares as a proxy or, at least, as a starting point. In the United States, the FTC underlines that:

> Courts look at the firm's market share, but typically do not find monopoly power if the firm (or a group of firms acting in concert) has less than 50 percent of the sales of a particular product or service within a certain geographic area.[18]

In Europe, the Guidance on the Commission's enforcement priorities in applying Article 102 states: "Market shares provide a useful first indication for the Commission of the market structure and of the relative importance of the various undertakings active on the market."[19]

Of course, market shares are not always sufficient. In the *Microsoft/Skype* merger decision, for example, the European Commission stated that "market shares only provide[d] a limited indication of competitive strength in the consumer communications services markets," since "competition in the consumer communications services markets is driven by innovation."[20] Still, market shares are where the analysis starts, and only after one defines them is it possible to say whether they are sufficient. When they are not, mainly because they are too low, other factors – such as barriers to entry, potential competition, price elasticity, the number of recent entries and the size of competitors – are expressly taken into account.

So, how should authorities and courts determine these market shares, especially when it comes to online products and services that are available throughout the world? In the *Google* decision, the European Commission used market shares by volume as a proxy for several reasons:

> First, market shares by value cannot be computed because general search services are provided free of charge to the user. Second, despite its best efforts, the Commission has been unable to obtain precise and verifiable values regarding the

---

[17] Discussing the methodology, *see* Dennis Carlton and Jeffry Perloff, *Modern Industrial Organization*, 4th ed. (Pearson, 2004): 642; Landes and Posner, "Market Power in Antitrust Cases," Harvard Law Review 94 no. 5 (1981). Discussing the pitfalls, *see* Louis Kaplow, "Why (Ever) Define Markets?" Harvard Law Review 124, (2010); and also, Daniel Crane, "Market Power Without Market Definition," The Notre Dame Law Review 90, no. 1 (2014).

[18] "Monopolization Defined," Federal Trade Commission, https://perma.cc/LDR6 -YJ2N.

[19] European Commission, "Guidance on the Commission's enforcement priorities in applying Article 82, 2009/C 45/02," Communication from the Commission (2009): para. 13.

[20] *Microsoft/Skype*, Case COMP/M.6281, C(2011)7279 (EC, 2011): paras. 74 and 84.

Revenue Per Search ("RPS") of the main general search services. Third, advertisers look at usage shares when deciding where to place their search advertisements ...[21]

A similar method is used in the United States. Volume is key, and ultimately, agencies end up comparing the turnovers of each company in the playing field. This is how market power is presumed, rather than established.

2.2 Blockchain Challenges

The classic analysis of market power translates poorly to blockchain. As a starting point, public permissionless blockchains do not enjoy coercive ability "to maintain prices above competitive levels for a significant period of time," since no user can impose such a decision. The indirect method for defining market power is not any easier. In fact, measuring market shares is challenging, whether for blockchain infrastructure or blockchain applications.

One indicator comes logically to mind: the value generated by each blockchain. The reward obtained by miners varies according to the amount of data that makes up a transaction. The larger the transaction, the larger the reward will be.[22] To this extent, the turnover generated by miners on a blockchain is correlated to the size (not the value) of the transactions carried out using the blockchain. This is valuable information when comparing blockchains.

But difficulties arise from the fact that one usually expresses the total value generated by one blockchain in the token created by that blockchain, such as in Bitcoin or Ether. Indeed, the values of most tokens register high fluctuation.[23] Comparing one token to another implies that they present a relatively stable picture of reality, but when the value of a token decreases sharply in just a few hours, the analysis is truncated. It could lead to considering one blockchain as being dominant one day and non-dominant the next. Figure 10.1 is a great example of tokens' high fluctuation (10,000 Bitcoins would amount to €140 million at the time of writing).[24]

Of course, agencies could calculate an average over the yearly value of a token, similarly to what they do when converting foreign currencies. For

---

[21] "Google Search (Shopping)," *Google Inc. v. Commission*, Case AT.39740, C(2017) 4444, (EC, 2017): 127, https://perma.cc/WXY2-R7YR. Please note that the fourth reason has been classified by the European Commission.

[22] Depending on blockchains, users could also decide to offer a higher reward for validating their transaction, therefore increasing the fees on a case-by-case basis.

[23] *See* CoinMarketCap, "All Cryptocurrencies" (listing 4166 active coins and tokens as of January 5, 2021).

[24] It would amount to €320 million at the time I am reviewing this writing, in early January 2021. And it would amount to over €400 million at the time I am re-reviewing it, in May 2021.

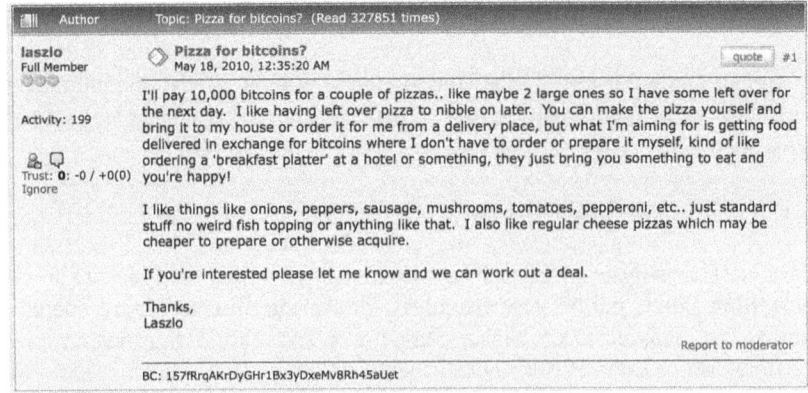

Figure 10.1   A bitcoin owner buying pizzas in 2010

example, when a merger is notified, the agency converts the annual turnover of
the entities based on average value (over the last 12 months) of the currency in
which their turnover is expressed. One could certainly do the same to convert
tokens, but ignoring the strong fluctuation would lead to ignoring market
reality. Indeed, one may easily conceive how unlikely it is that a blockchain
whose value fluctuates greatly from day to day would act as a company in
a stable dominant position. The average value of a cryptocurrency (over
a defined period) does not capture market volatility, which is highly problematic. It cannot stand on its own.

   One should therefore perceive market shares as a largely insufficient indicator for determining market power, especially when it comes to blockchains.
Other indicators will therefore have to be considered to compare the size of
players on the field. The question of which indicators to take into account will
become relevant in the coming months and years. The number of users and the
number of transactions seem to be two interesting values in that regard, as they
do a better job at capturing blockchain's market power.

   Generally speaking, one may argue that structural analysis shows its limits
when it comes to blockchain, and that behavioral elements will prove more
helpful. For instance, instead of assuming product substitutability by using
economic models, antitrust agencies could study the extent to which one
blockchain's miners and users are actually shifting their activities from one
blockchain to another – which could be based on empirical evidence, market
screening, or even agent-based modeling.

   The need for such an evidence-based approach is already recognized by
the DOJ and the FTC. In their Horizontal Merger Guidelines (2010), the two
agencies recognized the need to adopt a "flexible" definition of the market,

underlining that it may not be "always intuitive".[25] The same is true for the European Commission which, in its notice on the definition of relevant market, recognizes that:

> There is a range of evidence permitting an assessment of the extent to which substitution would take place. In individual cases, certain types of evidence will be determinant, depending very much on the characteristics and specificity of the industry and products or services that are being examined. The same type of evidence may be of no importance in other cases. In most cases, a decision will have to be based on the consideration of a number of criteria and different items of evidence. The Commission follows an open approach to empirical evidence, aimed at making an effective use of all available information which may be relevant in individual cases. The Commission does not follow a rigid hierarchy of different sources of information or types of evidence.[26]

In practice, however, the U.S. agencies and the European Commission often confine their approach to existing methods. As the agencies in the United States say:

> Even when the evidence necessary to perform the hypothetical monopolist test quantitatively is not available, the conceptual framework of the test provides a useful methodological tool for gathering and analyzing evidence pertinent to customer substitution and to market definition. The Agencies follow the hypothetical monopolist test to the extent possible given the available evidence.[27]

Adopting that approach increases legal certainty, but in trying to over-mechanize the definition of the relevant market, important factual criteria are left out of the picture. In the near future, it appears that it will be necessary to return to more evidence-based elements with regard to blockchain. Doing so makes sense in the field as blockchain generates public information that agencies could use, where other industries and ecosystems are more secret in nature.

3   CHAPTER SUMMARY AND BEYOND

In this chapter, I have first explained that evaluating market power entails defining the relevant market. This is generally done by studying two com-

---

[25]   *See* U.S. Department of Justice and Federal Trade Commission, "Horizontal Merger Guidelines" (2010), https://perma.cc/WT8K-E73G.

[26]   European Commission, "Commission Notice on the Definition of Relevant Market for the Purposes of Community Competition Law," *Official Journal of the European Communities* (1997): para. 25, https://perma.cc/L7KJ-VZV4.

[27]   *See* U.S. Department of Justice and Federal Trade Commission, "Horizontal Merger Guidelines" (2010), https://perma.cc/4TJF-2KR4.

ponents, whether in the United States or Europe. The first is the relevant product market – that is, the group of products and services substitutable to one another. The second is the geographical market, defining the zone within which each product and service competes.

When it comes to blockchain, assessing product and geographical markets is difficult. In that regard, it is necessary to draw a distinction between blockchain infrastructure and blockchain applications. First, for infrastructure, the theory of granularity helps determine the core activity of public blockchains, while private blockchains' core activities are generally easier to identify. Second, for applications, a similar analysis to that conducted outside of the blockchain space can be performed. In both cases, the geographical market follows the product or service market.

Overall, defining the relevant market implies that courts, agencies and regulators should adopt a "law + technology" approach. In turn, this would require that they analyze and understand blockchain's code. If they do not do so, they have no choice but to substitute the analysis of the underlying technology to one of business structure, leading to curious results that do not correspond to market realities.

Once the relevant market is identified, courts and agencies may study market power. Defined as the ability to raise prices above the competitive level or exclude competition, the concept of the relevant market is not easily transposable to blockchains insofar as they do not hold such coercive power. One may use market shares as the first indicator of power – as in non-blockchain cases – but I contend that this will be insufficient. Indeed, market shares are classically measured by the total value of transactions made by distinct entities. This implies the conversion of all the currencies in which they are expressed; but because the value of most tokens fluctuates dramatically, the analysis appears too random for lasting lessons to be learned. Things will change if and when the value of certain tokens stabilizes, or if stablecoins generalize. Still, the value of tokens is not always correlated to blockchains' market power, as speculation impacts these values. After all, the same is true for non-blockchain companies – one would not measure Google or Amazon's market power based on the value of its stocks.

One must take other variables into account – for instance, the number of users or transactions. Eventually, antitrust agencies will be required to analyze on a case-by-case basis the extent to which blockchain participants are moving from one blockchain to another. That information will become largely available to them as blockchain records are public and immutable, thus making it easier for agencies to observe whether a user (public key) is still active. This should lead to more factual analyses in the absence of mechanical criteria.

11. Blockchain and monopolization

1   PRACTICES RELATED TO BLOCKCHAIN ITSELF

This first section focuses on unilateral practices that are directly related to the blockchain infrastructure and governance. I have decided not to study practices at the application layer, as they resemble those outside blockchain. For the rest, Figure 11.1 helps identify which kinds of unilateral practices are the most likely to occur, with the understanding that consumer damage must always be proven on a case-by-case basis. This figure will have to be revised depending on the evolution of blockchain technology in the years to come, but one can use it as a first canvas.

1.1   Exclusionary Abuses

An important clarification is in order before I study the exclusionary practices that could take place on blockchains. As I shall show, public permissionless blockchains do not permit the implementation of unilateral practices by a single participant. For that reason, I must make a distinction between the initial possibility of carrying out such practices and the possibility of transforming these blockchains so as to implement them. It is thus necessary to consider whether the implementation of unilateral practices is technically possible and whether participants have incentives to do so. Finally, I make no general distinction between US and European law, because antitrust rules are similar in both jurisdictions. There are, however, some discrepancies that could have important ramifications in practice, including when it comes to the legal test being applied to these practices. I do my best to mention them.

1.1.1   Refusal to deal

Economic entities routinely refuse to do business with their rivals.[1] However, one would expect such practices to be rare in public permissionless block-

---

[1]   For a general overview on European refusal to deal, *see Oscar Bronner v. Mediaprint Zeitungs und Zeitschriftenverlag*, Case C-7/97, European Court Reports: 1998 I-7796 (ECJ, 1998); *European Night Servs. Ltd. (ENS) v. Commission*, Cases

Unilateral Practices related to Blockchain	Exclusionary Abuses							Exploitative Abuses	Discriminatory Abuses
	Refusal to deal	Tying	Predatory pricing	Margin squeeze	Exclusive dealing	Rebates & discounts	Predatory innovation		
Public Permissionless Blockchain	**Very unlikely** public blockchains run on open access, by definition	**Very unlikely** access to public permissionless blockchains are not submitted to conditions of buying/using another product or service	**Unlikely** implies two majority changes, first, to adopt the lower price to use the blockchain, then to raise it	**Very unlikely** access to public permissionless is free, and transaction fees apply the same to all participants	**Very unlikely** all participants can leave and rejoin the blockchain at will	**Very unlikely** implies a majority change in the blockchain, despite significantly reducing its attractiveness	**Unlikely** modifying the blockchain functioning is not possible without the agreement of a majority of all participants	**Unlikely** differentiating between participants is technically impractical, plus, access is free and easy, switching costs are low, and so are barriers to exit	**Unlikely** requires a majority vote, and any price discrimination is public, therefore significantly reducing the blockchain attractiveness
Private Blockchain	**Very likely** refusal to give access is one of the reasons why private blockchains exist	**Very likely** access to the blockchain can be easily subjected to conditions, such as creating another account / using another blockchain	**Likely** the price to use the blockchain can be easily changed, therefore facilitating such two-step strategies	**Unlikely** to date, no court or agency is imposing to grant blockchain access, removing in effect any incentive to squeeze the margins of those who have gained access	**Very likely** significantly increases the overall attractiveness and value of blockchains which have exclusive information	**Very likely** granting rebates could be used to incentivize specific users to join and use the blockchain	**Very likely** modifications to the blockchain functioning can be made effectively	**Likely** switching costs are high, especially in the absence of compatibility, strengthening the power of private blockchains as platforms	**Very likely** discrimination between users is likely, if only as an incentive to join the blockchain or stay active on it

Figure 11.1   The implementation of unilateral practices on blockchain

chains. Access to these blockchains is free by default. Should the access rights be modified to limit access, the blockchain would no longer be "public." One could thus say that refusal to deal or grant access is inconsistent with the inherent nature of public blockchains.

By contrast, the possibility to refuse access is an essential characteristic of private blockchains.[2] Their creators can indeed restrict entry (whether entirely or to certain functions such as validating transactions), see all information and use it as they see fit. Doing so, of course, is not necessarily illegal. In the United States, we know from *Aspen Skiing* (1985)[3] that "[t]he high value that we have placed on the right to refuse to deal with other firms does not mean that the right is unqualified." Although the *Trinko* decision (2017)[4] has since reaffirmed the absence of any duty to deal with rivals, it remains unclear whether the ruling applies to all situations or solely to regulated industries.[5]

As for European competition law, we know from *Commercial Solvents v. Commission* that:

> an undertaking which has a dominant position in the market in raw materials which, with the object of reserving such raw material for manufacturing its own derivatives, refuses to supply a customer, which is itself a manufacturer of these derivatives, and therefore risks eliminating all competition on the part of this customer, is abusing its dominant position.[6]

T-374/94, T-375/94, T-384/94 and T-388/94, E.C.R. II-3141 (1998); *Clearstream Banking AG v. Commission*, Case T-301/04, European Court Reports: 2009 II-3155 (CFI, 2009). In short, refusing to provide access to a facility is abusive if it is likely to eliminate all competition on the secondary market, if access is indispensable for entering the market in question and if access is denied without any objective justification. For an overview of American refusal to deal, *see Verizon Comm. Inc. v. Law Offices of Curtis V. Trinko, LLP*, 540 U.S. 398 (U.S., 2004), in which the court suggested that a refusal to deal motivated solely by a desire to eliminate competition, with no other purpose, might constitute illegal monopolization. To establish liability under the essential facilities doctrine, a plaintiff must show the monopolist's control over the essential facility, the plaintiff's inability to duplicate the essential facility, the denial of use of the facility and the feasibility of providing access to the facility.

[2]   The refusal to grant access to the blockchain could be an abuse of dominant position if decided by one company, but it could also be a cartel if the blockchain is run by a consortium.

[3]   *Aspen Skiing Co. v. Aspen Highlands Skiing Corp.*, 472 U.S. 585 (1985).

[4]   *Verizon Comm. Inc. v. Law Offices of Curtis V. Trinko, LLP*, 540 U.S. 398 (U.S., 2004).

[5]   For a discussion, *see* Andrew Gavil et al., *Antitrust Law in Perspective* (West Academic Publishing, 2018): 639–40.

[6]   *Istituto Chemioterapico Italiano S.p.A. and Commercial Solvents Corporation v. Commission*, Joint Cases 6 and 7-73, European Court Reports: 1974 -00223 (ECJ, 1974).

More specifically, the CJEU held that a refusal to deal might be punished when: (1) it concerns an input indispensable to do business; (2) the refusal is likely to eliminate competition; and (3) it is not objectively justified.[7] The General Court followed up with similar reasoning in *Microsoft v. Commission*, holding that:

> the refusal by an undertaking holding a dominant position to license a third party to use a product covered by an intellectual property right cannot in itself constitute an abuse of a dominant position within the meaning of Article 82 EC. It is only in exceptional circumstances that the exercise of the exclusive right by the owner of the intellectual property right may give rise to such an abuse.[8]

The following circumstances must be considered to be exceptional:

> in the first place, the refusal relates to a product or service indispensable to the exercise of a particular activity on a neighbouring market; in the second place, the refusal is of such a kind as to exclude any effective competition on that neighbouring market; in the third place, the refusal prevents the appearance of a new product for which there is potential consumer demand.[9]

One could easily see how these could play out in a blockchain environment: firms in a private blockchain could refuse access to it and thus eliminate competition in a downstream innovative market. This will surely happen.

Besides, there are similarities between refusals to grant access to a blockchain and refusals to grant standard-essential patents (SEPs). Concluding a license to use SEPs is deemed essential to compete on the market, because they are often integrated into norms. For that reason, the holders of SEPs are often encouraged by standard-setting organizations to license them on fair, reasonable and non-discriminatory (FRAND) terms, to avoid any breach of antitrust law. One can imagine that similar case law will be developed whereby private blockchain holders will have no choice but to grant access to their blockchains on FRAND terms if access is deemed essential to compete.

Generally speaking, should access to specific blockchains be recognized as a *de facto* necessity, the firms running such private blockchains would be prohibited from setting access terms that create a strong exclusionary effect. For these reasons, blockchain gatekeepers (those in control of private blockchains)

---

[7]   *See Oscar Bronner GmbH & Co. KG v. Mediaprint Zeitungs- und Zeitschriftenverlag GmbH & Co. KG, Mediaprint Zeitungsvertriebsgesellschaft mbH & Co. KG and Mediaprint Anzeigengesellschaft mbH & Co. KG.*, Case C-7/97, European Court Reports: 1998 I-07791 (ECJ, 1998).

[8]   *Microsoft Corp. v. Commission*, Case T-201/04, European Court Reports: 2007 II-03601 (CFI, 2007), para. 331.

[9]   *Id.* at para. 332.

should carefully consider, without further ado, whether their access conditions comply with antitrust law.

The same goes for gatekeepers located outside of the blockchain ecosystem.[10] In a recent case, a Brazilian association of cryptocurrencies operators (the National Association of Cryptocurrencies and Blockchain) asked the antitrust agency, in June 2018, to investigate Banco do Brasil's refusal to supply banking services to these operators.[11] In response, Banco do Brasil argued that it took precautions, and indeed refused to supply them, only to avoid any risk of financial crime by its clients.

The Administrative Council for Economic Defense initially closed the case in December 2018, but the agency tribunal asked for the investigation to be reopened in Summer 2020. The case is currently ongoing at the time of writing. Regardless of the outcome, it shows that blockchain antitrust issues also concern operators that can affect the ecosystem from the outside. Similarly, one could imagine antitrust actions against an exchange that would refuse to list a token for anti-competitive purposes.

1.1.2   Tying

"Tying" is the practice of subjecting the sale of one product (or service) to additional sales or obligations.[12] It may, for example, involve subjecting a contract to the acceptance of supplementary obligations.

Tying is unlikely to be seen on public permissionless blockchains. This type of blockchain can be accessed or used freely; submitting it to the use of another product or blockchain is unlikely. To this extent, and given the difficulty of modifying public blockchains, it is doubtful that one would find an abundance of such practices. They would have to be incorporated into the blockchain's

---

[10]   Discussing the subject, see Delrahim, "Never Break the Chain" ("consider seafood harvesters that establish a permissioned blockchain to track food through the supply chain and assure quality and sourcing. If multiple competing harvesters conditioned access to that permissioned blockchain on agreeing to certain prices or output, competition and consumers would suffer tremendous harm.")

[11]   Candil, "Cryptocurrency association".

[12]   For an overview of tying, *see Microsoft Corp. v. Commission,* Case 3/37.792, C(2004)900 (EC, 2004). For American cases, *see Jefferson Parish Hosp. District No. 2 v. Hyde,* 466 U.S. 2, 1 (U.S., 1984); *United States v. Microsoft Corp.,* 253 F.3d 34 (D.C. Cir. 2001). Though the United States seemed to adopt the rule of reason after *Illinois Tool Works Inc. v. Independent Ink, Inc.,* 547 U.S. 28 (U.S., 2006), "the general per se rule for tying arrangements when market power is present very likely still survives," per Herbert J. Hovenkamp, "The Rule of Reason," Florida Law Review 70 (2018): 81, 96. For more on bundling, *see* Nicholas Economides and Ioannis Lianos, "Elusive Antitrust Standard on Bundling in Europe and in the United States in the Aftermath of the Microsoft Cases", Antitrust Law Journal 76, (2010): 483.

code from the very first day. Also, such strategies can lead to a reduction in the potential number of users, which is contrary to the principal objective of public permissionless blockchains: to create network effects. Precisely because tied sales and the creation of network effects do not mix well, the modification of public permissionless blockchains to implement such practices is unlikely.

On the other hand, private blockchains may have an interest in imposing tying or similar practices. This may be the case, for example, where a company requires an account on another platform or the owning of tokens to connect to its blockchain.[13] This might also be the case where a blockchain gatekeeper requires that certain tasks be performed before becoming a validator. Here too, the desire to implement tying practices may be counterbalanced by the intention to generate strong network effects. However, private blockchains do not entirely rely on network effects to generate value. Indeed, their functioning is more centralized than that of public blockchains (as we established in Chapter 2), and, therefore, their integrity and scalability do not entirely depend on the number of users. One may therefore expect more tying on private blockchains.

1.1.3   Predatory pricing

Attempts to drive smaller competitors out of the market by systematically undercutting them have been the subject of numerous court decisions.[14] On blockchain, pricing occurs mainly in the form of transaction fees when a user submits a transaction to be registered into the chain.[15] Predatory pricing is very unlikely on public permissionless blockchains, because the practice will be possible only if enough users are convinced, first, to change the governance structure to lower the price, and second, to change it back to a profitable level.

The situation is different for private blockchains. Private blockchains can change the protocol and transaction fees at any point in time without having to convince anyone to adopt the change. The pricing can therefore be changed easily in response to a competitor's strategy. One could imagine, for example,

---

[13]   *Id.*

[14]   In the European Union, predatory pricing is considered abusive if the prices charged by the dominant undertaking are below average variable costs or if the prices charged by the dominant undertaking are below average total costs and they are set as part of a plan for eliminating a competitor. *See France Télécom v. Commission*, Case C-202/07 P, European Court Reports: I-2369 (2009). In the United States, in order to establish predatory pricing, the plaintiff must show below-cost pricing and a dangerous probability of recoupment by the monopolist once the rival has been driven from the market. *See Brooke Group Ltd. v. Brown & Williamson Tobacco Corp.*, 509 U.S. 209, 223–24 (U.S., 1993).

[15]   *See* "How Do Ethereum Smart Contracts Work?", Coindesk, https://perma.cc/74G6-D73W; *see also* Chris Dannen, *Introducing Ethereum and Solidity: Foundations of Cryptocurrency and Blockchain Programming for Beginners* (Apress, 2017): 3, 47.

a private blockchain offering its users low transaction fees to eliminate competing blockchains. The legal test for predatory pricing would then apply.

1.1.4 Margin squeeze

Margin squeeze occurs when a vertically integrated dominant company operates on upstream and downstream markets, and sets the upstream price high enough so that companies cannot compete sustainably in the downstream market.[16] This practice, by definition, cannot be implemented on public monocentric blockchains, as they allow only one application. The same cannot be said of public platform blockchains; but because access to this infrastructure is free, the implementation of margin squeeze is hard to conceive. Raising the costs of the transaction fees for the purpose of squeezing margins also appears implausible, as the new fees would apply to all use cases.

The situation is different for private blockchains. Different transaction fees could be applied to specific participants. The gatekeepers of private blockchains could thus implement a margin squeeze strategy. While this strategy seems unlikely in the development phase of blockchains, it will become more likely as the industry matures. It should be closely monitored.

1.1.5 Exclusive dealing

Another anticompetitive practice consists in granting retroactive rebates or discounts conditional on a customer getting all or most of its goods or services from the dominant entity.[17] One could include such terms in the user

---

[16] Commission of the European Communities, "Guidance on the Commission's Enforcement Priorities In Applying Article 82 EC Treaty To Abusive Exclusionary Conduct By Dominant Undertakings," COM(2008) (2008): para. 80, https://perma .cc/V7EC-C3TF (asserting that margin squeeze occurs when a dominant undertaking may charge a price for the product on the upstream market which, compared to the price it charges on the downstream market, does not allow even an equally efficient competitor to trade profitably in the downstream market on a lasting basis); *see also Konkurrensverket v. TeliaSonera Sverige AB*, Case C-52/09, European Court Reports: 2011 I-527 (ECJ, 2011); *Deutsche Telekom AG v. Commission*, Case C-280/08P, European Court Reports 2010: I-9555 (ECJ, 2010); *Telefónica and Telefónica de España v. Commission*, Case C-295/12, European Court Reports: 2013 619 (ECJ, 2013). In the United States, a margin squeeze does not constitute an independent cause of action under Section 2 of the Sherman Act. *See Pac. Bell Tel. Co. v. LinkLine Commc'ns, Inc.*, 555 U.S. 438 (U.S., 2009).

[17] For an overview of exclusive dealing, *see Tomra Sys. ASA & Others v. Commission*, Case T-155/06, European Court Reports: 2010 II-4361 (2010), and *Intel Corp. v. Commission*, Case C-413/14 P, European Court Reports: 2017 632 (2017). In the United States, exclusive dealing may constitute a violation of Section 2 of the Sherman Act if it forecloses competitors from accessing the market. The D.C. Circuit held that "a monopolist's use of exclusive contracts, in certain circumstances, may give

agreement, which is signed before using the blockchain.[18] It seems unlikely to see such exclusive dealings on a public permissionless blockchain, as, by definition, each participant may leave and rejoin the network at will, without restricting its use.

Again, the situation is different for private blockchains. Private blockchains are interested in increasing their attractiveness by obtaining data that they alone can provide. This increases the attractiveness – and the value – of the blockchain. Exclusive dealing could be easily imposed in the terms and conditions of these blockchains. The chances that exclusive dealing practices will be implemented on private blockchains are high for that reason.

1.1.6   Rebates and discounts

Dominant entities may also want to grant rebates and discounts in a way that is anticompetitive – that is, where this induces fidelity and hurts competition.[19] Granting such rebates and discounts on a public blockchain would imply a major change in its infrastructure, which appears unlikely to be accepted as it would benefit only a minority of users. For example, one might want to grant a rebate for reducing a user's costs to transact on a blockchain. This could be done by reducing the fees the user must spend for transactions to be validated. On the Bitcoin blockchain, these fees are calculated on the amount of data that makes up a transaction: the more data, the higher the fees. A rebate could be granted to reduce the fees a specific user has to pay while promising that her or his transactions will be rapidly validated.

Granting such a rebate would require giving specific users the right to change these fees, which is unlikely to be done in existing blockchains. But even where this could be done, it is important to remember that all practices are recorded and visible on public permissionless blockchains. One user's dis-

---

rise to a § 2 violation even though the contracts foreclose less than the roughly forty percent or fifty percent share usually required in order to establish a § 1 violation." *United States v. Microsoft Corp.*, 253 F.3d 34, 70 (D.C. Cir., 2001).

[18]   For an example, *see* "Ethereum Foundation, Legal Agreement", Ethereum.org, https://perma.cc/57TB-G4NU.

[19]   For an overview of loyalty rebates, *see Intel Corp. v. Commission*, Case C-413/14 P, European Court Reports: 2017 632 (ECJ, 2017); *Hoffmann-La Roche and Co. AG v. Commission*, Case 85/76, European Court Reports: 1979 461 (ECJ, 1979); *Irish Sugar v. Commission*, Case T-228/97, European Court Reports: 1999 II-2975 (CFI, 1999); *British Airways v. Commission*, Case T-219/99, European Court Reports: 2003 II-5925 (CFI, 2003). In the United States, discount and rebate scheme programs can violate Section 2 of the Sherman Act. *See LePage's Inc. v. 3M*, 324 F.3d 141, 157 (3d Cir. 2003); *Cascade Health Sols. v. PeaceHealth*, 502 F.3d 895, 905 (9th Cir. 2007); *Eisai Inc. v. Sanofi-Aventis U.S.*, Civil Action No. 08-4168, 2014 WL 1343254, at *12 (D.N.J. March 28, 2014).

count would be visible to all, and the grant of loyalty rebates or discounts could lead to push-back from users that do not enjoy the same discount. This would significantly reduce the blockchain's attractiveness. Therefore, one should not expect many of these practices on public blockchains.

Private blockchains may technically implement rebates and discount. They also do not necessarily suffer from the "visibility effect," which lets all users know about rebates and discounts, because they can determine what information is visible to each user. They may, in short, create the conditions for attracting reputable users by offering them discounts while keeping all others. Rebates are thus expected to arise on such blockchains.

1.1.7 Predatory innovation

"Innovation" is "the implementation of a new or significantly improved product (good or service)."[20] Each time one changes the blockchain infrastructure, the modification can be described as an innovation. And where there is innovation, there is a risk of predatory innovation: "the alteration of one or more technical elements of a product to limit or eliminate competition."[21] Predatory innovation mirrors positive innovation – it is, after all, a new version of a product or technology; but it does not bring any real improvements to users. It is simply… new. In short, predatory innovation encompasses all anticompetitive strategies that aim to eliminate competition without benefiting consumers or users under the guise of improving products.

While the initial choice of a blockchain's public or private nature should be exempt from antitrust scrutiny,[22] the chosen architecture affects the likelihood of anticompetitive practices. As far as public permissionless blockchains are concerned, predatory innovation could be implemented only if a majority of the miners adopted a new governance design. This seems unlikely, as the change would hurt part of the deciding community – but not impossible. That said, any change to a public blockchain's infrastructure requires coordination and consensus among most participants.[23] Thus, as a public blockchain's

---

[20] OECD and Eurostat, *Oslo Manual: Guidelines for Collecting and Interpreting Innovation Data* (OECD Publishing, 2005): 146.

[21] Thibault Schrepel, "Predatory Innovation: The Definite Need for Legal Recognition," SMU Science & Technology Law Review 21 (2018): 19, 22.

[22] Hanno F. Kaiser, "Are 'Closed Systems' an Antitrust Problem?", Competition Policy International 71, no. 1 (2011): 91, 102–03.

[23] No rule, however, is set in stone. They can all be modified with a broad consensus.

community grows, it becomes increasingly difficult to reach a consensus on changing their design.[24]

As is often the case, things are different for private blockchains. In the words of Ethereum creator Vitalik Buterin, "the consortium or company running a private blockchain can easily, if desired, change the rules of a blockchain, revert transactions, modify balances, etc."[25] This ability may lead to predatory innovation, where a change in the rules is easy and requires no user approval.[26]

Predatory innovation may become a common practice in private blockchains, for several reasons. First, one can implement a predatory innovation strategy at no cost merely by changing a blockchain's code. Its implementation can also be quick, as interactions and validations via blockchain usually take only a few seconds or minutes. And although transactions and modifications are not invisible on public blockchains, they can be on private blockchains. On top of that, predatory innovation on blockchain can have a radical effect – for example, excluding targeted users that are also competitors. Last, predatory innovation practices can take different forms with multiple effects beyond mere exclusion from the blockchain. A company that owns a private blockchain can change its governance design so that a user's access is simply denied or so that the user can no longer read all the information on the blockchain, register transactions or take part in the block validation process. In a nutshell, predatory innovation remains one of the most expected and dangerous anticompetitive strategies that can be implemented on private blockchains.

1.2   Other Abuses

1.2.1   Exploitative abuses

Exploitative abuses entail the direct or indirect imposition of unfair conditions on existing customers or suppliers.[27] Theoretically, these are not prohibited under US antitrust law. Still, some of these exploitative practices are sanc-

---

[24]   Patrick Murck, "Who Controls the Blockchain?," Harvard Business Review, April 19, 2017, https://perma.cc/EKK6-KWWT. Nevertheless, let us note that the future introduction of new governance models using off-chain and sidechain mechanisms in public blockchain may reduce these difficulties and therefore facilitate predatory innovation.
[25]   Vitalik Buterin, "On Public and Private Blockchains," Ethereum (blog), August 6, 2015, https://perma.cc/38UK-UFM8.
[26]   In fact, using a "godmode," the private blockchain owner can freeze any account or move the funds away, but the chances are that people will eventually discover it and sell all the stocks, securities or tokens.
[27]   Article 102(a) of the TFEU refers to the imposition of unfair purchase or selling prices as well as other unfair trading conditions. Consolidated Version of the Treaty on the Functioning of the European Union art. 102(a), 2008 O.J.C. 115/47. *See Rambus v.*

tioned – sometimes under different labels – on both continents, especially when it comes to intellectual property and digital markets.[28] As underlined by Harry First, "contrary to conventional wisdom, antitrust law is being used today to control the ability of intellectual property rights holders to exploit their licensees through excessively high prices or the imposition of particular nonprice terms."[29] Exploitative practices are therefore relevant in both Europe and the United States, although they remain arguably preeminent on the European side.

Blockchain's participants should keep informed about the activities of antitrust agencies in the field. For example, the creation of a dual blockchain environment with preferential treatment (paid prioritization)[30] – one for those who pay the most and another for those who pay less and whose transactions will lag behind[31] – might be questioned by agencies.

These dual environments are more likely to be implemented in private blockchain environments than public ones. The imposition of differentiated terms on just a few participants will prove difficult in public permissionless blockchains, as I have previously explained. On top of that, access is free and easy, switching costs and barriers to exit are low, creating a disincentive to engage in such practices. It follows that paid prioritization, where it exists, should not be seen as being systematically anticompetitive. Ethereum is a good example. Blockchain's participants can pay extra fees (called "gas fees") to

---

Commission, Case COMP/38.636, O.J. C 30 (EC, 2010) (the Commission had to deal with potentially abusive royalties for the use of patents).

[28]   *See* Harry First, "Exploitative Abuses of Intellectual Property Rights," in *The Cambridge Handbook of Antitrust, Intellectual Property, and High Tech*, eds. Roger D. Blair and D. Daniel Soko (Cambridge University Press, 2016): 222–23, 241 ("It is the standard view in the United States that … antitrust law does not reach acts of exploitation by a monopolist … [W]ithout denying this substantial divergence in general between the United States and the rest of the world, it turns out that there may be fewer differences between the United States and other jurisdictions when it comes to judging exploitative behavior by intellectual property rights holders with market power … [C]ontrary to conventional wisdom, antitrust law is being used today to control the ability of intellectual property rights holders to exploit their licensees through excessively high prices or the imposition of particular nonprice terms.") For cases, *see Microsoft Corp. v. Motorola, Inc.*, 795 F.3d 1024, 1033 (9th Cir. 2015); *Broadcom Corp. v. Qualcomm Inc.*, 501 F.3d 297, 310, 314 (3d Cir. 2007).

[29]   Harry First, *Exploitative Abuses of Intellectual Property Rights* (Cambridge University Press, 2017): 241.

[30]   Peder Østbye, "The Adequacy of Competition Policy for Cryptocurrency Markets" (2017), https://perma.cc/H8MH-C82A.

[31]   This issue is similar to that of net neutrality. *See* Falk Schöning and Myrto Tagara, "Blockchain: Mind the Gap! Lessons Learnt from The Net Neutrality Debate and Competition Law Related Aspects," Concurrences 3-2018 (2018): 6.

encourage their transaction to be validated first. This leads to the prioritiza-tion of those who pay the most, thus creating a procompetitive environment between users.

The picture is different with private blockchains. Paid prioritization can result not from a public process, but from abusive practices aimed at discour-aging certain users. Fee modifications can indeed be implemented unilaterally, beyond the participants' sight. The fact that switching costs are higher than they are in public blockchains (due to access fees and conditions) reinforces the assumption that paid prioritization could be detrimental to competition, even when the practice is known to users.

This type of abuse will undoubtedly be the subject of legal proceedings. In this regard, it is worth underlining that the rise of the term "fairness" at the European Commission[32] – whose definition and scope are still unde-fined[33] – could be seen as a sign of its willingness to tackle exploitative practices more aggressively. In an Impact Assessment, entitled "Fairness in Platform-to-Business Relations,"[34] the European Commission identified several issues related to platforms, including the negotiation of terms and con-ditions. One may find several indications that a similar direction is being taken in the United States.[35] Overall, everything suggests that antitrust agencies will tackle blockchain issues under this general policy.

1.2.2   Discriminatory abuses

Discriminatory abuses occur when parties apply "dissimilar conditions to equivalent transactions with other trading parties, thereby placing them at

---

[32] *See* Margrethe Vestager, "The Importance of Being Open—and Fair," in European Conference (Harvard University, March 2, 2018), https://perma.cc/7L78 -Q5QX.

[33] *See* Thibault Schrepel, "Antitrust Without Romance," NYU Journal of Law & Liberty 13 (2020). On the difficulty of defining "fairness," *see Mogul Steamship Co. v. McGregor* [1892] AC 25 (House of Lords, 1892): 49 (citing 23 Q.B.D. 625, 626): ("I adopt the vigorous language and opinion of Fry L.J.: 'To draw a line between fair and unfair competition, between what is reasonable and unreasonable, passes the power of the courts.'"). The scope of fairness is also unclear. *See* Louis Kaplow and Steven Shavell, "Fairness Versus Welfare: Notes on the Pareto Principle, Preferences, and Distributive Justice," The Journal of Legal Studies 32, no. 1 (2003): 331, 334 (fairness integrating all independent evaluative principles that are not purely welfarist).

[34] "Fairness in Platform-to-Business Relations," European Commission, https:// perma.cc/H5QS-VJK7.

[35] Federal Trade Commission, "FTC's Bureau of Competition Launches Task Force to Monitor Technology Markets," February 26, 2019, https://perma.cc/JDZ8 -XH3F; Makena Kelly, "Google Under Antitrust Investigation By 50 Attorneys General," The Verge, September 9, 2019, https://perma.cc/2XSX-FGUD.

a competitive disadvantage."[36] Price discrimination is the most common of these.[37] According to Judge Richard Posner:

> price discrimination is a term that economists use to describe selling the same product to different customers at different prices even though the cost of sales is the same. More precisely, it is selling at a price or prices such that the ratio of price to marginal costs is different in different sales.[38]

Price discrimination involves favoring specific customers. In practice, it occurs in two ways: (1) charging different customers different prices for the same product; or (2) charging customers the same price for different products.

Could price discrimination occur in the blockchain space? Of course it could. But let me recall that, first, the implementation of such practices on public permissionless blockchain would require approval by the majority, which is unlikely; and, second, because of the "visible effect" of public permissionless blockchains, price discrimination would be limited as it would reduce the blockchain's attractiveness. To be sure, one will find many instances in which different prices are charged to use the same blockchain. But so long as they correspond to different services or are applied to different users based on objective criteria, they will not be found to be discriminatory.

For private blockchains, one could easily implement discriminatory practices. Perhaps users will encounter discriminatory terms because they could help incentivize them to be active on the blockchain by offering lower prices, thus creating a potential discrimination claim for others. Once again, private blockchains will be the center of focus.

---

[36] *See* TFEU art. 102(c); *see also* 2008 O.J. C. 115/47; Robert O'Donoghue and A. Jorge Padilla, *The Law and Economics of Article 102 TFEU*, 2nd ed. (Hart Publishing, 2013): 789.

[37] In European judicial history, there are few cases in which price discrimination alone was found abusive. *See Clearstream Banking AG v. Commission*, Case T-301/04, European Court Reports: 2009 317 (CFI, 2009) (referring to anticompetitive foreclosure when an "as efficient competitor" cannot compete effectively with the price of the dominant undertaking); *see also Post Danmark A/S v. Konkurrencerådet*, C-209/10, European Court Reports: 2012 172 (ECJ, 2012) (clarifying that where prices are below average total costs while being above average incremental costs, a finding of abuse requires a demonstration of actual or likely exclusionary effects). In the United States, price discrimination by a monopolist violates Section 2 of the Sherman Act only to the extent that it is predatory or otherwise excludes competitors from the relevant market. *See Blue Cross & Blue Shield United of Wis. v. Marshfield Clinic*, 65 F.3d 1406, 1413 (7th Cir. 1995). Price discrimination may also violate the Robinson-Patman Act. *See Brooke Group Ltd. v. Brown & Williamson Tobacco Corp.*, 509 U.S. 209, 220 (U.S., 1993).

[38] Richard Posner, *Antitrust Law*, 2nd ed. (University of Chicago Press, 2001): 79–80.

2   PRACTICES USING BLOCKCHAIN

In this section, I analyze the extent to which blockchains can facilitate unilateral anticompetitive practices in the real space. In this regard, it is important to distinguish practices that merely use blockchain from those that involve smart contracts. This dichotomy is similar to that which I have used in the two chapters on collusive agreements. As I show, it seems highly unlikely that such practices could be created without the support of smart contracts.

2.1   Without Smart Contracts

Blockchain could theoretically be used without smart contracts to pursue unilateral anticompetitive purposes in the outside world. In practice, however, companies will use a blockchain when the technology's characteristics benefit their practice. Against this background, one must question whether blockchain characteristics could help abuses of dominant position. The answer seems negative.

I have shown that the immutable nature of blockchain creates trust between colluders, thus providing a technical answer to a classic cartel problem. But the same cannot be said of monopolization. Let me illustrate that claim by studying blockchain's key characteristics: encryption and immutability (*see* Chapter 2 for a technical explanation).

Thanks to encryption, the identity of users and the content of their transactions on the blockchain remain secret. This creates what I have called the "opacity effect," which complicates the detection of collusion. However, this does not protect monopolization practices with real-world impacts, as companies know the identity of their (dominant) business partners. As a result, one participant's public key can easily be correlated with its actual life identity. The same applies for the content of transactions. Decoding the hash value of transactions is undoubtedly complex, if not practically impossible considering the limits of computing power. Still, the fact remains that abused companies can easily establish a link between the problematic blockchain transactions and the real-world identity of the abuser. Encryption is not helpful for dominant companies.

The same can be said for immutability. Monopolization practices do not require a high level of trust between different players, as is the case with collusive practices. Accordingly, there is no need to transform any relationship into a cooperative game. Thus, except in limited cases, the immutable or unstoppable nature of smart contracts is indifferent to those who want to implement an illegal practice on their own. That feature could even create a negative effect. As I have previously discussed, one may not exclude that companies could fear their practice will be more easily discovered when implemented on a blockchain. The result is that neither of blockchain's two principal features encourage monopolization practices. But things are different when smart contracts are involved.

2.2 With Smart Contracts

Smart contracts can be useful allies in implementing various anticompetitive practices. Let me take a step back before analyzing each one of them. I have shown that smart contracts provide an important support to cartels by generating trust. Because companies do not encounter this trust problem in monopolization settings, one can logically expect that smart contracts will foster fewer unilateral practices than collusion. Still, I will try to draw up a risk map to help identify which practices are most likely to emerge.

As I shall explain, the distinction between public and private blockchains is not as essential here as it is for unilateral practices concerning the blockchain itself (such as those I studied in the previous section). The smart contracts I am about to discuss are implemented on top of existing layer 1 infrastructures. One does not need the approval of a majority to implement them. Finally, while many of these practices could be implemented using algorithms outside blockchain, blockchain's immutability may prove useful.

2.2.1 Exclusionary abuses

2.2.1.1 *Refusal to deal*
Refusal to deal or grant access often implies the absence of any contract. To that extent, explaining how smart contracts could help implement such practices might seem strange. But they can help. As we know, refusals to deal or grant access are not limited to sheer refusals. In practice, subjecting the signing of a contract to excessive (i.e., exclusionary) conditions may lead to a similar result. A dominant firm could impose such conditions on a smart contract.

2.2.1.2 *Tying*
A company may want to impose the use of a public permissionless blockchain when buying a product or service in the real space. In such a situation, access to the blockchain is free, but one could see the practice as a way of forcing people to use a product (here, the blockchain) they do not want. A company might also impose conditions to acquire tokens with the purchase of an independent product or service – effectively imposing additional costs on buyers. This will likely become a standard practice in the years to come, raising antitrust questions related to tying.

UNILATERAL PRACTICES USING BLOCKCHAIN (WITH SMART CONTRACTS)	EXCLUSIONARY ABUSES							EXPLOITATIVE ABUSES	DISCRIMINATORY ABUSES
	Refusal to deal	Tying	Predatory pricing	Margin squeeze	Exclusive dealing	Rebates & discounts	Predatory innovation		
PUBLIC PERMISSIONLESS BLOCKCHAIN	**Likely** by definition, a refusal to deal implies the absence of any (smart) contracts, but in practice, submitting the signing of a (smart) contract to excessive conditions may lead to a similar result	**Very likely** conditioning the sale of a product or service to the use of a specific blockchain or the purchase of tokens	**Likely** ensuring automatic price changes (first down, then up) via smart contracts, according to a set of predefined rules to exclude rivals	**Likely** ensuring automatic price changes via smart contracts according to a set of predefined rules (linked to the downstream price) to squeeze competitors' margins	**Unlikely** ensuring through smart contracts that a purchase is automated whenever a set of predefined conditions (indicating a need) are met.	**Very likely** ensuring through smart contracts that a discount or rebate is granted each time a set of predefined rules are met.	**Unlikely** automating by smart contract an action on a software or platform operating outside the blockchain.	**Likely** setting up an escrow that can be released at will by the dominant firm, but also, forcing the signing of abusive smart contracts.	**Likely** using smart contracts to impose differentiated conditions on partners
PRIVATE BLOCKCHAIN									

Figure 11.2   The implementation of unilateral practices via blockchain

2.2.1.3   Predatory pricing

Predatory pricing involves a two-step strategy (although only the first is required in European competition law):[39] a price decrease below the competitive level and a subsequent price increase above the competitive level, once competitors are excluded. In this respect, the use of smart contracts could allow price changes to be performed automatically, in either direction. The advantage that a dominant undertaking might gain in using a smart contract rather than a simple algorithm is that a smart contract could be considered a legally valid sale contract (if it meets specific requirements, depending on each national law). This interaction would then be recorded in the ledger. Besides, the dominant company could use different oracles searching for information on competitors' websites to adjust its strategy. This practice is likely to increase in the coming years.

2.2.1.4   Margin squeeze

As with predatory pricing, one can easily implement margin squeezes through smart contracts. Here, the dominant undertaking defines the rules of the contract in such a way that the price for access to an infrastructure (whether a private blockchain or another type of infrastructure) is a function of the price charged in the downstream market. The advantage of using a smart contract over a simple algorithm is the ability to create contracts directly through the blockchain and link different oracles to use variables on top of an immutable smart contract.

2.2.1.5   Exclusive dealing

Smart contracts could also automate purchases when predetermined conditions are met. For example, they could automate sending new supplies every time a company sells X number of products. One could indeed link smart contracts to inventories and ensure automatic transactions. One should nonetheless expect some reluctance from business partners to provide information promptly and grant access to their inventories.

2.2.1.6   Rebates and discounts

Smart contracts can also manage loyalty rebates and discounts, as they can automatically grant certain discounts whenever specific predefined conditions are met. For example, a smart contract may grant a retroactive payment when a predefined number of products have been purchased. It would allow the

---

[39]   *See France Télécom SA v. Commission*, Case C-202/07, European Court Reports: 2009 I-02369 (ECJ, 2009).

implementation of complex rebate systems while ensuring that the parties have full visibility of the system in place, and can trust its immutability.

2.2.1.7   *Predatory innovation*

Smart contracts, by definition, can be used to automate tasks within blockchain. It is thus hard to imagine how they could operate changes on products or platforms located outside of it. And even if this could be done, it is hard to see why this process would be superior to implementing predatory innovation without a blockchain.

2.2.2   **Other abuses**

2.2.2.1   *Exploitative abuses*

The number of cases involving exploitative abuses is increasing.[40] One should logically expect agencies to open related investigations in blockchain ecosystems.

To start with, dominant undertakings could use smart contracts to force a partner to provide an escrow which will be released depending on its behavior. The implementation of such a mechanism could be considered abusive under European competition law, as it strongly unbalances the relationship between the two companies that are parties to the transaction.

Dominant firms could also force their partners to sign pre-drafted smart contracts – so-called "adhesion contracts" (as defined at the beginning of the twentieth century by Raymond Saleilles).[41] Such contracts are not illegal by default, but they can be in several European countries when both parties have not freely consented to them. Smart contracts could also impose unfair terms of this sort.[42]

---

[40] *See*, for instance, "Antitrust: Commission Opens Investigations into Apple's App Store Rules," European Commission, June 16, 2020, https://perma.cc/3F3P-NK8J.

[41] Adhesion contracts are typically drafted by one party and signed by another party with lesser bargaining power, *see* Raymond Saleilles, *De la déclaration de volonté: Contribution à l'étude de l'acte juridique dans le code civil allemand* (Librairie Cotillon, 1901): 119 (defining an "adhesion contract" as a contract for which "there is an exclusive predominance of a will" forcing the co-contractor to "adhere to it").

[42] *See* Kevin Werbach and Nicolas Cornell, "Contracts Ex Machina," 67 Duke Law Journal (2017): 313 (smart contracts); Lin William Cong and Zhiguo He, "Blockchain Disruption and Smart Contracts" (2017): 11 (providing a functional definition of "smart contracts" as "digital contracts allowing terms contingent on decentralized consensus that are tamper-proof and typically self-enforcing through automated execution.")

2.2.2.2   *Discriminatory abuses*

As we have seen, discriminatory abuses arise when a company imposes dissimilar conditions on trading partners which are in similar situations. Smart contracts can be used to implement such practices, as they may facilitate complex and differentiated conditions. And because they are automatically executed, they eliminate a majority of the monitoring costs that one might incur for similar contracts outside the blockchain. There is thus a risk that smart contracts will be used for discriminatory ends, whether antitrust law is infringed upon signing of the contract or after several conditions are met.

3   CHAPTER SUMMARY AND BEYOND

The distinction between public permissionless blockchains and private blockchains is central to the practices impacting the blockchain itself. The gatekeepers of private blockchains hold unilateral powers, which significantly facilitates the implementation of anticompetitive practices. The presence of a pilot in the cockpit of private blockchains shows the need for antitrust agencies to focus on the latter. As for public blockchains, anticompetitive practices may be implemented only when the blockchain has allowed this from the outset (which is unlikely to be the case), or when a majority of the participants agree to alter the blockchain's rules.

The distinction between public and private blockchains is less useful with regard to anticompetitive practices using smart contracts. The constraints imposed by blockchain's architecture apply only to a limited extent in this case, as one can implement them on an upper level. Put differently, the blockchain's initial characteristics are important to allow smart contracts, but the two levels are not intrinsically linked. It follows that public blockchains can be almost as useful as private blockchains for the implementation of such unilateral practices. Two lessons emerge from this.

First, in terms of the practices directed at the blockchain, I would advise that antitrust agencies focus on behaviors that have the effect of concentrating the blockchain infrastructure by eliminating participants at this layer. Here, agencies should ensure that no anti-competitive practice impacts blockchain development and creates artificial centralization. As blockchain industries mature, this issue will become pressing – the technology will have a more significant impact on the overall economy, serving as one of its underlying foundations.

Second, the sanction of practices using blockchain for anticompetitive purposes (in the "real space") will help eliminate the artificial centralization of the economy while presenting little risk of indirectly affecting blockchain design. Thus, I advocate for the time being that antitrust agencies focus on these practices (section 2 of the present chapter) rather than on those concerning the blockchain itself (section 1 of the present chapter). Only if and when blockchains serve as the architecture for the global economy should agencies focus on inside practices.

12. Blockchain and merger control

1   CHALLENGES

In this first section, I introduce a typology of all blockchain concentrations. Some are technical by nature, as they concern the internal layers of two or more blockchains; while others are non-technical, as they concern the surrounding ecosystem.

1.1   A Typology of Blockchain's Operations

Figure 12.1   An overview of blockchain's concentrations

1.1.1   Technical concentrations
Blockchain concentrations may result from hostile takeovers. While these may look like proper acquisitions, I contend that the rules of merger control should not apply. On the contrary, when a blockchain concentration is mutually agreed upon, it might require a notification.

1.1.1.1   Hostiles
Hostile forms of blockchain concentrations – which we could also translate as forced takeovers – can be temporary or permanent. They are temporary when a blockchain nucleus takes "control" of a target Proof of Work blockchain for a specific period by devoting its computational power to it.[1] Of course, the nucleus can use its existing computational power; but it may also rent or borrow the mining power from a third party so to reinforce the takeover.

---

[1]   Joseph Bonneau, "Hostile Blockchain Takeovers (Short Paper)," in *Financial Cryptography and Data Security*, eds. Aviv Zohar et al (Heidelberg, 2018) (describing this practice of "rental attack").

Permanent takeovers are also possible, but require more sophisticated strategies. The first of these strategies relates to mining or validating activity. If the target runs on Proof of Work, a "building attack" may amount to taking control of it by obtaining a permanent majority of the mining power.[2] Where the target runs on Proof of Stake, a "buy-out attack" may be conducted by acquiring a majority of the existing capacity.

The second strategy is a "bribery attack."[3] In this situation, a blockchain offers (manually or by smart contract) tokens to all participants of another blockchain that agree to burn their own (i.e., sending them to non-spendable addresses or specific smart contracts).[4] When the vast majority of miners and users do so, one may consider that the takeover is complete. Prior coordination with miners and validators can help in completing such hostile takeovers – for example, by ensuring and explaining that the revenues from the mining activity will be higher in the acquiring blockchain.[5] At the same time, disclosing the willingness to carry out a hostile takeover too far in advance could cause the operation to fail, as the target will have time to organize.[6] Moreover, the more coordinated the strategy between blockchain participants, the more the operation will be considered mutually agreed upon.

In any case, one may question whether these hostile takeovers should be subjected to merger control. Those related to mining and validating activities are successful in the medium and long run only if the "acquired community" agrees to keep on mining or validating transactions in the chain. There are examples in which hostile takeovers have failed, and where blockchain communities have forked the blockchain after the takeover to seize back their own governance.[7] Furthermore, in these "building attacks," there is no proper

---

[2]   Liehuang Zhu, et al., "Research on the Security of Blockchain Data: A Survey," Journal of Computer Science and Technology 35, no. 4, (2020) (describing the process).

[3]   Joseph Bonneau, "Hostile Blockchain Takeovers (Short Paper)," in *Financial Cryptography and Data Security*, eds. Aviv Zohar et al. (Heidelberg, 2018).

[4]   Andy Bromberg, "What the First Token Hostile Takeover Could Look Like," Medium, March 15, 2018, https://perma.cc/8JFE-FH3F.

[5]   Coordination with exchanges could also help, *see* Michael, "Altcoin Merger Season—Coming Spring 2019," November 4, 2018, https://perma.cc/AG35-D5AY.

[6]   Discussing how to prevent such hostile takeovers, *see* Andy Bromberg, "What the First Token Hostile Takeover Could Look Like," Medium, March 15, 2018, https://perma.cc/8JFE-FH3F ("One way to apply this to this token hostile takeover would be to encode in the token's original smart contract that if a certain percentage of tokens outstanding are burned within a specific time period, those tokens are re-issued and distributed pro rata to all the remaining holders.")

[7]   Vitalik Buterin, "Coordination, Good and Bad," Vitalik Buterin's website, September 11, 2020, https://perma.cc/FBX5-R59E (explaining that forks are "a major and crucially important form of counter-coordination," preventing a few blockchain

change in control of the entire blockchain, as only mining and validating activities are impacted.

As for hostile takeovers by way of bribery ("buy-out attacks"), they are successful only when the vast majority of users move to the other (more profitable) blockchain. These takeovers result from the interplay of competition. Anticompetitive practices could eventually be punished along the way, but in neither case is there a shift of power over the same entity (an essential criterion in merger control). Users are simply leaving for another blockchain. Hence, subjecting hostile takeovers to the obligation to notify, regardless of the procedural issues (i.e., their unpredictable and secret nature), would be nonsensical.

1.1.1.2   Mutually agreed

One may expect that mutually agreed concentrations will mainly take the form of "chainmergers," at least for the time being.[8] Here, two blockchains merge their transaction histories and gather all new transactions in a single chain. The new entity may keep the identity of one of the two parents (the concentration would then be an acquisition), or it may also take on a new identity (the concentration would then be a merger).[9] At least, that is the theory. In practice, however, these deals present several difficulties.

First, the two blockchains might not run on the same type of architecture.[10] That being said, this technical problem will most likely end up with technical solutions. Second, the hard cap (if any) on the number of blockchain tokens must be maintained at equivalent levels.[11] In other words, if one blockchain

---

users from colluding against the majority interest). For example, part of the Steem community – a social blockchain – has implemented a fork to escape a harmful collusion, *see* Paddy Baker, "Steem Hard Fork Confiscates $6.3M, Community Immediately Takes It Back," CoinDesk, May 20, 2020, https://perma.cc/L6ZF-PDPH.

[8]   *See* Jonathan Jones, "JP Morgan Consider Blockchain Merger with Consensys," February 12, 2020, https://perma.cc/4HXB-BTVP. Also, discussing the possibility that setting up a blockchain consortium may be "subject to approval or at least scrutiny by merger control authorities," *see* Law Society and London Advocates, "Blockchain: Legal and Regulatory Guidance Report" (2020): 56.

[9]   For an example, *see* Yogita Khatri, "Polygon Acquires Hermez in $250 million Deal that Includes First-Ever Token 'Merger'," The Block, August 13, 2021, https://perma.cc/C34C-U34D (describing the acquisition of Hermez Network by Polygon and the merging of their native tokens).

[10]   Eric Lombrozo, "Consensus Rules – Changing Them Without Changing Bitcoin," YouTube, September 10, 2017, https://perma.cc/348B-BHRR ("We don't have a merge process in Bitcoin. There might be some future ideas eventually in other cryptocurrencies that might allow for merges but as Bitcoin stands right now, there really is no way to merge two chains that are incompatible").

[11]   Paddy Baker, "Chainmerger: Could BTC And BHC Ever Become One Again?" Crypto Briefing, September 24, 2018, https://perma.cc/GGB9-M3RA.

has a cap of 20 million tokens and the other has a similar one, the merged blockchain should maintain that 20 million token cap instead of doubling it (its value would otherwise decrease dramatically). Further problems arise, for example, when one blockchain has a 20 million token cap while the other is limited at 3 million. Third, token holders would have to commit to burning their tokens to receive new ones.[12] During this process, smart contracts could automatize the distribution of new tokens, depending on the number of old tokens being burned. This could also be done manually.[13] Issuing tokens is called an "airdrop" where they are created out of thin air and distributed "for free" for a limited period of time, under specific conditions. The process could reward the adoption of the new blockchain – for example, by distributing 1.2 tokens per 1 burned token.[14] These chainmergers also present challenges such as ensuring proper conversion, implementing the airdrop and verifying whether the tokens have been permanently burned before distributing new ones. Fourth, mechanisms would have to be put in place after the merger to convince the users remaining on one of the old chains to use the merged one instead.[15] Let us recall that blockchains are immutable, and for that reason, one cannot erase them. They can only be abandoned.

Ultimately, mutually agreed concentrations will also take other forms than chainmergers – many of which are yet to be invented. For example, when two blockchains implement perfect interoperability, ensuring their protocols and operations are fully compatible, their ecosystems will be *de facto* combined into one (despite the continued presence of two entities).[16] As a result, miners will mine blocks on either of these two blockchains without two core clients. This would achieve a concentration.

---

[12]   Chris Herd, "Why Blockchains Could Become Hostile Takeover Targets for Other Blockchains and How They Could Pull it Off," Medium, December 22, 2017, https://perma.cc/JD5H-EYQ2. One could also envision that they would transfer their old tokens to "the acquiring network's management team, which would then sell those tokens and take the proceeds," *see* Andy Bromberg, "Paying to be Bought: A Token Network Acquisition Blueprint," Medium, July 5, 2018, https://perma.cc/GT2T-HELB.

[13]   Michael, "Crypto to Crypto Merger—It's Possible!" Medium, December 11, 2018, https://perma.cc/KH93-BNV2.

[14]   Issues may arise if fewer of the new tokens are delivered compared to what had been promised.

[15]   Domocoin took over the Heptacoi, *see* Michael, "Crypto to Crypto Merger—It's Possible!" Medium, December 11, 2018, https://perma.cc/KH93-BNV2 ("The Domocoin <> Heptacoin is the first recorded 'merger' between open source crypto projects (if there were others please let me know) and proves that M&A is a viable growth hacking strategy for crypto projects.")

[16]   Discussing interoperability in this context, *see* World Economic Forum, "Building Block chain(s) for a Better Plane" (2018), https://perma.cc/3FKJ-UDQS.

1.1.2 Non-technical concentrations

Non-technical mergers do not affect the infrastructure or the governance of blockchains,[17] but include the surrounding environment, such as media, exchanges, wallets, investment funds, hardware manufacturers, analytics firms, think-tanks and foundations. These operations create classic problems in terms of competitive analysis. For example, if a single exchange became so dominant that it captured 90 per cent of exchange activities, competition law concerns would logically arise. Also, mining companies could regroup to capture a larger share of the market. Finally, such concentrations could be vertical – for example, an exchange could acquire core developers.

On top of analyzing the relevant markets at stake, antitrust agencies should ensure that these transactions do not indirectly reduce the competitive pressure or lead to artificial centralization within blockchain markets. This will rarely be the case. Being outside of the blockchain ecosystem (such as I have presented in Chapter 4), these concentrations are unlikely to impact one or multiple blockchain layers. But the possibility cannot be entirely excluded, as outside operations could eventually impact blockchain's infrastructure. For example, when the incentive to invest knowledge, time or money in a blockchain is reduced because of a non-technical merger, this indicates the need to consider the competitive impact on the entire ecosystem.

1.2 Evaluating Concentrations

1.2.1 Change in control

1.2.1.1 The logic

In the United States, Section 7 of the Clayton Act (1914) governs mergers and acquisitions. It prohibits those transactions where "the effect of such acquisition may be substantially to lessen competition, or to tend to create a monopoly." On top of the Clayton Act, the Hart-Scott-Rodino Antitrust Improvements Act of 1976 ("HSR Act") gives the FTC and the DOJ Antitrust Division the power to review all operations concerning assets, non-corporate interests or voting securities.

Although none of the abovementioned texts is explicitly limited to transactions that involve a change of control, that element is central to the analysis. First, all acquisitions of less than 50 percent of a non-corporate entity are not reportable under the HSR Act. There is also an exemption for up to 10 percent of a corporation's voting securities. Furthermore, the element of control is

---

[17] Nat Nead, "Tracking Reverse Mergers in Crypto & Blockchain," Investment Bank, https://perma.cc/X7HZ-EA6T.

essential when analyzing the "acquiring" and "acquired" persons. Put differently, two zones of control must be involved in the transaction and a transfer must be realized from one to another.

In Europe, the element of "control" is defined as the power to exercise decisive influence over an undertaking based on rights, contracts or other means. Control is characterized:

> either separately or in combination and having regard to the considerations of fact or law involved, in particular by: (a) ownership or the right to use all or part of the assets of an undertaking; (b) rights or contracts which confer decisive influence ...[18]

All concentrations involving a lasting change of control must be notified. The change can be *de jure* or *de facto*; it can include negative (e.g., veto rights) or positive (e.g., voting rights) capacities. Measuring that transfer is challenging when it comes to blockchain.

1.2.1.2   In practice

As I have shown, distinct forms of horizontal control are exercised within blockchains, as opposed to the firm, where control is vertical by nature. This makes pinpointing who controls the blockchain more complex.

As a matter of fact, there are few assets linked to a blockchain. Acquiring a blockchain means acquiring its key usage (miners and users), and its expertise (core developers). To be sure, blockchain concentrations can take different forms, but they all lead to a similar result: merging two blockchain nuclei into one. In other words, a takeover is complete whenever one blockchain nucleus ensures the survival of another blockchain. When the nucleus participants refuse to do so, their blockchain conserves the means to survive and keeps on exerting competitive pressure on the others. Participants' behaviors are central to the analysis for that reason.

Identifying the behavioral factors that suggest a possible change in control will help agencies. As I have explained, the participants in the nucleus have the power to influence the blockchain. By collaborating and therefore evading (some of) the constraints imposed by others, they may decide to acquire another blockchain. For instance, a nucleus could start an airdrop and set up a smart contract to offer freshly minted tokens to the users of another blockchain. One nucleus could also agree with another to start a fork with the ambition of joining the two chains.

They could also achieve their objective by setting up sufficiently high incentives for the operation to succeed, as they cannot impose the takeover on

---

[18]   European Commission, "EC Merger Regulation Guidelines," Council Regulation (EC) No 139/2004.

other members (Chapter 7 explains how members of the nucleus can impose these strategies). These apply to both public permissionless blockchains and private ones.

In the end, agencies will have to decide which mechanisms are sufficiently robust and effective to incite blockchain nuclei to approve and complete takeovers. Doing so will help agencies identify which actions could succeed and, therefore, trigger the need for prior notification. This is no easy task, but it is a crucial one. Agencies do not want to impose notifications in situations where the incentives are not good enough, nor do they want to do so once the concentrations have been completed. Meeting this challenge will require agencies to carefully analyze existing blockchain code and ecosystems in search of answers.

1.2.2   Analyzing thresholds

Not all operations that involve a change of control are subject to a notification requirement. They must also pass relevant thresholds. In both the United States and Europe, these thresholds are linked to the turnover of the entities involved in a transaction. Transposing these thresholds to both public permissionless and private blockchains will, once again, prove challenging. Determining the (representative) turnover of these blockchains, as I have explained, is difficult. Indeed, their value is initially expressed in their native tokens. One can certainly convert these into fiat currencies and one can calculate their average over a year; but this would negate their numerous fluctuations.

Simply converting tokens to express a blockchain's turnover could end up in a situation where agencies might find that one blockchain enjoys significant market power because its turnover, converted into dollars or euros, is high on average, despite substantial fluctuations. On the contrary, agencies might find that another blockchain enjoys lesser market power because its average turnover, once converted, is lower despite its stability. This situation would paint an erroneous picture of the market reality. A blockchain whose value soars for a few months before collapsing does not necessarily benefit from significant market power. Therefore, new analyses must supplement the metrics that are currently used. The second section of this chapter deals with this question.

2   OPPORTUNITIES

Despite the challenges blockchain creates for the control of concentrations, it also opens up opportunities. Embracing the advent of blockchain ecosystems will notably lead antitrust agencies to adopt a more technological approach to merger analysis and modernize existing procedures.

2.1   A Technological Approach

2.1.1   Analyzing technology (for real)

Analyzing blockchain concentrations requires a good understanding of the technology. Acquiring this knowledge is a challenge as much as an opportunity to modernize merger control.[19] That applies to notifications and assessments of anticompetitive effects.

Most notifications are triggered by a change in legal structure (e.g., the acquisition of shares), but one may also take on legal instruments (e.g., contracts) to analyze the acquisition of *de facto* control. Such analyses neglect the intention behind the operation; while, as I have shown in the first section, the concentration of public permissionless blockchains is a matter of implementing the proper incentives. Blockchain concentration will thus require more from agencies – namely, to study not only how blockchain code is used or changed for the purpose of an operation, but also the effects of these changes (i.e., if they create sufficient incentives or not).

Assessing the competitive effects of blockchain concentrations also requires agencies to understand the underlying technology. Merely looking at market shares will be insufficient. Antitrust agencies occasionally look at other metrics, such as competitors' size, the number of recent entries and so on. But those are poor substitutes for analyzing the technology at stake in digital mergers. Code and programming may reveal some potential for growth, compatibility diversification outside one relevant market, network effects and potential consumer lock-in (or absence thereof).

Put differently, analyzing blockchain's code will allow agencies to assess its dynamic capabilities[20] – that is, the capacity to absorb and integrate external knowledge. In fact, one may talk about dynamic technical capacity – that is, the ability to develop new technical capability on top of or using an existing technology.[21] That is crucial in assessing dynamic competition and monopoly

---

[19] Robert Zev Mahari, Sandro Claudio Lera and Alex Pentland, "Time for a New Antitrust Era: Refocusing Antitrust Law to Invigorate Competition in the 21st Century," Stanford Journal of Computational Antitrust 1 (2021): 57 (showing how technological analysis can inform antitrust agencies in merger control).

[20] David J. Teece, Gary Pisano and Amy Shuen, "Dynamic Capabilities and Strategic Management," Strategic Management Journal 18, no. 7 (1997), https://perma.cc/DVE6-8QMF?type=image.

[21] Mary Tripsas, "Surviving Radical Technological Change through Dynamic Capability: Evidence from the Typesetter Industry," Industrial and Corporate Change 6, no. 2 (1997). As I explained (*see* Chapter 10), Ethereum's code is Turing complete, meaning that one can use its Virtual Machine to compute anything computable. Bitcoin's current code is not Turing complete, which provides Bitcoin's blockchain with less dynamic technical capacity.

power.[22] This will ultimately generate enough expertise to update merger control guidelines and institutionalize a technological assessment both for blockchain and outside.

2.1.2 Blockchain unicorns and killer acquisitions

The subject of killer acquisitions has become increasingly important to antitrust policy debates. In the absence of empirical studies documenting the frequency of the phenomenon, let me simply explain what is at stake. A "killer acquisition" is the purchase of a company by a competitor to end its products or services, where the costs of the acquisition are recovered by the absence of competition.

Part of the antitrust academic community has made the point that most of these acquisitions escape merger control. Indeed, only concentrations above a certain threshold must be notified. In the United States and Europe, these thresholds concern at least two entities involved in the operation – typically the acquirer and the target. When a company acquires an emergent (and small) competitor, the operation is likely to fall below the threshold. Austria and Germany have introduced alternative thresholds linked to the value of the transaction to remedy this issue – the idea being that the acquisition of a small competitor for several hundred million euros is something that antitrust agencies may want to study.

When it comes to the blockchain industry, one could argue that the price of setting up the right incentives equals the value of the transaction. But that value goes directly to the blockchain's participants, not to a handful of owners, as is the case with firms. For this reason, one should not be too worried about killer acquisitions – the purchase of dynamic blockchain unicorns by other blockchains or firms – within the blockchain sphere, as it takes more than convincing a few individuals to sell. Considering how unlikely it is that the vast majority of participants would agree to a killer acquisition, the price that an acquirer would have to pay to compensate each of them and the fact that blockchain's participants could reactivate their blockchain should the acquisition turn out to be for "killing" purposes, the priority for antitrust agencies seems to be elsewhere. Blockchain escapes this issue thanks to the lack of centralized control.

---

[22] That importance is increasing, as most of today's new technologies result from "new combinations" of past technologies, *see* W. Brian Arthur, *The Nature of Technology: What it Is and How it Evolves* (Free Press, 2009) (explaining that "technologies … arose as combinations of other technologies").

2.2   Modernizing Procedures

2.2.1   Improving assessments

Blockchains can facilitate the exchange of pre-transaction information between parties. This can be done in two ways. The first is to use blockchains as a trusted database. M&A transactions involve due diligence, which is lengthy and costly – the target provides information to the potential acquirer to assess the risks associated with the acquisition. Private blockchains could be used in that regard to replace data rooms, as they are more secure.[23] Specific rights of access could be granted, with or without editing rights. The second is to create smart contracts that verify information or automate transactions.[24]

Blockchains can also facilitate exchanges between the parties and antitrust agencies. They could notably be used to standardize the information agencies require from the parties or to facilitate the transfer of complete and verified information. One could imagine a world where companies and antitrust agencies use blockchains to facilitate the analysis of operations. Antitrust agencies currently suffer from the incompleteness of the information they receive.[25] Blockchain could assist agencies should they require companies to document their market shares into private blockchains. Deleting information from these blockchains – for instance right before a merger – would leave a trace in the ledger.

One may also question whether the information provided by the parties is always accurate, if only because they must estimate the market shares of their competitors. To remedy this issue, agencies could require companies to centralize all information they send to various administrations in private blockchains. Antitrust agencies would then obtain a more comprehensive view of markets. They would be able to cross-reference different sets of data and, in the end, get a clearer view of the industry.

---

[23]   SS&C, "Blockchain in M&A: Hope or Hype?" December 4, 2018, https://perma .cc/A83B-W3MQ.

[24]   Ataullah Khan, "How Mergers and Acquisitions Could Occur on the Blockchain," Hackernoon, March 2, 2018, https://perma.cc/5PV2-Q2PK; "Blockchain & the Future of M&A," The Non Executive, June 2, 2020, https://perma.cc/VD45-KXCQ.

[25]   *See Olympic/Aegean Airlines*, Case COMP/M.6976, C (2011)316 (EC, 2011) (underlining the "poor quality, incomplete and/or inaccurate" information, because the ferry operators' databases were "not as developed as the sophisticated systems/ databases used by airlines.") *See* also *Ryanair/Aer Lingus*, Case No COMP/M.4439, C(2007) 3104 (EC, 2007) in which the Commission explained that it did not have sufficient information regarding several routes. More recently, *see* Merck/Sigma-Aldrich, COMP/M.8181, to be published (EC, 2021) ("Not only was the project not disclosed and discussed in remedy submissions, but information about it was also withheld in replies to specific requests for information").

Agencies could also use blockchains to centralize their data in a single shared space. Access (but not necessarily writing rights) to one agency's private blockchain could be granted to another one – for example, if a company is simultaneously filing a merger in two jurisdictions. Access to an agency's blockchain could also help when several proceedings follow one after another over time, as blockchain immutability ensures that records cannot be altered (whether voluntarily or involuntarily). This immutability would strengthen the trust agencies have in each other and would ultimately allow better-informed analysis of merger proceedings and anticompetitive practices.

Smart contracts could also speed up procedures by automating the request of additional information based on that provided by the parties. This would avoid a considerable amount of back and forth. And should the agencies be comfortable enough with the technology, smart contracts could force parties to implement specific commitments – for example, by automating divestitures in case of noncompliance with behavioral remedies. That being said, smart contracts will most likely be used not only to ensure better monitoring of obligations, but also to survey all the firms' behaviors post-transaction. Data about the new entity could be automatically transmitted to antitrust agencies, which would considerably enhance their knowledge of the market.

In sum, blockchain could provide antitrust agencies with better information and will simplify interactions with companies. Today, a significant amount of data is sent by the parties (e.g., the relevant market shares) in the form of unverifiable Excel sheets. Monitoring is difficult. Blockchain's capacity to ease merger procedures will surely be explored for these reasons.

Let us also note (if I may take this little detour) that blockchain will help antitrust agencies in other fields than merger control. First, blockchain will most certainly be used to identify nascent practices. Antitrust agencies continuously point out the difficulty of detecting anticompetitive practices because their databases are incomplete.[26] Public permissionless blockchains could provide a remedy – at least a partial one – to this difficulty by enabling antitrust agencies to monitor final prices to consumers and detect anticompetitive trends.[27] This will lead them to discern patterns and thus increase their knowledge of the cycles in which anticompetitive practices are committed

---

[26] Underlining that "not all facts can be observed or measured with high accuracy and most datasets are incomplete or otherwise imperfect," European Commission, "Best Practices For The Submission Of Economic Evidence And Data Collection In Cases Concerning The Application Of Articles 101 And 102 TFUE And In Merger Cases," Staff Working Papers (2011), https://perma.cc/675N-7374.

[27] OECD, "Executive Summary of the Hearing on Blockchain and Competition Policy," DAF/COMP/M(2018)1/ANN8/FINAL (2019): 3, https://perma.cc/L2F8 -JXKY.

(this process is often referred to as "cascade analysis"). Second, blockchains could also speed up and improve the accuracy of proceedings once a practice has been identified. Antitrust agencies could ask incriminated companies to provide specific information by way of smart contracts.

2.2.2   Improved monitoring

Blockchains could help enforcers monitor companies' behavior – specifically, when they impose remedies and commitments that seek to restore competition on the merits (anticompetitive cases) or ensure that markets will remain competitive (in merger cases).[28] In either case, agencies need to identify effective solutions that they can follow up on. Here again, blockchain could help.

As far as the design of the commitments and remedies is concerned, one could use smart contracts to ensure that they are correctly implemented.[29] Structural commitments could be set up by way of smart contracts so that they are activated only under certain conditions.[30] For example, one could force a company to sell specific assets or undertakings if a product's price exceeds a pre-defined level. Smart contracts could also improve behavioral commitments. These usually take the form of an obligation to provide access to an essential facility or intellectual property rights;[31] smart contracts could enable agencies to ensure that these are well observed.

Other smart contracts could help in implementing more detailed obligations. A smart contract could combine behavioral and structural commitments, activating one depending on the other. For example, a smart contract could require prices to be kept below a certain level; otherwise antitrust agencies would receive a signal and another smart contract would trigger structural remedies. And without going that far, one may expect that companies will observe

---

[28]   The implementation of remedies can be observed with regard to both *ex post* conduct through Articles 7 and 9 of Council Regulation 1/2003, 2003 O.J. (L 1) 46 and *ex ante* conduct pursuant to Articles 6(2) and 8(2) of Council Regulation 139/2004, 2004 O. J. (L24) 29.

[29]   Generally speaking, the European Commission prefers behavioral commitments to address anti-competitive practices and structural remedies in merger control, *see* Benjamin Lörtscher and Frank P. Maier-Rigaud, "On the Consistency of the European Commission's Remedies Practice," in *Substance, Process and Policy*, eds. Damien Gerard et al. (Wolters Kluwer, 2019): 2.

[30]   *See* Chris Pike, OECD, "Blockchain Technology and Competition Policy," DAF/COMP/WD(2018)47 (2018): 9, https://perma.cc/MGJ5-NH7Y (discussing the potential "cost reduction effect" using smart contracts).

[31]   Generally, behavioral remedies take the form of access remedies, interoperability obligations and internal remedies such as firewalls and corporate governance measures.

stricter compliance, since smart contracts increase antitrust agencies' ability to monitor commitments.[32]

But before this happens, several challenges will be encountered along the way. First, implementing smart contracts will require (some) familiarity with code, although several services are being developed to allow easy smart contract design (called "no code"). A psychological barrier could nonetheless exist. Second, smart contracts are unstoppable, and accordingly, they may create disparities with the actual world in case of unforeseen events. Third, smart contracts are written in computer languages. This has advantages and limits, as it provides companies with some form of (extreme) certainty but reduces flexibility. Finally, one may be concerned that public blockchains could split or be altered by majority votes, and that all smart contracts would be extinguished. The use of private blockchains run by agencies seems safer in that regard.

3   CHAPTER SUMMARY AND BEYOND

In this chapter, I have studied all the different forms of concentrations that may occur in the blockchain ecosystem and in relation thereto. I have shown that technical concentrations can be hostile – whether they result from a "building attack," in which a majority of the mining power is captured, or from a "bribery attack," in which the participants are incentivized to move to another blockchain. These operations should not, however, be subjected to notification requirements, as they generally result from the interplay of competition and entail no change of control. At most, they might sometimes amount to anti-competitive practices.

Things are different with mutually agreed concentrations. They mainly take the form of chainmergers, where two blockchains or more merge their entire transaction histories. I have shown that these concentrations raise many practical difficulties, yet remain likely to happen. Then, I moved on to the study of non-technical concentrations – that is, all operations concerning the blockchain environment, but not blockchain itself. I explained that existing merger control rules more easily capture these concentrations, and that agencies should pay attention to their impact on the chain.

After exploring these different forms of concentrations, I studied the two main criteria of merger control: the change in control and the relevant transaction thresholds. I explained that because blockchains – public permissionless ones and most private ones – exert no coercive power over their participants,

---

[32]   Ajinkya M. Tulpule, "Enforcement and Compliance in a Blockchain(ed) World," CPI Antitrust Chronicle 1 (2017).

one blockchain can take control of another only when the participants consent to the operation. Here, I argued that agencies should study which incentives are convincing enough for participants to agree to the takeover. As for the threshold requirements, I explained that one cannot rely on blockchains' turnover expressed in native tokens that poorly represent their market power.

The first section of the chapter led me to conclude that a more technical analysis is required. This was further discussed in the second section. I started by proposing that analysis of the underlying technology is essential for antitrust enforcers. It helps not only the notification process, but also the assessment of these operations. Indeed, antitrust agencies will be better equipped to understand competitive forces if they understand the technology's capacity to generate network effects, mutate, be combined and so on. The analysis of the technology reveals, for example, that killer acquisitions are unlikely to happen in the blockchain ecosystem.

Lastly, this technological approach could also be used to modernize merger control procedures. Blockchain could help standardize the process and give agencies access to more complete sets of data. The use of smart contracts could also require specific information to be placed on the ledger to improve the monitoring of remedies and commitments. And smart contracts would enable parties and agencies to craft more accurate and complete remedies. In a nutshell, these are the benefits of the cooperation between law and technology, on top of those I have already described when dealing with anticompetitive practices. In Part 3 of this book, I explore how this collaboration can be fostered.

PART 3 – ALLIES

In the third part of this book, I discuss how I think antitrust law should be enforced in the blockchain space. In order to do so without undermining blockchain ecosystems, a shift in legal and technical paradigms is necessary. This notably entails transforming mentalities, legal tools and competition policy.

In fact, implementing a collaborative approach will become increasingly necessary. On the one hand, "the cyberspace is no longer some peripheral dimension. It increasingly has become the place where people organize themselves and define what happens in the real world."[1] On the other hand, the digital space is putting up a strong resistance to legal enforcement by constantly increasing the speed of activities. That resistance is particularly relevant when it comes to blockchain. If law and technology are at odds, both will fail to maximize social welfare. For that reason, West Coast code (programming) and East Coast code (laws and regulations) can no longer oppose each other; they must collaborate.

Against this backdrop, I first detail what it takes to make blockchain and antitrust work together from a conceptual point of view (Chapter 13). I show that this raises unique challenges and offer a solution to them, using the full scope of the so-called "law is code" approach. Second, I discuss what needs to be done to ensure cooperation between blockchain and antitrust from a practical perspective (Chapter 14). To this end, I introduce a proactive agenda for regulating blockchain activities. As I explain, this approach would lead policymakers to establish comfort zones – that is, innovation hubs (allowing firms to raise questions and seek clarifications), regulatory sandboxes (testing grounds for businesses supervised by regulatory bodies) and safe harbors (similar to sandboxes, but with no limit in time or scale). They would also switch the focus of their enforcement activities on certain practices.

I then discuss how blockchain can be used to support antitrust agencies' activities. I contend that regulators should use blockchain technology to make regulatory enforcement more horizontal, and I discuss the decentralization of decision-making mechanisms. In support of this, I explain what futarchy is

---

[1]   Brad Smith & Carol Ann Browne, *Tools and Weapons: The Promise and the Peril of the Digital Age* (Penguin Books, 2019): 22.

and show how it could support authorities. If they collaborate, blockchain and antitrust can create a strong infrastructure upon which markets may thrive, including the Internet of Things and artificial intelligence (Chapter 15).

13. Law + technology

1   INTRODUCTION

Policymakers often see laws and regulations as the ultimate instrument to improve the common good. In this vision, laws prevail over architecture (the design of analog and digital things), markets (economic incentives) and social norms (what is acceptable). A combination of laws and regulations with these other constraints is rarely implemented. By contrast, many developers consider technology as deterministic (i.e., the determining factor of society). This belief might explain why it is so common for developers to start by putting a product on the market, hoping that it will make an impact, and only afterward consider its compliance with laws and regulations.

Neither of these two approaches is optimal. One cannot apply the law to all illegal practices (some remain undetected; and jurisdictions might be mutually unfriendly, as I explained in Chapter 5). Conversely, technology cannot systematically trump the law (as the exponential number of litigations shows, even within the blockchain ecosystem). It is thus necessary to achieve a compromise.

2   UNIQUE CHALLENGES

Blockchain is not a horse – at least, not in the sense of Frank H. Easterbrook. It follows that the digital fortress created by blockchain brings unique challenges which require specific regulatory responses. But regulators and policymakers are also required to facilitate blockchain development, as the technology can benefit the common good. One must therefore discuss regulatory principles for the field.

2.1   Blockchain Is No Horse

2.1.2   Decentralized horses

In 1996, Judge Frank H. Easterbrook presented his paper entitled "Cyberspace and the Law of the Horse" at the University of Chicago, in which he argued that there is and should be no dedicated law for cyberspace. He stated that the law as we know it (contract law, tort law) is good enough for cyberspace, the same way it was when horses began to be used as a means of transportation. Lawrence Lessig, who was in the audience, explained: "As is often the case when my then colleague spoke, the intervention produced an awkward silence, then some polite applause, and then quick passage to the next speaker."[1]

Time has shown that the regulation of the Internet has developed based on existing general principles. In fact, regulation in this sphere mainly relies on the same principles today as it did 20 years ago. Antitrust law is but one example of this. That being said, new regulations such as the European Digital Markets Act and the Artificial Intelligence Act are now going in Lessig's direction.

The technological foundations of blockchain constitute a radical change in the way transactions are implemented; it requires a dedicated approach. The Internet – which is primarily a communications technology – challenged the legal system by substantially increasing the speed at which the law needed to be applied, as Judge Richard A. Posner explained in his famous "Antitrust in the New Economy."[2] With blockchain, it is not just about speed; it is also about the substance – as I show in Part 2, blockchain raises fundamental new questions (e.g., how to handle "cooperative" collusion).

Judge Easterbrook's recommendation to first "[d]evelop a sound law of intellectual property, then apply it to computer networks" falls short with blockchain. One needs to start with the specifics so the general principles can apply. Blockchain is no horse for that reason.

2.1.2   Digital fortress

Every time a new fundamental technology appears, enforcement is questioned. When the Internet went mainstream, some announced the end of antitrust law, which they predicted would become useless or impracticable.[3] A couple of decades later, antitrust is still working; the fines imposed by agencies against tech companies have never been so high, and so frequent.

Why should things be any different with blockchain? As I have explained, unlike the Internet, which is an information technology, blockchain is a transaction technology, built around two key features: encryption and immutability. This is a game-changer for antitrust, which is transactional by nature.

---

[1]   Lawrence Lessig, "The Law of the Horse: What Cyberlaw Might Teach," Harvard Law Review 113 (1999).

[2]   *See* Richard Posner, "Antitrust in the New Economy," Antitrust Law Journal 68, no. 3 (2001): 925, 939 (explaining that "the rapidity of innovation in the new economy" has very important institutional implications, and that the "mismatch between law time and new-economy real time is troubling").

[3]   *Id.* at 206 ("[L]egal scholars thought that the rule of code would ultimately prevail on the Internet.")

Blockchain is indeed constructed as an encrypted fortress against the outside world where the rule of law applies. To be sure, the distinction between real space and the blockchain space is not always crystal clear, as I have addressed when discussing blockchain layers in Chapter 4. In fact, most blockchain activities involve using services that are already covered by the rule of law.[4] For example, several regulations require that exchanges which convert tokens into fiat currencies ask for proof of actual identity. In other cases, blockchain users' real-life identities are already known to others – for example, when two companies decide to move their business relationship to blockchain. Pseudonymity does not protect blockchain users against all types of detection and identification.

That said, interactions between the real space and the blockchain space are not fully transparent. Indeed, blockchain uses encryption techniques that anonymize not only the identify of participants, but also that of transactions – that is, the content and purpose of transactions are unknown to external parties. Those who predict the lack of pseudonymity on blockchain often forget to address this point.[5] It stands even in the face of deanonymization services which apply to participants, not transactions.

And as I have explained in Chapter 2, blockchain analytics services and cyber-forensics might be accessible to governments, but not to individuals, creating issues in terms of private enforcement. We often think of antitrust agencies and government (public enforcement) when we talk about questions of enforceability. But issues surrounding private enforcement are just as important. The characteristics of blockchain, such as pseudonymity, pose significant constraints to private actions. Often, private parties have more limited forensics capacities at their disposal than public authorities.

The immutability that results from the lack of centralized control within blockchain creates another problem: it might be practically impossible to stop a transaction (regardless of the identification of persons and transactions). This is true for both individuals and states. This shortcoming results from the

---

[4] Generally, *see* Lawrence Lessig, "The Zones of Cyberspace" Stanford Law Review 48 (1996): 1403, 1406 (arguing for the regulation of cyberspace through "real space regulation to the extent that it affects real space life, and it will quite dramatically affect real space life"). For an opposite point of view, *see* David G. Post, "Anarchy, State, and the Internet: An Essay on Law-Making in Cyberspace," Journal of Online Law, Article 3 (1995) (arguing that the Internet is a network of networks, and that each network carries its own rule set).

[5] Arguing that "[t]he level of anonymity available is directly proportional to the discretion and skill level of the user seeking it," *see* Jonathan Lane, "Bitcoin, Silk Road, and the Need for a New Approach to Virtual Currency Regulation," Charleston Law Review 8 (2014): 511, 521.

technical translation of blockchain's original ideology – that is, to prevent state control over private activities. It is still very much present to this day.

A court cannot initiate, alter or prohibit transactions successfully;[6] at least, not on its own. No "technically skilled people of goodwill"[7] are needed to maintain and manage the blockchain. If one implements an anticompetitive smart contract on a blockchain with no kill function or preprogrammed technical solutions, the blockchain will continue to perform the transactions for as long as the terms apply and assets are made available. The same goes for D-Apps, as there is no server to shut down[8] (except for shutting down all the computers running the blockchain). As a result, even if antitrust agencies identify an anticompetitive practice, there is no directly enforceable remedy. This could be problematic, as smart contracts and D-Apps can be deployed at scale. Indeed, they are easily accessible, as they do not require a trusted intermediary.

This partial ineffectiveness of the rule of law creates room for another set of rules – here referred to as the Lex Cryptographia ecosystem[9] – in which the technology is central to regulating behaviors. Its interaction with the rule of law remains to be defined. In that regard, one may underline the existence of two different trends among blockchain communities: one group is working hand in hand with regulators to ultimately benefit from the rule of law, while the other is working in the spirit of the cypherpunks to protect citizens from governments.[10] In this second group, as I explained in Chapter 2, we find

---

[6]   *See* Thibault Schrepel, "Is Blockchain the Death of Antitrust Law? The Blockchain Antitrust Paradox," Georgetown Law Technology Review 3, no. 2 (2019) (arguing that ways must be found to incentivize developers and users to facilitate legal enforcement by integrating the code proposed by the regulator). Discussing the different technics for altering blockchains, *see* Thibault Schrepel, "Smart Contracts and the Digital Single Market Through the Lens of a 'Law + Technology' Approach," European Commission (2021).

[7]   Jonathan Zittrain, *The Future Of The Internet—And How To Stop It* (Yale University Press, 2008): 242 ("Our generative technologies need technically skilled people of goodwill to keep them going, and the fledgling generative activities above— blogging, wikis, social networks—need artistically and intellectually skilled people of goodwill to serve as true alternatives to a centralized, industrialized information economy that asks us to identify only as consumers of meaning rather than as makers of it.")

[8]   Siraj Raval, *Decentralized Applications: Harnessing Bitcoin's Blockchain Technology* (O'Reilly Media, 2016): 21 ("Data in a dapp is decentralized across all of its nodes. Each node is independent; if one fails, the others are still able to run on the network.")

[9]   *See* Aaron Wright and Primavera De Filippi, "Decentralized Blockchain Technology and the Rise of Lex Cryptographia" (2015).

[10]   *See* Thibault Schrepel, "Is Blockchain the Death of Antitrust Law? The Blockchain Antitrust Paradox," Georgetown Law Technology Review 3, no. 2 (2019): 322–23. Also, *see* Arvind Narayanan, "What Happened to the Crypto Dream? Part

blockchains such as Monero, which uses "ring signatures" – a technology that groups a real cryptographic signature with fake ones – to make identification harder.[11] Zcash uses "zero-knowledge proofs," which also severely limits the information available to third parties and therefore complicates the task of antitrust agencies and governments.[12]

Overall, blockchain creates what some have called "temporary autonomous zones" (TAZs) – that is, zones in which the state's power cannot be fully enforced.[13] This inevitably leads to games of cat and mouse, where states manage to bring their power to bear on some TAZs, while new ones appear elsewhere. Satoshi Nakamoto described this situation. When told that one cannot "find a solution to political problems in cryptography," he answered: "Yes, but we can win a major battle in the arms race and gain a new territory of freedom for several years." He further underlined that although "[g]overnments are good at cutting off the heads of a centrally controlled networks like Napster ... pure P2P networks ... seem to be holding their own."[14]

2.2   The Magic Four

Policymakers and regulators must enter the domain of blockchain without sacrificing the tremendous potential of the technology. If they do not, part of blockchain communities will constantly seek to escape the rule of law – or, at least, undermine its enforcement. It is thus crucial to consider four key principles and the tradeoffs they entail.

2.2.1   Principles

Different types of regulations can be implemented to stop anticompetitive practices on blockchain. Here are four criteria to ascertain the extent to which

2," IEEE Security & Privacy (2013): 2 (drawing a distinction between Cypherpunk Crypto, "the dream of wielding crypto as a weapon for social and political change," and Pragmatic Crypto, "a more down-to-earth view that seeks to engineer modest privacy enhancements in specific applications.") Originally, the cypherpunk group described "a loose, anarchic mailing list and group of hackers," *see* Timothy C. May, "Crypto Anarchy and Virtual Communities," December 1994, https://perma.cc/6CMV-YMFT.

[11]   Monero, "Ring Signature," https://perma.cc/WGU2-V8L2.

[12]   ZCash, "What are zk-SNARKs?", https://perma.cc/3RJU-LMVZ ("Zero-knowledge proofs allow one party (the prover) to prove to another (the verifier) that a statement is true, without revealing any information beyond the validity of the statement itself.")

[13]   Hakim Bey, "The Temporary Autonomous Zone," in *Crypto Anarchy, Cyberstates, and Pirate Utopias*, ed. Peter Ludlow (MIT Press, 2001): 401.

[14]   Satoshi Nakamoto, "Re: Bitcoin P2P e-cash Paper," The Mail Archive, November 7, 2008, https://perma.cc/S7MV-75NB.

they will preserve the vitality of the ecosystem:[15] (1) manageability, (2) objectivity, (3) accuracy, and (4) flexibility (MOAF).

From the regulators' point of view, "manageability" refers to the costs of implementing and enforcing regulation. For instance, simpler forms of regulation might drive down enforcement costs, but they may also allow private actors to find ways around them. On the contrary, more precise regulation can be effective, but designing and enforcing such regulation might prove costlier for policymakers. Complying with complex laws is also costlier for private actors; it may benefit large ones that can afford good legal advice. "Accuracy" refers to the idea that regulation should minimize false positives and false negatives. A false positive occurs when regulation restricts practices that increase the common good. On the contrary, a false negative is when a practice or behavior decreasing the common good is deemed legal. Ideally, regulations should prohibit only socially undesirable behavior.

From the private actors' point of view, "objectivity" implies that a regulation's objectives should be transparent and known to all of them. It also requires that enforcement activity be consistent. This is essential to build trust and, eventually, cooperate with enforcers. "Flexibility" implies that regulation should achieve its aim in the least intrusive way possible. It generally involves setting a goal to be achieved by private companies without top-down management of their activities. By leaving private actors free to decide how to achieve this objective, they can compete and innovate in heterogeneous ways.

2.2.2 Tradeoffs

The MOAF approach is illustrated in Figure 13.1.

When trying to position an existing regulation on this graph, one quickly realizes that important tradeoffs are involved.

On the one hand, there is a tradeoff for regulators between accuracy and manageability. The more accurate a regulation (i.e., it generates few false positives and false negatives), the costlier it is. One may easily understand this tradeoff by considering the following example. Let us imagine that a regulation prohibits all trading activities on public permissionless blockchains. The enforcement costs[16] of applying that regulation would be low, as no differentiation between trading activities would have to be made. It would, however, create many false positives whose effects cannot be measured. Similarly, if

---

[15]   Many methodologies have been developed over the years, *see,* for instance, Better Regulation Task Force, "Principles of Good Regulation" (2003), https://perma .cc/D4JK-QWY9; OECD, *Better Regulation in Europe: United Kingdom* (2010): 37–54, https://perma.cc/8H7Q-3836.
[16]   They differ from the social costs, evidently.

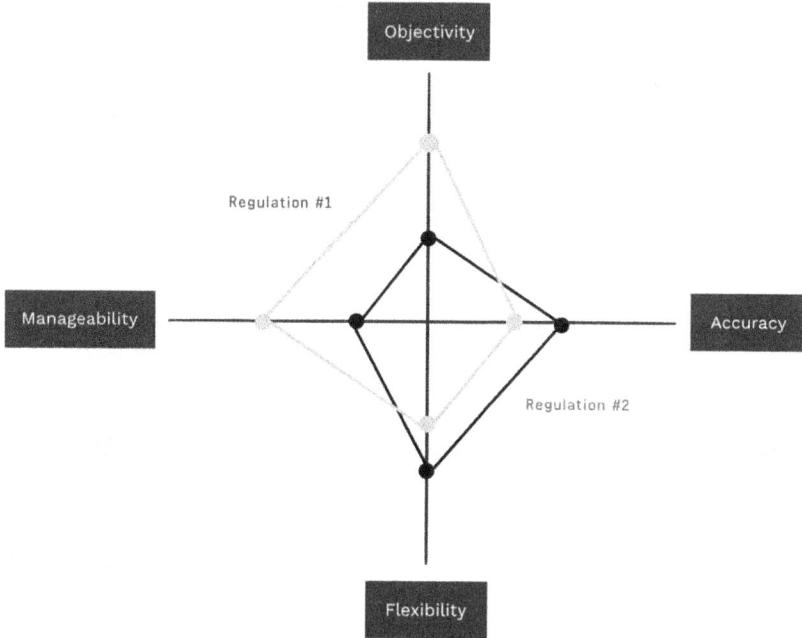

Figure 13.1   Principles for balanced regulations

the Internet had been banned in the 1990s, the common good would have been reduced without it being possible to measure the extent of the phenomenon.

The contrary is also true. A regulation holding all blockchain activities as legal would impose even fewer enforcement costs (in fact, they would disappear), but would create significant false negatives. Granting all blockchain transactions a free pass would in fact create a strong incentive to use the technology to carry out illegal transactions. It would engender even more false negatives. The tradeoff between accuracy and manageability is real.

On the other hand, there is a tradeoff between increasing objectivity and flexibility. The less a regulation is flexible, the more regulators and companies can apply it (or comply with it) in a consistent and certain way. And yet both objectivity and flexibility are necessary to ensure innovation on the market: objectivity is required to provide private actors with legal certainty, while little coercion is necessary to let them pursue business activities in the way they find best.

3   UNIQUE RESPONSE

In this section, I analyze different strategies for policymakers and regulators to enter the blockchain fortress without hampering the growth of blockchain ecosystems. I consider the temptation to create *ex ante* regulation and explain that collaboration with tech communities will prove mutually beneficial.

3.1   Finding a Way

3.1.1   Theoretical primacy
Can the law take up the challenge on its own? Can it lift all barriers protecting blockchain? If it engages in this direction, can it maximize the four MOAF criteria?

As I mentioned, blockchain raises several issues regarding the theoretical applicability of the law (see Chapters 6 and 7) and its actual enforcement. Even if applicability issues could be resolved, enforcement issues would still pose problems that cannot merely be addressed by recalling the theoretical primacy of the rule of law. Blockchain requires special rules that enable the application of legal rules.

I have explained that blockchain is immutable and unstoppable. While exceptions to these principles can be identified, they remain marginal. For that reason, upstream regulation is necessary to catch up with the technology. However, if the law wanted to solve this problem on its own, it would clash with blockchain ecosystems. There is a strong temptation to follow that road; after all, why should policymakers look for solutions in the architecture and governance of the technology that is causing the issue? The answer is that not doing so would lead to destructive policies.

One confrontational idea that seems to come up quite often, for example, is the creation of an identity management system that would require the setting up of a database linking public keys to real-life identities and revealing these links when necessary.[17] But what is "necessary?" When is it so? And who would keep the register? If that were a private entity, it could gain a commercial advantage. If that were the government, this would crush some users' trust in the blockchain and would cause privacy concerns.

Scholars have also suggested that a regulatory node could be added to blockchains to spy on them.[18] Or that policymakers could introduce backdoors on

---

[17]   Brad Finney, "Blockchain and Antitrust: New Tech Meets Old Regs," Transactions 19, no. 2 (2018).

[18]   Lin William Cong and and Zhiguo He, "Blockchain Disruption and Smart Contracts," Review of Financial Studies 32 (2019). In this article, the authors suggest

individual computers to monitor citizens' behavior. First, there is every reason to believe that many blockchains would refuse that node or backdoor. And even if one were added, it would not make enforcement of the law any easier; in fact, it would solve only the encryption "problem," but not the immutability "problem." Concomitantly, it would create a strong deterrent effect on blockchain activities.

Other proposals include criminalizing core developers' activities and imposing fines on them when a blockchain is used for illegal activities.[19] But as I have shown, core developers do not enjoy a coercive power they could use to stop unlawful practices. And again, should they create the mechanisms to secure such power, this would generate distrust within the system by reinserting vertical control, the absence of which is the precise reason why blockchains are thriving.

Furthermore, some are defending the necessity of allowing governments to "filter" the data held by Internet service providers.[20] The basic idea is to regulate the Internet layer rather than blockchain architecture or governance layers. Such a proposal would most likely infringe individual freedoms, such as the right of access to the Internet.[21] Lastly, proposals have been tabled to ban the

---

that "regulators can also potentially participate in the protocol design," which is even more coercive. See also, Samuel Weinstein, "Blockchain Neutrality," Georgia Law Review 55 (2021).

[19] *See* Aaron van Wirdum, "A Primer on Bitcoin Governance, or Why Developers Aren't in Charge of the Protocol," Bitcoin Magazine, September 7, 2016, https://perma .cc/CAG2-K9WD (stating that this is based on the idea that the developers control the blockchain, which is misguided). Also, Aaron Wright and Primavera De Filippi, "Decentralized Blockchain Technology and the Rise of Lex Cryptographia" (2015): 51.

[20] Although this would have to be done at a worldwide level, which seems very unlikely to happen anytime soon. Jeff John Roberts, "The Law of Blockchain: Beyond Government Control?" Fortune, May 11, 2018, https://perma.cc/NX7S-WSLJ ("Even though blockchain ledgers like bitcoin are decentralized and run by computers across many countries, state authorities can still target chokepoints in their infrastructure to exert control. In the same way governments have targeted intermediaries like search engines and ISPs to tame unruly aspects of the Internet, they could do the same to put pressure on blockchain networks.")

[21] See Jay P. Kesan and Rajiv C. Shah, "Shaping Code," Harvard Journal of Law & Technology 18, no. 2 (2004): 319 ("In considering regulatory actions, prohibitions can be an effective method of regulation, but current export prohibitions on encryption code are impractical. Similarly, there are regulatory trade-offs involved with technology-forcing regulation.") But it is not even certain that these measures would be effective because the technology will keep developing. *See* Siraj Raval, *Decentralized Applications: Harnessing Bitcoin's Blockchain Technology* (O'Reilly Media, 2016): 31 (on decentralized bandwidth: "The latest example is the Firechat app for iOS, created by a company called Open Garden. Firechat lets phones speak to each other directly, peer to peer, using the iOS multipeer connectivity feature. No ISP is required. Firechat

creation of anonymous crypto accounts[22] or prohibit the issuance of stablecoins by anyone else but banks.[23] These proposals would also endanger blockchains by reintroducing centralization through the creation of ledger holders, slowing down innovative dynamism and forcing institutionalized actors to become the only players.

In short, none of these coercive measures is appropriate.[24] Yet proposals to simply regulate blockchain use cases will do the trick only at the application layer, leaving untouched all the structural issues that will keep on appearing.[25] Architectural problems demand architectural solutions.[26]

3.1.2   Departing from confrontational law

Opting for a confrontational approach will put blockchain ecosystems at risk. Let me generalize my findings and return to the MOAF approach to explain why that is.

First, a confrontational approach would not be desirable from the regulators' point of view. Aggressive law enforcement would indeed threaten the fundamental principles of encryption and immutability. While that might deter some illegal behaviors, it would also threaten all sorts of beneficial practices that rely on either of these two principles. Thus, the accuracy level would remain low because it would entail numerous false positives and eventually

---

is an example of a mesh networking application. Mesh networks are the decentralized version of the standard centralized Internet. In a mesh network, users don't need to go through a central gateway to access a site; they can connect directly to the nearest router, which would be a nearby computer.")

[22]   Helen Partz, "France Moves to Ban Anonymous Crypto Accounts to Prevent Money Laundering," CoinTelegraph: The Future of Money, December 10, 2020, https://perma.cc/ZA4E-JVJ9.

[23]   *Stablecoin Classification and Regulation Act of 2020*, prepared by The United States Congress (Washington, D.C., 2020), https://perma.cc/K6PX-KC8K.

[24]   None of these proposals considers the possibility and impact of governmental failures.

[25]   Arguing for use-case regulations, *see* OECD, "The Policy Environment for Blockchain Innovation and Adoption: 2019 Global Blockchain Policy Forum Summary Report," OECD Blockchain Policy Series (2019): 43. Also, *see* Hossein Nabilou, "How to Regulate Bitcoin? Decentralized Regulation for a Decentralized Cryptocurrency," International Journal of Law and Information Technology 27, (2019): 266.

[26]   Discussing how the regulation of use cases could impact the underlying technology to some degree, *see* A. Michael Froomkin, "Flood Control on the Information Ocean: Living with Anonymity, Digital Cash, and Distributed Databases," Journal of Law & Commerce 15 (1996): 395, 476 ("digital cash is banned by a government, many corporations active in that jurisdiction will be reluctant to use it because they are subject to audit and disclosure requirements, and have assets to lose if subjected to civil or criminal penalties. At a minimum, a ban would raise the cost of using anonymous digital cash, perhaps to the point where few people were willing to trade in it.")

deprive regulators of blockchain's contribution to the common good. In terms of manageability, a confrontational approach would put blockchains under the regulator's control. Enforcing and monitoring costs would be extremely high. This approach would require costly deanonymization services and expansive practices altering the registers, stopping smart contracts and carrying out forks.

Second, this approach would also be detrimental to blockchain communities. In terms of objectivity, regulations of this sort could be relatively predictable for private actors, but objectivity would suffer from the resistance of certain blockchain communities. Technical innovations would rapidly emerge to escape regulation, forcing the regulator to continually adapt its regulations and apply them inconsistently. In terms of flexibility, this confrontational regulation would open the blockchain fortress with a tank. It would be highly coercive. New regulations would forcibly impose enforcement mechanisms on all blockchain communities – or, at the very least, on a (large) part of them – by eliminating some of the technology core characteristics. In other words, implementing regulations of this sort would be like using a sledgehammer to crack a nut.

This is not a pretty picture.[27] Blockchain is still a burgeoning technology and adopting a confrontational approach would end up removing some essential features for its survival against other species (i.e., centralized ecosystems).

Alternatively, these regulations would be ineffective, as communities would work to escape the rule of law. If confrontational law lags behind the technology, its enforcement will partially be held in check for the reasons I have discussed. If, on the contrary, confrontational law is ahead of technology, the latter will circumvent and escape it by eliminating control mechanisms and changing governance and incentives (not always for the better). This will be limited, as only the most advanced part of the community would succeed; but that fraction would take a chunk of the users with it. The rule of law would not regain its full primacy. In fact, we have seen this already. When the New York State Department of Financial Services imposed a requirement to obtain a "BitLicense" before engaging in Bitcoin activities,[28] several startups moved to New Jersey. If developers cannot vote with their computers, they vote with their feet by relocating their operations. This affects all users.

---

[27] Aaron Wright and Primavera De Filippi, "Decentralized Blockchain Technology and the Rise of Lex Cryptographia" (2015): 52 ("The result would be a gross abuse of government power, and many of these approaches would likely chill the economic gains that permissionless blockchain technology offers. It would represent a retreat from current attempts to support the free exchange of information, ideas, and commerce on the Internet, which might ultimately raise significant constitutional issues.").

[28] Kevin Werbach, *The Blockchain and the New Architecture of Trust* (MIT Press, 2018): 175.

In a nutshell, one must reject the confrontational approach because it allows neither the law (here, antitrust) nor the technology (here, blockchain) to fully achieve its objective. One must find another way to enter blockchain ecosystems. I offer an alternative option in that regard.

3.2   Law + Code

3.2.1   Why together?

We are facing a conundrum. On the one hand, blockchain architecture requires us to find ways to prohibit illegal behaviors (and only those). On the other hand, confrontational law may hamper the technology and therefore reduce the common good or stay ineffective. It is crucial that we find a way around this conundrum. Blockchain code reveals, probably more than ever, the need for collaboration between law and technology: between policymakers, regulators and blockchain communities. This may spark a pivotal moment in legal history, forcing the creation of a new paradigm that leads to the emergence of hitherto unexplored synergies.[29]

If they work together, these two communities can put in place mechanisms to stop and punish anticompetitive practices once committed by creating a way for legal enforcement instead of trying to prevent all illegal practices from happening in the first place.[30] That requires us to find a way for blockchain communities, alongside the regulator, to take practical actions when necessary and give them incentives to do so.

The code that underlies blockchain ecosystems is an ideal candidate to achieve this aim. Code is the language of technology and the principal determinant of behavior within a digital ecosystem. The maxim "code is law" describes that reality.[31] As I have explained, blockchain's architecture creates trust between participants. It is the same architecture that can build "too much trust," leading to illegal practices because it creates (a sentiment of) impunity from the law. The occurrence of these practices therefore implies that one must adapt the architecture. If policymakers and regulators want the help of

---

[29]   This issue has long existed. As Foucault underlined in 1977, the state is not the only institution to exercise constraint, *see* "Truth and Power: an interview with Michael Foucault," Critique of Anthropology 4, no. 13–14 (1979).
[30]   *See* Thibault Schrepel, "Computational Antitrust: An Introduction and Research Agenda," Stanford Computational Antitrust 1 (2021) (discussing the impossibility of preventing all illegal practices).
[31]   *See* Lawrence Lessig, *Code: And Other Laws of Cyberspace, Version 2.0* (Basic Books, 2006): 121 ("[I]n real space, we recognize how laws regulate—through constitutions, statutes, and other legal codes. In cyberspace we must understand how a different 'code' regulates—how the software and hardware (i.e., the 'code' of cyberspace) that make cyberspace what it is also regulate cyberspace as it is.")

blockchain communities, they must translate the law into code so they can implement it and monitor its application.

This is the "law is code" ex-post approach I am arguing for,[32] which I distinguish from other "law is code" ex-ante solutions that lead to the prohibition of practices before they even occur or automatic enforcement by code.[33] In practice, ex-ante solutions suffer from the rigidity of code language and, above all, from our cognitive and imaginative limits.[34] Instead, the "law is code" ex-post approach I am offering relies on, and allows, other constraints (law, market, norms) to play a part in deterring most illegal practices; and, when implemented, creates a gateway for legal enforcement.

3.2.2   Blockchain code

The "law is code" approach I suggest strikes what I find to be a satisfying MOAF balance. In terms of accuracy, modifying code to allow other constraints creates few false negatives and even fewer false positives. There is no need for overreaching regulations or to break the blockchain door altogether. This "law is code" approach is more surgical. In terms of manageability, it gives power to blockchain communities which are the first to implement and enforce blockchain code. Policymakers and regulators will trust new blockchain architectures; only the costs of verification will remain.

In terms of objectivity for private actors, one can trust that blockchain communities will know the rules they enforce. The extent to which these communities should enforce the rules on their own, or with the supervision of regulators, is debatable (see below). In terms of flexibility, that "law is code" approach is non-coercive, as it is agreed upon, implemented and enforced by blockchain

---

[32]   *See* James Mohun and Alex Roberts, "Cracking the Code: Rulemaking for Humans and Machines," OECD Working Papers on Public Governance 42 (2020), https://perma.cc/6T3Z-5NST (discussing the process of coding the law); also, Meng Weng Wong, *Rules as Code – Seven Levels of Digitisation* (Research Collection School of Law, Singapore Management University, 2020) (discussing the different degrees of codification).

[33]   Discussing the limits of automatic enforcement, *see* Pedro Quintais et al., "Blockchain and the Law: A Critical Evaluation," Stanford Journal of Blockchain Law & Policy 2, no. 1 (2019): 106. Part of the doctrine argues that law is code equals necessarily having machines applying the law, but that is incorrect. *See*, for instance, Joe McIntyre, "CSIRO Wants Our Laws Turned into Computer Code. Here's Why That's a Bad Idea," The Conversation, January 19, 2020, https://perma.cc/2QN2-JAYF.

[34]   If only because unexpected elements cannot be computed in advance, *see* Nassim Nicholas Taleb, *The Black Swan: The Impact of the Highly Improbable* (Penguin Books, 2010): 1–10 (explaining that inductive reasoning does not allow us to tackle never-before-seen events – the "Black Swans").

communities. The more significant the role of the community agreeing to enforce these rules, the less top-down and coercive they will become.

In the end, there is every reason to believe that such as "law is code" ex-post approach will achieve proper deterrence. If mechanisms are in place to deter and punish illegal practices, and if blockchain participants are made aware of these mechanisms, then the number of such practices will be significantly reduced. Again, as Beccaria said:

> one of the greatest checks on crime is not the cruelty of punishments, but their inevitability ... the certainty of a chastisement, even if it be moderate, will always make a greater impression than the fear of a more terrible punishment that is united with the hope of impunity.[35]

Two mechanisms can be used in that regard: a first that allows communities to discourage and sanction anticompetitive practices, and a second that enables courts and regulators to "enter" blockchains. Both come with specific challenges. The first will partially recentralize blockchain, but it proves to be best for "targeting." The second requires participants to trust the rule of law on top of the rule of code, but maximizes "objectivity," since the regulator has no financial interest in the blockchain, unlike the other participants.

4   CHAPTER SUMMARY AND BEYOND

In this chapter, I started by analyzing the new challenges that blockchain creates for policymakers and regulators. I showed that blockchain has singular characteristics that require specific regulations in response. In the absence of such regulations, blockchain creates a nearly impenetrable fortress. One must then find a solution to make the law applicable. With that in mind, I introduced four principles against which to assess potential regulation: (1) accuracy, (2) manageability, (3) objectivity and (4) flexibility. I explained that one cannot maximize them all at once, as significant tradeoffs are involved.

Against this analytical framework, I have assessed distinct types of regulatory approaches. I concluded that a classic confrontational approach would not lead to good results. I explained this confrontational approach would either threaten the survival of blockchain technology or simply prove to be ineffective. Conversely, when law and code are combined, the results are more satisfactory. This collaboration implies that blockchain communities and regulators must find common ground to introduce mechanisms that sanction illegal practices when they are committed and, even before that, prevent them from taking

---

[35]   *See* Cesare Beccaria, *On Crimes and Punishments*, trans. David Young (Hackett Publishing Co., 1986): 46.

place by relying on other constraints. In the next chapter, I detail the terms of this arrangement and explore how blockchain communities would ultimately agree to take part in the "law is code" approach that I have advocated for.

14. Running the formula

1 A POSITIVE AGENDA

In this section, I introduce a positive agenda that would lead agencies to create comfort zones and to direct legal enforcements toward certain specific practices. The objective is to create the right incentives for blockchain communities to implement the "law is code" approach described in Chapter 13 – that is, translating the law into code in a way that opens up *ex post* enforcement. This approach would lead to a cooperative relationship between law and technology. The result would be better legal protection for blockchain communities (which would suffer from fewer anticompetitive practices) while ensuring blockchain creates a positive impact outside the ecosystem.[1] But getting there will require mutual concessions.

1.1 Comfort Zones

1.1.1 The legal side

Agencies and regulatory bodies face the challenge of understanding blockchain code and programming.[2] Without a comprehension of the ecosystem, most illegal activities on blockchain will remain undetected, creating a legal loophole and encouraging anticompetitive strategies using coding instead of contracts.[3] This explains why former Assistant Attorney General Makan

---

[1] *See* generally Tom R. Tyler, *Why People Obey the Law* (Yale University Press, 1990) (stating that people tend to obey the laws that they perceive as fair). Similarly, blockchain results from a desire for decentralization, and in this regard, the use of decentralized mechanisms by antitrust agencies could reinforce their acceptance.

[2] Several antitrust agencies have started to learn about blockchain technicalities to meet future challenges, *see*, for instance, Makan Delrahim, "'Video Killed the Radio Star': Promoting a Culture of Innovation," the United States Department of Justice, October 8, 2020, https://perma.cc/T672-37A6. Also, Authority for Consumers & Markets, "2018 ACM Conference," https://perma.cc/8MMU-EEXK.

[3] This does not mean that antitrust and competition agencies must convict dozens of companies overnight based on the programming of their software. They must first gain expertise, notably by hiring software developers in their litigation teams.

Delrahim stressed in a speech about blockchain that it is "vital for antitrust enforcers to understand how the emerging technology works."[4]

I contend that the creation of comfort zones would be a great way for agencies to familiarize themselves with the ecosystem, whether they are innovation hubs (allowing firms to raise questions and seek clarifications and non-binding guidance),[5] regulatory sandboxes (testing grounds for businesses supervised by regulatory bodies)[6] or safe harbors (legal provisions exempting liability on the fulfillment of certain conditions, such as Section 230 of the Communication Act in the United States).[7] These comfort zones would also allow agencies to test different modifications of blockchain code. This testing capacity would prove extremely beneficial for law enforcement. Initiatives such as the European Commission planning a pan-European blockchain regulatory sandbox that might become operational in 2022 are laudable in that respect.[8]

But of course, most blockchains will not enter sandboxes for the sake of improving regulation: they must find it advantageous to do so. Being opt-in by nature, sandboxes require the creation of proper incentives. They could

---

[4]   Makan Delrahim, "Never Break the Chain: Pursuing Antifragility in Antitrust Enforcement," the United States Department of Justice, August 27, 2020, https://perma.cc/NEZ8-WC5E.

[5]   *Regulatory Sandboxes and Innovation Hubs for FinTech: Impact on Innovation, Financial Stability and Supervisory Convergence*, prepared by European Parliament (Brussels, 2020): 20 (underlining that "[i]nnovation hubs are often a compelling first step in the innovative regulatory journey;" indeed, "innovation hubs provide a platform to exchange knowledge and informal guidance, a regulatory sandbox usually implies some lenience or supervisory discretion about the way in which the regulatory framework applies to innovative products or services").

[6]   For instance, the Financial Conduct Authority is using sandboxes in the United Kingdom, *see* "The Financial Conduct Authority Unveils Successful Sandbox Firms on the Second Anniversary of Project Innovate," Financial Conduct Authority, November 7, 2016, https://perma.cc/3HQS-FBWS. *See also Regulatory Sandboxes and Innovation Hubs for FinTech: Impact on Innovation, Financial Stability and Supervisory Convergence*, prepared by European Parliament (Brussels, 2020): 21 (listing all the European countries with operational or planned sandboxes, such as Denmark, the Netherlands, Norway, Spain, Italy and Poland). Lastly, *see* Her Majesty's Treasury, "Ambitious plans to boost UK fintech and financial services set out by Chancellor," Gov.uk, April 19, 2021, https://perma.cc/K54K-GZLC (introducing the concept of "scale boxes" as a package of measures to enhance regulatory sandboxes and enable firms to test different products and services).

[7]   According to Section 230 of the Communications Act, online intermediaries are not liable for the content they display.

[8]   *Regulatory Sandboxes and Experimentation Clauses as Tools for Better Regulation: Council Adopts Conclusions*, prepared by General Secretariat of the Council of the European Union (Brussels, 2020), https://perma.cc/X5G2-WW93.

be legal by nature. Typically, entities that enter comfort zones benefit from a flexible application of the law. They are sent "no enforcement action" letters in return for their collaboration and may ask agencies to help them assess the legality of grey practices. These firms may also benefit from having to comply with legal obligations tailored to their activities and therefore proportional to their business practices. Last, these incentives might be economic – for instance, in the form of tax breaks.

Ideally, regulators will enroll the blockchains (and related entities) that are expected to benefit society the most. Blockchains that are public, resilient to well-known attacks and free to use could be first to enter these comfort zones. Indeed, they offer optimum decentralization and lessen the risk of anticompetitive practices, as I have previously discussed in Part 2 of this book.

1.1.2   The tech side

On the tech side, opt-in sandboxes would increase developers' familiarity with legal mechanisms.[9] They would also allow blockchain communities to enjoy related legal and economic advantages, plus to benefit from the rule of law.[10] First, sandboxes would end up protecting them from anticompetitive practices, as they would implement relevant mechanisms to stop (most of) them. Though they might be tempted to try to achieve that objective with only code, this approach would fail. Code simply can't solve all problems on its own; blockchain needs the law.

Second, the law will provide blockchain participants with legal certainty and protection. This applies in the short and long term. In the short term, entering sandboxes provides legal certainty, as the dialogue with agencies and regulators is made easy. In the long term, sandboxes help the creation of well-defined legal systems. They help to shape legal rules to engage liability only in appropriate situations – here, when blockchain communities have control.

But of course, entering sandboxes would require developers to experiment with new blockchain designs that might make legal enforcement possible, fast and cost effective. One must distinguish between two possibilities in this regard. In the first, a public permissionless blockchain enters a sandbox at the stage of project development (before it hits the market). Here, experimentation is easy to implement, as core developers still have control over the blockchain. In the second, a public, permissionless blockchain that has already hit the

---

[9]   Which is not without creating a risk of regulatory capture. To remedy this, sandboxes results should be made open to all.

[10]   This is also true outside of antitrust law – for example, the Coin Center has applied for an exemption from the rules applying to money transmitters, *see* Peter Van Valkenburgh, "Bitcoin Innovators Need Legal Safe Harbors," Coin Center, January 24, 2017, https://perma.cc/774A-N7XB.

market opts into a sandbox. Here, experimentation is more complicated, as developers will have already lost much of their control over design choices. Only the blockchain nucleus will have the power to implement them, constraining regulators to specific experiments.

Developers might also want to conduct experiments that alter different blockchain characteristics. For example, they could study whether a blockchain in which smart contracts can be stopped unilaterally by a handful of users would generate the same trust as unstoppable blockchains.[11] They might also want to explore the impact of having a central entity collecting all real-life identities before allowing access to the blockchain. And one could imagine governance mechanisms that allow regulators to submit blockchain modifications to the community.[12] These are just three examples of the need to assess which features can be modified without deteriorating blockchain differentiation (i.e., chances of survival) from centralized systems.[13]

The greater the effect of these modifications on the fundamental features of a blockchain, the more blockchain communities will be reluctant to implement them. To remedy that, the involvement of blockchain participants will be crucial. Regulators should thus determine what incentives should be granted for each mechanism. Eventually, the results of these experiments will be generalized to other blockchains – regulation could then leave the realm of sandboxes (which only concern a few) in favor of safe harbors (which apply to all).

1.2   Enforcement

1.2.1   Not this…

Enforcement is the second pillar of a collaborative approach between law and tech, antitrust and blockchain. I realize that this may seem counterintuitive; enforcement is, by definition, confrontational. In reality, distinct types of enforcement can lead to varying degrees of confrontation: some harm the entire blockchain, while others target the sole perpetrators of illegal practices. One should avoid the former, as it would reduce blockchain's usefulness and thus deprive policymakers and regulators of an important ally. It is in the interests of both communities to encourage the latter.

I concluded the first part of this book by underlining that making law and tech work toward the same objective implied bearing with some assaults by

---

[11] *See* Aaron Wright and Primavera De Filippi, "Decentralized Blockchain Technology and the Rise of Lex Cryptographia" (2015): 50.

[12] These mechanisms could be similar to those of Decred, *see* Kevin Werbach, *The Blockchain and the New Architecture of Trust* (MIT Press, 2018): 549.

[13] Proposing the introduction of a decentralized "supreme court," *see* Vitalik Buterin, "Decentralized Court," Reddit, https://perma.cc/K5CQ-URMK.

each on the other. This means that blockchain communities should not only tolerate antitrust sanctions, but also facilitate them, because they ultimately lead to further decentralization. It also means that antitrust agencies and courts should direct their enforcement activities in a specific way. Overall, they should seek to preserve blockchain. This will be challenging, as agencies generally conduct their enforcement activities one case after the other, without such a long-term objective. That being said, agencies could still achieve the overall goal of enabling blockchain technology to flourish while ensuring case-by-case enforcement.

For that, agencies should avoid enforcement activities against practices that directly arise from the intrinsic characteristics of a blockchain. For example, public permissionless blockchains distribute information throughout the marketplace, including the number of transactions implemented by specific users, the fees being paid and so on. This transparency could lead to antitrust concerns, especially when it comes to tacit collusion.[14] Nevertheless, because this essential feature makes markets more fluid and mitigates information asymmetry,[15] enforcement activities should not be directed at it.

The same goes for the opacity that blockchains create. As we have seen together, the identity of a blockchain's participants and the content of their transactions are protected by encryption. Yet one should not consider this a relevant element in European competition law for presuming the intention to collude (moral component), for systematically making cartelization on blockchain a restriction "by object" rather than "by effect," or for easing the burden of proof on antitrust agencies. Doing so would deter legal uses of blockchain.

More generally, it is important to underline that all blockchain participants agree to the same set of rules. That should not be seen as an illegal agreement between them, even though it affects their economic behavior. Agreeing to the same rules is, in fact, necessary for blockchain's survival, as it creates consistency in the blockchain ledger in the absence of central coordination. It solves the Byzantine Generals Problem, according to which a central power is always needed to coordinate actions and maximize outcomes. That applies to forks, which should only rarely be seen as illegal (as I discussed in Chapter 8), because they create checks and balances within each blockchain. Let me reiterate that without consensus regarding the rules and their modification, the whole system would collapse, as the ledger integrity could not be maintained. All practices engaged by the blockchain nucleus to ensure survival, such as

---

[14]   See Lin William Cong and Zhiguo He, "Blockchain Disruption and Smart Contracts" (2017): 9 (underlining that decentralization facilitates collusion by distributing information).

[15]   *Id.* at 3

their forks and modifications of the core client, should thus be presumptively legal as far as antitrust enforcement is concerned.

1.2.2   ...but that!

I recommend that antitrust agencies focus their enforcement activities on practices that affect the "real space", and on practices that defeat blockchain's purpose.

As I discussed in Chapters 9 and 11, the first type of practice covers the use of blockchains to support firms' efforts to collude or monopolize markets. These practices have a strong and direct impact on consumers. Detecting this type of behavior will require proactive actions by antitrust agencies. If they engage in such actions, enforcement in the field will increase consumer welfare.

The second category concerns practices that centralize blockchain ecosystems artificially. More specifically, agencies should target practices that centralize the infrastructure level of a blockchain. As I have explained, that level has a critical influence on the decentralization of other levels. Prohibiting artificial forms of centralization at that layer will free most of the ecosystem from coercive forms of power. In doing so, it will make blockchain a more potent ally to antitrust law. Furthermore, this type of enforcement will prove increasingly important over time. If blockchain adoption continues to increase, it could very well become a key infrastructure for the world economy. At that point in time, the artificial centralization of blockchain will become antitrust agencies' top enforcement priority.

Overall, directing enforcement activities toward these two types of practices would free blockchain, and its economic ramifications, from the most restrictive practices without diminishing its usefulness or creating resentment within blockchain communities. Antitrust would thus become the ally of blockchain ecosystems and would start being perceived as such.

2   REGULATION BY BLOCKCHAIN

Up to this point, I have discussed an agenda for blockchain and antitrust to benefit from one another while staying in separate silos. In this section, I focus on how combining the two could strengthen their link on a long-lasting basis and lead to the emergence of a decentralized regulator. In a way, I propose a merger between law and technology.

2.1   Sketch of a Decentralized Regulator

2.1.1   The endgame

Tensions between law and technology benefit neither of them. To remedy these frictions, the first part of this chapter put forward a proposal that would foster cooperation between them. But would it be possible to alleviate these tensions in a more sustainable way? The answer lies in the chosen methods of regulatory governance.

Absent a decentralization of antitrust agencies, the law is enforced top-down. It maintains a mistrust within blockchain communities and put the terms of their cooperation with regulators at risk. The decentralization of antitrust agencies could, on the contrary, bring the two spheres closer together. And as I shall explain, blockchain could allow for a more democratic and efficient decision-making.[16]

2.1.2   Futarchic antitrust

In what follows, I explain why and how antitrust agencies should use "futarchy" augmented by blockchain. But first, what is futarchy? To put it simply, futarchy is a system of governance based on the "wisdom of the crowd" which is using prediction markets – a way of making the future outcome of an event tradable.[17]

We know from the work of Friedrich Hayek that prices reflect the information distributed in the market. Prediction markets use this feature by putting a price on future outcomes in order to evaluate their likelihood.[18] More specifically, they identify sincere beliefs[19] by forcing participants to "put their money

---

[16]   *See* Marta Poblet et al., "From Athens to the Blockchain: Oracles for Digital Democracy" (2020); Melanie Swan, *Blockchain: Blueprint for a New Economy* (O'Reilly Media, 2015): 54 ("It might seem harder to let go of centralized authority in matters of government ... but there is no reason that social maturity could not develop in similar context").

[17]   Discussing other "wisdom of the crowd" technologies, *see* Robin Hanson, "Insider Trading and Prediction Markets" (2007) (they also include "wikis, blogs, collaborative filtering, link-popularity-based-search").

[18]   Robin Hanson, "Shall We Vote on Values, But Bet on Beliefs?" The Journal of Political Philosophy 21, no. 2 (2013): 5 ("Betting markets are speculative markets that trade assets that are specifically designed to allow people to bet on particular matters of fact, such as which horse will win a race"); also, Kenneth J. Arrow et al., "The Promise of Prediction Markets," Science 320, (2008): 877 (defining "prediction markets" as "forums for trading contracts that yield payments based on the outcome of uncertain events").

[19]   Robin Hanson, "Could Gambling Save Science? Encouraging an Honest Consensus," Social Epistemology 9, no. 1 (1995): 3, 7–9. Also, Michael Abramowicz,

where their mouth is,"[20] and differ in this respect from traditional voting mechanisms that record what the voters want, as opposed to what they think will happen.[21] These have been successfully applied in practice.[22]

In practice, one attributes the probability that a future event will occur between 0 and 1, and creates a bet in which the entry price equals the perceived probability. After the event has (or has not) occurred, only those who bet on the correct outcome receive a payoff. Let me take an example. The likelihood that person X will be elected president of the United States is 70 percent. It follows that one will have to spend 0.7 (dollars, or euro, or tokens) to bet on person X's election. Conversely, one will have to put 0.3 to bet on person X's non-election. Once the result is known, the value corresponding to the correct result is converted into 1. Here, if a participant has bet 0.7 dollars that person X would be elected, the bet is converted into 1 dollar, earning a payoff of 0.3. Those who have bet against person X election lose their 0.3 dollars. This loss discourages bad gamblers from taking part in similar prediction markets (unless they enjoy losing money), which is why prediction markets are becoming more accurate over time.[23]

Now, let us focus on futarchy. Futarchy uses these bets to determine a governance strategy in the private and public sectors alike: participants bet on whether a specific outcome will occur after a specific decision is taken. One may distinguish between two distinct mechanisms.

In the first mechanism – the original form of futarchy introduced by Robin Hanson – two votes are submitted in parallel. Let us assume that the goal is to choose the best president for increasing a country's gross domestic product (GDP) one year after the election. Two bets are created regarding the odds that person X (one bet) and person Y (another bet) will reach that goal once

---

Predictocracy: Market Mechanisms for Public and Private Decision Making (Yale University Press, 2008): 7.

[20] Robin Hanson et al., "Decision Markets," IEEE Intelligent Systems 14, no. 3 (1999).

[21] If one wants to change the outcome, a prediction market is not the right tool.

[22] See Frank M.A. Klingert and Matthias Meyer, "Comparing Prediction Market Mechanisms: An Experiment-Based and Micro Validated Multi-Agent Simulation," Journal of Artificial Societies and Social Simulation 21, no. 1 (2018); Also, Colin F. Camerer et al., "Evaluating Replicability of Laboratory Experiments in Economics," Science 351, no. 6280 (2016); Finally, *see* Pavel Atanasov et al., "Distilling the Wisdom of Crowds: Prediction Markets vs. Prediction Polls," Management Science 63, no. 3 (2016).

[23] Marti A. Hearst et al., "Building Intelligent Systems One E-Citizen at a Time," IEEE Intelligent Systems 14, no. 3 (1999): 16.

elected president. They are both conditioned on the election,[24] meaning that once a candidate is elected, the bet regarding the other candidate is automatically canceled and gamblers are refunded. Now, let us assume that the president-elect has achieved the goal of increasing the country's GDP at the end of the specified period (one year in this case). Those who had bet on her or his success see their values converted to 1; the others to 0. In the second mechanism, a single bet is created[25] – for instance, will person X increase the country's GDP one year after her or his election? If the bets are overwhelmingly positive, this indicates the desirability of electing that person. After a year, those who voted for the correct outcome earn a gain and the others take a loss. If person X is not elected, the bets are canceled.

That being cleared up, I realize that readers may still have a few interrogations regarding prediction markets and futarchies. For that reason, I shall address them in the form of questions and answers.

First, who creates these prediction markets? It can be a decision maker who is using them as a way to govern. For example, a company's shareholders could choose a CEO using a prediction market for evaluating the likelihood that she or he will increase the company's value. But in the original form of futarchy, the outcomes of the bets are simple indications that can be ignored. This enables non-decision makers to create prediction markets. In either case, futarchy allows for the decentralization of the decision-making process, enabling individuals with information to bet on outcomes and contributing their expertise to the decision.[26]

Second, who can bet? Three variants can be distinguished here. In the first, only specific participants can bet (e.g., members of a company or a governmental agency). This method gathers only limited expertise. In the second, specific participants and designated experts can submit bets, bringing external yet selective expertise to the process. In the third, bets are open to everyone.[27]

---

[24] These markets are called "Conditional Prediction Markets," because they are contingent on some events, *see* Michael Abramowicz, *Predictocracy: Market Mechanisms for Public and Private Decision Making* (Yale University Press, 2008): 141.

[25] *See* Justin Wolfers and Eric Zitzewitz, "Prediction Markets," Journal of Economic Perspectives 18, (2004): 107, 120 ("the new prediction markets in announcements of economic statistics operate more like the pari-mutuel systems that are common in horse-race betting. In a pari-mutuel system, all of the money that is bet goes into a common pot and is then divided among the winners after subtracting transaction costs").

[26] For one implementation, *see* Vitalik Buterin, "Prediction Markets for Content Curation DAOs," Ethereum Research, https://perma.cc/D22J-DNJK.

[27] Tom W. Bell, "Government Prediction Markets: Why, Who, and How," Penn State Law Review 116, no. 2 (2011): 403, 416.

This brings together broad expertise, but opens up a risk of manipulation – I will come back to this.

Third, how do blockchain ecosystems fit within this picture? It appears that, regardless of its form, the benefits offered by futarchy are increased by blockchain.[28] Blockchain provides transparency to the participants, which motivates fair behaviors. Blockchain is also censorship resistant, which allows for the creation of market predictions that cannot be altered or stopped by their creators. Once the result is registered, the funds are immediately transferred to those whose bet was correct, avoiding the lengths of centralized prediction markets where a financial institution must order the transfer. Conversely, those whose bets were incorrect cannot cheat – that is, the combination of cryptography and immutability forces voters to bear the costs and benefits of their bets.

In fact, blockchain also allows for mechanisms to be put in place to ensure that correct outcomes are being recorded. For example, several decentralized prediction markets are forcing the participants challenging an outcome (e.g., person X wasn't elected, person Y was) to place a financial stake that will be lost if they are proven wrong by the majority.[29] This is the process used by Augur, a decentralized prediction market launched on the Ethereum blockchain. Augur enables the creation of prediction markets that work with a reputation token (called "Rep") where users are randomly chosen to verify outcomes. They win new tokens if they do the verification accurately.[30]

Lastly, blockchain allows the use of tokens instead of fiat currencies for betting purposes.[31] The advantage of using fiat currencies is their immediate appeal to attract gamblers, thus increasing expertise. That being said, the use of tokens – which did not turn out to be leading to less accurate outcomes when they have been used[32] – might still create proper financial incentives. Using

---

[28] Melanie Swan, *Blockchain: Blueprint for A New Economy* (O'Reilly Media, 2015): 53 (describing prediction markets as "a quintessential example of the potential transformative power of blockchain technology").

[29] Ben Davidow, "The Ultimate Guide to Decentralized Prediction Markets," Medium, August 22, 2019, https://perma.cc/3W7C-2BZN.

[30] *See* Dr. Jack Peterson and Joseph Krug, "Augur: a Decentralized, Open-Source Platform for Prediction Markets" (2015); and, also, Pete Rizzo, "Augur Bets on Blockchain-Powered Prediction Markets," CoinDesk, March 1, 2015, https://perma.cc/SKV3-3C2T ("[a]fter the election happens, because there's not a centralized source that confirms that it's happened, there has to be a decentralized reporting system. That's where reputation comes in. Reputation holders are asked to report on the outcome of events and that ensures the integrity of the system").

[31] One may see nonetheless a recent decline of prediction markets, *see* State of Adoption, "Report 2019/2020" (2020), https://perma.cc/PZA9-X92Y.

[32] Emile Servan-Schreiber et al., "Prediction Markets: Does Money Matter?" Electronic Markets 14 (2004): 243 ("the play-money markets did not perform any worse than the real-money markets. We speculate that this result reflects two oppos-

tokens also allows for the creation of betting markets in which reputation is at stake rather than financial gains. These tokens can indeed be public tokens such as Ether, but they can also be created for betting and used only within a firm or agency. They do not necessarily need to be convertible in fiat currencies or other tokens. A simple reputation system can suffice to create a strong incentive for participants to bet only when they possess inside information. Furthermore, using tokens instead of fiat currencies might allow the triggering of smart contracts.

2.2   Decentralized Regulator in Action

Thomas B. Leary, a former FTC commissioner, underlined in 2011 that "virtually all antitrust analysis involves predictions."[33] In recent years, competition law has undergone radicalization in that regard. Two camps seem to have formed: the first extols markets' ability to correct failures, while the second argues for systematic governmental intervention to do so. Futarchy can help balance these two camps by forcing them to bet not on their beliefs or desires, but on what they expect to become reality. Futarchy will reward only those who are right, creating an incentive not to take a purely ideological stance.[34] I take three examples: (1) merger control; (2) commitments and remedies; and (3) the design of competition policies. I explain that futarchy could benefit these three areas of antitrust law, whether they concern blockchain antitrust or not. In a sense, this section is about how blockchain could help regulators by allowing trustful futarchies.

2.2.1   Merger control
Futarchy can help improve merger control analysis in which antitrust agencies are tasked to address whether "the effect of [an] acquisition may be substantially to lessen competition or to tend to create a monopoly."

Let us assume a merger between two companies, X and Y. The relevant antitrust agency creates two prediction markets to discover whether, one year after the merger, the average price of the product at stake has greater chances of increasing if the merger is authorized. The first assumes that the merger

---

ing forces: real-money markets may better motivate information discovery while play-money market may yield more efficient information aggregation").

[33] Thomas B. Leary, "The Inevitability of Uncertainty," *Competition Law International* 3 (2007): 27. On this, *see* Albert A. Foer, "Prediction and Antitrust," The Antitrust Bulletin 56 (2011): 505.

[34] Discussing the use of prediction markets to anticipate court outcomes, *see* Michael Abramowicz, *Predictocracy: Market Mechanisms for Public and Private Decision Making* (Yale University Press, 2008): 232.

is accepted and the second that it is prohibited. After the betting period has expired, it presents the antitrust agency with two probabilities. One shows 80 percent of the gamblers betting that the price will increase over a certain value if the merger is accepted, and the other only 30 percent that it will reach the same value if the merger is prohibited. The agency could bind itself to these results, here prohibiting the merger. Evidently, companies and competitors will have a strong incentive to try gaming the bets; but again, should they succeed, and should the future prove them wrong, they will lose the money corresponding to their bets.

In fact, this mechanism could incentivize companies to recognize the possible effects of their merger on the market, rather than argue systematically that there are no competitive issues. As a result, they could propose commitments and submit them to the prediction market to influence it in their favor. For example, they could offer to divest part of their activities for influencing the bets or come up with behavioral remedies.

Once the period stated in the prediction market has elapsed (here, one year), the real-life outcome will be shown (the price has increased or not). Those who have bet on the right decision (the merger was allowed or prohibited) and the right outcome (the price has gone up or down) make a profit. Those who have bet on the right decision but the wrong outcome record a loss. And all those who have bet on the wrong decision get their money back.

Evidently, the company could maintain prices artificially low until the end of the period and raise them after it has expired. Should the period be lengthened in response, the prediction market could be less liquid, as the incentive to bet over a longer period will be diminished. However, one could create several prediction markets for different periods and make a decision (on allowing the merger or not) based on them all. In any event, a company raising prices right after the period embedded in prediction markets would severely jeopardize the likelihood of obtaining approvals without commitments in future cases.

So, who should vote? These bets could initially be submitted to the personnel of antitrust agencies alone. One could use an internal token for voting rights, the objective being to prevent decision makers from bringing financial considerations among their members. One could also imagine opening bets to the market. Again, the financial incentive would force all participants to bet on the outcome they think will happen, rather than an outcome they say will occur for the sake of forcing a decision. Lastly, the bet need not be as binary as allowing or preventing the merger. One can create a prediction market about the commitments, as I am about to explain.

2.2.2   Remedies and commitments

It is not uncommon for antitrust agencies to impose remedies on companies in the context of investigations concerning anticompetitive practices. In the case of merger control, companies can "propose" commitments to address the agency's concerns and get their deals through.

These measures are, by definition, forward looking and predictive. While antitrust agencies have long preferred structural commitments (e.g., divestitures) because they entail relatively low monitoring costs, they generally impose behavioral remedies and commitments (e.g., an obligation to grant access to certain infrastructure or IP rights) when an anticompetitive practice has not led to a change in market structure. Companies often perceive such behavioral measures as less constraining than structural ones, although they can be just as coercive.

Both structural and behavioral measures are predictive. For that reason, futarchy can help antitrust agencies achieve their goal: to restore or maintain competition on the market. In practice, futarchy first requires agencies to clarify what measures they want to impose and their objectives. Second, it implies that antitrust agencies submit commitments that are not excessively coercive or unrelated to the harm they are seeking suppress. When these two prerequisites are met, prediction markets could be created for betting on the possible outcomes of various solutions – for example, a price decrease below a certain threshold or a certain number of firms entering the market. Antitrust agencies would then choose the policy that has the highest probability of creating the outcome(s) they are actively seeking to achieve.

2.2.3   Competition policies

Futarchy can also be used to design competition policies. By definition, these policies affect a vast number of market players, often in different countries. They have economic implications, but also sociological and philosophical ones. Their design requires complex analyses, which is a substantial reason to bring in the extensive expertise of prediction markets.

Prediction markets could be used to evaluate the opportunity to introduce new guidelines, tools and enforcement priorities.[35] They could also predict the chances that a decision will be overturned on appeal. Here again, futarchy will require an unambiguous definition of the objective being pursued. Achieving such clarity will present some difficulties, as I will explain. In the meantime, it will also make policies more transparent, which will benefit all market players (and citizens at large). This transparency will prove particularly helpful for preventing policies from being used for strictly *politikè* (party politics) or

---

[35] Explaining that prediction markets could also be used to draft regulation, *see* Michael Abramowicz, *Predictocracy: Market Mechanisms for Public and Private Decision Making* (Yale University Press, 2008): 258.

personal purposes.[36] It will increase public awareness concerning these policy choices while leaving agencies in charge of deciding the objectives.[37]

2.2.4 Challenges

Up until now, I have focused on futarchy's potential to decentralize antitrust agencies. But futarchy also has challenges that require careful consideration.[38] Addressing (most of) them will prove crucial to futarchic governance and implementing what I call "futarchic antitrust." I explore them from the least to the most complex.

The first of these challenges relates to prices and, more specifically, their ability to capture all market information.[39] In fact, some question whether the value of each bet in a prediction market gives a reliable view of the probabilities. But a consensus has emerged in recent decades that there is very little information that the price does not reflect.[40] This accuracy is visible in real life where prediction markets have proven accurate.[41] Furthermore, even if prices do not capture all information, they certainly capture more than one can without them.

The second challenge concerns the creation of coalitions to rig the outcome of bets and manipulate markets.[42] One could indeed create bets on top of prediction markets. Although such a risk cannot be excluded, several observers

---

[36]   Thibault Schrepel, "Antitrust Without Romance," NYU Journal of Law & Liberty 13 (2020).

[37]   Michael Abramowicz, *Predictocracy: Market Mechanisms for Public and Private Decision Making* (Yale University Press, 2008): 193. Discussing how prediction markets could constitute "the machinery" of governments, *see id.* at 283. For a more radical view, *see* Daniel Larimer, interviewed by Sparkes, 2014 (governments are "going to be losing legitimacy as more open, transparent systems are able to provide that function without having to rely on force").

[38]   Explaining that the main limits of prediction markets can all be resolved, *see* Justin Wolfers and Eric Zitzewitz, "Five Open Questions about Prediction Markets," Federal Reserve Bank of San Francisco Working Paper 2006-06 (2006): 23.

[39]   *See*, for instance, Justin Wolfers and Eric Zitzewitz, "Prediction Markets," Journal of Economic Perspectives 18 (2004): 107, 112 (discussing the "accuracy of prediction markets").

[40]   In 1999, *see* M.A. Hearst, R.D. Hunson and D.G. Stork, "Building intelligent systems one e-citizen at a time," IEEE Intelligent Systems 14, no. 3 (1999): 16 ("On accuracy, decades of research on the efficiency of financial markets have found little price-relevant information that is not reflected in market prices.")

[41]   Robert S. Erikson and Christopher Wlezien, "Markets vs. Polls as Election Predictors: An Historical Assessment," Electoral Studies 31, no. 3 (2012). Also, Michael Abramowicz, *Predictocracy: Market Mechanisms for Public and Private Decision Making* (Yale University Press, 2008): 26.

[42]   Although, *see* Robin Hanson et al., "Information Aggregation and Manipulation in an Experimental Market," Journal of Economic Behavior & Organization 60, no. 4

have underlined that manipulators actually improve prediction market accuracy by inducing gamblers to be better informed.[43] On top of that, supervised machine-learning methods have also proven efficient in detecting market manipulation.[44] Also, let us remember that manipulating prediction markets is very costly, as would-be manipulators lose their money when real-life outcomes do not match their predictions.[45] In short, futarchic decision making can be influenced by market manipulation, but several factors mitigate this risk.

The third concerns the need to identify easily verifiable outcomes that can be expressed in binary terms ("Boolean values"). Let me break this down. One part relates to quantity: should a prediction market be created to test several objectives (outcomes) instead of just one, the number of participants willing to bet would be most likely reduced.[46] The other part relates to quality: although one could easily measure a price or GDP increase, some outcomes would be more complex to assess. For example, in a prediction market that questions whether a merger or policy will increase innovation, evaluating the outcome is difficult. To be sure, agencies could choose several metrics for measuring innovation. Still, questions will emerge regarding their capacity to correctly measure the outcome. Also, should the evaluation of these metrics be more subjective, it would create a risk for prediction markets to register incorrect outcomes (e.g., an increase in innovation while innovation has decreased).[47]

(2006): 449 (attempts to manipulate prediction markets generally increase market accuracy by improving liquidity).

[43]   Robin Hanson and Ryan Oprea, "A Manipulator Can Aid Prediction Market Accuracy," Economica 76, no. 302 (April, 2009); Patrick Buckley and Fergal O'Brien, "The Effect of Malicious Manipulations on Prediction Market Accuracy," Information Systems Frontiers 19 (2017); Eric Huang and Yoav Shoham "Price Manipulation in Prediction Markets: Analysis and Mitigation," AAMAS (2014).

[44]   Aihua Li, Liede Wu and Zhidong Liu, "Market Manipulation Detection Based on Classification Methods," Procedia Computer Science 122 (2017).

[45]   Joyce E. Berg and Thomas A. Rietz, "Market Design, Manipulation, and Accuracy in Political Prediction Markets: Lessons from the Iowa Electronic Markets," Political Science and Politics 47, no. 02 (2014).

[46]   Also, on the question of the combination of conditional events, *see* Walter A. Powell et al., *Combinatorial Prediction Markets: An Experimental Study in Scalable Uncertainty Management* (International Conference on Scalable Uncertainty Management: 2013): 283; Joyce E. Berg and Thomas A. Rietz, "Prediction Markets as Decision Support Systems," Information Systems Frontiers 5 (2003): 79 ("Valuations from 'prediction markets' reveal expectations about the likelihood of events. 'Conditional prediction markets' reveal expectations conditional on other events occurring").

[47]   Michael Abramowicz, *Predictocracy: Market Mechanisms for Public and Private Decision Making* (Yale University Press, 2008): 270.

That being said, prediction markets will force reflection on how to achieve specific goals and measure success. This process will be beneficial in the long run.

Perhaps the most salient barriers to prediction markets are legal ones. Prediction markets are not far from gambling activities (quite heavily) regulated in the United States and Europe.[48] In 2008, numerous Nobel laureates and economists wrote about "The Promise of Prediction Markets," calling for legal rules to facilitate them.[49] This has not been done yet.

Against this background, one should discuss creating safe harbors for these markets.[50] Several fundamental questions will have to be answered along the way to address precisely how to design these comfort zones. For example, one could argue that allowing private gamblers to make money based on prediction markets created by governments requires some safeguards. I am confident that we can, collectively, design such safeguards; the widespread of economic relationships between private and public sectors indicates we have done so in the past. Perhaps the fact that futarchy creates business activities (gambling) that complement or replace state functions raises more critical questions.[51]

Overall, you may have noticed that these criticisms mainly concern prediction markets that are open to everyone. These demand more research. In the meantime, I would recommend starting with small implementations – for example, with the creation of non-binding futarchies whose access is limited to each antitrust agency and using internal blockchain-based tokens. I see this as a great way of attaining the end goal of bringing regulated communities closer to the regulators themselves.

3   CHAPTER SUMMARY AND BEYOND

In this chapter, I discussed how cooperation between law and technology could take shape. The first step is to set up a positive agenda that turns their

---

[48]   Kenneth J. Arrow et al., "The Promise of Prediction Markets," Science 320, no. 5878 (2008) (asking to free prediction markets of "unnecessary government restrictions").

[49]   *Id.*

[50]   *Id.* at 877 ("Unfortunately, however, current federal and state laws limiting gambling create significant barriers to the establishment of vibrant, liquid prediction markets in the United States. We believe that regulators should lower these barriers by creating a legal safe harbor for specified types of small-stakes markets, stimulating innovation in both their design and their use.") For instance, the Commodity Futures Trading Commission granted Intrade an exemption to operate in 2005.

[51]   See Marcella Atzori, "Is the State Still Necessary?" Journal of Governance and Regulation 6, no. 1 (2017): 54 ("Decentralization through distributed blockchains mostly means privatization of public functions, with the transformation of government services and citizens' rights into a new profitable private business").

differences into mutual benefits. I argued that creating comfort zones fosters cooperation between lawmakers and industry participants. In parallel, I also argued that it is necessary to shift enforcement activities toward certain malicious practices that threaten the underlying value proposition of blockchain ecosystems. For the time being, agencies should avoid dealing with practices that stem directly from blockchains' core features.

This cooperation between law and technology also requires them to merge on a more practical level. Regulators (here, antitrust agencies) could use blockchains to improve their assessments and monitoring. The technology could also enable antitrust agencies to foster decentralized decision making, blurring the boundaries between law and technology, private entities and governments. In this respect, I have argued that futarchy augmented by blockchain should play a central role because it is efficient and democratic. Whether it concerns merger control, remedies and commitments or antitrust policies, futarchy could play an important role. There are limits to this approach; but instead of waiting for them all to be solved, one could start with carefully designed futarchic governance. This new regulatory environment would foster the integration of blockchain and antitrust. It would simultaneously allow all the other technologies running on blockchain to benefit from this integrated approach. I explore the topic in Chapter 15.

15. Blockchain's future

1   BLOCKCHAIN'S EXTERNAL FACTORS

The future of blockchain depends on external constraints. The first is competition from centralized platforms and services. It causes mutations within the blockchain ecosystem, which is forced to adapt in order to survive. But the future of blockchain also depends on friendly relations, particularly with the Internet of Things (IoT) and artificial intelligence (AI). The complementarity of these technologies will indeed require blockchain to evolve and, in the end, to face internal struggles.

1.1   Blockchain and Centralized Platforms (Competition)

1.1.1   The "token effect"

Today, competition between tech companies – such as Google, Facebook, Uber and Amazon – garners significant public attention.[1] In the future, one may expect competition between blockchain and non-blockchain platforms or applications to become a topic of considerable interest. For example, blockchain-based services could compete with social media (e.g., Instagram and TikTok) and aggregators (e.g., Amazon and eBay) by allowing direct interaction between sellers and buyers, without an intermediary taking a cut in the middle. The intensity of this competition will depend in particular on the network effects from which blockchain applications will benefit.

There has been much discussion of network effects in the economic literature on digital industries.[2] These effects are twofold: direct and indirect.[3] The theory is that the more a specific product or service is used, the more

---

[1]   *See* Juan Manuel Sánchez-Cartas and Gonzalo León, "Multisided Platforms and Markets: A Literature Review" (2018), https://perma.cc/M6FQ-DLS6.

[2]   *See* Michal S. Gal, "The Power of the Crowd in the Sharing Economy," Law and Ethics of Human Rights 13 no. 1 (2018), https://perma.cc/44RM-D6JG.

[3]   Matthew T. Clements, "Direct and Indirect Network Effects: Are They Equivalent?" International Journal of Industrial Organization 22 (2004): 633.

it encourages new users to join the group.[4] This scaling effect, described as Metcalfe's Law in the context of information technology, calculates the value of a network to be approximately proportional to the squared number of nodes (be they people or machines) that it connects. Once a certain number of users is reached (called "critical mass"), new users derive enough value from the product or service to be willing to join the network. And because of that cyclical mechanism, competing against the entity benefiting from network effects becomes more difficult. With that in mind, one may ask how blockchain could compete with centralized applications already enjoying strong network effects.[5]

With public permissionless blockchains, data is open and shared in the distributed ledger. This accessibility creates an incentive to spread blockchain information (1) to make it effective against third parties and; (2) to encourage other users to join.[6] The more users join the blockchain, the more it creates an incentive for new ones to do the same and derive increasing utility from it.

On top of that, public blockchains also benefit from what I call the "token effect," creating a powerful inducement to join by releasing free or cheap tokens whose value may increase rapidly. By doing so, blockchains create a disconnect between the number of users and the willingness to join. Indeed, new users will derive financial utility from the blockchain (should the tokens' value go up), regardless of the utility they derive from its use. Although the token value will increase only if the blockchain proves to be successful, and in that sense, is linked to the network effect, it adds a way to reach the tipping point. One can summarize it as illustrated in Figure 15.1.

---

[4]   John M. Newman, "Complex Antitrust Harm in Platform Markets," CPI Antitrust Chronicles 3 (2017) ("reputation has emerged as one of the most vital facets of competition in many modern markets").

[5]   *See* Neil Gandal and Hanna Halaburda, "Can We Predict the Winner in a Market with Network Effects? Competition in Cryptocurrency Market," Games 7, no. 3 (2016): 16; *see* Abeer El Bahrawy et al., "Evolutionary Dynamics of the Cryptocurrency Market," Royal Society Open Science 4 (2017): 11.

[6]   *See* Eric A. Posner, *Law and Social Norms* (Harvard University Press, 2009): 221 (explaining that Marx and Weber have argued that markets – or capitalism – undermine community).

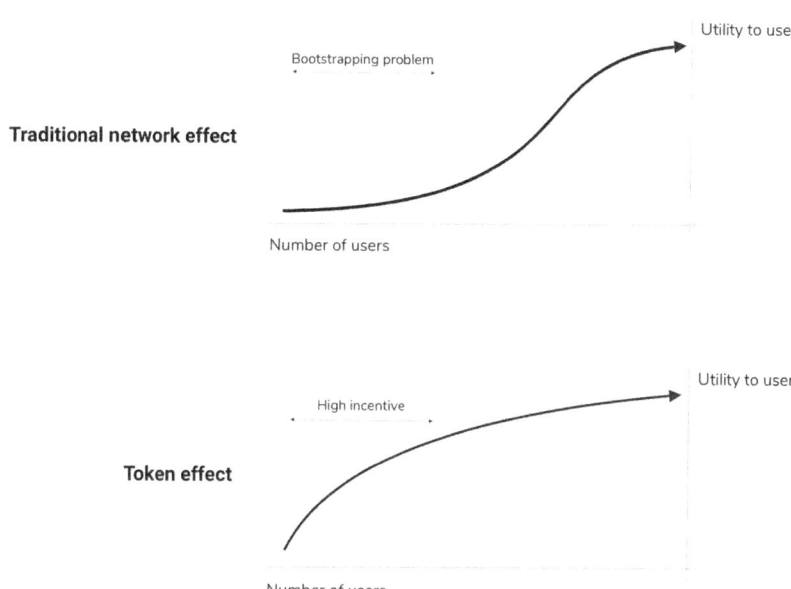

Figure 15.1   Network effect vs. token effect

The token effect may manifest itself in distinct ways. It can be via ICOs,[7] in which tokens are sold at a low price. It can also be via "airdrop,"[8] in which one gives away free tokens. The latter generally demands that the user acquiring the tokens make the blockchain known to her or his network – for example, by referring email addresses, joining Telegram groups or posting on social media.[9]

Of course, centralized firms could create similar incentives, but they would face difficulties in convincing users that, despite their control power, they

---

[7]   Christian Catalini and Joshua S. Gans, "Initial Coin Offerings and the Value of Crypto Tokens," MIT Sloan Research Paper 5347-18 (2018): 3 ("ICO mechanism allows entrepreneurs to generate buyer competition for the token, which, in turn, reveals consumer value without the entrepreneurs having to know, ex ante, consumer willingness to pay."); *see* also Paul Vigna, "What's an Initial Coin Offering? ICOs Explained in 11 Questions", Wall Street Journal, October 2, 2017, https://perma.cc/ HT67-3FZV.

[8]   This is also called a "coin drop," *see* Melanie Swan, *Blockchain: Blueprint for A New Economy* (O'Reilly Media, 2015): 73.

[9]   *See* "Kasko2Go ICO Review & Rating," Top ICO List, https://perma.cc/9UYF -CCY9; "Avinoc Rating & Review," Top ICO List, https://perma.cc/YQY5-K4DJ.

would never change the token value, function or integrity. This trust issue may explain why such initiatives are not as common in that field as they are in the blockchain ecosystems. And because blockchain creators can issue these tokens without incurring any costs, one may expect that they will soon compete fiercely with centralized platforms.

But let me underline the importance of the legal qualification given to tokens in the matter. A debate is raging as to whether tokens are utilities or securities. The methodology for distinguishing between the two is quite simple, on paper at least. In the United States, tokens are securities when their acquisition passes the Howey Test ("a person invests his money in a common enterprise and is led to expect profits solely from the efforts of the promoter or a third party").[10] These acquisitions are subject to federal securities and regulations whose related requirements are known to discourage some investors. Unsurprisingly, most blockchain communities oppose the qualification of tokens as securities, because it may chill the token effect. In Europe, there is no standardized distinction, as token taxonomy is still fragmented across different EU countries.[11] Yet the most common classification[12] identifies tokens as securities when they provide their holders with economic rights.[13] Securities tokens are regularly considered financial instruments under applicable EU regulations, such as the Second Markets in Financial Instruments Directive – as long as they meet with features such as tradability, negotiability on capital markets and standardization.[14] Tokens are considered utilities when they represent a tokenized right to access a future product or service.[15] Generally, utility tokens do not qualify

---

[10]   Referring to Supreme Court, *SEC v. W.J. Howey Co.*, 328 U.S. 293 (U.S., 1946).

[11]   That said, "MiFID II" regulates the tokens considered as securities, while "MiCA" will regulate utility tokens, *see* Directive 2014/65/EU of the European Parliament and of the Council of 15 May 2014 on markets in financial instruments and amending Directive 2002/92/EC and Directive 2011/61/EU (MiFID II), and the Proposal for a Regulation of The European Parliament and of The Council on Markets in Crypto-assets, and amending Directive (EU) 2019/1937 (MiCA). For an explanation of these regulations, *see* Patrick Hansen, "New Crypto Rules in the European Union – Gateway for Mass Adoption, or Excessive Regulation?" Stanford Law School Blogs, RegTrax, January 12, 2021, https://perma.cc/A9BU-2R47.

[12]   Although they vary depending on each national authority, *see* ThinkBLOCKtank, "Position paper on the regulation of tokens in Europe (version 1.0)", June 2019, https://perma.cc/PA5H-FKCD.

[13]   Thijs Maas, "Initial Coin Offerings: When Are Tokens Securities in the EU and US?" (2019).

[14]   Valeria Ferrari, "The Regulation of Crypto-Assets in the EU – Investment And Payment Tokens Under The Radar," Maastricht Journal of European and Comparative Law 27, no. 3 (2020).

[15]   *See* Thijs Maas, "Initial Coin Offerings: When Are Tokens Securities in the EU and US?" (2019).

as a financial instrument and will not be subject to the same rigorous regulation. In the end, the legal treatment of a token will depend on a case-by-case analysis, as many of them have a hybrid character that can hinder a smooth classification.[16]

The strength of "token effect" greatly depends on this classification, because calling tokens a security, with all it entails, may hinder the desire to acquire them. This shows that the collaboration between law and technology necessitates a global view that considers legal fields other than antitrust alone.

1.1.2   Blockchain vs. centralized platforms

Although the term "platform" is often used to describe all tech giants, some are more accurately described as "aggregators."[17] Platforms are the infrastructure on top of which one may build a product or service. Microsoft and Apple's operating systems are prominent examples of platforms. On the contrary, aggregators such as Facebook and Google merely sort out existing information.[18] Against this background, blockchain layer 1 is a platform which serves as an infrastructure for developers to plug applications. For that, one may expect a stronger competition between blockchain and centralized platforms than aggregators.

The token effect will facilitate the growth and expansion of blockchains against these platforms. But it will not suffice to ensure the long-term survival of blockchain ecosystems. Other factors will be necessary to compete effectively with centralized ecosystems.[19]

Blockchain survival is indeed not a given. Decentralization comes with the drawback of requiring a consensus each time an important decision is taken. That explains why blockchains can't be as reactive as centralized platforms. While Google could change its functioning in just a few days (time for the board to meet and vote, if even necessary), Ethereum needs several years to switch from Proof of Work to Proof of Stake. Steve Jobs put it better than

---

[16]   *See* Valeria Ferrari, "The Regulation of Crypto-Assets in the EU – Investment And Payment Tokens Under The Radar," Maastricht Journal of European and Comparative Law 27, no. 3 (2020).

[17]   Analyzing the distinction between platforms and aggregators in antitrust law, *see* Thibault Schrepel, "Platforms or Aggregators: Implications for Digital Antitrust Law", Journal of European Competition Law & Practice 12 (2021).

[18]   On the distinction between platforms and aggregators, *see* Ben Thompson, "Aggregation Theory," Stratechery, https://perma.cc/8XKS-QJAH.

[19]   Raising the possibility, see Neil Chilson, "It's time for a FTC Blockchain Working Group," Federal Trade Commission, March 16, 2018, https://perma.cc/ 7EAY-Y6JX ("Cryptocurrency and blockchain technologies could disrupt existing industries.").

I can: "Our job is to figure out what they're [consumers] going to want before they do."[20] Centralized platforms have a clear advantage on that front.

Also, centralized platforms could control some of the infrastructures necessary for blockchain services to be developed. For example, one could imagine that controlling cloud services or advertising channels could be leveraged to prevent the emergence of blockchain applications. Antitrust agencies will therefore have a role to play in ensuring that blockchain applications are not prevented because of anticompetitive practices at the infrastructure level.

That being said, blockchain will compete with centralized platforms by means of other unique features that, depending on the type of application, will provide them with a strong competitive advantage. Differentiation will be key to blockchain survival.

First, the absence of middlemen naturally comes to mind, as it removes the need to trust a single economic agent.[21] Given, for example, that the primary reason why people do not use Facebook is that they do not trust the company, the absence of intermediaries could prove a central feature in fostering the adoption of blockchain.[22] And it will benefit antitrust agencies. By removing ecosystems' gatekeepers, blockchains eliminate *de facto* all anti-competitive practices they can engage in. This, once again, explains why blockchain and antitrust should work together.

The absence of middlemen also reduces certain transaction costs, such as intermediary costs for putting the two sides of the market in touch. To be sure, blockchain transaction fees can be quite high; but in many situations, these fees will remain smaller than the costs of transacting through an intermediary. This observation led former Assistant Attorney General Makan Delrahim to underline the following:[23]

> Importantly, blockchain solutions provide a means for dramatically decreasing networking costs, which relate to the value created for users when more users join a network. In traditional networking solutions, the company that owns the network infrastructure can raise the cost of doing business on the network as the network

---

[20] Henning Meyer, "Left Out: How Europe's Social Democrats Can Fight Back," *Foreign Affairs* 92, no. 6 (2013): 18.

[21] Stephen Graves, "Bitcoin Lightning Network on Twitter 'Only A Matter of Time': Jack Dorsey," *Decrypt*, June 11, 2021, https://perma.cc/BSQ9-2WXA (discussing the integration of the Lightning Network into BlueSky, Jack Dorsey's new decentralized social media).

[22] Casey Newton, "The Verge Tech Survey 2020," *The Verge*, March 2, 2020, https://perma.cc/UK72-3R49.

[23] Makan Delrahim, "Never Break the Chain: Pursuing Antifragility in Antitrust Enforcement," the United States Department of Justice, August 27, 2020, https://perma .cc/NEZ8-WC5E .

becomes larger and more ubiquitous. The potential of blockchain is the ability to operate a marketplace or network without a centralized intermediary. Again, the ability to lower networking costs has important implications for markets the Division regularly considers in the context of conduct or merger investigations. ... At the core of these inquiries lies a central question for antitrust enforcers: whether this new way of organizing interactions can prevent or limit the concentration of market power. Many have argued that blockchain solutions might do just that. ... The dream for blockchain developers is that it will enable all the benefits of network effects, while minimizing or eliminating the market power that usually comes with those benefits. There is still a long way to go, however.
The absence of leveraging power will create a strong incentive to build products and services on top of blockchain rather than centralized infrastructures. The first will remain free from economic coercion in that sense, here again, preventing related illegal practices by design.[24]

Second, blockchain could impact centralized platforms from the inside. There is a potential scenario where centralized social media, for example, could hold the data generated by the use of the service (e.g., likes and other activities), while blockchain would provide users with "self-sovereign identity."[25] They would leave users with control over their data (e.g., photos, status updates), which could be stored on their private blockchain or across many hard drives throughout the blockchain network. This would leave the product or service developers with less data in hand.[26] Centralized platforms would then be pressed to find alternative ways to reward their users for accessing their data and using their services.

Third, and perhaps most importantly, one may expect blockchains to compete fiercely with centralized products and services by adding financial value. Blockchains may ensure that only one individual can transfer (sell) a piece of code. This is made possible by the traceability of all transactions. The ledger can be used to identify the current owner of anything digital if it has been transacted (and therefore get assigned an identity) on a blockchain. It follows that the transfer of a piece of code (embodying a Bitcoin, a crypto-currency or, in fact, anything digital) by someone other than its owner will be rejected. For example, cryptokitties – digital cats created on the basis of the

---

[24] *See* Vitalik Buterin, "Coordination, Good and Bad," Vitalik Buterin's website, September 11, 2020, https://perma.cc/FBX5-R59E (discussing the absence of such leveraging power and concluding that "the blockchain experience shows how designing protocols as institutionally decentralized architectures, even when it's well-known ahead of time that the bulk of the activity will be dominated by a few companies, can often be a very valuable thing").
[25] Alex Preukschat, "Self-Sovereign Identity—A Guide to Privacy for Your Digital Identity with Blockchain," Medium, January 11, 2018, https://perma.cc/SYS5-QMZ3.
[26] Kevin Werbach, *The Blockchain and the New Architecture of Trust* (MIT Press, 2018): 238.

Ethereum blockchain[27] – are all unique and each one is owned by a single user. If anyone copies the code underlining a cryptokitty, that user will be unable to transfer it. Other use cases of non-fungible tokens have emerged in recent months,[28] all pointing toward the same end: empowering users by offering them financial benefits.

By doing so, blockchain reintroduces the concept of uniqueness in the digital environment. This is another feature of blockchain that explains why it changes the nature of digital transactions. This uniqueness gives value to digital assets and distribute value capture on top of value creation. This should concern non-blockchain operators as they cannot offer the same economic incentive to use their products and services. Indeed, centralized operators cannot create something similar by ensuring, on their own, that all digital assets are transferable only by the owners. Such a mechanism could not scale. They are forced to face this new type of competition – which already represents billions of dollars in video games related-markets.[29] And if, of course, centralized players could also use blockchains to introduce uniqueness, doing so will benefit these blockchains by increasing the number of transactions, and thus the value of their token.

Furthermore, blockchain applications will retain another competitive advantage over centralized players using blockchain: the former will not need to establish a link between the asset being sold (e.g., a cryptokitty) and the identity assigned to that asset on the blockchain. This will facilitate sales by allowing blockchain applications to automate the transfer of assets that are native to the blockchain. Conversely, selling an asset located outside the blockchain (e.g., a tweet) could amount to enforceability issues, should the owner retain its possession or... not truly be the owner.

Overall, blockchain platforms have great survival potential if they focus on their strengths. And, as I explained already, benefiting from the rule of law will also help to prevent centralized platforms from employing anticompetitive practices against them.

---

[27]   CryptoKitties, "CryptoKitties: Collect and Breed Digital Cats," CryptoKitties, https://perma.cc/5LJ2-B2QT.

[28]   *See* Melanie Kramer and Daniel Phillips, "Non-Fungible Tokens (NFT): Beginner's Guide," Decrypt, February 4, 2021, https://perma.cc/8XZZ-3XU7.

[29]   Josh Williams and Russell Roberts, "Josh Williams on Online Gaming, Blockchain, and Forte," The Library of Economics and Liberty, July 13, 2020, https://perma.cc/H5RV-TKL9.

1.2   Blockchain and Other Technologies (Collaboration)

1.2.1   Blockchain and the Internet of Things

Technologies tend to accelerate each other,[30] and for that reason, it is useful to analyze how they interact. Blockchain has direct implications for quantum computing, 3D printing, biotech and nanotechnologies, among others.[31] In the subsequent developments, I will limit myself to discussing the IoT and AI, as blockchains may serve as an infrastructure for these two technologies, therefore shaping their use and developments.

To put it simply, the IoT is all about connecting the analog world to the digital one. Physical products are equipped with sensors or connectors that can send information or be controlled by online applications. There are over 20 billion IoT devices in circulation today and this number will likely triple by 2025.[32] Each of these devices generates information that is then turned into data, thus accelerating the already exponential production of data. In fact, the world is expected to produce six times as much data in 2025 as in 2019.[33]

Blockchains could boost IoT. First, blockchains could be used as the infrastructure layer on top of which IoT ecosystems are built. Second, blockchains, combined with algorithms, could help monitoring devices and spot anomalies. Should, for example, a product malfunction, blockchain ledgers could help identifying why–without permitting the constructor to tamper it. Third, smart contracts could allow IoT devices to interact with each other on specified terms and ensure that they stick to them.[34] Most of all, blockchain technology provides IoT systems with security. By eliminating a single point of failure, blockchains ensure continuity even when a server is down. Not so surprisingly, 86 percent of blockchain adopters are combining the technology with IoT solutions and this number will likely grow in the future.[35]

If blockchain technology does indeed become the infrastructure upon which most IoT systems are built, it will be necessary to ensure that the technolo-

---

[30] Mark Fenwick and Erik P.M. Vermeulen, "Technology and Corporate Governance: Blockchain, Crypto, and Artificial Intelligence," Texas Journal of Business Law 48 (2019): 1–2.

[31] *See* the European Union Blockchain Observatory & Forum, "Convergence of Blockchain, AI and IoT" (2020): 7.

[32] *Id.* at 9.

[33] S. O'Dea, "Data Volume of IoT Connected Devices Worldwide 2019 and 2025," Statista, October 26, 2020, https://perma.cc/B2PS-QCDH.

[34] *Id.* at 5. Also, *see* Nick Bostrom, *Superintelligence: Paths, Dangers, Strategies* (Oxford University Press, 2014): 129 (explaining that one may want to constrain AI capabilities).

[35] "Gartner Survey Reveals Blockchain Adoption Combined with IoT Adoption Is Booming in the U.S.", Gartner, December 12, 2019, https://perma.cc/JJG2-LPG9.

gy's internal layers are free from economic coercion. If not, artificial forms of centralization will impact IoT markets – for example, notably through anticompetitive practices that affect the validation of transactions or that raise prices. We can find a direct relationship between these external applications and blockchain's fourth and fifth layers.

1.2.2   Blockchain and AI

Blockchain also proves useful for developing AI systems. Its immutability is a central feature of cybersecurity. As I have explained, the ledger cannot be hacked by accessing a single copy; it does not have a single point of failure. Let us consider autonomous cars in this context. These cars carry sophisticated AI systems that make constant use of data.[36] If they used blockchains, hackers would need to alter all the copies of the ledger instead of a single database to interfere with the cars on the road. Moreover, the public nature of blockchain would ensure the transparency of the data used in AI systems. This would be useful when auditing databases used to train and operate the AI, especially in case of an accident.

Smart contracts are complementary. First, they can ensure that the flow of information is maintained as imagined, therefore creating more trustful databases for AI to function. Second, they build trust in transferring data that can be automated when specific conditions are met. Third, they ensure the traceability of the transfer. And fourth, they help prevent hacking of that transfer as they are as censorship-resistant as the blockchain that supports them.

Against this backdrop, it is unsurprising to see the European Parliament calling on the European Commission to "explore the use of blockchain-based cybersecurity protocols and applications to improve the resilience, trustworthiness, and robustness of AI infrastructures."[37] In fact, the importance of blockchain in creating reliable AI products and services will only increase in the years to come. The world produced 47 zettabytes of data in 2020.[38] Some estimate that this will increase to 175 in 2025, over 600 in 2030 and over 2100 in 2035. A large chunk of that data will be critical to people's daily lives, while monitoring it will not become any easier. Blockchain features could become a central piece of the puzzle.

---

[36]   Generally speaking, the typical AI product or service involves recording data (input) into a production method (training models) to obtain a result, *see* The European Union Blockchain Observatory & Forum, "Convergence of Blockchain, AI and IoT" (2020): 13.

[37]   *Report with recommendations to the Commission on a framework of ethical aspects of artificial intelligence, robotics and related technologies*, prepared by the European Parliament (Brussels, 2020), https://perma.cc/V8Y4-ZJ2F.

[38]   One zettabyte equals 1 trillion gigabytes.

In the meantime, AI will also help blockchain. First, tomorrow's smart contracts will surely embed machine learning instead of simple expert rules.[39] Doing so will bring smart contracts closer to reality by activating them (i.e., calling their functions) only when complex real-world events have been verified. Second, AI will search blockchains and smart contracts for flaws, ensuring they are valid and complete before putting them on the chain. In fact, artificial intelligence will help verify the validity of smart contracts, whether it is technical or legal. For example, AI systems will ensure the security of blockchains' core code and detect intrusions. They will improve the performance of hash functions, help to upgrade the design of hardware, etc.[40] AI systems will be used for technical testing, assisting with formal verifications, and search-based software engineering. Other AI-based technologies, such as natural language processing, will help analyze the content of smart contracts and ensure their compliance with legal rules.[41]

With this in mind, one cannot overemphasize how important it is that antitrust agencies free blockchain from anti-competitive practices; otherwise, AI systems built on top of blockchains will suffer from such practices.

And as I just explained, AI could assist agencies for this purpose.

2 BLOCKCHAIN INTERNAL FACTORS

The evolution of blockchain also depends on internal balances in terms of design and governance. Overall, choices that will be made within each blockchain will prove important for their evolution. As I show, it all comes down to human interactions.

2.1 The Trifecta: Intra-blockchain Evolution

A blockchain trilemma has emerged in the literature over the last several years. It can be summed up as follows: ensuring blockchain's decentralization, scalability and security entails tradeoffs, at least in the short term. Although this makes sense on a technical level, it does not capture the entirety of our subject. Let us take a closer look. I have discussed decentralization at length throughout this book. It is blockchain's central feature, in terms of both architecture and philosophy. "Scalability" refers to the ability to validate large volumes

---

[39] Riccardo De Caria, "The Legal Meaning of Smart Contracts," European Review of Private Law 6 (2019): 737.
[40] Tshilidzi Marwala and Bo Xing, "Blockchain and Artificial Intelligence," CoRR (2018): 6.
[41] *See* The European Union Blockchain Observatory & Forum, "Scalability Interoperability and Sustainability of Blockchains" (2020): 17.

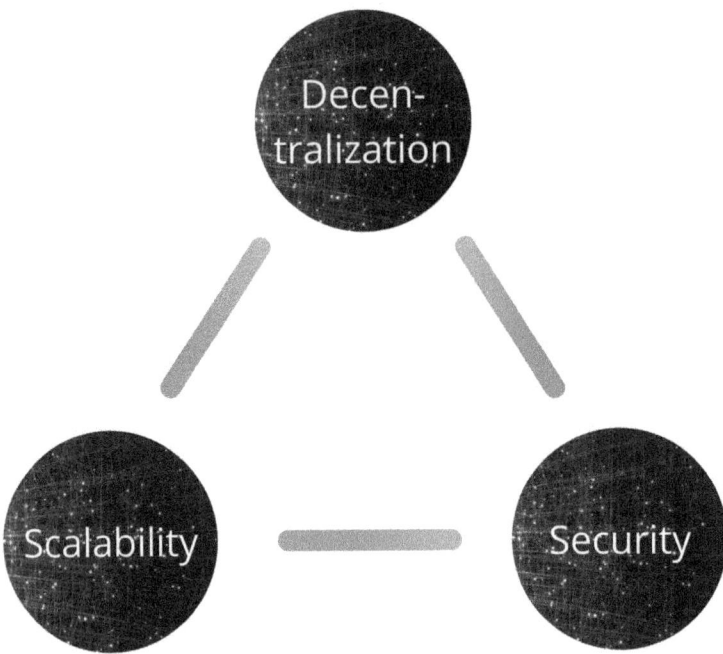

Figure 15.2   The blockchain trifecta

of transactions rapidly. Last, blockchain's security hinges upon its ability to maintain integrity: that only desirable transactions take place – for example, by preventing double spending.[42]

To a certain extent, we have seen together that the mechanisms that ensure decentralization at different blockchain layers may conflict with security.[43] This is what Awemany's story in Chapter 1 revealed. Decentralization implies the distribution of power, limiting the ability to act unilaterally in case of an

---

[42]   Nick Szabo, "Money, Blockchains, and Social Scalability," Unenumerated, February 9, 2017, https://perma.cc/36CT-JT6J ("Whereas the main social scalability benefit of the Internet has been matchmaking, the predominant direct social scalability benefit of blockchains is trust minimization. A blockchain can reduce vulnerability by locking in the integrity of some important performances (such as the creation and payment of money) and some important information flows, and in the future may reduce the vulnerability of the integrity of some important matchmaking functions.")

[43]   *See* The European Union Blockchain Observatory & Forum, "Scalability Interoperability and Sustainability of Blockchains" (2020): 10.

emergency. At the same time, decentralization can also affect the scalability of blockchain: Proof of Work is decentralized by nature, but it prevents the rapid validation of large transaction numbers. Conversely, a private blockchain can restrict access to the ledger or certain functions, raising security and scalability issues.[44]

In the long run, however, these three objectives are mutually reinforcing. The more a blockchain is decentralized, the more it stands out from the central-ized platforms and services that readers know only too well. By differentiating themselves, blockchains attract users by offering a different value proposition. In turn, this generates scalability. The same goes for security, as the more participants use a public blockchain, the harder it becomes to alter the registry or perform a 51 percent attack. The blockchain trilemma is thus useful for thinking about what needs to be done, but it cannot provide a coherent ana-lytical framework in the long term. It will become less relevant with technical advances, to the point where some blockchains will maximize these three objectives. Those who manage to do so will prosper.

2.2   Interoperability: Evolution between Blockchains

Blockchain's ability to survive in the face of centralized applications depends not only on the trifecta (which is specific to each blockchain), but also on interoperability between different blockchains.[45]

Interoperability can be enabled by a trusted third party that validates the information in one blockchain and records it in another.[46] Interoperability can also be achieved without an intermediary;[47] but in either case, a mechanism to duplicate the information is necessary. For instance, the value transfer from blockchain A to blockchain B would entail a fundamental alteration to

---

[44]   *Id.* at 11. The same feature, however, may also be used to enhance privacy, *see* Mary Lacity and Remko Van Hoek, "What We've Learned So Far About Blockchain for Business," MIT Sloan Management Review, February 3, 2021, https://perma.cc/ 38RK-A3TF (with certain private blockchains, the owner cannot "interpret the data ... unless authorized by the data owners").

[45]   World Economic Forum, "Bridging the Governance Gap" (2020): 17 (insisting on the necessity for blockchain environments to become interoperable, and discussing the interoperability between blockchain, including Cosmos and Polkadot). Also, *see* Information Technology and Automation Office, Blockchain Standardization Research Symposium Held in Beijing, November 8, 2019, https://perma.cc/RS75-K9TC (docu-menting General Secretary Jin Ping's interest in blockchain standardization).

[46]   *Id.*

[47]   Making a distinction between a cross-chain communication protocol and a cross-blockchain communication protocol, *see* Rafael Belchior et al., "A Survey on Blockchain Interoperability: Past, Present, and Future Trends" (2020): 6.

the receiving blockchain, since the total number of tokens would increase.[48] Gartner predicts that such transfers will soon be possible,[49] either with the help of simple application programming interfaces[50] or thanks to blockchains allowing the implementation of relays – that is, allowing one blockchain to read another.[51]

Technical difficulties aside, interoperability at all costs is debatable. On the one hand, interoperability increases options for users. If it were possible for a user to create an Ethereum smart contract using Bitcoin for payment purposes, the entire ecosystem would be more flexible. Interoperability also increases the ecosystem's scalability, since compatible blockchains could share the benefits from the network effects of other compatible blockchains, making the entire ecosystem more attractive. Vitalik Buterin has called the current limits "embarrassing" for these precise reasons.[52]

On the other hand, *imposing* interoperability can be a dangerous exercise. First, it may create negative effects for the blockchain trilemma, as it may reduce decentralization by compelling acceptance of (centralized) data coming from outside. This could also create security loopholes. Second, interoperability can reduce competitive pressure. When standards ensure interoperability, they may lock in all market players into an inferior technology, as Jean Tirole has previously underlined.[53] This phenomenon is reinforced by the "winner takes all" nature of standards, because when one is adopted it tends to be

---

[48] Pascal Lafourcade and Marius Lombard-Platet, "About Blockchain Interoperability," Information Processing Letters 161 (2020): 1.

[49] Make no mistake: the days of seamless blockchain interoperability at the "atomic" level are not here yet. Nor are the days of cross-chain functionality, where a single smart contract can update multiple blockchain platforms using a single process. Likely, we will not see these functions go mainstream for a couple of years, *see* Avivah Litan, "Top Trends in Blockchain Technology; inching towards Web 3.0," Gartner, September 19, 2019, https://perma.cc/93QP-6C72.

[50] Rebecca Liao, "How Interoperability Establishes Blockchain's Utility and Effectiveness for Trade Finance," World Economic Forum, May 18, 2020, https:// perma.cc/UT8Z-5TYA.

[51] *See* Aleks Larsen, *A Primer on Blockchain Interoperability*, Blockchain Capital, December 20, 2018, https://perma.cc/75HN-V2VE; *see* also Avivah Litan, "Top Trends in Blockchain Technology; Inching Towards Web 3.0," Gartner, September 19, 2019; and Vasilios A. Siris et al., "Interledger Approaches," IEEE Access 7 (2019) (presenting a survey of interledger approaches).

[52] *See* Vitalik Buterin, (@VitalikButerin), March 24, 2020, https://perma.cc/J442 -ZXR3, "We should put resources toward a proper (trustless, serverless, maximally Uniswap-like UX) ETH <-> BTC decentralized exchange. It's embarrassing that we still can't easily move between the two largest crypto ecosystems trustlessly").

[53] Jean Tirole, "Normes et Propriété Intellectuelle : la vue d'un économiste," Lettre de l'Autorité de Régulation des Communications Electroniques et des Postes 51 (2006).

applied across the entire industry.[54] And on top of all that, they may also encourage anticompetitive strategies, such as holdup – that is, not reporting the incorporation of a patent into a standard in order to claim royalties later on.[55] One must therefore weigh these adverse effects against procompetitive ones. Still, it seems that *emerging* interoperability (without standards) is more desirable early in an ecosystem's lifespan, as it is more organic and results only from the needs of that ecosystem.

2.3   Blockchain at War with Itself

The ability of each blockchain, and the ecosystem as a whole, to solve the trilemma and enable interoperability will depend on further technical advances, but also on their governance mechanisms.

Different methods of governance are argued for within the sphere of public permissionless blockchains. To be fair, debates on system organization were taking place long before the emergence of blockchain technology. Back in 1840, Tocqueville noticed that his contemporaries were "incessantly tormented by two hostile passions: ... the need to be led and the desire to remain free."[56] Blockchain has simply crystallized that tension once again.

Two different perspectives are developing here. On the one hand, part of the blockchain community advocates the need to maintain on-chain governance. According to them, keeping the governance such as we saw together in Chapter 7 is an absolute necessity. They see this as the best way to preserve blockchain's decentralization, which they value over other blockchain features.[57] For them, "code is absolute law," and it should stay as it is. But another part of the community favors integrating off-chain governance – tools and mechanisms that function outside the blockchain ecosystem, but that affect it.

---

[54]   Michael J. Schallop, "The IPR Paradox: Leveraging Intellectual Property Rights to Encourage Interoperability in the Network Computing Age," AIPLA Quarterly Journal 28, no. 3 (2000): 195; also, Michael A. Carrier, *Innovation For The 21st Century: Harnessing The Power Of Intellectual Property And Antitrust Law* (Oxford University Press, 2009); and Jean Tirole, *The Theory of Industrial Organization,* (MIT Press, 1994): 405 (explaining that standardization may reduce diversity).

[55]   Richard M. Steuer, "Standard setting: can be rife with opportunities for anticompetitive activity," Mayer Brown, June 23, 2011, https://perma.cc/T6AA-C3VK; *Am. Soc'y of Mech. Eng'rs v. Hydrolevel Corp.*, 456 U.S. 556, 571 (U.S., 1982). *See* specifically *Allied Tube & Conduit Corp. v. Indian Head, Inc.*, 486 U.S. 492, 495–98 (U.S., 1988).

[56]   Alexis de Tocqueville, *Democracy in America*, trans. James T. Schleifer (Liberty Fund, 2012): 1255.

[57]   *See* The European Union Blockchain Observatory & Forum, "Governance of and with Blockchain" (2020): 13.

They see these as the best way to ensure that blockchain ecosystems function properly. They often insist on favoring blockchain scalability over decentralization, to the point where some argue for completely centralized governance.[58]

In the end, these different governance structures will lead to different ways of solving the blockchain trilemma and ensuring interoperability. Darwin's evolutionary theory will play out eventually, eliminating all forms of blockchain governance that do not achieve an efficient balance while maintaining enough differentiation with centralized systems.

For now, I simply want to recall that centralizing blockchain governance is a dangerous game. That being said, blockchain communities have a strong interest in ensuring cooperation with the law, which is very much an off-chain (and, for now, centralized) tool. In the end, it all comes down to guessing what balance best maximizes the potential of blockchain technology.

3   CHAPTER SUMMARY AND GOODBYES (FOR NOW)

In this last chapter, I have attempted a most perilous exercise: guessing what the future will hold for blockchain ecosystems. Surely, I will come to regret some of my prognoses as they encapsulate my current vision of a rapidly evolving ecosystem.

I started by discussing the pressure of external factors. Blockchain will undoubtedly compete with centralized platforms and services in the coming years. My best guess is that although the "token effect" will help attract users, the long-term survival of blockchain ecosystems will require maintaining decentralization at the architectural and governance layers. Without it, non-blockchain platforms will take over because of their speed and handiness. But if blockchain remains decentralized, all activities for which decentralization creates efficiency will thrive. Besides, other external factors will shape blockchain's future – not in competing with it, but in requiring cooperation.

---

[58]   CleanApp and Crypto Law Review, "The Wood-Zamfir Governance Debates," *Medium*, November 27, 2018, https://perma.cc/26CV-L99F; Alyssa Hertig, "Why This Dev Built a 'Centralized Ethereum' on Top of Bitcoin's Lightning," *CoinDesk*, June 12, 2020, https://perma.cc/5KED-ESUL ("Pseudonymous developer Fiatjaf has created Etleneum, which he describes as a 'centralized' version of Ethereum that runs on payments from Bitcoin's Lightning Network ... But it is not decentralized. Fiatjaf controls it all — as he is quick to note. ... Finally, contrary to Ethereum's tenet of decentralization, many of its apps have back doors that can be used to switch them off in case of a critical bug. Similarly, with one ruler, Etleneum allows that party to just shut down a contract if it isn't working properly.")

Most specifically, IoT and AI will benefit from using blockchain as infrastructure. This will enable blockchain to prosper.

I then studied how blockchain's internal factors could shape the technology. First, I showed that the blockchain trilemma sheds some light on what blockchain communities need to achieve to ensure their long-term survival. On that basis, I explained that blockchain interoperability – that is, blockchain's interaction with others – will generate crucial efficiencies. But make no mistake: imposing interoperability at all costs is a dangerous exercise.

In the end, it all comes down to human interactions and choices to be made in the context of uncertainty. It is closer to an art form than it is to science. On that note, it is time for me to thank you for your interest; and now, let us push together for the "law + technology" approach to develop further – whether it concerns blockchain + antitrust, AI + privacy law, or technologies that do not yet exist.

Index